MANAGED PROFESSIONALS

SUNY Series

FRONTIERS IN EDUCATION

Philip G. Altbach, Editor

The Frontiers in Education Series draws upon a range of disciplines and approaches in the analysis of contemporary educational issues and concerns. Books in the series help to reinterpret established fields of scholarship in education by encouraging the latest synthesis and research. A special focus highlights educational policy issues from a multidisciplinary perspective. The series is published in cooperation with the School of Education, Boston College. A complete listing of books in the series can be found at the end of this volume.

MANAGED PROFESSIONALS

UNIONIZED FACULTY AND
RESTRUCTURING ACADEMIC LABOR

GARY RHOADES

State University of New York Press

Excerpts from "Reorganizing the Faculty Workforce for Flexibility: Part-time Professional Labor" by Gary Rhoades from the Journal of Higher Education (67, 6:624–59). Copyright © 1996 Ohio State University Press. Reprinted by permission.

Published by
State University of New York Press, Albany

For information, address State University of New York Press,
State University Plaza, Albany, N.Y., 12246

Production by Marilyn P. Semerad
Marketing by Dana E. Yanulavich

Library of Congress Cataloging-in-Publication Data

Rhoades, Gary.
    Managed professionals : unionized faculty and restructuring academic labor / Gary Rhoades.
        p.   cm. — (SUNY series, frontiers in education)
    Includes bibliographical references and index.
    ISBN 0–7914–3715–9 (hardcover : alk. paper). — ISBN 0–7914–3716–7 (pbk. : alk. paper)
        1. College teachers—United States.   2. College teachers––Salaries, etc.—United States.   3. College teachers' unions—United States.   4. Collective bargaining—College teachers—United States.
    5. College teachers, Part-time—Salaries, etc.—United States.
    6. Universities and colleges—United States—Administration.
    I. Title. II. Series.
    LB2331.72.R56 1998
    378.1'22—dc21   97–22368
                                                                           CIP

10 9 8 7 6 5 4 3 2 1

To all those
who seek dignity and respect
in their work;
And to all those
who in big ways and small
have dignified my work and life.

Contents

Acknowledgments   ix

Chapter 1
Academics as an Organizationally Managed, Stratified
     Professional Work Force   1

Chapter 2
Restructuring Professional Rewards: The Structure,
     Stratification, and Centrality of Faculty Salaries   29

Chapter 3
Retrenchment and Reorganization: Managing Academic
     Work(ers) for Productivity   83

Chapter 4
Reorganizing the Faculty Work Force for Flexibility:
     Part-Time Professional Labor   131

Chapter 5
The Production Politics of Teaching and Technology:
     Deskilling, Enskilling, and Managerial Extension   173

Chapter 6
Managerial Domain and Academic Employees: Outside
     Employment, Intellectual Property, and Faculty's
     Own Time   211

Chapter 7
Unionized Faculty: Managing the Restructuring of
     Professionals and Production Work in Colleges
     and Universities   257

Notes   281

Bibliography   321

Index   341

SUNY Series, Frontiers in Education   349

Acknowledgments

Though my words are simple and few, my debts—intellectual, emotional, and otherwise—are profound and many.

This book could not have been written without the good work of Chris Maitland and Rachel Hendrickson of the NEA and John Lee of JBL Associates, in gathering several hundred collective bargaining agreements and organizing them into a user-friendly, sophisticated CD-ROM package, the Higher Education Contract Analysis System. My thanks to them, to Harold Weschler, and to numerous other colleagues/authors in the NEA's Higher Education Almanac series, on whose work and insights I have drawn considerably.

My thanks as well to the numerous union members and contract negotiators at the AAUP, AFT, and NEA, with whom I have talked over the years. Particular thanks go to Ernst Benjamin of the AAUP, for his excellent and thorough comments and advice, and to Perry Robinson of the AFT for his good thoughts and work.

I am especially appreciative of the thoughtful and useful comments of the reviewers selected by State University of New York Press to read my manuscript. And special thanks for the statistical advice and suggestions of Ken Kempner, that sheep with wolf's knowledge, who ably bridges the not-so-separate worlds of quantitative and qualitative research.

Throughout my career, my "conditions of employment" have been extraordinary, chiefly because of my colleagues, both close and far. Bob Clark hired me as a "postdoctoral research scholar," introducing me to the study of higher education and to the significance of the organizational level of analysis. He told me to "write books; they stand up on shelves by themselves," and I have finally complied. Larry Leslie and Clif Conrad, a pair to beat any full house, hired me as a tenure-track faculty member at the University of Arizona's Center for the Study of Higher Education. They have modeled for me in distinct ways the careful craft of scholarly production and much more. Sheila Slaughter arrived at the University of Arizona, as I did, in 1986, from which time we have engaged in an ongoing conversation that has touched my work and life in ways that may not always be seen but always are felt. Her work and insight have expanded the horizons and refined the analysis of my study of professionals and of unions. To her, and to all my colleagues, both at Arizona and in that "invisible college" beyond, I offer the best of my thanks and my work.

A special thanks to Don and Vivian, for (to paraphrase Virginia Woolf) a "room of my own," an alcove in an idyllic coastal southern Maine summer cottage, in and from which creative juices and much pleasures flow.

To my parents, for as Thomas Hardy's *Jude the Obscure* noted, "it takes two or three generations to do what I tried to do in one." As I have written them, "From much love learned young, much derives."

To Janet, for whom and in whom love ever thrives. And to Elizabeth and Olivia, whom I did *not* ignore while writing this book, for playing with, reading to, and being with them are among the greatest and sweetest joys I know.

CHAPTER 1

Academics as an Organizationally Managed, Stratified Professional Work Force

What are the terms of work for unionized faculty? Within that one general question are several specific ones. What criteria are built into unionized faculty's salary structures? How secure are their jobs, and what are the conditions governing layoffs? To what extent do full-time faculty influence the use of part-time faculty? Have unions negotiated rights, controls, and limits surrounding the use of instructional technology? What claims do faculty have on their own time, as professionals, and on the intellectual property they produce?

In exploring these particular terms of work for unionized faculty I am interested in two overarching issues with regard to faculty as a work force. First, what measure of professional autonomy do faculty enjoy, and what measure of managerial discretion are they subject to? In other words, what is the balance between faculty self-governance and managerial flexibility in the contracts? Second, what are the dimensions and bases of professional stratification? In other words, what are the internal divisions among faculty that are evidenced and built into the contracts?

Such questions are timely. Faculty emerged as a profession in the United States, as did many other professions, in the last decades of the nineteenth century.[1] Now, in the last decades of the twentieth century, we are witnessing a fundamental restructuring of many professions. Perhaps the most dramatic example of such restructuring is the most prestigious of the liberal professions in the United States, medicine. Indeed, the health professions in general are being reshaped as an increased proportion of health care is provided by large, private health management organizations. Physicians have gone from being indepen-

1

dent practitioners to being salaried employees of large organizations run by administrators interested as much or more in efficiency and revenues as in quality of health care.[2] Corporatization and privatization are having an adverse impact on the salaries of physicians and their control over decision making about health care. They also likely will lead to a reconfiguration of physicians' numbers, in relative and absolute terms, across specialties. Privatization is having a particularly adverse impact on the unionized profession of nursing, effecting the layoff and replacement of nursing personnel with less qualified and lower paid workers. The same effects may soon be felt by primary care physicians and even by specialists. At the time of this writing an ophthalmologist in Tucson, Arizona, filed suit against a health maintenance organization—FHP Inc.—that is diverting his glaucoma patients away from him—there is only one local ophthalmologist with his level of training—to a cheaper, for-profit eye care group. FHP Inc. also now requires patients to first see an optometrist—nonphysicians who test vision and who are licensed to prescribe medication, but who deal only with minor problems.[3]

The extraordinary changes in the working conditions of physicians have led to an extraordinary response. In December 1996 Tucson physicians of Thomas-Davis Medical Centers, owned by FPA Medical Management Inc., voted by nearly a 3–1 margin to unionize, to be represented by the Federation of Physicians and Dentists, an affiliate of the American Federation of State, County, and Municipal Employees. The issues at stake included control over decisions regarding patient care and contracts that now give management the right to lay off physicians at will, without cause. These Tucson physicians are not the first to unionize. Nor, perhaps, will they be the last. But their action highlights the extent to which the conditions of employment for even those most prestigious of professionals—physicians—have changed.

The academic profession also is undergoing restructuring. The terms and position of faculty's professional labor are being renegotiated as managers seek to reform, reinvent, re-engineer, redesign, or reorganize colleges and universities. Part of such restructuring is an increased emphasis on efficiency and on generating revenues. Privatization in higher education has not been as dramatic as in medicine. Yet, it has involved academic managers reallocating resources to strengthen institutions' connection to various markets. It also has meant institutions pursuing various strategies to generate new revenues, including encouraging faculty to pursue commercially relevant activities. In this context, higher education executives have sought greater flexibility in shaping and controlling the configuration, distribution, activity, and output of the academic work force. Such efforts have implications for faculty's reward structures, their job security, the ratio of part- to full-timers, the use of technology in delivering curriculum, outside employment, and intellectual property rights.

Managerial efforts threaten faculty even in the most prestigious sectors of higher education. Witness the year-long tenure dispute at the University of Minnesota, a top ten research university in terms of federal research grants and contracts. In 1996 the Board of Regents proposed changes in the tenure code which would enable the administration to retrench tenured faculty if an academic program was being "reorganized" (proposed changes also would enable the administration to cut a faculty member's salary for "adequate cause"). The reaction of faculty was so strong and so negative that faculty threatened to unionize. That effort led to a formal drive to organize a collective bargaining unit (with the American Association of University Professors), which undermined regental efforts to push through the proposed changes in tenure (although a watered down version of the changes was approved for the law school, which was not part of the unionizing effort). The vote to unionize was extremely close: 666 for, and 692 against. The margin of defeat (or of victory, depending upon your point of view) has been attributed to two factors: first, a group of twenty-six regents professors circulated a letter before the vote urging faculty to vote against a union, arguing that having a union would hamper the new president who would be starting his term of office in the coming year; second, the engineering faculty voted overwhelmingly against the union. Two layers of stratification are evidenced *within* even this top research university: senior, tenured research stars versus others; and highly paid engineering (and law professors) versus faculty in the arts and sciences and in less wealthy professional schools. It is not clear at this point what will become of the unionizing effort. As for the tenure policy, it appears that with a new president, and particularly a largely new board (five new members in a board of twelve), substantial changes are off the agenda, at least for now.

The union drive at the University of Minnesota is fascinating. Not nearly as dramatic, but equally fascinating to me, is the retrenchment policy that pre- and post-dates the tenure dispute. Prior to the dispute, tenured faculty could be retrenched if their department or college was reorganized. That policy remains in place. The proposed change that occasioned an outcry was to shift the unit of analysis to the "program," below the level of an entire department. Not a minor change. But there are two points worthy of note. First, management already enjoyed much flexibility in laying off tenured faculty and yet still sought greater discretion. Second, faculty are already subject to managerial discretion in reorganization and retrenchment actions, and yet seem oblivious to the fact.

Many, if not most, faculty are unaware of the scope and significance of the restructuring that is ongoing in higher education. Indeed, many faculty seem to think of themselves as independent professionals. It makes no difference that the history of American higher education is of top-down institution building. Instructors were hired by college presidents. Presidents were hired by boards of trustees.[4] It makes no difference that in the public sector, faculty are state or municipal employees and that their paychecks bear the signature of the state treasurer or county comptroller. Or that in the private sector, faculty are employed by boards of trustees and that their paychecks bear the institutional comptroller's signature. (In fact, many faculty have direct deposit of their paychecks, from one big organization to another, and never see their paychecks.)

Many faculty still believe that they are independent professionals. At least they act as such. In fact, that is part of the ongoing criticism of faculty in the popular literature and press. It is also part of the criticism of them by higher education administrators and leaders.[5] Faculty are too independent. They are self-interested careerists. They devote too little time to lower division undergraduate teaching. They are committed more to themselves than to their clients or institution. They are inflexible and resistant to change. (Or, in neoconservative accounts, they are too radical and too quick to cast off time-honored traditions and values.)[6] They enjoy the lifetime job security of tenure and thus are not accountable.

Perhaps. Yet for all that, faculty are managed professionals. By and large, faculty work in medium and large organizations, of hundreds, thousands, even tens of thousands of employees. Faculty work in complex enterprises. In the public sector, they generally work in large systems of multiple organizations encompassing entire cities, counties, or states. Colleges and universities are often among the major employers in their locale.

College and university administrators may not find faculty particularly "manageable." They may not always or ever be able to get faculty to do what administrators want. And faculty for their part may actively or passively resist managerial efforts, somewhat successfully. Nevertheless, faculty are managed professionals.

Of course, faculty have various forms of influence in colleges and universities. The closer one gets to classroom decisions (and to students' academic lives), to decisions about the content of academic programs, and to evaluations of peers, the stronger is that academic influence. There are various forms of faculty influence, and they can be exercised in various ways. Influence may involve ongoing, proactive efforts within one's program or department to update and reform the subject matter and intellectual work of higher education. It may involve grading students, reviewing colleagues' dossiers, or offering votes of censure regarding particular administrators. It may involve participating in countless committees and governance activities, or it may consist of faculty's ability to stage effective, long-term resistance to managerial initiatives. But for all of this, faculty members are professional employees who are managed by others.

It is not faculty members who manage college and university budgets. They do not set the salaries of administrators or themselves. They do not have final authority over who gets laid off. They do not decide whether to approve or eliminate academic programs. By and large, they do not control how many full- and part-time faculty members are hired (nor how many students are admitted). Faculty do not purchase and set up new instructional technologies (nor do they determine how many students will be served by these technologies). Faculty neither set nor enforce (nor, some would say, follow) outside employment policies. They must negotiate with the organization regarding intellectual property rights. None of this is to say that faculty want, should have, or could handle any or all of these responsibilities. I simply note that all of these matters are ultimately decided by those who manage faculty, by administrators and boards.

In this book I examine the negotiated *formal* conditions of academic work in unionized higher education. The principal primary data for my study are 212 collective bargaining agreements for faculty in the 1990s, about 45 percent of all faculty contracts. (The contracts have been collected and put on CD-ROM by the National Education Association—contracts negotiated by the American Association of University Professors, by the American Federation of Teachers, and by independent bargaining agents are also included. The data base is called the "Higher Education Contract Analysis System" (HECAS); it has search capabilities for contractual analysis.[7]) I conduct thematic and rhetorical analysis of contractual language regarding various terms of faculty labor, concentrating on contracts' themes, rhetoric, specific terminology, and emphases. My analysis is primarily a close reading and systematic content analysis of the contracts. In addition, I conduct some statistical analyses of the incidence of various provisions by institutional type and in chapter 4 by type of faculty included in the unit.

My principal theses are as follows: (A) academics are managed professionals and are increasingly so. Managerial discretion is broad and expanding. Professional involvement in decision making is limited, as are professional constraints on managerial discretion; (B) academics are highly stratified professionals and are increasingly so. Managerial flexibility serves to heighten the hierarchy and divisions within the academic profession, which are already considerable, and are growing.

However, there are important shades and subtleties to the general patterns that I posit above. Faculty are not passively submissive to the missives and actions of their managers. Passive-aggressive, perhaps. But not submissive. As professionals, and as a unionized workforce, faculty have struggled with some success to build protections, constraints, and a considerable measure of professional autonomy and influence into the contractual conditions of their work. That is what makes the story interesting. In the social relations of work between managers and faculty, the balance of managerial discretion on the one hand, and of professional autonomy and involvement on the other, is weighted in the former direction. But there is some counterbalance: the relations are not one-sided.

Organization of the Book

The book is organized around various terms of faculty labor. I open with the issue that is most identified with union negotiations and perhaps most dear to faculty—salaries. In chapter 2 I analyze salary structures embedded in the HECAS contracts. I focus on three criteria for making salary adjustments for faculty—merit, market, and equity. In closing the chapter, I analyze the dispersion of faculty salaries as an indicator of increasing professional stratification. I also briefly address the centrality of faculty salaries relative to the costs of other professional personnel. In doing so, I set the stage for chapter 3, which deals with restructuring and retrenchment. In justifying such actions, academic managers often refer to institutions' financial conditions. They state that expanding labor costs are the major budget item, and they presume that faculty salaries account for the overwhelming proportion of personnel costs.

Chapter 3 examines the programmatic and job security of faculty, focusing on the reorganization of academic programs and the retrenchment of faculty. I focus on faculty involvement and managerial discretion in making judgments surrounding reorganization and retrenchment. My analysis essentially replicates my 1993 *Journal of Higher Education* article, in which I examined 42 contracts from the 1980s, with an expanded data base of 212 contracts.[8] I apply a similar analytical framework of focusing on financial exigency and administrative discretion. Restructuring academic institutions involves reallocating faculty resources. I address the job security of various types of faculty and their involvement in decision making surrounding reorganization and retrenchment. In short, how much flexibility do managers have in reconfiguring the faculty work force? That issue relates to the next chapter's focus on faculty over whom managers have much control.

Chapter 4 focuses on the use of part-time faculty. This cuts to the heart of faculty self-governance and to their professional position—the ability to choose one's colleagues and to ensure future jobs for full-time, tenure-track faculty. I analyze collective bargaining agreements to determine first the extent of managerial discretion and of professional constraint in the use of part-time faculty. Then I examine work-force issues, the politics of professional work evident in the political struggle between management and labor over faculty positions, and the proportion of the academic workforce that is part-time. I also explore the profession's internal stratification between full- and part-time faculty and among various gradations of part-timers. My analysis of the contractual terms surrounding the use of relatively cheap, part-time academic labor—which is being utilized increasingly—sets the stage for the next chapter, which discusses another managerial strategy for reducing the costs of faculty labor.

Chapter 5 concentrates on the use of technology in delivering curriculum. Such use represents a managerial challenge to faculty control and ownership of the curriculum. In considering whether and how the introduction of new instructional technologies affects the social relations of work I draw on several theories that have addressed this issue regarding blue-, pink-, and white-collar workers, but not in regard to professionals or to faculty. Does technology lead to a deskilling of workers, degrading their skills and reducing their autonomy? Does it instead lead to an enskilling of workers, upgrading their skills and expanding their autonomy? Or does technology lead to managerial extension, with skills being increased but autonomy being reduced? I consider these three theories in an analysis of contractual provisions surrounding the use of instructional technology to deliver curriculum. My findings lead me to generate my own thesis of "marginalization": technologically delivered curriculum may marginalize track faculty, who are largely peripheral to the use of new instructional technologies (when track faculty are involved, it is simply to deliver instruction). New production workers in education (educational technology and curriculum specialists) are emerging, as the process by which education is produced—the means of production—changes. Such workers have an increasingly prominent role in various curricular areas that are outside the purview of full-time faculty. As a further measure of faculty's position, I consider the extent of their ownership claims in regard to their instructional work. For example, if faculty are videotaped for a telecourse, who owns the tape and who controls whether and how it will be revised and/or reused? In addressing ownership issues, I foreshadow the book's final empirical chapter.

Chapter 6 addresses ownership issues in regard to faculty members' time and intellectual property. I analyze contractual provisions regarding outside employment and intellectual property. What are the organization's claims on faculty, the extent of what I call "managerial domain"? To what extent is faculty's time controlled by the organization? That is a factor that shapes outside employment policy. It is also a factor that figures prominently in the calculus of faculty ownership of intellectual property. As in previous chapters, my focus is on the extent of professional autonomy that can be claimed by faculty. However, I also focus on the extent of managerial claims on the work and intellectual products of faculty. In closing this chapter, I consider the findings for unionized faculty in light of past research on outside employment and intellectual property policies in nonunionized colleges and universities.

Chapter 7 summarizes my findings. I come back again and again to the variegated themes I have developed regarding the management and stratification of faculty. And though I stay close to my data on collective bargaining agreements, I note parallels to developments in higher education generally. I conclude as I open. Unionized faculty are managed, stratified professionals. Yet I draw attention to variations on that theme, particularly in terms of unions' efforts to constrain managers and to the effects of union strategies on professional stratification. I then speak to the implications of my findings for the literatures on which I have drawn. I suggest that sociological research on professions and higher education research on college and university faculty would benefit analytically and substantively by attending to intervening organizational levels between "the campus" and "the state." Both fields also would benefit from an exploration of the politics of professional work, embedded in negotiations between professionals and their managers. Finally, I close with some thoughts about the restructuring of faculty as a work force. I address four major studies of academe over the past twenty-five years and use my contractual findings to extend that work. I close by addressing major issues and challenges confronting unions in particular and faculty in general.

Unions and Faculty

Why focus on faculty members who are unionized? More to the point, as I have often been asked by university colleagues: *Are* there any faculty who are unionized? To paraphrase Shakespeare, me thinks they doth project too much. With a few exceptions—for example, the State University of New York system— research university faculty (who do the most writing about higher education) are not unionized. Such faculty assume that their condition is universal. It is not. In 1994, 242,221 faculty on 1,057 campuses were represented by collective bargaining agents. That is about 44 percent of full-time faculty (and 26 percent of full- and part-time faculty) nationwide. It is 29 percent of all campuses. The percentages would be much higher if one counted only faculty in public institutions—which account for over 95 percent of unionized faculty (in 1995, only 10,725 faculty in private institutions were covered by collective bargaining agreements). About 63 percent of full-time faculty, and 60 percent of institutions in the public sector have faculty union contracts (if you factor out research universities, which with a few exceptions are not unionized, the percentages are 89 percent of faculty).[9] As a work force, a higher percentage of faculty are unionized than of workers in the private sector of the economy (12 percent) or the general workforce (16 percent).[10]

Limits of the Higher Education Literature

Despite these numbers, one can read much higher education literature and not discover that faculty unions exist. One can read many of the most widely read books on higher education and not learn that faculty unions exist. One can get a master's or doctoral degree in many Higher Education programs, and gain no knowledge of faculty unions.

There is some literature on faculty unions, but it tends to be dated, having emerged with the rise of faculty unions in the late 1960s and 1970s. It is also a literature that tends to be limited in perspective and scope. Most of it adopts a managerial and/or a functionalist perspective on professions. Unions are regarded as a threat to managerial prerogatives and flexibility or to professionalism. In its scope, the managerialist literature is policy oriented and nonempirical—as in studies of and commentaries on how leaders can prevent, control, and effectively negotiate with faculty unions. The functionalist literature regards unions as antithetical to central values and mechanisms of professions—that is, meritocracy (and high salaries) and "traditional" "collegial" mechanisms of governance. Much of the literature seeks to assess the impact of unionization on salaries and faculty governance structures such as senates.[11] Such work is relevant to some of my interests, yet it does not speak to the specific conditions or broad scope of my interests in the contractual terms of faculty labor in unionized institutions.

In contrast to most work on resource allocation, restructuring, and retrenchment, some recent work acknowledges collective bargaining. For example, Gumport analyzes "academic program reduction" at two institutions, one of which is unionized.[12] The union is mentioned generally and in passing, as a factor fostering a collective sense among faculty. But collectively bargained terms of labor and the ways in which they influence decision-making are not included in the analysis. Slaughter analyzes patterns of retrenchment in the 1980s, focusing on cases reported to the AAUP.[13] In the context of a couple of cases, faculty unions' inability to protect faculty positions is noted. But there is no analysis of specific and widespread contractual terms of labor. We have a limited understanding of these terms.[14]

Rationale for Focus on Unionized Faculty

I focus on unionized faculty for several reasons. One, as noted above, is that such faculty are many in number and largely overlooked in the literature. Another is the convenience and breadth of the available data. Yet another reason is that the types of colleges and universities that are most likely to be unionized often are overlooked in the literature. Such institutions are especially relevant for studying restructured terms of academic labor because they are part of higher education sectors that have been the most financially squeezed in recent years. Moreover, unions represent an important strategy utilized by many occupations to control the terms of their labor, through collective bargaining that yields formal provisions and contracts regarding work. Such formal agreements provide an excellent vehicle for exploring the balance between managerial discretion and professional control or constraint.

Several years ago, when I began analyzing retrenchment, I discovered dozens of collective bargaining agreements on microfiche. Such records enabled me to study retrenchment clauses in forty-two institutions, systems, and districts.[15] Subsequently, higher education analysts at the NEA became aware of my work and I became aware of (and gained access to) the NEA's contract analysis system, HECAS. No comparable data base is available for such a number and range of nonunionized institutions.

However, I have focused on unionized faculty for more than just reasons of numbers and convenience. The types of colleges and universities that are most likely to be unionized often are overlooked in the higher education literature. Higher education scholars are much more likely to focus on the more than 100 research universities in which they are employed than on the more than 3,200 other institutions that make up American higher education. There is much literature on small, selective private colleges, but the literature on public comprehensive state colleges and universities, and on community colleges, is limited, particularly in the area of faculty.[16] At the time I began studying unionized faculty and institutions, I felt that this "top heavy" bias marked not just "the literature" in general, but my work as well. I wanted to explore the terms of academic labor in often overlooked settings. Examining unionized institutions was one way of accomplishing this task. The most heavily unionized sector in higher education in terms of contracts is community colleges: 94 percent of public-sector community-college faculty are represented by bargaining agents. Nationwide, 70 percent of all collective bargaining agreements—and 78 percent of agreements in the public sector are in two-year colleges. The distribution in the population of HECAS contracts is similar: 68 percent are in two-year institutions, 25 percent in four-year institutions, and 7 percent in technical colleges (designated by title, technical colleges are all two-year institutions).[17] Yet, more faculty in four-year than in two-year institutions (138,254, versus 103,967) are covered by collective bargaining agreements. Why? Because large state systems of comprehensive colleges and universities tend to be unionized (85 percent of faculty in public four-year institutions other than research universities are unionized). In such a system, one contract may cover ten to twenty thousand faculty members. So there are more contracts in two-year than in four-year institutions, but these tend to be smaller colleges (and districts) in their total faculty numbers.

Such institutions are excellent sites for studying the restructuring of academic labor. It is the two-year and comprehensive four-year state college sectors that have been the most financially squeezed in recent years. Public-sector institutions in particular have been squeezed by reductions in the share of state budgets going to higher education. In absolute terms, state appropriations to higher education have not grown at the rates they did in previous years. The comprehensive state universities and two-year institutions have somewhat fewer and less lucrative alternatives than do research universities in generating additional revenues. In some states, in the early 1990s, there were absolute cuts in state appropriations to higher education.[18] Such cuts have been especially acute in many of the larger and industrial states, having an impact on big public state and municipal systems of higher education such as the California State University System, City University of New York, the Florida State University System, the Los Angeles community colleges, the Massachusetts State College and Regional Community College systems, the Minnesota community colleges, the Pennsylvania

State system, and State University of New York. All of these systems are unionized and are found in the data base used for this study.

In unionized institutions, the balance between managerial discretion and professional autonomy and constraint in academe on the one hand and the terms of faculty work on the other hand are clarified in various contractual provisions. Unionization has been a strategy not simply to increase wages but to enhance the collective faculty's voice in college and university governance. It also has been a strategy to restrict managerial discretion in regard to various conditions of employment. Indeed, one of the criticisms of unions is that they make it more difficult for managers to creatively restructure institutions. Unions are said to inhibit managerial flexibility with formal rules and structures that standardize and set constraints on working conditions and decision-making processes. Such formal conditions, embedded in college and universities' collective bargaining agreements, reflect the politics of professional work between faculty and management, writ *formally.*

Limitations of Data, Contractual Provisions

Of course, there are *informal* conditions, processes, and power structures that formal agreements neither fully define nor constrain. Not everything is in the contract. Just because something is not formalized in the contract does not mean it does not exist. However, that in itself is significant. For example, in January 1996 I presented data from chapter 5 on instructional technology at the annual meetings of the American Association for Higher Education, an association consisting largely of higher education administrators.[19] In response to my finding that very few contracts had clauses providing any kind of training in instructional technology for faculty, one dean of Arts and Sciences at a unionized institution stated that such training existed at her campus but was not in the contract. I asked her why she thought a training provision was not in the contract. She replied that management wanted to retain "flexibility." "What does that mean?" I asked. "Does it mean that management wants the 'flexibility' not to commit resources to such training if it so chooses, for budgetary reasons or otherwise?" Smiling, she replied that yes, that was certainly part of the reasoning.

What are the implications of such a situation for my study? That contractual provisions about training in instructional technology do not reliably measure the number of such training programs in unionized institutions. Some programs exist, but are not specified in the contracts.

That is fine, because that is not my analytical focus. However, the presence and the absence of such provisions *are* reliable indicators of managerial flexibility and professional rights in this area. That is good, because that is precisely my analytical focus.

Similarly, some contracts have "Past Practices" provisions. Such provisions acknowledge the validity of policies and practices that predate the contract. Depending on the nature of the provision, particular policies and practices may be specified, or the clause may speak generally and inclusively to a range of past policies and practices. Of course, it is worth noting that in general one of the reasons for unionization was to give faculty more control and managers less discretion over a range of work place matters. Thus, extensive past practices that favor professional rights and privileges are not likely. At any rate, only twenty-seven contracts in HECAS have such a provision. Of these, seven indicate that past policies do *not* apply. "Nothing contained in this agreement shall be interpreted as to imply or permit the invocation of past practices, or tradition, or accumulation of any employee rights or privileges other than those expressly stated herein." (Blue Mountain Community College, Article 36) Thus, less than 10 percent of HECAS contracts have past-practices provisions that support the continuation of previous policies/practices. About half of the provisions are statements about past practices in general.

> The parties agree to continue all past practices as defined above concerning faculty rights, privileges and terms and conditions of employment except as expressly modified by this Agreement or by mutual written consent; where the terms of this agreement and past practices are in conflict, the terms of this Agreement shall govern. (Western Michigan University, Article 5)

The other half specify particular practices and/or policies, such as scheduling of classes, release time for chairs, work load, nontraditional working patterns, formation of educational policy, overload priority, patent and copyright policy, and academic freedom.

What are the implications of such provisions for my study? Although in relative terms, the provisions are few in number, it would be extraordinarily difficult to go to each of the twenty contracts and determine first what policies and practices are recognized and then determine exactly what those policies are. For the purposes of this book, though, that is not necessary. Past-practices provisions are a strategy used by union negotiators to ensure some recognition of pre-existing terms of faculty labor. Union negotiators may choose not to negotiate contractual language for a certain policy for fear that the outcome will be less favorable for faculty than the terms of the past policy. Thus, they will leave the policy to be included under a past-practices provision.[20] The downside of such a strategy is that it accords management much more discretion than if the policy or practice were specified in a contractual article. (After all, it is often fear that contractual language would not be so favorable to faculty that leads union negotiators to pursue a past-practices strategy.) Managerial discretion is what I am interested in.

The strategy or tactic that is most clearly identified with unions is the strike. A strike is the most powerful, direct tool that most unions utilize (if only, sometimes, as a threat). It is an action that most publicly and plainly constrains managerial discretion.

However, the strike is not an action that many unionized faculty have often pursued (although many readers may be surprised by the total numbers). From 1984 to 1994, there were forty-eight strikes in colleges and universities nationwide. One-quarter of those took place in 1987. The mid-1980s were a period of greatest strike activity, with six strikes in 1986 and nine in 1985. After this period, the number of strikes has tapered off: three in 1988, four in 1989, one in 1990, five in 1991, three in 1992, none in 1993, and two in 1994.[21] From 1984 to 1994, there have been strikes at thirty-seven institutions of higher education. Two institutions—University of Bridgeport and Wayne State University—have had as many as three strikes each in that period.

One factor that contributes to the limited strike action among faculty is the "no-strike" provisions found in most faculty collective bargaining agreements. Faculty unions have relied more on grievance and arbitration than on strikes as the ultimate weapon inhibiting arbitrary or capricious managerial actions. Generally, no-strike provisions bar the union from engaging in or supporting strike action *during the term of the contract* (the union can strike after the contract expires; thus, some institutions with no-strike clauses nevertheless have had strikes).

The specifics of no-strike provisions vary in detail and scope. In the HECAS population of 212 contracts, 124 have such clauses. The largest number (61) of these prohibit not just "the union," but also its members, from engaging in or supporting any strike activity. The California State University System's contract offers one example of a prohibition.

> During the life of this Agreement, faculty unit employees shall not engage in strikes or other concerted activity which would interfere with or adversely affect the operations or the mission of the CSU. The CFA shall not promote, organize, or support any strike or other concerted activity. The CFA shall endeavor to prevent faculty unit employees from participating in a concerted activity which would interfere with or adversely affect the operations or the mission of the CSU. During the life of this Agreement, the CSU shall not lock out faculty unit employees. (Article 9)

The closing sentence points to a quid pro quo in many such clauses. Management agrees not to lock out workers if the union agrees not to strike. However, nearly one-third of the "no-strike" clauses lack a "no-lockout" clause.

Of the sixty-one provisions that prohibit unit members' involvement in a strike, 25 (41 percent) call for disciplinary action against faculty who do become involved. In five of those cases, termination also is identified as a managerial response to faculty involvement.

> No full-time faculty member covered by this agreement will instigate, sponsor, or participate in any strike, sympathy strike, slowdown, stoppage of work, or any other interruption of the operations of the College, regardless of the reason for so doing. Any or all full-time faculty members who violate this provision may be terminated or otherwise disciplined by the Board. (Illinois Eastern Community Colleges, Article 8)

All five provisions with termination language are in the contracts of community colleges (two other contracts have provisions preventing reprisals against faculty who engaged in a strike). Similarly, nine of eleven provisions prohibiting "sympathy strikes" (as in the above provision) are in the contracts of two-year institutions (the two others are from the Rhode Island School of Design, in the contracts for part- and for full-time faculty).

Statistical analysis reveals that the incidence of no-strike clauses is associated with institutional type ($x2=14.57$, significant at .005 level).[22] Such clauses are overrepresented in four-year institutions and underrepresented in two-year and technical colleges. The contracts of four-year institutions account for 25 percent of HECAS contracts, but 34 percent of no-strike provisions; whereas the contracts of two-year and technical colleges account for 68 percent and 7 percent respectively of HECAS contracts, and 60 percent and 6 percent of no-strike provisions. No-strike provisions are found in 81 percent of contracts in four-year institutions, 52 percent of those in two-year institutions, and 44 percent of contracts in technical colleges. In this regard, then, faculty in four-year institutions are more restricted in the strategies they can utilize to constrain managers' exercise of discretion.

Why are no-strike clauses significant? Consider the case of the Chicago City Colleges' contract. In summer 1995, the Illinois legislature passed HB 206, known as the Chicago School Reform Act. Attached to that bill—now Public Act 89-0015—is an amendment that undermines the collective bargaining rights of unionized teachers and faculty in Chicago. It prohibits Cook County College Teachers Union and schoolteachers' unions from bargaining issues including the following: layoffs, class size, class staffing and assignment, hours and place of instruction, use and staffing of programs to deliver instruction with new technology, and contracting work out to third parties.[23] The Illinois legislation is similar to that passed in some other states. Perhaps Michigan has gone the furthest, with legislation that not only limits the scope of bargaining (unions cannot bargain student contact time, privatization, and experimental and pilot programs, among other matters) but also prohibits strikes. Similarly, legislation passed in Oregon limits the scope of bargaining in areas such as class size, evaluation, discipline, scheduling (and arbitration standards were revised to give priority to the "public interest"). Many other states have considered or have pending comparable attacks on bargaining rights, including reform bills that provide for privatization, charter schools, and home rule districts that will bypass collective bargaining processes and rules.

At the NEA's annual higher education meetings in early March 1996, the president of the Cook County Teachers Union (AFT) spoke to this national pattern. He then delineated the bargaining rights that would be lost to Chicago City College faculty when the current contract expired (in July 1996). A member of the audience asked, "Why haven't you struck?" The president responded, "We can't strike. Our contract has a no-strike clause. So we are pursuing a political route first."[24]

The case of Chicago's city colleges points to the tremendous impact that the state legislature has on the legality and scope of collective bargaining in higher education (and to the import of the contract). Of course, the emergence of collective bargaining in the public sector was dependent on enabling legislation at the state level. However, other levels and branches of government have a significant influence on collective bargaining as well. For example, collective bargaining in private-sector higher education has been impacted by the Yeshiva decision (the meaning and impact of which have been much debated). The federal and state courts have influenced the scope and nature of collective bargaining. The executive and administrative branches of government also have influenced collective bargaining profoundly. For example, President Reagan's actions in the PATCO strike affected the extent of strike activity generally and management's response to strikes in particular (for example, the use of replacement workers or scabs). At the state level, governors have long played a major role in collective bargaining, often breaking strikes by calling in state troopers and the national guard. The actions (or inaction) of the National Labor Relations Board, and of state labor relations boards, also have influenced strike activities and managerial practices. Moreover, they have influenced what sorts of workers (for example, part-time) can be represented by unions.[25] Various domains of the state are embedded in contractual conditions. For example, managerial rights clauses often invoke state statutes. And layoff clauses are influenced by the language and outcomes of past court cases.[26]

By the time this book is published, there will no doubt have been new developments in the state's actions relative to collective bargaining. State legislation affecting collective bargaining rights will have been passed. New legislation may be pending. Cases will have been filed in state and federal courts. Some decisions will have been rendered and some appealed, and others may be in the process of being heard. Rulings by labor relations boards at the state and national levels will have been tendered. New disputes and complaints will be in the process of being filed and deliberated. In short, the actions and roles of various branches and levels of government are important and are in flux. The "state," writ large, plays a critical role in shaping unionization, practices of labor and management, and language and provisions of collective bargaining agreements.[27] However, analysis of the various levels and branches of the state and of the broader political economy as they relate to academic unions and the terms of faculty labor must await another book. Here, I concentrate on the contracts.

For the purposes of this study, the collective bargaining agreements themselves are an excellent data source. Contractual conditions are primary factors establishing the legal parameters of managerial discretion and of professional autonomy, involvement, and constraint in the academic work place. Agreements cover much that is central to the terms of faculty labor. They constitute and define much that contributes to stratification among faculty. Topics covered by contracts include wages and salary structures; personnel procedures and work-force matters such as retrenchment and layoffs and the use and ratio of part- to full-time faculty; use of instructional technology; outside employment and intellectual property; academic freedom; affirmative action; benefits such as leaves, insurance, professional development and training; rights of management and the association; and grievance and arbitration procedures. The agreements speak directly to and provide plenty of fodder for pursuing my central analytical interests—managerial discretion, professional autonomy and constraint, and professional stratification.

Professions and (Unionized) Faculty

There are many interesting and important questions surrounding faculty unions, many of which relate to pressing questions about unions in general. Have unions benefitted workers, and are professionals better off for having unionized? What negotiating (and organizing) strategies and priorities have unions adopted, and should these change in the future? What is the future of unions, or in their present form do unions have any future? Given recent attacks in the judicial, legislative, and executive branches of government on unions, what broader political strategies should unions pursue to increase their legitimacy in the public eye and ensure the future of collective bargaining? What reforms of colleges and universities should unions pursue? How do unions of professionals function in their internal organization and politics? Are they more or less democratic and independent than unions of other workers?

Yet this book is not about unions as such. It is about the conditions of employment of unionized faculty. It is about managerial flexibility and professional autonomy/self-governance, and about the restructuring and stratification of academic labor. I speak in part and indirectly to some issues about unions, per se. For example, I refer in places to strategies of unions and management that are evident in collective bargaining agreements. But my primary data is the contracts, as one set of parameters defining the terms of professional work. This is not a study of unions' forms and activities based on interviews with national union leaders or on analyses of union archives. My primary focus is on faculty who are unionized, not on unions that organize faculty.

My questions and central analytical interests stem from a particular sociological perspective on professions. I am a sociologist by training and a sociological scholar of higher education by profession. What does that mean? It means that I have been grounded in sociological research on professions. The perspective that I adopt in this study expresses elements of major debates in sociology surrounding professions. (Of course, it also expresses elements of the professional life I experience as a university academic.) I hope that a brief review of that sociological literature will help readers understand where I am coming from and where I am trying to go with this study.

Professionalization Theory

My graduate training in sociology in the mid to late 1970s was coincident with the rise of professionalization studies.[28] These studies challenged the functionalist perspective, which characterized and analyzed professions in terms of traits such as technical expertise, meritocracy, codes of ethics, values learned in professional education, and altruism.[29] Dating back to Durkheim, functionalists have regarded professions as a functional adaptation, a way of organizing work that better serves the needs of clients and society. By contrast, professionalization scholars have portrayed professions first and foremost as groups seeking to establish and maintain monopolies of expertise. These groups seek autonomous control of various terms, conditions, and domains of work. Professions are cast as self-interested groups that serve the interests not of their clients and of society, but of themselves, of powerful groups and/or classes, of capitalism, and of patriarchy.[30] The focus is on the political strategies by which professions establish or maintain license, autonomy, and prerogatives vis-à-vis lay society.

To some extent, I pursue related matters. I focus on professional autonomy, on faculty's control of and involvement in decisions surrounding key terms of academic labor. However, most professionalization work examines the social negotiation between profession and laity/society. By contrast, I examine the organizational struggle between professionals and the managers of the organizations in which they work.[31] Hence, the title of my book, *Managed Professionals.*

My analysis diverges from professionalization theory in another regard. I study professional autonomy and managerial discretion not as political strategies or efforts. Rather, I analyze them as negotiated terms of labor within organizations. Thus, I do not study the pronouncements, positions, and political activities of major faculty unions and of the major associations of administrators, though such a topic merits investigation. I study collective bargaining agreements.

The professionalization perspective has much to recommend it. I share much of its critique of professions. That academic critique has been matched by broader social challenges to professions, evident in women's, consumer, and environmental movements that have questioned the autonomy, practices, and expertise of professionals. I share much of these critiques as well.

Yet professionalization studies overlook important dimensions of and questions about professions. Their critique is limited. Professions are changing, as the social compacts between various professions and society in the United States are being renegotiated. So, too, sociological studies of professions are changing. In recent years, scholars have focused on reform movements within professions, on competition among professions, and on changing modes and ideologies of professionalism.[32]

Recent Sociological Research on Professions

Insights from recent work on professions inform my research. First, professions and the organizations in which they are employed are structures and places of work. Professionals are employees. The tasks of their work and the terms of their labor are important. The focus of professionalization studies on political strategies and interests blinds us to the nature of work and to the quality of work-life issues. In a systems model of professions, Abbott concentrates on work and on the negotiation of task control.[33] He also details professions as a competitive system, focusing on disputes between professional groups over jurisdictional boundaries. As a functionalist systems theorist, Abbott offers an "equilibrating model" that suggests such disputes are determined not by an exercise of power (as argued by professionalization theorists) but by objective and subjective qualities of the work of professions. A key dimension of jurisdictional disputes and settlements is in the control of tasks. Such control is established publicly, through claims in the public media, in legal discourse, and in workplace negotiation.

However, Abbott's work-place focus is on informal, private negotiations that allow internal adaptation and change in work while maintaining the profession's external public image. I modify Abbott's conceptual contributions in exploring faculty collective bargaining agreements. I examine competition and jurisdictional disputes not between professions, but between professionals and their managers. The workplace negotiation I study is grounded not in the informal domain of private adaptations and fluctuations, but in the formal domain of contracts. I focus on professional autonomy and constraint and on managerial discretion. What does that mean? In studying salary structures I ask what criteria shape salaries, to what extent are faculty involved in decisions surrounding salaries, and to what extent do managers have discretion to make salary adjustments on the basis of their own judgment? In studying retrenchment and reorganization I ask to what extent and at what point are faculty involved in decisions surrounding layoffs, and to what extent are managers free to make decisions on their own? In studying the use of part-time faculty I ask to what extent can full-time faculty determine the extent and ways in which part-time faculty are utilized; and to what extent do managers have discretion to act on their own in regard to the hiring, firing, and use of part-time faculty? In studying the use of instructional technology I ask to what extent and at what point are faculty involved in decisions surrounding the use of instructional technology, and to what extent are managers free to make decisions on their own? In studying policies regarding outside employment and intellectual property I ask to what extent do faculty have rights to their own time as independent professionals, and to the products of their labor; and to what extent do managers and institutions have claims on faculty as full-time, salaried employees? As a student of professions and as a faculty member, these are what I regard as some of the key terms of academic labor: who and what determines faculty *salaries*; who, and what conditions, determine a faculty member's *job security*; who controls *entry into and the shape of the professional work force*; who controls what dimensions of *deliv-*

ering curriculum; and what claims does a faculty member have to his or her *time* and *work products*.

A second sociological insight from recent work on professions is that they are internally stratified. The dichotomous focus on profession versus laity of professionalization studies blinds us to internal gradations and divisions, which are addressed in recent research. Instead, Brint focuses on stratification among and within professions, attributing professional position in the hierarchy to location in markets and organizations. He also focuses on divisions among professionals in their professional and political beliefs.[34] Finally, he points to the changing mode of professionalism in society, which is linked to patterns of internal stratification. In his view, professions are changing from "social trustee professionalism"—which emphasizes moral dimensions of work and casts professionals as guardians of socially important knowledge—to "expert professionalism"—which emphasizes technical dimensions of work and casts professionals as applying formal, technical knowledge. Brint suggests that professionals no longer mitigate the excesses of the marketplace—the ideology justifying the rise of professions. Rather, they are now directly implicated in and defined by marketplaces.

The application of Brint's concepts to the internal stratification of faculty by academic field is relatively straightforward. For example, there is an increasing emphasis on academics conducting research that has commercial relevance.[35] There is also a related redefinition of the terms of academic labor—for example, of intellectual property rights— and of the ideology of how universities serve the public interest.[36] In analyzing the contracts, then, I devote special attention to matters of the market, of intellectual property rights, of technology, and of professional stratification. I address the role of market criteria in faculty salaries. I consider the extent to which market considerations can be used to justify retrenchment or the hiring of increased numbers or proportions of part-time faculty. I consider the control of new technologies. I consider claims on faculty's commercially relevant activities and products. And in each case, I consider the extent to which there are divisions among different types or categories of faculty—for example, part- versus full-time or faculty in two-versus four-year institutions.

The sociological research on professions in general, then, is rich and useful. But recent sociological scholarship largely overlooks faculty. It ignores unionized faculty. Indeed, the sociological research on professions is divorced from sociological research on unions and labor relations.

Sociological Research on Faculty

There are many sociological studies of faculty. Many are classics, including analyses of academic recruitment, self-censorship in the McCarthy Era, meritocracy, academic values in education, scientific norms, academic divisions in political beliefs, distribution of faculty effort in research and teaching, and the increased power of research university faculty and their values.[37] More recently, scholars have studied faculty demographics, stratification of faculty in their work and values, the gendered nature of the profession, and the changing economic realities and dependencies of the work of professors and the revenue portfolios of institutions.[38]

The work cited above is excellent. It has informed and enriched my work. Nevertheless, there are limits to and gaps in the sociological literature on faculty. For example, much of the literature concentrates on faculty in elite research universities. In fact, much higher education literature reflects a view articulated by David Riesman four decades ago, that American higher education is a "snakelike procession," with the snake's body following the head.[39] Whether explicit or implicit, the assumption is that the majority of higher education is, to mix metaphors, a tail that follows (or aspires to follow) the dog(ma) of elite universities. Some scholars have analyzed the attitudes/aspirations of faculty in less prestigious settings, whether in community colleges or in comprehensive state colleges and universities.[40] For the most part, however, such settings are overlooked, and the presumption about the snakelike procession is not put to the test empirically.

I am a research university professor. When I discuss hierarchy in American higher education I place research universities at the top. I believe there are many patterns of upward aspiration. I know of colleagues who wish that they were at more prestigious institutions. I know of colleges that seek to become universities. Yet I also believe that there are alternative aspirations. Not all liberal arts colleges want to become research universities, and not all community colleges want to become four-year schools. There is much to be learned from the less prestigious levels of the higher education hierarchy.

Ironically, one of the key figures in the sociology of the professions, Everett C. Hughes, argues *against* a clear, objective distinction between professions and other occupations. In his view, *profession* is more of a subjective attribution by society (of value and status) than an objective characterization by social scientists of distinct traits that professions have but occupations do not. The similarities among professions and occupations are such that Hughes advocated studying the least prestigious realms of work in order to best understand the most prestigious ones.

> I have come to believe that it is a fruitful thing to start study of any social phenomena at the point of least prestige. For, since prestige is so much a matter of symbols, and even of pretensions . . . there goes with prestige a tendency to preserve a front which hides the inside of things; a front of names, of indirection, of secrecy. . . . On the other hand, in things of less prestige, the core may be more easy of access.[41]

Similar, some dimensions of the politics of professional work may be concealed in the more prestigious realms of academe and be more apparent in the less prestigious ones.

Such a sociological approach also can apply to different strata within a profession. I see collective bargaining as an occupational strategy to enhance a group's terms of work. It is worth exploring contracts to find the outcomes of that strategy. Yet I also see collective bargaining agreements—which are overwhelmingly found in American higher education's less prestigious sectors—as providing a window into the academic profession as a whole. At least the terms of academic labor in unionized institutions are suggestive in regard to what is happening generally with respect to salary structures, retrenchment and reorganization, the use of part-time faculty, the use of instructional technology, outside employment, and intellectual property rights. There may be parallels.

I do not look to compare the terms of faculty labor in unionized and nonunionized institutions. I lack a comparable data set for nonunionized settings. What is more important, the two sectors are not entirely independent. And therein lies a conceptual shortcoming of comparative salary studies in the higher education literature. They fail to address/model interactive effects between wages in unionized and nonunionized institutions, although there is substantial evidence of

such interactive effects in comparable settings outside of higher education.[42] Unionization has positive effects on wages in nonunionized
organizations and institutional sectors. In higher education, then, one
might expect that the existence (and threat) of faculty unions could lead
to increased salaries in nonunionized colleges and universities. Indeed,
there are certainly cases in which management has sought to undermine
organizing efforts by offering faculty salary increases. Yet interactive
effects are not incorporated into the higher education studies, which utilize linear regression in matched comparisons of institutions. Unionized and nonunionized institutions are treated as independent. (A
remarkable and ironic oversight in that such studies have been utilized
by management, unions, and scholars in the debate over the desirability
and effects of unionization, in an effort to inhibit or promote organizing
efforts.) Although empirical data do not support such a view, this work
generally regards unionization as a threat to professionalism and to faculty salaries.

At any rate, sociological studies of faculty as a profession neither
focus on unionized faculty nor utilize unionization as a major explana-
tory variable. Professions and unions are seen as antithetical structures.
This is true also in the higher education literature, with a few important
exceptions.[43] For example, Schuster and others follow a long and significant tradition in higher education of governance studies grounded in
pluralist political science, studies interested in "what works" in ensuring "shared governance."[44] They analyze a particular, innovative governance mechanism in unionized and nonunionized settings—"strategic
planning councils." They do not see unions as antithetical to the success
of such councils. Indeed, they see some "mature collective bargaining
units" playing a "strong and positive role in decision making."
However, they see unions as being fitted to sharing governance more in
the negotiation of wages, benefits, and working conditions than in
"strategic governance" in curricular and educational matters.

Sociological Literature on Labor Relations

There is, of course, a rich literature on labor relations and unions in
general. Yet it is focused largely on blue-collar, private-sector workers.
Indeed, despite the rise and growing prominence of white-collar, public-sector unions, the sociological literature on unions virtually ignores

feminized occupations/(semi?)professions such as nursing and teaching. It completely overlooks unionized faculty.[45]

Some of the exceptions to the blue-collar, private-sector focus of the sociological literature pose interesting issues for faculty unions. For example, Johnston's study of "social-movement unionism" concentrates on the distinctive political strategies and negotiating positions of public-sector workers.[46] Worker strength is said to lie more in strategic alliances and political resources than in economic market position. Successful movements and organizing efforts frame negotiations in ways that extend beyond the worker to the public agenda and public needs. Although I do not focus on strategies, Johnston's analysis sensitizes me to terms of labor that invoke needs and concerns beyond those of faculty. For example, to what extent do matters of quality figure into the contracts—such as, in the use of part-timers or of instructional technology? Johnston also features gender in his analysis, particularly in discussing leadership and coalitions within unions in various strikes. Other literature has addressed gender issues confronting unions, from membership and leadership issues to particular terms of labor—for example, salary structures and the wage gap, family policy, and part-time labor.[47] Such work is suggestive for my analysis of the terms of faculty labor. To what extent are gender equity and issues built into the contracts—for example, in salary structures and policies affecting control of faculty's private time?

Another exception to the private-sector focus of most sociological literature on unions is Murphy's study of "blackboard unions."[48] Her book is more on teacher unionism, per se, than on the histories of the AFT and NEA. Yet the reader gets a good sense of these two unions' different characters, traditions, strategies, and political positions over time. In addition, Murphy speaks a bit to the classic issue of democracy in unions—that is, unions studied as organizations, in terms of their governance structure.[49]

My data set is not suited to making comparisons among AAUP, AFT, and NEA negotiated contracts. I do not tell the reader which agent negotiates the best terms of labor for faculty, the best salaries, and so on. Even if I wanted to I could not conduct a *Consumer Reports* analysis of which union to choose. The 1994 HECAS data that I use does not allow for reliable comparisons along these lines. It includes some of the major contracts negotiated by each of the three big faculty unions, as well as by independents. But the NEA is overrepresented. Nationally, it is the agent for 46 percent, the AFT for 31 percent, and the AAUP for 11 percent of all collective bargaining agreements. In the HECAS population of 212 contracts, the NEA accounts for 58.5 percent, the AFT for 20 percent, and the AAUP for 6 percent of the agreements (the rest are independent bargaining agents).

The three major faculty unions are competitive organizations. In talking with officials and negotiators of each of them, such competitiveness is apparent, even as the AFT and NEA move toward a millennial merger. People emphasize differences among unions in negotiating strategies. However, any differences that exist may have a good deal to do with the types of institutions the three unions tend to represent. For example, the AAUP tends to be the agent in four-year and private institutions, whereas the NEA is more typically the agent in public and two-year institutions.

The HECAS data set allows for analysis of differences between the terms of faculty labor in four and two-year institutions. My principal reason for conducting this analysis is to get a sense of professional stratification in academe. To what extent and in what ways do the terms of faculty labor vary by institutional type? Such findings also may be useful in understanding any differences that others might suggest exist among the three major unions.

Principally, however, in this book, I pursue one of the central issues in labor history, generally, in David Brody's terms, "the efforts of laboring people to assert some control over their working lives, and . . . the equal determination of American business to conserve the prerogatives of management."[50]

I do not intend to cast faculty as proletarianized "workers." They are not. They are professionals. But in the context of colleges and universities that are increasingly privatized and capitalistic in their orientation, faculty are increasingly managed professionals. And the story of social relations between faculty and managers is one of the ongoing negotiation of professional autonomy and managerial discretion.

Restructuring Professional Rewards: The Structure, Stratification, and Centrality of Faculty Salaries

Not too long ago, a cabbie driving me from a conference hotel to the airport asked what I did for a living. I told him I was a college professor. His next question was, "How much more does your boss make than you?" A natural social scientist. Right to the heart of occupational stratification—salaries.

There are many studies of unionized faculty's salaries. However, they compare the salaries of unionized faculty to those of faculty in nonunionized settings, not to the salaries of their "bosses." Most scholars expect nonunionized faculty to be better paid, for unionization is considered a sign and/or cause of *de*-professionalization, and thus of lower pay. However, the findings do not support these expectations.

In this chapter, I, too, pose questions about salaries and bosses. Yet they are different questions than those posed by either the cabbie or by higher education scholars. I am interested less in salary comparisons than in salary structures. What criteria and factors in contracts shape faculty salaries? Who controls the application of those criteria? What degree of faculty involvement and managerial discretion is evident in decision-making processes and criteria surrounding salary adjustments?

To return for a moment to the cabbie, my first reaction to his question about my boss's salary was, "*What* boss? *I* don't have a '*boss.*' " I have been steeped in the profession's ideology of autonomy. Of course, I do have a boss. More than one. And like most academics I know, I kvetch about the salaries of the president, provost, vice-presidents, vice-provosts, deans, and so on at my institution. (I cannot bring myself to write "*my* president").

Academics' ideological sensibilities are offended by administrators' salaries: *our* sense is that *their* salaries are based more on formal location in the organization (position) than on performance (merit). We see ourselves as more qualified and meritorious. Meritocracy is a key element of academic ideology. Faculty, as with other professionals, seek to establish and maintain autonomous, collegial control of professional review. We call it "peer review." Systems of reward (and punishment) and reviews for promotion and salary adjustment should be run by professional peers exercising judgment on the basis of criteria that can best (and should only) be interpreted by peers.

Much to our surprise and chagrin, in recent years the prevailing public perception is that faculty members are overpaid and underworked. That view is shared by many administrators, those eleven-month contract, 8:00 A.M. to 6:00 P.M. salaried persons who increasingly seem to be exercising powers to assess the value and centrality of individual academics' work and of entire academic units. *Their* sense is that *faculty* are often not at work in designated workspaces (that is, offices on campus). We are not working hard enough, or we are not working hard enough for the institution (in lower division undergraduate teaching) versus for our own interests or careers (in upper division and graduate vanity courses and in research—writing articles and books).

To what extent is merit embedded in contracts as a key criteria shaping unionized faculty's salaries? To what extent do faculty and administrators influence the definitions and decision making surrounding the reward of merit? From a managerial perspective, do contracts accord managers discretion to encourage and reward what they regard as meritorious performance? From a faculty perspective, do contracts allow for peer review and reward according to professional merit?

Of course, occupational stratification and academics' sensibilities are grounded in more than merit and income differentials between administrators and faculty. Faculty are sensitive to other income comparisons. For instance, at my university everyone's salary is a matter of public record, on file at the library. Many faculty members review this record. Sometimes the review is part of a faculty member's effort to support his or her case for a raise. Sometimes it is simply morbid curiosity. First faculty look in outrage at administrators' salaries. Then we compare our salaries with those of faculty colleagues we know.

"Can you believe what so and so makes?" "I'm more productive than he is." "How did he rate a bigger salary increase than I got last year?" The indignation arises from our sense that "meritocracy" has not been served.

How do we react to salary differentials among departments? Differences across departments and colleges are far greater than those within. Although we bemoan these differentials, we are more likely and able to justify them by "the market." It may gall education faculty that their colleagues in business, law, and engineering have far higher salaries. But we can attribute the differences to a sense that faculty in these fields can move into the private sector and command higher salaries. Such faculty are more "marketable." Or education faculty can attribute salary differences to "society's"—and the "market's"—failure to sufficiently value education.

Thus, a second criteria on which I focus is the market. To what extent is the market embedded in contracts as a key criteria shaping unionized faculty's salaries? To what extent do faculty and administrators influence the definitions and decision making surrounding market-based adjustments? From a managerial perspective, do contracts accord managers discretion to differentially reward individual faculty and units that are perceived as being close to the market? From a faculty perspective, do contracts enable marketable individuals to negotiate higher salaries, or faculty as a collective to review, monitor, and define what units are close to the market? Such questions are relevant now, when managers are seeking to make their colleges and universities more productive and to link them more closely to various external markets.

Some groups of faculty have taken salary comparisons to a collective level. Women faculty have undertaken comparisons of men's and women's salaries, charging that there is gender discrimination and inequity in the professional reward structure. Meritocracy is violated if salaries are influenced by faculty's particularistic characteristics (such as gender or ethnicity), and not only by their achievements. As a result, some institutions have created systems for making "equity adjustments" (these often apply not just to women but also to minorities and veterans). Generally, the criteria and process for determining the existence of an inequity apply to individual faculty, to comparisons of their salaries with those of comparable peers in their fields. The greatest salary stratification between men and women (and faculty generally) is field based.[1] It is linked to the fields in which women are more likely to work (for example, education, English, and nursing versus engineering, physics, and medicine). If most administrators and faculty attribute such salary differentials to "the market," some faculty have pursued the issue in their scholarship and/or institutions as a matter of comparable worth.[2]

Not all equity adjustments are specific to gender or to other personal characteristics such as race or ethnicity. Internal equity related to market-induced distortions of salary profiles has emerged as a significant issue for faculty in general. The market violates meritocracy. The problem may take various forms. It may be "inversion": new faculty's salaries being higher than those of recently hired faculty. It may be salary "compression" experienced by faculty who have been at the institution a long time. It may be the effect of a few faculty receiving counteroffers that jump them ahead of comparable peers.[3] Or, at a collective level, inequities may refer to salary inequalities among faculty within and/or across fields. Some institutions have established equity adjustment policies to reduce the inequitable effects of the market.

To what extent, then, is equity embedded in contracts as a key criteria shaping unionized faculty's salaries? Are equity considerations specific to gender (or to race/ethnicity) or market effects, or do they apply generally to salary differences? To what extent do faculty and administrators influence the definitions and decision making surrounding equity adjustments? From a managerial perspective, do contracts accord managers the discretion to adjust salaries to reduce internal inequity? From a faculty perspective, do contracts enable faculty, as individuals or as a collective, to review, monitor, and define salary inequities and to ensure adjustments accordingly? Such questions are quite relevant in a time when managers are seeking to exercise more flexibility in allocating revenues and faculty resources to academic units.

In this chapter, then, I concentrate on the salary structures found in collective bargaining agreements. I consider the extent to which they incorporate merit, market, and equity into the salary structure of full-time faculty. I also consider the extent to which managerial discretion and professional involvement are built into the structure of faculty salaries.

Addressing such issues represents a useful empirical contribution. Many, if not most, people (especially scholars/faculty in nonunionized settings) associate unions with standardized reward structures in which salaries are uniform and are based on seniority. From a traditional faculty perspective such a structure violates the profession's principle of meritocracy. From a managerial perspective such a structure violates managerial prerogatives. (Of course, from yet another perspective, such a structure might serve to protect the collective interests and unity of the academic profession.) Yet we lack a comprehensive empirical analysis of salary structures in faculty contracts.[4]

Analytically, I explore professional reward structures as a way of yielding insight into the management and restructuring of academic labor. Salary structures in collective bargaining agreements offer insight into the terms of academic labor and patterns of managerial discretion in rewarding and thereby influencing the academic work force. However, analytically, I also am interested in professional stratification. For this issue, salary patterns of actual salaries, not structures, are the relevant indicator.

As for academic analysis, so for professional practice. Current efforts to restructure academic institutions and labor are grounded in two assumptions about faculty salaries: (a) managers require more flexibility in personnel and salary matters to foster merit and respond to the marketplace; (b) personnel costs account for the overwhelming proportion of an institution's costs, and faculty account for the overriding proportion of such personnel costs. An empirical analysis of salary structures is obviously relevant to (a). However, consideration of actual salaries is necessary to address (b).

Thus, in closing this chapter, I review data on salary stratification among fields (as a way of addressing managers' ability to respond to the market) and on faculty salaries' centrality in institutional expenditures—that is, faculty's share of higher education's professional personnel work force costs. I come full circle, then, to finally address the cabbie's question of how faculty salaries compare to the salaries of their "bosses." Data on stratification patterns among fields, and on faculty salaries' share of institutional expenditures, yield insight into restratification among faculty and restructuring of faculty's position relative to administrators and other professionals in higher education's work force.

Existing Research on Salaries and Restructuring Professions

Although there is considerable research on faculty salaries in general, research on faculty salaries in unionized institutions is relatively limited. Most of this work compares salaries in unionized and nonunionized settings. Some addresses merit pay in the two settings.

For the most part, comparative studies of faculty salaries in unionized and nonunionized institutions are dated (based on data from the 1970s and early 1980s) and are limited in analytical scope. Soon after faculty unions emerged, scholars began conducting studies comparing average faculty salaries in unionized and nonunionized settings. Some found that average salaries were higher in unionized settings. Others found no significant impact of unionization on salaries. Still others suggested that if salaries were adjusted for differences in cost of living by state, the wage benefits of unionization would disappear. Virtually all of the studies share two limitations: the focus is on average salaries for all faculty, and the analytical methods underlying the comparisons (that is, the regression models) do *not* model interactive, "spill-over" effects of wages in unionized and nonunionized institutions. On the latter point, one set of investigators acknowledged that after an initial significant benefit to unionized faculty, the salaries of unionized faculty probably have an 'inflationary' effect on those of nonunionized faculty. That would explain why salary differentials had declined over time.[5]

Comparative salary studies do not tell us much about the structure of salary adjustments for unionized faculty. Other than that the structures may not be vastly different from those in nonunionized institutions, for average salaries in the two settings are comparable. Such studies do not offer insight into salary criteria, procedures, and mechanisms in collective bargaining agreements. Nor do they speak to salary stratification among fields or to differences between faculty salaries and those of their bosses and of other professionals on campus.

Some research exists on merit pay in collectively bargained agreements in higher education. Unfortunately, it too is rather dated. However, it does identify a baseline pattern in the past with which I can compare findings from the contractual analyses regarding merit provisions. Reviewing earlier studies, Mortimer contrasts unionized and nonunionized institutions in terms of the prevalence of merit criteria in shaping salary.[6] He indicates that less than half of unionized colleges and universities utilize meritocratic criteria in determining annual salary increases. Further, he points to a decline over the previous decade in the presence of merit in faculty contracts. Similarly, Douglas and Goldsmith find that only thirty-four of about two hundred faculty contracts have merit pay provisions. More recently, Hansen finds twenty-four of fifty AAUP contracts have some information on merit pay.[7] Such work benchmarks merit practices. Yet it does not address the scope of my analytical interests, from market and equity provisions to faculty and administrators' role in applying them.

Much scholarship tracks faculty salaries nationally, over time. Salaries are tracked by faculty rank, field, gender, ethnicity, state, and institutional type. But the salaries of unionized faculty are not treated separately as a distinct data point in such studies, even in the annual faculty salary report of a premier union, the AAUP.[8]

A number of studies analyze factors shaping faculty salaries. Many variables have been considered—age, rank, gender, publications, prior administrative experience, prestige of institution, and more.[9] Yet studies do not consider the differential play of such factors in unionized and nonunionized colleges and universities.

Nevertheless, general salary studies and salary trend data are useful. In closing the chapter, I review the literature on faculty salaries in general as a foil for summarizing my results about salary structures in the contracts. I also use the literature and trend data as a foil for considering prevailing assumptions about the effects of unionization on salaries. Finally, I utilize trend data to suggest some patterns in the stratification and centrality of faculty salaries, yielding insight into the restructuring of academic labor.

What patterns of salary structure and restructuring might one expect to find, given restructuring in professions generally and higher education in particular? As discussed in chapter 1, much sociological research on professions has emerged in recent years. Although little of that work speaks directly to the academic profession, the major theses coming out of it have clear implications for faculty salary structures. If, for example, Brint's "expert professionalism" is transforming and even replacing "social trustee professionalism," then one would expect to find considerable and increasing emphasis on market considerations in the salary structures of collective bargaining agreements.[10] In higher education, patterns of policy change and organizational restructuring suggest the increased importance of certain markets and actors in shaping colleges' and universities' internal allocation of resources. Indeed, decision-making processes and choices about reallocating resources to academic programs are being guided less and less by programs' reputations and quality (merit) and more and more by their closeness to academic, student, and corporate markets.[11] Therefore, one might expect merit to be less of a consideration than market in shaping salaries. One might also expect to find greater managerial prerogatives in implementing market-based salary adjustments than in merit-based ones.

At the same time, research on the political strategies of less powerful professional groups suggests that faculty unions might work to counter the managerial emphasis on the market in a couple of ways. For example, if faculty members adopt the "inclusion" strategies of the female health professionals studied by Witz (that is, working through the state to change policy and law), then one would expect to find considerable evidence of gender- (and race or ethnicity) based equity mechanisms for prohibiting discrimination and/or providing redress to counter the effects of past discrimination.[12] And if faculty unions follow the political strategies of the public sector unions studied by Johnston, then one would expect to find evidence of mechanisms that appeal to universalistic norms—for example, equal treatment and salary equity for faculty, and comparable worth as gender justice.[13]

Of course, much of the recent sociological work retains the conventional functionalist separation of professional and unionized workers. Unions are considered antithetical to professionalism. In which case one would expect to find little emphasis on merit or on professional markets in the salary structures of faculty unions' collective bargaining agreements.

I now turn to my analysis of merit, market, and equity, and of managerial discretion and professional involvement, in the salary structures of contracts. Each analysis is grounded in a term-based search of HECAS contracts (that is, searches on merit*, market*, and equit*/inequit*), and in a contract by contract reading of all clauses having to do with salaries and compensation.[14]

Merit

Merit is the most common of the three salary structures found in collective bargaining agreements. A search on merit* yielded 48 contracts with provisions that explicitly refer to the term *merit* in salary clauses. That is more than the combined total of contracts with equity (26) or market adjustment (21) provisions. (Nevertheless, of the 203 contracts for full-time faculty in HECAS, 76 percent do *not* have provisions using the term *merit*.)

Merit figures into contracts in three other regards. First, some clauses use terminology (for example, "performance based") other than merit. Salary increases may be linked to scholarly performance and/or productivity. Second, many contracts award salary credit for proxy measures of merit—completion of college/graduate courses and advanced degrees. (If that sounds like the salary schedule of K through twelve schoolteachers, it is. Yet it is also consistent with the fact that degree is directly related to pay in postsecondary institutions.[15]) Third, union-negotiated salary structures—such as steps, across-the-board pay raises, and the like—did not simply replace existing academic structures, they were often layered on top of a pre-existing professional career/reward structure—the rank structure of assistant, associate, and full professor, with tenure and attendant salary adjustments. Movement through those statuses is governed by decisions regarding the merit of candidates.

Merit Specified in the Contracts

Of the 48 contractual provisions on merit, over half (27) are in the agreements of 4 year institutions (one is in the agreement of a technical college). The incidence of such provisions is dependent on institutional type. Collapsing two-year and technical colleges into one category, the association is significant at the .005 level ($x2=34.01$). Four-year institutions are overrepresented: 52 percent of the contracts in such institutions utilize the term *merit* as compared to 14 and 6 percent of the contracts in two-year and technical colleges (see table 2.1).

The merit provisions speak primarily to pay (11 contracts address only promotion). Of those provisions, by far the most call for changes in base salaries (29 contracts) rather than for one-time bonuses (4 contracts). That runs counter to Hansen's findings with 50 AAUP contracts.[16]

TABLE 2.1
INCIDENCE OF MERIT PROVISIONS

	Explicit merit	Faculty involvement	Merit in other words	Merit by proxy
Two-year	20 (14%)*	2	6	94
Technical	1 (6%)	0	0	0
Four-year	27 (52%)	10	6	6
Total	48	12	12	100

* The percentage of all such contracts in HECAS

Merit provisions take various forms. They are relatively evenly divided in terms of faculty involvement in the process: in 8 contracts, decisions are made by administration, with no meaningful faculty consultation; in 9 cases there is joint administrative and faculty involvement in the decision; and in 3 cases faculty committees are the principal evaluators of whether merit monies are awarded a faculty member. The numbers are too small for meaningful statistical analysis. Nevertheless, it is suggestive that 8 of the 9 contracts in which there is joint decision making, and 2 of the 3 in which faculty committees decide, are contracts of four-year institutions. Faculty appear to be more likely in four-year than in two-year institutions to enjoy some measure of professional involvement in decision making about merit awards.

Most merit provisions attach to decisions surrounding regular step or ladder increases. Movement up a step salary scale is governed by merit. Such provisions are much more common than set-aside programs/payments for rewarding meritorious performance that do not become part of the base salary. Both types of provision are built into the California State University System contract.

Merit salary adjustments (MSAs) refer to annual upward movement between steps on the salary schedules. Such adjustments shall be one step annually, and shall be limited to four MSAs following appointment or the most recent promotion. No MSAs will be granted beyond step 20 on the appropriate schedule. Upon the determination by the appropriate administrator that an employee has performed with merit in carrying out the duties of his/her position, the employee shall receive a merit salary adjustment. Such a determination shall be after consideration of material in the employee's Personnel Action File. (Articles 31.11,31.12)

The parties are committed to provide special incentives for meritorious performance and professional promise in the areas of teaching, other professional accomplishments and service to the University community. This program is dedicated to that end. Criteria to be used in the evaluation of faculty applications for these incentive awards shall be developed mutually by the academic senate or council and the campus President or designee. In each fiscal year of this Agreement, there shall be 1870 awards, and each award shall be in the amount of $2,500. This amount shall not accrue to the base salary of the recipient. . . . The faculty of a particular school, college, or appropriate administrative unit shall, after consideration of applications therefore, forward, in a timely fashion to the Dean or appropriate administrator recommendations as to individuals designated to receive the award. (Articles 31.17,31.18,31.19,31.22)

Provisions regarding step increases take a variety of forms.

Movement through the schedule at the rate of one increment per year to Step VII (where applicable) shall be based on merit. (Erie Community College, Article 68)

A merit increment of 4.2 percent of the faculty member's class and step placement will be granted upon completion of nineteen years of satisfactory service to the District or upon completion of five years of satisfactory service at Step 14 of the Basic Faculty Salary Schedule. Satisfactory service is defined as a rating of Satisfactory on the annual/biannual evaluation. (Kern Community College, Article 5I10A)

Each academic department head shall annually evaluate the teaching, research, and professional service of each tenured, probationary, and term faculty member for the purpose of merit salary increases. (University of Northern Iowa, Article 3.43)

Yet all involve some form of regular review governing movement on the salary schedule. Faculty do not automatically move up by virtue of seniority.

Allocation of merit money may involve professional judgment. But there is much managerial control and discretion built into these provisions. Some clauses explicitly accord discretion to the administration in such matters. "The College shall be authorized to grant, at its discretion, merit/equity salary increases beyond the increases stipulated in the Agreement; application of this provision would be limited to up to ten faculty members and a total of $5,000 in each year of the Agreement" (Hudson Valley Community College, Article 12D).[17]

Most clauses do not make decision making explicit, thereby leaving discretion in managers' hands. Other evidence of managerial flexibility is that in nearly one-third (14) of merit provisions decisions are not grievable (or in a couple of cases, not subject to binding arbitration).

Contrary, then, to prevailing characterizations of unions, a substantial minority (24 percent) of faculty collective bargaining agreements overall, and a majority of contracts in four-year institutions (54 percent) have provisions utilizing the term, *merit*. Even by this narrow measure, that represents a greater incidence of merit provisions than found by Douglas and Goldsmith for two- and four-year institutions (17 percent) and by Hansen for four-year institutions (48 percent).[18]

Depending on one's professional position and view of professionalism, such evidence might be seen as good or bad news. Whatever the case, it contradicts prevailing views of reward structures in the contracts of unionized workers. Similarly, for better or worse, there is evidence of much room for managerial discretion in decision making surrounding merit adjustments. That contradicts the prevailing view that unionization prevents managers from rewarding what they regard and label as "meritorious performance."

Merit in Other Words

Of course, clauses may be grounded in conceptions of merit without actually utilizing the term. In reading through the salary sections of the HECAS contracts, many clauses are merit provisions in other words. In addition to the 48 provisions that use the term *merit*, another twelve contracts address merit in other words. Thus, one in three (30 percent) of the HECAS contracts have merit provisions in the traditional sense of the word—that is, salary supplements for individual faculty due to exemplary achievement. Of the additional twelve clauses, six each are in the contracts of four-year and two-year institutions. Overall, then, merit provisions are found in over two-thirds (68 percent) of contracts in four-year institutions, as compared to 19 percent of the contracts in two-year institutions (only one technical college contract has a merit provision). The incidence of such provisions is associated with institutional type ($x2=42.19$, significant at .005 level).

Most of the twelve provisions that address merit in other terms speak to salary adjustments for outstanding performance. Those adjustments range from advanced placement on a salary schedule for "demonstrating a superior contribution to the educational goals and endeavors of the College" (DuPage Community College) to selective salary increases and performance-based adjustments (for example, Wayne State University, Western Oregon State College). Four provisions have to do with identifying and rewarding "distinguished professors" (for example, Adirondack Community College, Youngstown State University).

One factor that may account in part for the greater presence of merit provisions in the contracts of four-year than of two-year institutions is evident in two contracts from the University of Nebraska system. The contract of the University of Nebraska, Omaha, long a part of the system, has a merit clause.

> Salary Increases for Exceptional Performance. $137,356, less any amount required to meet promotion increases specified above, shall form a salary increase pool to be distributed to the Colleges for allocation to Unit Members based on performance. The dollars allocated to the Colleges shall be proportional to the salary base of Unit Members as of April 25, 1994. (Article 4.2.6)

The contract of the University of Nebraska, Kearney, recently transitioning from a state college to part of the University System, reveals the pressure to incorporate a similar merit clause.

> The UNKEA recognizes that performance-based pay is a concern of the Board and acknowledges that pay plan which recognizes and rewards exceptional performance on the part of the University faculty members can be a legitimate means to foster and promote excellence in the pursuit of the institution's mission. The parties further acknowledge that the validity of any performance-based pay plan depends, of necessity, on the integrity of the underlying evaluation mechanism and their mutual agreement as to the method by which performance dollars are identified

and distributed among eligible faculty. In light of the foregoing and in recognition of the fact it is appropriate to explore and, if possible, develop a performance-based pay plan as part of the transition of Kearney from a state college to a part of the University of Nebraska System, the Board and the UNKEA hereby agree to establish a joint committee composed of six individuals, three of whom shall be appointed by the UNKEA and three of whom shall be appointed by the Board, and to undertake a comprehensive examination of performance-based pay. . . . The Committee . . . shall make its final recommendation regarding performance-based pay prior to the commencement of negotiations for the 1995–97 Collective Bargaining Agreement. (Article VII, Section 4)

Most obvious in this provision is the belief that merit-based pay is in some sense more appropriate as one moves up higher education's prestige hierarchy. (Some would argue that increased reliance on merit mechanisms as one moves up the hierarchy reflects the wider range of professional responsibilities and greater differentiation of skills and roles in research universities versus in community colleges.) Equally important is the role played by faculty in ensuring the "integrity of the underlying evaluation mechanism" and in shaping the process. Merit provisions not only draw on professional criteria, but they also often involve faculty in decision making surrounding salary adjustments.

Proxy Measures of Merit

In addition to conventional merit provisions there are proxy measures of merit. Such proxies shape salaries by awarding salary points or bonuses or by making salary schedule placement or advancement based on education, degrees, and professional development. Proxies for merit most often are found in the contracts of two-year institutions, where salaries are typically structured by salary schedules. Such structures replace the career ladder of assistant, associate, and full professor with annual steps. Over two thirds (69 percent) of the 137 contracts covering full-time faculty in two-year colleges have such schedules, versus 12 percent of contracts in four-year institutions. (The difference is statistically significant: $x2=47.02$, significant at the .005 level). Most other two-year college contracts establish salary minimums, maximums, or ranges. Placement on schedules generally is determined not just by seniority, but by degrees and/or course credits, among other criteria.

Thus, educational achievement and certification serve as proxies of merit.

The most common proxy measures are degrees and course credit. Over two-thirds of two-year college contracts provide for salary adjustment and/or salary schedule placement or advancement based on degrees; 64 percent make such provision based on college or graduate course credits. Far fewer contracts in four-year institutions have such proxies—12 and 40 percent respectively.[19] Overall, including technical college contracts (11 provisions for degrees, 10 for course credits), such proxies are found in over half of the contracts. Provisions regarding degrees are in 126 (62 percent), and those regarding course credits in 107 (53 percent) contracts.

Other proxy measures are mentioned in contracts but are not nearly as common. In twenty-three (11 percent) contracts (twenty-two in community colleges, one in a technical college), salary credit is awarded for various professional development activities. In nineteen (9 percent) contracts (twelve in community colleges, five in four-year institutions, two in technical colleges), provisions indicate that movement up the salary schedule is contingent upon satisfactory performance. Another six contracts mention research or publications. (Many contracts have more than one proxy measure: thus the total is greater than the number of contracts.)

Obviously, the existence of set salary schedules inhibits managerial discretion in shaping faculty salaries. Similarly, proxies of merit represent set criteria that minimize managerial discretion. More than that, such criteria reflect achievement as judged and determined by faculty, who teach the courses and gatekeep the earning of degrees. The manager's role is largely to monitor/verify the validity of faculty members' claims to course and/or degree completion. Such a function serves not to reduce professional autonomy, but to protect it. It is based on an acceptance of professional claims.[20]

Perpetuating Existing Professional/Career Structures

Merit figures into salary structures of faculty in unionized institutions in an additional regard. The salary structures of contracts are often layered on top of existing professional career and reward structures. Many contracts specify salary adjustments for promotion up the traditional ranks of the academic career—from assistant to associate to full professor. Such promotion generally is based on peer review. Professional input outweighs or counterbalances managerial discretion. (The extent to which promotion and tenure decisions are in the hands of faculty peers, department heads, deans, and provosts varies by institutional type. On the one hand, this is a very significant dimension of faculty self-governance. On the other hand, faculty control over such matters is far from total. Even in the most prestigious of universities administrators can and sometimes do override faculty decisions. Moreover, the link between such decisions and salaries is generally not specified and not always direct.)

The incidence of provisions for promotion up the traditional academic career ladder is dependent on institutional type ($x2=34.88$, significant at the .005 level). The contracts of four-year institutions are overrepresented. Of the seventy-two such provisions (36 percent of the HECAS contracts), thirty-six are in the contracts of four-year institutions—which represents 72 percent of the four-year HECAS population. The set salary schedules of two-year institutions are far less likely to have the traditional rank structures of faculty built into them: thirty-four promotion-based adjustment clauses are in the contracts of two-year colleges (two others are technical college contracts), representing 25 percent of the two-year HECAS contracts.

Merit: Summary

In sum, the findings contradict the view that unions are antithetical to meritocracy. Merit provisions are embedded in the salary structures of most collective bargaining agreements. They take various forms, and many contracts contain various such provisions. Yet there is a significant pattern in the incidence of different sorts of merit provisions. The mechanisms that provide for the reward of merit and achievement vary by institutional type.

A substantial majority (68 percent) of contracts of four-year institutions have merit provisions that allow for salary adjustments of individual faculty for their job performance. A comparable number (72 percent) provide salary adjustments for promotions in academic rank. By contrast, for two-year colleges, the numbers are 19 and 25 percent, respectively.

A substantial majority of contracts of two-year institutions base salary schedule placement and/or adjustments on the meritocratic proxies of degrees (69 percent) and course credits (64 percent). Other proxies, such as publications and professional development, are factored into faculty's salary adjustments in 29 percent of the contracts. By contrast, for four-year institutions, the numbers are 40, 12, and 12 percent, respectively.

In the contracts of four-year institutions one is more likely to find merit provisions that follow a conventional model of merit-based pay that is defined in the literature. In the contracts of two-year institutions one is more likely to find merit provisions that diverge from the merit pay literature.

To many academics, certification-based proxies of merit that govern movement up the ladder of a set salary schedule may not seem to fit a professional model of merit. They might instead seem more typical of schoolteachers' salary structures. One colleague, upon reading a draft of this chapter, said that I was on "thin ice" in identifying such mechanisms as proxies of merit. Perhaps. But I am married to a former schoolteacher. I teach schoolteachers. And from that perspective, I see conventional models of merit-based pay as being very much like models of merit pay for schoolteachers.[21] They are no less problematic than are proxy measures in this regard. And in some regards the merit pay model is *more* problematic than set schedules in that they accord extensive discretion to managers. (For example, in spring 1996 the New Jersey State College Locals/AFT reached an agreement on a new four-year contract, averting a potential strike. The principal point of contention was a proposal by the college presidents that would have replaced a system of regular salary increments with smaller merit steps awarded according to the discretion of the presidents.) More to the point, it is hardly novel to reward professionals by certification. Certification has a more powerful effect on the salaries of research university faculty than do publications, which are arguably weak proxies of merit.[22] Further, in many professions (such as those in the medical field), continuing education is required throughout one's career in order to maintain one's professional standing. So, too, for many faculty in unionized two-year institutions. Pursuing an advanced degree is an important way of keeping up in one's field and of maintaining or enhancing expertise.

In conventional, explicit provisions for merit pay, faculty often are involved in the process surrounding merit adjustments. However, there is also much room for the exercise of managerial discretion, contrary to prevailing views of the effects of unions on salary structures. By contrast, in the case of certification, proxy measures of merit, managers have less room for exercising discretion vis-à-vis reward structures shaped by faculty. Ironically, such discretion tends to be greater in the contracts of four-year institutions.

Market

To what extent does the market appear in salary structures in collective bargaining agreements? Roughly 10 percent of HECAS contracts (twenty-one) have provisions that explicitly link salaries to the market conditions of the field or faculty member. A reading of the salary sections of all the contracts reveals another nineteen contracts with market clauses that do not use the term *market*. (One of these—in the CUNY contract—is of special interest because of the number of faculty affected and because it reveals the recency of the market's inclusion in at least some agreements.) Moreover, union-negotiated salary structures have been built on existing patterns of market-based variations in salaries. Bargaining agents worked from a pre-existing base of salary differentiation, which has been perpetuated. Finally, there is some evidence of an increased emphasis on market considerations in collective bargaining agreements. Of the twenty-one current contracts with market provisions, in nine cases I have copies of earlier contracts. In seven cases there are substantial differences between the earlier and the current contracts.

Market Specified in The Contracts

As with merit provisions, over half of the contractual provisions specifying market considerations are in the agreements of four-year institutions. Of twenty-one provisions, eleven are in the contracts of four-year institutions, seven in those of two-year colleges, and three in the contracts of technical colleges (21, 5, and 19 percent respectively of four-year, two-year, and technical college HECAS contracts). There is a dependent association between the incidence of market provisions and institutional type ($x2=12.67$, significant at .005 level). Salary structures that emphasize market are far less likely to be found in contracts of two- than of four-year institutions and of technical colleges: two-year institutions account for 68 percent of the relevant contracts, but only 33 percent of market provisions; four-year institutions and technical colleges account for 25 and 7 percent of the contracts, but 52 and 14 percent of market provisions (see table 2.2).

TABLE 2.2
INCIDENCE OF MARKET PROVISIONS

	Explicit market	*Faculty involvement*	*Market in other words*
Two-year	7 (5%)*	0	8
Technical	3 (19%)	0	0
Four-year	11 (21%)	4	12
Total	21	4	20

* The percentage of all such contracts in HECAS

    Provisions specifying market considerations take different forms. In the vast majority of cases, provisions give managers considerable discretion to respond to the demand of external labor markets in the profession. (Some provisions also invoke the market negatively; I address these in the section on equity provisions.) In one exceptional case, a clause invokes the market to afford the union leverage in ensuring wage increases.

    All but one of the provisions address base salary rather than bonuses. Most (sixteen) speak to salary adjustments (or adjustments up a set salary scale).

> The board may accelerate advancement of existing faculty members on the salary schedule in case of tight labor market conditions. (Hutchinson Community College, Article 10)

> It is recognized that situations may arise which will make it necessary for the University to make special salary adjustments for individual faculty members in addition to the annual increases provided in Articles 12.1 and 12.2. Such adjustments may be implemented by the University under the following situations: . . . 2) when a salary adjustment is necessary to retain a faculty member at the University. (University of Delaware, Article 12.7)

> MARKET ADJUSTMENT–CRITICAL AREA ADJUSTMENT. The market adjustment pool of not less than $x for 1991–92 and for 1992–93

shall be made available to provide compensation increases to faculty in academic disciplines where external markets have made competitive recruitment or faculty retention difficult. (Western Montana College, Article 12.126)

A considerable minority (nine) speak to initial salaries (or schedule placement) (some contracts speak both to initial salaries and to adjustment).

For positions where the current base does not attract qualified employees due to existing market value, the College may award up to an additional two years service credit on the salary schedule at the College [sic] discretion. (Jefferson Technical College, Article 24)

No one will be placed above Step 8. The College reserves the right to make exceptions above this maximum initial placement at the College President's discretion for unusual situations, such as high market rates for a specific instructional discipline. (Rogue Community College, Appendix A)

Market demand generally is treated in a collective, not individualistic, sense. That is, adjustments are grounded in and legitimated by the labor market of a field more than by an individual faculty member's marketability. A clear, important example of this is the California State University contract, which builds adjustments for "Designated Market Disciplines" into its salary schedule (Article 31.3).

Managerial discretion is far broader in market than in merit provisions. In seventeen of the twenty-one contracts, administrators have broad discretion to make market-based adjustments in placement or in existing faculty's salaries. For example: "The College shall exercise its best judgment" (Terra Technical College, Article 12); "It is the exclusive right of the administration to determine" (Kirtland Community College, Article 4); "This market adjustment amount may be apportioned among those academic units of the College deemed appropriate by the administration" (Western Montana College, Article 12.126); and "If in his judgment [the vice-president, administration and finance, sic.] the market and other factors warrant such action" (Washtenaw Community College, Appendix B-1). Such phrasing affords managers extensive flexibility. It is the exceptional case, like that of Saginaw Valley State University, in which a committee with faculty representation has substantial input into the process (all four exceptions are found in the contracts of four-year institutions).

> The Market Committee shall consist of two faculty members appointed by the President of the Faculty Association, two administrators appointed by the Vice-President for Academic Affairs, and the Vice President for Academic Affairs or his/her designee who shall chair the committee with vote. The Market Committee shall be responsible for determining the distribution to faculty members of base salary adjustments to the extent that funds are assigned in order to appropriately recognize marketability in faculty salaries. Recommendations of the Market Committee will be determined by majority vote. (Article N.6.2.1–6.2.3)

Managerial discretion, is the rule, enhanced by the fact that in ten of the twenty-one provisions market decisions are explicitly *not* grievable—as in Saginaw Valley State University's contract: "Decisions to grant or not to grant an adjustment in the base salary of a faculty member as well as the amount of the adjustment are final and binding and are not grievable" (Article N.6.2.4).

In one exceptional case the *union* uses the market to leverage the salaries of faculty, by comparing their salaries to those of faculty in similar programs.

> An amount equal to 1.0 percent of the previous year's 2 semester base salaries will be funded for making market salary adjustments. This allocation shall be made for each year of the Agreement. For 1992–93 the University shall make market salary adjustments based on the program salary survey presented during negotiations. For 1993–94 and 1994–95, the University, in consultation with the Association, will design a study to examine salaries of all Association full-time faculty members to determine whether Association represented faculty are paid at or below the mean of faculty in similarly situated academic programs. . . . Salary adjustments will be made to faculty members who are shown to be the furthest from the surveyed salary mean in the faculty member's respective discipline. (Northern Michigan University, Memorandum of Understanding No. 3)

Significantly, the point of reference is the department or discipline, the unit at which academic labor markets operate, not average faculty salary by rank. The provision also prioritizes market over merit: "For the life of the 1992–95 Master Agreement only, no merit shall be distributed due to the necessity of adjusting salaries on a market comparison basis" (Article 16.4.1).

Market in Other Words

A contract-by-contract reading of all agreements reveals an additional twenty provisions not captured in the market* search. These provisions do not utilize the term *market*, but invoke professional labor markets and department differentials in setting faculty salaries. In closing this section, I focus on one of these contracts—for the CUNY system—which underscores the recent introduction of market considerations in agreements.

Summing the market provisions and the market provisions "in other words" yields a total of forty-one provisions, 20 percent of the HECAS contracts covering full-time faculty. There is a dependent association between these provisions' incidence and institutional type ($x2=28.05$, significant at .005 level). Provisions are more common in the contracts of four-year (twenty-three) than of two-year (fifteen) institutions (three are in technical colleges): 46 percent of the HECAS contracts in four-year schools have market provisions, as compared to 11 percent of those in two-year schools and 19 percent of those in technical colleges.

Most market provisions (eleven) in other words address recruitment and/or retention. The provisions take different forms, but all speak specifically to the managerial need for flexibility in making salary offers. In the contracts of two-year colleges this means adjusting placement on the set salary schedule:

> It is recognized that the possibility exists, based upon the needs of the college and supply and demand considerations, that the Board may have to hire a non-degree or lesser degreed candidate (possibly with less experience) at a higher salary than higher degreed personnel in disciplines where more numerous candidates are available. (Kirtland Community College, Appendix A)

> Unlimited step placement up to five excess increment steps may be made by the President after a review with the SCCHEA President, SCCHEA Vice President and the Personnel Officer if the following determinations have been made by the administration: A survey of edu-

cational institutions and when appropriate, business and industrial concerns produces valid evidence that the standard salary/wage scale in effect at the college is quite obviously deficient to meet the demand of qualified candidates for the position. (Southeastern Community College, Article 23.6.2.A)

Some provisions reveal union efforts to monitor or restrict such discretion:

> When hiring new employees, the Board retains the right to offer salaries which are competitive with those of industry and which are higher than those on the salary placement guide. The Board will make every effort not to hire new employees at a rate higher than current employees in that discipline with similar educational credentials and work experience. The Board will notify the Association of such hirings. (Kirkwood Community College, Article 2.B.3)

> All new instructors will be hired at a salary capable of attracting quality people. However, a new employee will be placed no higher than $350 above current faculty in the department with equal experience and degree. (Cloud Community College, Article 46.2)

Similarly, the contracts of four-year institutions reveal tension between managerial discretion and professional constraint in making market adjustments.

> During the term of this Agreement, a University may appoint regular full-time faculty members at Step Z of any rank then in effect for which they are legally qualified if the following conditions are met: The faculty member is in a specialty or discipline which has been identified by agreement at local meet and discuss for that academic year as a specialty or discipline in which the university has had difficulty recruiting. Such specialties and disciplines must be identified and agreed to at local meet and discuss each academic year; and, the final appointment must be reported to local meet and discuss for notification purposes. (Pennsylvania State System of Higher Education, Article 22)

> The maximum salary levels stated in the above tables may be exceeded by up to 5 percent (10 percent for the Assistant and Associate Professor ranks) when the initial salary is established for a new member joining the University, if, in the judgment of the appointing authorities, the individual possesses critical needed skills, the lack of which will seriously inter-

fere with University progress towards its goals, and if the higher salary range is essential in the recruiting of the individual. Individuals so hired shall be ineligible for additional salary adjustments until such time as their salaries are below the adjusted maximum of Unit ranks. . . . . The number of such new hire exception appointments shall not exceed 25 percent of the new hires in any one fiscal year. Whenever a salary offer is made to an individual under this provision, notice of same shall be provided by the Vice-President for Academic Affairs to the MSP through its President. (University of Lowell, Article 19.E.2.a)

Of course, some professional constraints are quite limited. The University of Lowell clause allows managers to make exceptions one-quarter of the time, violating our everyday, commonsense definition of an exception.

All four of the provisions for making counteroffers are in the contracts of four-year institutions. Perhaps faculty in these institutions are more likely to operate in a national academic marketplace than are two-year college faculty. Two examples illustrate different conditions surrounding counteroffers.

In the event that the College wishes to make salary or fringe benefit adjustments which are more favorable than those called for in the Agreement to any individual member of the bargaining unit for purposes [sic] matching a bona fide offer from a rival institution, the College may do so. The Association will be informed of such action. (Delaware State College, Article 17.10)

During the term of the 1992–95 collective bargaining agreement the President, with the approval of the Board of Governors, may grant exceptional salary increases in order to retain particularly valuable faculty members. . . . Such increases . . . shall be funded only with available uncommitted resources. In no event shall the total ESI awards exceed $35,000 per year over the life of the contract. Matters under this letter are not grievable except on the basis of Article III, Non-Discrimination. (University of Rhode Island, Letter of Agreement)

Constraints on discretion vary, from notice to limits on monies allocated.

The remaining market provisions speak to collective adjustments based on designations of three different markets. Two provisions reflect the union's effort to utilize the *academic marketplace of comparable institutions* to raise faculty salaries. The California State University System contract bases salary raises on a salary index of peer institutions:

> Salary rates on the schedule in Appendix C which pertain to members of the unit shall be increased by that percentage identified and officially adopted by the California Post-Secondary Education Commission as the salary lag between CSU faculty and those at CSU's comparison institutions (6.9 percent). This percentage shall be applied across-the-board to rates on the schedule. (Article 31.6)

Union use of peer institutions is not exclusive to four-year schools— though for San Joaquin Delta Community College, comparison districts are in California.

> In exchange for the salary being set with respect to the third quartile of the sixteen comparison districts, the bargaining unit accepts an instructional average of 17.4 ADA per FTE per semester. For purposes of this article, the non-doctorate top salary of each comparison district without special increments for the previous year will be used to determine the third quartile. (Article 18)

One provision invokes the differential value of *various fields in the academic marketplace*. Somewhat like the "Designated Market Disciplines" of the California State University System (which had a different salary scale), Oakland University's contract establishes "pay area factors," which consist of differential weightings for calculating salaries in different fields.

> Each academic unit shall constitute a pay area and have a pay area factor, with the exception that when a school constitutes the academic unit it may consist of more than one pay area. Each pay area factor shall be no less than 1.000. Pay areas are shown in Appendix B, "Pay Area Factors." Pay area factors for the following academic year adjusted for both personnel changes and other reasons shall be announced by Oakland by August 15 and shall not be grievable. . . . No pay area factor may decrease in one year (for reasons other than personnel changes) by more than the greater of 0.015 or 20 percent of the amount by which the pay area factor exceeds 1.000. (Article 11)

For 1991 through 1992 pay-area factors ranged from 1.025 to 1.225, with thirteen different factors identified for twenty-five areas.

In four other market provisions the market in question is the *student market*.[24] Changes in enrollments are identified as one basis for raising the salaries of faculty in the appropriate units. Unlike most other market provisions, such adjustments are one-time bonuses. For example:

> Ownership Bonus. In addition to the annual wage increase, in any year during the length of this contract that the actual full-time equivalent, tuition paying students . . . exceeds budgeted FTE students by 100 FTE's, a bonus will be paid to all unit members. This will be a flat dollar amount calculated by taking Ok of the total salaries . . . and divide [sic] it by the total number sharing in this bonus. . . . This bonus shall not become part of the unit member's base salary. (Cumberland Community College, Article 6.B.6)

> Beginning with the fall quarter of 1991, an enrollment bonus shall be earned in any year in which the following goals are attained: 1991 Fall Term, the FTE enrollment exceeds the 1990 FTE by 5 percent; 1992 and successive years of the contract, the FTE exceeds the previous year's FTE by 5 percent if the actual final high count FTE. The bonus will be calculated as 2 percent of the total base pay of the bargaining unit members, excluding any lump sum bonus, as of the end of the calendar year in which the enrollment goal is attained. (Detroit College of Business, Article 8.2.3)

Given the current emphasis on productivity and efficiency in higher education, one might have expected more such clauses providing faculty an incentive to contribute to increased enrollment growth or graduation rates.

I close this discussion of explicit market provisions with the case of CUNY, whose market provision highlights the recency and extent of the market's introduction into collective bargaining agreements. Few institutions have figured more prominently than has CUNY in major work-force actions, either historically, with massive layoffs in the 1970s, or presently, with massive early cuts and early retirements.[25] By virtue of its size and special role in providing access to populations that historically have been denied access to higher education, CUNY has a distinctive place in higher education history. Currently, we are seeing a challenge to CUNY's traditional access function, as part of an assault on public institutions launched by politicians in New York and nation-wide.[26] The challenge is internally driven as well, evident in actions of CUNY's managers and emergent in CUNY's 1990 through 1996 contract.

> The University and the Professional Staff Congress agree to establish a joint task force to study and review the need for and feasibility of establishing differential salary scales for teaching members of the instructional staff in particular academic fields or disciplines. The recommendations of the task force shall be advisory and shall be made jointly to the Chancellor of the City University of New York and the President of the Professional Staff Congress. (Article 24.5)

The provision underscores the recency of such considerations in collective bargaining agreements. The push is for more managerial discretion to effect internal differentiation among faculty to respond to market demand.

Perpetuating Existing Salary Stratification

Collective bargaining for faculty arrived after professional labor markets had worked their effects on salary differentiation among academics in different fields. In the 1970s and 1980s, when faculty unionized, it would not have been attractive to many faculty to level down salaries to a common denominator. Bargaining agents thus worked within and built on pre-existing stratification (table 2.3).

From 1976 through 1977, in 21 fields, the salary range—difference between the top and bottom fields in average salaries—for full professors was $8,906; for new assistant professors it was $7,340. The top average salaries were 40 and 57 percent higher than the bottom average salaries for fulls and new assistants. The coefficient of variation was .082 and .110 for fulls and new assistants, a considerable degree of inequality.[27] In short, there was already much salary dispersion among faculty in different fields.

In salary negotiations, bargaining agents were and are confronted with this differentiated structure. In response, they almost universally negotiate across-the-board percentage increases. A case by case analysis of contracts reveals that all but 3 of the contracts covering full-time faculty have salary provisions for across-the-board percentage-based increases. In those contracts with set salary schedules, the percentage

TABLE 2.3
AVERAGE SALARIES OF FULL AND NEW ASSISTANT PROFESSORS,
BY DISCIPLINE, 1976–77*

DISCIPLINE	FULL	DISCIPLINE	NEW ASSISTANT
Law	$30,951	Law	$20,297
Computer sc	27,149	Business	16,701
Business	25,800	Engineering	15,939
Mathematics	25,762	Public affairs	15,561
Public affairs	25,533	Computer sc	15,526
Engineering	25,209	Tech & occup	15,517
Physical sc	25,183	Home economics	15,169
Psychology	24,959	Agriculture	15,030
Social sc	24,831	Library sc	14,602
Area studies	24,304	Biological sc	14,564
Foreign lang	24,266	Communications	14,360
Library sc	24,174	Mathematics	14,296
Biological sc	23,841	Education	14,283
Letters	23,440	Architecture	14,052
Communications	23,377	Physical sc	14,050
Architecture	23,202	Social sc	14,017
Home economics	22,955	Psychology	13,876
Education	22,928	Area studies	13,510
Agriculture	22,418	Letters	13,321
Tech & occup	22,114	Foreign lang	13,263
Fine arts	22,045	Fine arts	12,957

* Source: American Association of University Professors (1985, Table 1). Based on data from *1984–85 Faculty Survey of Institutions belonging to the National Association of State Universities and Land Grant Colleges,* conducted by the Office of Institutional Research, Oklahoma State University (February 1985 edition).

increase applies to the schedule as a whole. In those contracts that lack set schedules, the percentage increase applies to all faculty salaries (and to any minimums, maximums, or ranges that are defined). Such provisions either perpetuate or in absolute terms increase salary inequities. When the increase is a percentage of current salary, the fields with higher salaries obviously get larger raises than do fields with lower salaries. The differentials between top and bottom increase in absolute dollars. At the same time, such increases mitigate against further salary dispersion in that they are across the board.

However, one pre-existing salary structure—promotion adjustments—mitigates against increased salary dispersion. As noted earlier, many contracts—most in four-year schools—build on the existing structure of faculty ranks—assistant, associate, and full professor—setting salary adjustments for each promotion in the academic career. Typically, such adjustments are flat figures: amounts are different for promotions at different levels, but are the same regardless of field and salary. Salary adjustments for promotions are found in thirty-six (72 percent) of the contracts in four-year institutions. In thirty of those cases the adjustment is a flat figure. Such adjustments are found in thirty-four (25 percent) of the contracts in two-year colleges (two contracts in technical colleges have flat adjustments). In twenty-eight of those cases the adjustment is a flat figure. Such flat adjustments reduce salary stratification, for they represent a larger increase percentage-wise for lower than for higher paid fields and faculty.[28]

If union-negotiated across-the-board raises limit the discretion of managers to make market-based salary adjustments, most contracts enable managers to set initial salaries for individual faculty. In seventy-two (36 percent) of the contracts (many with set salary schedules) that discretion is made explicit.

> Faculty members will be hired at Step 1 of the Salary Schedule (Appendix A), except that the Board reserves the right to hire employees at higher steps of the schedule in particular circumstances. (Belleville Area Community College, Article 7)

> Basic salary upon initial appointment shall be at an amount which is commensurate with the credentials and experience of the candidate and his/her anticipated value to the College in the judgment of the Board. (Mohawk Valley Community College, Article 9.1.B)

> Bargaining unit employees hired by the Employer to commence work on or after the effective date of this Agreement shall be accorded placement on the Salary Schedules attached as Appendix A in accordance with the following. . . . The Administration reserves the discretion to award "Steps" of credit in excess of the foregoing mandatory levels both for outside teaching experience and with respect to nonteaching experience. (North Central Michigan College District, Article 14, Section 61)

The Director is authorized to evaluate the prospective faculty member's past educational, occupational, and instructional experience and competency, and place the individual on the salary schedule at a step that, in his [sic] opinion, is fair and just. (Northcentral Technical College, Article 3)

Sweeping managerial discretion to set initial salaries exists even in the face of seemingly rigid salary schedules. Nearly half (45 percent) of 110 contracts with set salary schedules have explicit provision for such discretion.

Contracts that establish salary minimums, maximums, or ranges both set a cap on and perpetuate pre-existing stratification. If minimums, maximums, and ranges delimit the extremes of differentials, they also accord discretion to set initial (and other) salaries. Of 70 contracts with such salary structures, 19 explicitly afford managers such discretion. Sometimes the discretion extends to exceeding established maximums/ranges.[29] Even when not specified, the discretion exists. Managerial discretion to set initial salaries means that salary negotiation is basically between the new hire and the institution. The union is left to negotiate raises from the point at which initial salaries are set, which can contribute to furthering salary dispersion.[30]

Increased Emphasis on the Market

Over time, the contractual emphasis on market considerations appears to have increased. In nine of the agreements with market provisions I have copies of earlier contracts. In seven cases, the market provisions have either been newly introduced or enhanced in the later agreements. This is obviously a small number of contracts. Yet four contracts are for large systems: California State University System, City University of New York, Florida State University System, and Pennsylvania State University System. One contract—Washtenaw Community College—is for one of the oldest cases of faculty unionization. Finally, the recency of the introduction of market considerations is highlighted by Western Michigan University's case: the 1987 through 1990 contract makes no mention of the market; the 1993 through 1994 contract introduces two different sorts of market provisions.

The contracts for Washtenaw Community College provide the longest term perspective on contractual change—I have the institution's initial collective bargaining agreement (1969–71).[31] The initial contract makes no reference to labor market demands requiring managerial discretion to adjust salaries for recruitment or retention in particular fields. However, it does, establish a point system for the salary schedule that is found in the current contract. The key difference between the contracts lies in the manager's discretion in the current provision to award points to enhance recruitment.

> The Vice-President, Administration and Finance, shall have the option of placing newly appointed faculty members up to a maximum of 25 points on the salary schedule if in his [sic] judgment the market and other factors warrant such action. This discretionary action shall be applicable when the following two conditions are satisfied: (1) the applicant qualifies, by education and years of experience, for 21–25 points and (2) the labor market for the position involved makes it difficult to hire at the twenty point salary. (Appendix B-1)

The case of the Pennsylvania State University System, for which I have contracts dating back to 1971, also provides good historical perspective. The 1990 through 1996 contract provides for managerial discretion in placing faculty who are in designated specialties or disciplines. That clause is also found in the 1987 through 1990, but not in the 1985 through 1987, contract.

The California State University System's initial collective bargaining agreement was for 1983 through 1986. It incorporates market factors in setting faculty salaries, but the provision is not routinized as part of the salary schedule. Instead, "Market Condition Salary Supplement" reads as an add-on.

> The purpose of a Market Condition Salary Supplement (MCSS) shall be to ameliorate critical recruitment and retention problems . . . in a teaching specialization. . . . A department or equivalent unit or administrator may recommend approval of an MCSS for a specific teaching specialization. Such recommendation shall include complete documentation and rationale supporting the critical nature of recruitment and/or retention problems within the teaching specialization. . . . An MCSS authorization shall be expressed as a supplement to the base salary, not as a change in the faculty unit salary schedule. (Articles 31.20, 31.21, 31.31)

In the 1991 through 1993 contract, adjustments are not supplements. They are built into base salaries in a separate schedule for "Designated Market Disciplines."

Moreover, the 1983-86 contract establishes many constraints on managerial discretion in making market adjustments.

> If the Legislature appropriates funds to ameliorate recruitment/ retention problems in specific disciplines and such funds are made available to the CSU, these funds shall be utilized to implement this Article to the extent such an appropriation allows. Beginning with the 1983–84 academic year, MCSSs may be authorized for new faculty unit employees only. Funds for MCSSs during the 1983–84 academic year shall not exceed 10 percent of the instructional salary savings obligation. Beginning with the 1984–85 academic year, MCSSs may be authorized for all faculty unit employees in authorized teaching specializations. Funds for MCSSs during the 1984–85 academic year shall not exceed 30 percent of the instructional salary savings obligation. Beginning with the 1985–86 fiscal year, authorization of MCSSs shall be contingent upon the availability of categorical funds provided by the Legislature for purposes consistent with this Article. (Articles 31.32, 31.34–31.37)

Such restrictions are not found in the 1991–93 contract. In place of the year-to-year requirement of the earlier contract, disciplines now remain on the "Designated Market Disciplines" schedule until the Chancellor or CSU decide to remove the specialization from the list. (The one professional constraint is that additions/replacements to the current list are not allowed.)

Changes in the contract of the Florida State University System are even more recent and dramatic. Market clauses are absent in the 1988 through 1991 contract. The 1994 through 1995 contract accords managers discretion to make "counteroffers."[32]

The recent introduction of market considerations is also clear in the case of Western Michigan University. The 1987 through 1990 contract makes no mention of the market. The 1993 through 1994 contract introduces two kinds of market provisions. One gives managers discretion in making salary adjustments. "In the event Western wishes to employ a new faculty member on terms more favorable than those specified herein, it may do so. In cases involving a faculty member already employed by Western, Western may give salary increments for market considerations" (Article 14.5.1).

A second contingency for adjustment involves linkage to research markets.

"Contract/Grant Full, Associate, Assistant Professors and Post-doctoral Fellows" are ranked faculty, including bargaining unit faculty, so designated by Western to conduct research and other programs sponsored by external agencies and in so doing perform work different from and additional to the usual faculty duties and responsibilities. Contract/Grant faculty may be compensated for the specified portion at "market value," in accordance with the policy for the establishment of Contract/Grant Professorships approved by the president of the University on September 13, 1988, as long as the support for their compensation is derived entirely from externally-funded grants or contracts. (Article 2h)

Market: Summary

In sum, specific market provisions are not as common as merit provisions, but are found in a substantial number (20 percent) of contracts. Market provisions are more likely to be found in the contracts of four-year institutions than of two-year and technical colleges. There is some evidence that such provisions are increasingly being introduced into faculty contracts.

Yet the market shapes faculty salaries in far more pervasive, powerful ways. Perhaps the greatest market influence is the salary stratification that predated the emergence of faculty unionization. The union practice of across-the-board percentage raises for all faculty, found in virtually all contracts, perpetuates such stratification. It also delimits further salary dispersion.

The salary structures prevalent in four-and in two-year institutions differ. Yet they serve both to perpetuate and to delimit salary dispersion. The salary minimums and ranges and the system of promotion adjustments up the academic ladder, found mostly in four-year institutions, enable and even ensure further dispersion. They also delimit it. Similarly, the set salary schedules found in the contracts of most two-year institutions delimit further differentiation of faculty salaries. Yet they often afford managers discretion to effect further dispersion. In nearly half of the contracts with set schedules, there is explicit provision for managerial discretion in setting initial salaries. In 70 percent of all contracts there is evidence of such managerial discretion embedded either explicitly or implicitly in salary provisions.

To the extent that there is a move towards the increased import of the market, there is also a move toward increased managerial flexibility. In market driven personnel decisions managers have far more discretion than they have in merit provisions. Faculty involvement in decision making surrounding the marketplace is extremely limited. The principal professional constraints lie in salary structures that limit the extent to which managers can exercise discretion in moving toward the market. In the ensuing section I explore more active professional constraints on managerial prerogatives in this regard, equity adjustments intended to reduce faculty salary dispersion.

Equity

Equity is the least common of the three salary structures found in collective bargaining agreements. A search on "equit*/inequit*" yielded twenty-six contracts (13 percent of the population) with provisions that explicitly use the term *(in)equity* in salary clauses.

What is meant by the term *equity*? Some provisions speak to gender and other forms of discrimination. Others are more general references to equity in faculty salaries. Still other interpretations refer to inequities stemming from the market. Whatever the interpretation, equity provisions are efforts by faculty as a collectivity to counter the effects of managerial discretion and external forces to differentiate faculty salaries.

Some provisions relevant to equity issues do not use the term *(in)equit**. These emerge from a full reading of the agreements. The clearest example are so-called nondiscrimination clauses.[33] Finally, in closing this subsection I review a few longitudinal cases suggesting the relative recency of equity provisions in collective bargaining agreements.

Equity Specified in the Contracts

As with merit and market provisions, equity clauses are more common in the contracts of four-than of two-year institutions. There is a dependent association between their incidence and institutional type ($x2=22.73$, significant at the .005 level). Of twenty-six equity provisions, seventeen are in the contracts of four-year institutions and nine are in those of two-year colleges. That is a reversal of the contract distribution in HECAS: two-year colleges account for 68 percent of the HECAS contracts, but only 35 percent of those with equity provisions; four-year institutions account for 25 percent of HECAS contracts, and for 65 percent of those with equity provisions (see table 2.4).

TABLE 2.4
INCIDENCE OF EQUITY PROVISIONS

	Explicit equity	*Faculty involvement*	*Equity in other words*
Two-year	9 (7%)*	5	3
Technical	0	0	0
Four-year	17 (33%)	12	5
Total	26	17	8

* The percentage of all such contracts in HECAS

Contrary to what one might expect, only three equity provisions speak primarily to gender. For example:

> Those individuals who have been identified through the gender equity salary study as requiring an adjustment in salary to equalize pay, shall have their base contract salary adjusted according to the negotiated salary adjustment schedule. (Central Community College, Article 1.A.i)

> A committee of three bargaining unit members representing the noninstructional faculty will, as a group, be allocated a total of $4,100 prior to the end of fall term 1990–91 to address equity issues . . . for non-instructional faculty. This allocation will occur in such a manner that the equity position of women, relative to men, remains in approximate relative balance or improves. The assessment of progress of women relative to men will be determined by a regression analysis performed by the committee by the University and monitored by the President of the FFA. (Ferris State University, Article 14.3)

Significantly, these two clauses call for empirical study in which faculty have some involvement to guide managerial decision making (yet none of the three equity provisions invokes conceptions of comparable worth).

Three contracts speak to discrimination that includes race and gender. The Florida State University System's provision is detailed in establishing a process for conducting a salary study and ensuring appropriate adjustments.

> No later than October 1 each university President shall notify employees of the procedures adopted by the university to conduct the salary study. The notification shall include the following statement: "In any year, an employee may seek to resolve a salary inequity due to discrimination based on race or sex either by filing a grievance under Article 6— Nondiscrimination—or by conducting a salary equity study according to this procedure. But the employee cannot do both." Pursuant to notification . . . an employee who perceives that the factors of race or sex may have affected the employee's salary may request a meeting with the department chair . . . to review salary data and to request assistance in preparing the employee's salary study. The employee may be assisted by a colleague, or by a representative of the UFF, at this and all subsequent meetings. . . . The administrator shall provide reasonable assistance to the employee, including copies of available documents that the employee may request. (Article 23.4.1.1, 2)

The provision goes on to detail deadlines and appeals (adjudicated by the president). Individual faculty can initiate their own salary study. But the contract also requires administrative review and study of salary equity.

> Each university shall conduct an administrative review of salaries to ensure that any significant differences in the salaries of female and minority employees, when compared with those of male and white employees, respectively, are attributable to factors other than race or sex. The university shall ensure that the data used in the review are accurate. The administrative review shall consist of a statistical analysis and an administrative salary analysis. . . . Each university shall use a statistical model to review the salaries of all full- and part-time ranked faculty in class codes 9001–9004. Each university may include other comparable ranked faculty classes in the statistical analysis. The universities shall use the statistical model in Appendix "F" as a framework for analysis, adapting it as appropriate to each university. The university's model, and the ranked faculty classes to be included in the statistical analysis, shall be provided to the UFF Chapter no later than October 1 for review prior to the university's conducting such analysis. The Chapter shall provide written comments regarding the model to the university within two weeks after the model has been transmitted to the Chapter. Salaries of

female and minority employees that are more than one standard deviation below the salaries predicted by the statistical model shall be reviewed further, as discussed in paragraph (3) below. Female and minority employees included in the analysis whose salaries are more than one standard deviation below the predicted value shall be notified by December 1 and offered the opportunity to conduct a self-study. (Article 23.4.b.1, 2)

In other words, the burden is not on the shoulders of individual faculty. The Chapter is involved, and the administration must follow established procedure.

Nebraska State College's provision is not nearly so detailed. It states the priority in which adjustments will be made. Similarly lacking in detail, Pittsburg State University's provision simply identifies the type of adjustment to be made and specifies the amount of monies to be allocated.

The largest number of equity provisions (12) refer in general terms to salary inequities, not specifying their causes. Thus, Lincoln University's provision establishes an equity committee and a salary equity fund but does not specify factors or causes of the inequities being redressed.

Lincoln and LUC-AAUP agree to establish an equity committee consisting of three persons designated by the University and three persons designated by LUC-AAUP. The committee shall conduct a salary-equity study to ascertain the extent of possible inequities in the salary's compensation. It is understood and agreed that the University may select an expert to perform such services as are necessary to assist the committee in carrying out the study. Based on the findings of the study the committee shall make recommendations for salary adjustments to the President of the University. Lincoln agrees to establish a salary equity fund from which up to $50,000.00 for both the 1992–93 and 1993–94 academic years will be deducted to remedy such inequities. (Article 16)

Unequal salaries are apparently, in themselves, an inequity. Hudson Valley Community College's contract clarifies the equation of equality and equity.

Equity adjustment to which a returning probationary or tenured faculty member shall be entitled each year of this Agreement shall be determined in the following manner: An equity unit shall be the sum of $100.00 or less by which a returning tenured or probationary faculty member's base salary for the preceding year was below the average base salary of all tenured and probationary faculty members of the same rank for the same (preceding) year. The number of units so determined shall be multiplied by the number of his/her years of continuous full-time service at the College and thereafter divided by the number representing the mean years of full-time continuous service in his/her rank. The number of such units for all faculty members in all ranks shall be divided into a sum equal to $33,425.00 in 1992/93, $14,325.00 in 1993/94. (Article 12.A)

Some people might justify unequal salaries in terms of the unequal performance of various faculty. Inequality is legitimate, not inequitable. Not so in the above provisions. Inequalities are by definition inequities to be adjusted.

Another seven provisions specify market-based inequities. Many are alongside provisions for market adjustments. After a provision for adjustments to retain faculty, the University of Delaware contract speaks to "disparities": "when salary disparities occur, relative to market demands, which adversely effect the quality of an academic unit" (Article 12). The first conditions cited as justifying adjustments are salary inversion and compression. Nebraska State College's contract has provision for "Adjustments to compensate for 'salary compaction' present in long term bargaining unit member salaries" (Article 9) just prior to a provision that allows for "market-place adjustments." The Florida State University System contract has a provision allowing for salary increases for reasons of "counteroffers." It also has a detailed provision on "Salary Compression/Inversion."[34]

Funds of approximately 1.1 percent shall be distributed to eligible employees in the following manner to address salary compression and inversion: (1) Each College or equivalent unit shall be allocated salary increase funds in the amount of approximately 1.1 percent of the base salary rate of its employees to be distributed to those eligible employees in accordance with the college's model as described in (3), below. (2) The Dean of each college/equivalent unit, in consultation with the departments/equivalent units, shall develop a model to be used in distributing the salary increase funds which are provided under this Section. (3) The college's salary compression/inversion model shall include the following elements: a. comparisons of employee salaries to appropriate national market salaries by rank and discipline; b. evaluations of employee performance; c. an employee's years of service in the State University System. . . . (8) The parties agree to review the models developed by the colleges, as well as other models they may identify, during their 1994–95 negotiations, and to carefully assess which models may be used in distributing salary increase monies in subsequent years. (Article 23.1.b)

Decisions regarding market based salary adjustments lie almost entirely in the realm of managerial discretion. By contrast, equity-based salary adjustments afford considerable influence to faculty. Of the thirteen clauses specifying who decides, eleven identify joint committees or a process that includes faculty input. For example, Central Michigan University's clause (Article 28.10) calls for a "Salary Equity Study Committee" with three members each appointed by the faculty association and by the institution. Similarly, Saginaw Valley State University's contract (Article N.6.1.1) establishes an "Equity Committee" of two faculty appointed by the faculty association, two administrators appointed by the vice-president for academic affairs, and a chair who is the president or designee of the Faculty Association.

Equity in Other Words

A careful reading of the contracts reveals equity provisions not identified in the initial term search. The most common of these are "nondiscrimination" clauses. Some other provisions also speak to equity concerns such salary compression/inversion without using the term *equity*.

Most contracts (64 percent) have some sort of nondiscrimination clause. Such clauses speak broadly to equity issues in employment, prohibiting employment discrimination based on a range of personal characteristics. In addition to general clauses in 135 contracts, 7 others speak only to age discrimination, and 3 others address discrimination involving pregnancy.

General nondiscrimination clauses vary considerably in detail and in what conditions are included. Some are minimalist statements covering sex, race, and religion. More typically, a range of characteristics are identified.

The provisions of this Agreement shall be applied equally to all employees eligible for membership in the bargaining unit without discrimination as to age, sex, sexual orientation, marital status, race, color, creed, national origin, political affiliation, or handicapping conditions. (Hudson Valley Community College, Article 6)

The District shall not discriminate against unit members with respect to wages, hours of employment, and other terms and conditions of employment as defined in Government Code 3540 et seq., or application of the provisions of this Agreement with respect to age, color, creed, residency, marital status, membership in an employee organization, national origin, physical handicap, race, sex, or religion. (Rio Hondo Community College, Article 13)

Some characteristics are relatively common. Others are not. For example, the reference to sexual orientation in Hudson Valley Community College's contract is *not* covered in most contracts.

However, for my purposes, nondiscrimination clauses are significantly different from other equity provisions in the contracts. They are *not* specific to salary. They do *not* provide for salary adjustments. They do *not* constitute an effort to readjust salaries/structures to redress the effects of past practices and conditions. They simply prohibit discriminatory practice.

In addition to the twenty-six provisions that use the term *equity*, another eight contracts address equity in other words. Thus, 17 percent of the contracts have explicit equity provisions. Equity provisions in other words are more often found in the contracts of four-year institutions—in five of these eight provisions (and thus in twenty-two of all thirty-four equity provisions). There is a dependent association between explicit equity provisions and institutional type ($x2=31.19$, significant at the .005 level). Overall, 44 percent of HECAS contracts covering full-time faculty in four-year institutions have equity provisions, as compared to 9 percent of contracts in two-year colleges.

As with provisions utilizing the term *equity*, most (six) equity provisions in other words do *not* focus on gender. They address salary compression and inversion. Ediston State Community College's contract provides differential salary adjustments based on time of employment to redress compression.

In order to address the faculty's concern relative to the phenomenon of salary compression, the College agrees to make the following adjustments to faculty salaries: Faculty members whose initial full-time employment began before January 30, 1979, and who have remained continually employed as a full-time faculty member with the college, exclusive of periods of authorized leave, shall have $1000 added to their 1992–1993 base year salary. This one-time payment of $1000 will be applied before any across the board adjustment and will become part of their 1992–1993 base salary. (Article 6)

Different levels of adjustment are based on faculty's date of initial (and continuous) full-time employment: faculty hired between 1979 and 1982 receive a $750 adjustment; those hired between 1982 and 1985 get $500; and those hired between 1985 and 1988 receive $250. Northern Montana College's contract offers inversion adjustments, explicitly relating them to managerial discretion to adjust new faculty members' salaries based on market considerations.

The President at his/her discretion may offer up to 20 additional points to a new faculty member where a difficulty of recruitment has been established. . . . If the candidate accepts the offer and that candidate has equal or less-than-equal qualifications of a faculty member who is currently teaching the same subject area, the current faculty member's total points will be adjusted equal to the new faculty member's total points. Current faculty teaching in the same subject area who have less-than-equal qualifications than the candidate and who have fewer total points than the total points offered the candidate shall be granted at least one (1) additional point. The determination of qualifications will be made on the basis of point assignment. (Article 9.10)

Only two equity provisions in other words speak to gender. One is like a nondiscrimination clause but is specific to salaries and fringe benefits ("The Board shall agree that the principle of equal pay be observed, as defined in the Contract Salary Schedule provision, for comparable work and duties." Wisconsin Indianhead District, Article 2.C.1). A second (Rhode Island College, Memorandum of Understanding) establishes a salary study committee, which is charged to address gender and race, among other factors.

The latter point is important. Equity in other words provisions tend to provide far more in the way of professional involvement and constraint than do market provisions. Of eight provisions, six entail faculty involvement in decision making, and/or they specify in detail factors that should shape administrative decisions. Overall, then, seventeen of the twenty-one equity provisions have professional involvement in decision making, or constraints on managerial discretion.

Equity Provisions Over Time

The timing of the introduction of equity provisions having to do with gender and race is clearly a matter of the timing of the establishment of legal statutes and rulings regarding discrimination. For example, the salary equity study provision of the Florida State University System contract indicates that "the procedures for conducting the Salary Equity Study required by Section 240.247, Florida Statutes shall include: . . . " (Article 23.4). Similarly, many nondiscrimination clauses refer explicitly to state statutes and/or to federal law.

Yet most of the equity provisions do *not* have to do with gender and/or race discrimination/equity. They focus generally on equality of salaries or specifically on phenomena such as salary compression and inversion. The timing of the introduction of these equity provisions is less clear. The recency of many market provisions suggests that equity provisions aimed at redressing market effects might also be fairly recent. For example, the provision in Western Michigan University's 1994 through 1995 contract for a "Salary Study Committee" to "study the problems of salary compression and inversion and to report its findings to the provost and the Chapter" (Article 32.7) is not in the 1987 through 1990 contract. But that is only one case.

Equity: Summary

Equity provisions are less prevalent than either merit or market provisions: 17 percent of the contracts have such provisions, as compared to 30 percent with conventional merit and 20 percent with market provisions.[35] However, as with merit and market provisions, equity provisions are far more common in the contracts of four-year than of two-year institutions—44 percent of the former, and only 9 percent of the latter. Most equity provisions do *not* focus on gender and race (although 64 percent of contracts have nondiscrimination clauses). The most common provisions establish adjustments to ensure greater equality among salaries. The second most common speak to redressing the market's adverse effects.

Faculty involvement and professional constraints are evident in most equity provisions. Provisions can be read not so much as a direct check on managerial discretion as an effort to redress adverse affects of the exercise of the market and managerial discretion.

Two further sources of equity-based constraint on managerial discretion in the name of equity were discussed in the subsection on market. Set salary schedules, most common in two-year schools, and salary ranges, more common in four-year schools, inhibit the ability of managers to differentiate salaries. Indeed, equity provisions may be less commonly found in the contracts of two-year institutions because they are less necessary given the existence of standard salary indexes. A second equity constraint, typical of all union contracts, is across-the-board percentage raises.

However, the professional constraints established by faculty unions in the area of working to ensure more salary equity should not be overestimated. Half of equity provisions do *not* specify "who decides," thereby according managers much discretion. Further, 87 percent of the contracts lack provision for equity adjustments. Finally, decisions in 27 percent of the twenty-six equity provisions either are explicitly "not grievable" or are not covered by binding arbitration.

Unionized Faculty's Salary Structures: Conclusion

In closing my analysis of salary structures I address three assumptions that underpin most scholarship on faculty salaries. First, salary should be a function of merit. Second, salaries should reflect faculty's attractiveness in the academic marketplace—marketability is a proxy of merit. Third, salary structures in unionized settings are largely grounded in seniority, with little consideration of merit. That minimizes the play of merit and market. Faculty salaries thereby are depressed. In short, unions are antithetical to professional salary structures and to faculty salaries.

These assumptions persist although they lack empirical support. In regard to merit, the prestige of the department or institution in which faculty members work and from which they graduated is positively related to pay. Yet, for all faculty, there is little evidence that scholarly productivity in itself is highly correlated with pay. Quite the contrary. Seniority is the strongest predictor of salary in nonunionized settings.[36] Moreover, there is much evidence that particularistic characteristics such as gender significantly shape salary. The salaries of female faculty, and of fields with relatively large percentages of female faculty, are less than those of male faculty and male dominated fields, holding constant measures of merit and market. Such effects are strongest at the peak of higher education's meritocracy, elite research universities.[37] Finally, presumptions about the significance of merit ring rather hollow in an occupation whose purchasing power has declined in real terms in the past two decades.[38]

There is little empirical evidence of external *academic* labor markets' effect on salaries. Of course, some fields may have higher salaries because it is believed faculty may leave academe for jobs in external *professions*, often in the private sector. The effects of such professional labor markets are widely evident. However, such marketability in a profession external to academe can hardly be seen as a proxy of merit within academe. Moreover, the mechanisms by which markets operate have not been fully explicated.[39] For example, to my knowledge, no one has analyzed the extent or influence of offers from institutions within or outside of academe on faculty salaries.

By contrast, there is empirical evidence of the positive effect of previous administrative experience on faculty salaries. A sure route to professional rewards is not to leave (or threaten to) the organization for another faculty position, but to leave the profession for a stint as an administrator (often within the same organization) and then to return to the faculty ranks at a higher salary in recognition not of professional merit but of previous position.[40]

Finally, assumptions about reward structures in unionized institutions, and their depressing effect on faculty salaries, do not hold up to empirical examination. My content analysis speaks directly to the first assumption. I posed two general questions about faculty salary structures in collective bargaining agreements: To what extent are considerations of merit, market, and equity built into contractual provisions regarding salaries?; and To what extent do contracts accord faculty and managers involvement and discretion in decision making surrounding salary adjustments?

What did I find? The extent and location of merit and market provisions in contracts do not support the view that unionized salary structures are antithetical to professional reward systems. They point instead to the effects of institutional type more than of unionization. I find considerable differences between the contracts of four- and two-year institutions. Overall, one in three contracts has conventional merit-based provisions. However, over two-thirds (68 percent) of four-year institution contracts have such provisions, as compared to 19 percent of two-year institution contracts. In addition, merit is built into contracts in various other forms, from promotion through the traditional rungs of the academic career ladder to proxy measures of merit.

As with merit, so with the market. A substantial minority of contracts (20 percent) contain market-based provisions, which in recent years appear to have become increasingly prevalent. Again, there are considerable differences in the contracts of four- and two-year institutions: 46 percent of contracts in four-year institutions have such provisions, as compared to 11 and 19 percent of those in two-year and technical colleges. In addition, market is built into the contracts in other forms, from pre-existing salary differentiation that is perpetuated, to managerial discretion to set initial salaries, found in 70 percent of contracts. Market provisions are much more likely to accord managers discretion than are merit provisions. The latter are more likely to ensure faculty involvement in decision making and some professional constraint on managerial discretion.

As for equity, about one in six (17 percent) contracts has such provisions. Again, there is much difference between institutional sectors. In four-year institutions, 44 percent of contracts have such provisions, as compared to 9 percent of two-year institutions. Equity is also built into contracts in across-the-board raises and set salary schedules. Some such equity measures have been introduced to mitigate the market's distorting effects on faculty salaries. The differentiating effects of the market may constitute at least as great a threat to academe as the presumed standardizing structures of unionization.

Stratification among and Centrality of Faculty Salaries

Contractual provisions are one matter. Actual salaries are another. Has unionization depressed faculty salaries? No. Repeatedly, scholars have found that if there is any difference between faculty salaries in unionized and nonunionized settings the results favor the former. (Such findings match those found for the work force in general and for public-sector workers.)[41] There is no evidence of a depressing effect of unionization on salaries.

Has unionization led to a standardization of faculty salaries? Most research on faculty and professions would lead one to expect considerable and growing salary stratification in academe. General studies of faculty point to various dimensions of stratification among faculty.[42] Recent studies of professions in general, and of academe in particular, point to increased stratification, salary and otherwise.[43] Has unionization overridden this pattern for unionized faculty? No. As I noted in discussing market factors, union salary structures were overlaid on pre-existing stratification.

The most significant salary stratification among faculty is by field. That dates back at least to the 1970s (see table 2.3). Using data for unionized and nonunionized institutions alike, that dispersion among average faculty salaries by field had increased by the 1990s (see table 2.5).

In 1976/77, the difference between average salaries for full professors in the highest and lowest paid fields was $8,096, with average salaries for full professors in law being 40 percent higher than average salaries for fulls in fine arts. By 1993/94, the difference between average salaries for full professors in the highest and lowest paid fields was $37,318, with average salaries for full professors in law being 71 percent higher than average salaries for fulls in performing arts.

Such a pattern is remarkable. Faculty salaries in the 1970s declined in real terms and relative to salaries of all college graduates. In the 1980s, they rebounded both in real and in relative terms, although they still remained below real salary levels of 1972/73.[44] The fate of faculty salaries somewhat mirrored the financial condition of many postsecondary institutions in the 1970s and 1980s. Similarly, one decade experienced a glut and the other an impending shortage in the academic labor pool. Salary dispersion among fields is often justified in terms of "the market." Yet it increased in the 1970s *and* in the 1980s, which represented different market environments for faculty in general, as well as for faculty in particular fields.[45]

TABLE 2.5
AVERAGE SALARIES OF FULL PROFESSORS,
BY DISCILIPINE, 1993–94*

DISCIPLINE	FULL PROFESSORS
Law	$89,777
Engineering	77,985
Health sciences	77,913
Business & management	77,535
Computer and information	75,964
Physical sciences	65,914
Mathematics	63,776
Psychology	62,567
Public affairs	62,435
Social sciences	62,351
Library science	61,827
Interdisciplinary studies	61,808
Architecture	59,322
Agribusiness	59,178
Communications	58,933
Philosophy & religion	58,424
Foreign languages	57,344
Home economics	57,157
Letters	56,744
Education	56,605
Performing arts	52,459

* SOURCE: Daniel S. Hamermesh, "Plus Ca Change: The Annual Report on the Economic Status of the Profession," *Academe* 80,2(1994):5–13, Table 5; data derived from the Faculty Salary Survey by Discipline of Institutions belonging to the National Association of State Universities and Land-Grant Colleges, conducted by the Office of Institutional Research, Oklahoma State University. Some of the fields differ from the 1976–77 data.

The pattern of salary dispersion by field suggests that academic managers have been willing and able to respond to field-defined labor markets. Some fields have fared either well or poorly over the past two decades, maintaining their position in the salary hierarchy; the relative position of others has shifted (see tables 2.3 and 2.5). Many of the highest paying fields in 1976/77 (e.g., law, engineering, business, computer sciences) remain at the top of the salary hierarchy in 1993/94, and have realized greater percentage increases in average salaries than have fields at the bottom of the salary hierarchy (e.g., education, arts, home economics, and communications). Salaries in law, engineering, business, and computer sciences, increased 190, 209, 201, and 180 percent respectively. By contrast, salaries in education, arts, home economics, and communications increased by 157, 149, 138, and 156 percent respectively (these figures are not indexed against the cost of living or the consumer price index). Not only has the position of many fields in the overall hierarchy persisted, but the gap between the top and the bottom of the hierarchy has increased, a slight variation on Merton's "Matthew effect." The rich get richer.[46]

Remarkably, another salary gap that is increasing in academe is the gender gap. There is little question that faculty salaries are stratified by gender.[47] The average earnings of faculty men continue to be 25 percent higher than those of women, a difference that is higher than the wage gap in the work force as a whole, but considerably less than the differential for professional women.[48] In 1992, the salary gap between faculty men and women was $9,725: the average salary of faculty men was $49,098, for women, $39,373.48 That gap *increased* from 1972 to 1992 by $1,192. The pattern in academe is all the more remarkable given that during a comparable period the gender gap between men and women in the general work force decreased by approximately 10 percent, as did the wage gap for men and women with five or more years of education.[49]

The increased faculty salary dispersion by field indicates that academic managers have helped to effect systematic differential resource allocation by field within their colleges and universities. The major expenditure item in instructional expenditures is personnel. A major personnel cost in academic units is faculty. Thus, a pattern of increased faculty salary dispersion by field suggests a pattern of increasingly stratified investment in different academic departments.[50] Such a pattern represents a selective restratification of the academic profession and of academic units in institutions. It runs counter to managers' claims of having effected across-the-board cuts for many years prior to undertaking selective "tough choices." Assuming that the quality of faculty within various academic fields remained relatively constant in the 1980s, increased dispersion suggests that salaries (and thus resource allocations within colleges and universities) were increasingly shaped not by merit but by market considerations.

Salary Stratification by Field in Unionized Institutions

To what extent is there comparable salary stratification by field in unionized institutions? Given the salary structures found in collective bargaining agreements, one would expect less stratification among faculty salaries by field in unionized colleges and universities. The data support that expectation. Yet they also reveal much dispersion in unionized institutions in 1993/94 (see table 2.6).

TABLE 2.6
AVERAGE FACULTY SALARY BY ACADEMIC DEPARTMENT,
COLLECTIVE BARGAINING VERSUS NON-COLLECTIVE BARGAINING,
1993–94*

PROGRAM	SALARY NONBARG	SALARY BARG	DIFFERENCE
Engineering	53,718	61,960	9,354
Accounting	52,583	57,550	4,967
Marketing	52,461	57,540	3,677
Business admin.	51,136	57,062	5,926
Comp/info sc	47,999	56,631	8,632
Physics	46,283	58,976	12,693
Physical sc	45,694	48, 294	2,600
Edtl admin	45,636	49,238	3,602
Geology	44,901	55,142	10,241
Chemistry	44,796	54,894	10,098
Architecture	43,390	52,160	8,770
Ethnic/clt st	42,929	54,439	11,510
Phys therapy	42,615	46,542	3,927
Anthropology	42,512	52,553	10,041
Phil/religion	42,458	53,119	10,661
Biol sc	42,337	54,714	12,377
Psychology	42,314	52,478	10,164
History	42,303	52,428	10,125
Political sc	42,189	53,544	11,355 *(Con't)*

TABLE 2.6 (Continued)

PROGRAM	SALARY NONBARG	SALARY BARG	DIFFERENCE
Eng rel techs	42,156	48,704	6,548
Geography	41,975	51,105	9,130
Agribusiness	41,543	55,795	14,252
Sociology	41,241	49,543	8,302
Edtl counsel	40,930	59,009	18,079
Mathematics	40,727	53,335	12,608
Education	40,512	47,104	6,592
Speech/lang	40,487	47,014	6,527
Protective services	39,833	50,258	10,425
Industr arts	39,661	49,930	10,269
Edtl curric	39,634	51,792	12,338
Reading/tch ed	39,618	49,216	9,598
Social work	39,474	50,258	10,784
Interdisc stud	39,298	48,416	9,118
Music	39,254	47,549	8,295
Special ed	39,126	46,667	7,541
Social sc	39,051	52,980	13,929
Public health	38,881	52,369	13,488
General art	38,672	49,009	10,337
Teacher ed	38,576	44,496	5,920
Home econ	38,573	46,421	7,848
Drama/thtr	37,812	46,643	8,831
Occuptl ther	37,667	42,269	4,602
Parks/rec	37,505	46,974	9,469
Visual/perf art	37,449	46,779	9,330
Communications	37,294	46,173	8,879
Foreign lang	37,223	48,838	11,615
Engl/lit	37,103	48,129	11,026
Nursing	36,388	43,249	6,861
Library sc	35,544	47,455	11,911

* SOURCE: John B. Lee, "Faculty Salaries, 1993–94," *The NEA 1995 Almanac of Higher Education* (Washington, D.C.: National Education Association, 1995), Table 10; data from College and University Personnel Association, 1993–94 National Faculty Survey by Discipline and Rank in Public Colleges and Universities (Washington, D.C.: CUPA, 1994). Departments are listed in order of salary in noncollective bargaining units.

Engineering is the highest paid field in both sectors. In nonunionized institutions, the average engineering salary is 51 percent higher than the average salary in the lowest paid field (library science). In unionized institutions, the average engineering salary is 47 percent higher than the average salary in the lowest paid field (occupational therapy).[51]

There is some evidence that the gender gap in faculty salaries is less in unionized than in nonunionized settings, again matching the pattern for the general work force.[52] There is still a significant gender differential for all ranks of faculty in unionized institutions, but the differential is less than that found in nonunionized institutions. The reduced gender gap cannot be attributed to higher salaries in non-unionized colleges and universities. As evidenced in my contract analysis, neither can the difference be attributed to widespread equity adjustment provisions that focus on gender. (There are a significant number of equity provisions in collective bargaining agreements that either are general or that focus specifically on redressing the adverse effects of the market. Such provisions, along with the common across-the-board percentage raises, may work to slow down the pace and extent of salary dispersion, thereby inhibiting the expansion of the gender gap.[53])

If this is true, the irony is that critics of unions feared that unions would bring standardization which would threaten professionalism. Instead, it turns out that the greater threat to professional community in academe has been salary dispersion and stratification—by field, gender, and institution—which appears to be somewhat mitigated by unionization. Such patterns also undermine another dimension of professionalism—collegial governance—that critics believed would be imperiled by unionization. Expanding dispersion and steeper stratification not only contribute to tension and resentment within the collegium, but they make it more difficult and unlikely for faculty to form common cause and to act in a collective faculty interest. For in material reality, as market overrides merit in shaping salaries (and as it leads to greater dispersion and stratification), the interests of faculty in different parts of the institution are becoming increasingly divided. In other words, unions may strengthen faculty's position as *one* profession.

One other point about faculty salaries. I return to the cabbie's question with which I started the chapter, with a few modifications. The cabbie asked, "How much more does your boss make than you?" Let me be "scholarly" (that is, abstract) and raise the analytical level above me and my boss, to faculty and managers in general. And let us extend the question back in time: What kinds of raises in recent decades have bosses received as compared to faculty? The study has been done, for the years 1971-72 to 1984-85. Though not great, the differences favor administrators. "The relative earnings position of administrators vis-à-vis faculty improved by 3.5 percent."[54]

Now let me further rephrase the cabbie's question to fit the current context of organizational restructuring in higher education: How much of institutional expenditures do managers' salaries account for as compared to faculty salaries? and Has that changed over time? I am not aware of any direct study of that question. But we can reason out an educated estimate from existing research and data. Managers' share of institutional expenditures has to have increased over time, because their salaries have increased at a greater rate than have the salaries of faculty. Unless there are now fewer administrators relative to faculty (wishful thinking). The reverse is true. The number of administrators in the work force of higher education increased by 36.9 percent between 1977 and 1989, compared to 19.3 percent for faculty.[55]

More dramatic is the growth in the number of nonfaculty professionals, so-called other or support professionals (what I call "managerial professionals").[56] From 1977 through 1989, the number of such staff increased by 91.1 percent.[57] Unfortunately, I am not aware of any comprehensive salary data on these personnel.

At any rate, faculty account for a declining share of the academy's professional work force and of institutions' personnel expenditures. I cannot break such data out by unionized/nonunionized institutions. However, the pattern holds for every institutional sector in higher education. In 1977, faculty accounted for 64 percent of the professional work force, and 34 percent of all personnel on campus. By 1989, the numbers were 55 and 32 percent.

The point is that faculty and their salaries are not as central and overriding a part of the institution's portfolio and expenditures as they once were. I emphasize this point in closing because academic managers, and others in and outside the academy, tend to believe that restructuring requires major reallocations and/or reductions in academic departments and personnel because faculty are the overwhelming source of personnel expenditures, which in turn account for an overwhelming share of institutional expenditures. Not true.

As a final note, there is much talk currently about academic managers' need for greater "flexibility" in dealing with academic personnel. It would appear from my analysis of salary structures that at least in this personnel area, managers enjoy a great deal and an increasing measure of flexibility in unionized institutions, though perhaps less than they enjoy in nonunionized colleges and universities.

CHAPTER 3

Retrenchment and Reorganization: Managing Academic Work(ers) for Productivity

The myth is that tenured faculty cannot be fired. The myth is strong. Many faculty believe it, as do many people outside the academy.

Many administrators believe the myth too. Sort of. In (re)telling the story, managers complain that tenure is a job guarantee that makes faculty unaccountable. It restricts managers' flexibility in motivating faculty, in deploying faculty resources, and in reorganizing academic programs.

The myth of the untouchable tenured faculty member is false. Tenured faculty can and have been fired, in large, public research universities and in small, private colleges, unionized and in nonunionized institutions.[1] Legally. With a few notable exceptions, the courts have generally supported colleges and universities in their retrenchment actions.[2]

But the managerial moral is true. With two key modifications. First, tenure makes it *procedurally* and *politically* more difficult, but not illegal, to fire faculty. Second, most faculty—49 percent of full-timers (and 75 percent of all faculty)—do not have tenure.[3]

Tenure is a strategy and structure developed by faculty as a professional group to protect their job security and professional autonomy. As with academic freedom, tenure's explicit aim and eventual impact was to reduce managerial discretion in personnel actions. Largely through the efforts of the AAUP, tenure and academic freedom have been inscribed in institutional policy and case law in higher education.[4]

As managers realize, their degree of discretion in personnel actions affecting individual faculty is related to their flexibility in reorganizing academic programs. Tenure protects individual faculty. It thereby inhibits managerial flexibility in moving faculty and in changing academic programs. It also establishes a measure of faculty self-governance over individual personnel decisions. Furthermore, it strengthens faculty's position as a collectivity in governance decisions surrounding the mission and strategic directions of the institution. (Even so, criticism of the administration is one of the principal reasons, over time, for faculty firings in academic freedom cases.)[5]

Of course, not all faculty enjoy the same professional protections. A large number are untenured assistant professors. Many others are not even on the so-called tenure track. Many are part-time. Managerial flexibility is much greater in dealing with these categories of faculty (see chapter 4).

Moreover, as noted above, the protections of tenure are far from absolute. From the inception of tenure, managers have been able to justify retrenchment for reasons of cause and financial exigency, and with a strategy increasingly being utilized in recent years—program reorganization. Nevertheless, historically managers have challenged the legitimacy of tenure, as they currently are doing, in order to increase their discretion. Managers want the flexibility to reduce personnel and resources in some areas and reallocate them to others in order to increase productivity. Tenure and retrenchment are interwoven with managerial discretion and reorganization.

Several questions, then, focus my contractual analysis of retrenchment clauses. What conditions are identified as justifying retrenchment? Do such conditions suggest the possibility of widespread, systematic reorganization rather than isolated, crisis-induced layoffs? What measure of discretion do managers enjoy, and what measure of involvement do faculty have in defining and acting in those conditions? What structures, professional and otherwise, protect faculty job security? What strategies have faculty unions employed to inhibit managerial discretion in retrenchment? And to what extent does managerial flexibility vary with respect to different strata of faculty?

There is no national data base by which to track faculty layoffs over time. The AAUP's longitudinal data base, consisting of academic freedom cases reported in *Academe* from 1915 to the present, is valuable more for the identification of trends and examples of practices than for an indication of the total number of cases.[6] The cases investigated by

Committee A of the AAUP, and reported in *Academe* generally involve retrenchment that violates academic due process, constitutes breach of contract, and/or annuls tenure. The number of cases is small—forty-eight in the 1980s. So, too, is the total number of faculty dismissed in these cases—less than three hundred between 1980 and 1990. That is less than 10 percent of estimated layoffs in this period, between four and seven thousand faculty. One survey reported in 1983 indicates that over four thousand faculty (twelve hundred with tenure) had been laid off in four-year institutions in the previous five years.[7]—not a large percentage of the work force; not an insignificant number either. At least it demonstrates that the myth about tenured faculty having lifetime guaranteed jobs is false.

Despite their limitations as a data set, the *Academe* cases suggest an important pattern. The 1980s mark the emergence of managerial strategies for effecting not just retrenchment, but reorganization. Strategic planning and programmatic restructuring came to be principal mechanisms of retrenchment, superseding claims of institutional financial exigency.[8] Managers could retrench faculty in some programs even as they expanded and built other programs. Rather than reducing faculty numbers in the face of financial crisis, managers could reallocate faculty resources from one part of the organization to another, eliminating departments (and retrenching faculty) even as total faculty numbers grow, in order to reposition the institution for the future (in part, such rationales underlay the administration's proposals at the University of Minnesota). Financial considerations still could be invoked, but in a less dramatic, constraining fashion—for example, not as present exigency but as future possibility.

Financial exigency has played a historically significant role in colleges and universities' retrenchment actions. In the 1970s, it accounted for a large portion (85 percent) of the academic freedom cases (involving 1,356 faculty) reported by the AAUP surrounding faculty layoffs.[9] It figured in the two most prominent cases of mass dismissal, in the CUNY and SUNY systems. (And it continues to figure in CUNY: in a May 1996 New York Supreme Court ruling, in Polishook—the president of the Professional Staff Congress—vs. CUNY, the court held that CUNY had improperly declared a financial exigency and it ordered the board of the institution to revisit its definition and implementation of exigency.) The AAUP developed and advanced its own definition of financial exigency in its *1976 Recommended Institutional Regulations on Academic Freedom and Tenure*, as "an imminent financial crisis which threatens the survival of the institution as a whole and which cannot be alleviated by less drastic means." (Its *1940 Statement of Principles on Academic Freedom and Tenure* was as follows: "Termination of a continuous appointment because of financial exigency should be demonstrably bona fide."[10])

Several retrenchment cases involving exigency have been litigated. At issue has been academic freedom, faculty involvement in decision making, and the definition and existence of exigency. Faculty have not fared well on any of these counts. Academic freedom is an individualistic concept. Courts tend to presume administrative neutrality in dismissals stemming from exigency (which often involve more than one faculty member)—no individual is being targeted for his or her views. The one exception—Bloomfield College—is a case of extraordinary administrative incompetence in revealing bad faith: thirteen tenured faculty were laid off, allegedly for reasons of exigency; tenure was revoked for all faculty, who were put on one year contracts; twelve new untenured faculty were hired to replace the thirteen fired faculty, based on program plans that were developed *after* the thirteen had been laid off.[11] The procedural requirements for ensuring that actions are "bona fide" (taken in good faith) are minimal. Moreover, courts have accepted various institutional definitions of exigency, including quite moderate fiscal difficulties and conditions applying to departments or colleges within the institution rather than to the institution as a whole. In the one exception—Pace v. Hymas (1986)—the faculty handbook phrased exigency as "a demonstrably bona fide, imminent financial crisis," and the administration had made no efforts to explore alternatives to retrenchment or to demonstrate exigency.[12]

In short, with a few exceptions, managerial prerogatives to direct their institutions' educational and programmatic courses have largely been upheld in court. Those prerogatives suggest the need to rethink traditional conceptualizations of collegial self-governance in curricular matters. It would seem that not only faculty job security, but also the faculty control of the curriculum, is something of a myth. It is certainly unsupported legally.

Nevertheless, institutions prefer to stay out of court. Managerial groups and individuals not only rejected the AAUP's definition of exigency. They suggested that institutional policies and contracts *not* invoke the term *financial exigency*.[13] One former legal counsel to a board made the rationale underlying the shift explicit.

> Under the former Board policy, tenured faculty could be terminated only for financial exigency . . . or discontinuance of an entire program or department. . . . However, as the Montana University system began to experience enrollment and budget problems in the late 1970s, the Board of Regents directed the management bargaining team to negotiate a procedure whereby university administrators could sensibly reallocate positions to departments where they were needed, without waiting for bankruptcy of the institution or discontinuing entire programs or departments. First, management proposed to substitute "retrenchment" for the term "financial exigency." The term "financial exigency" had been largely undefined in prior Board policies, but during the 1970s courts throughout the country were beginning to interpret it, sometimes very restrictively. The Board sought to define for itself the conditions under which reductions of faculty might occur, rather than deferring entirely to the courts.[14]

The terms of the struggle shifted.

If "financial exigency" historically has been important in retrenchment actions, the meaning and use of financial exigency has changed over time. At one point, financial exigency was defined as a condition of fiscal crisis for the entire institution. Then it was a condition of fiscal crisis for a particular unit within the institution. Then it was an imminent crisis. Then it was a perceived threat of impending crisis. Then it became the possibility of a perceived threat of future crisis.[15]

Each step down this path obviously extended managerial discretion. It also reduced the scope of tenure's protections. No longer an immediate condition, the facts of which could be examined, exigency came to be a judgment about the future. Moreover, the arena in which managerial judgment was to be exercised expanded. Short- and medium-term interpretations surrounding mere economic conditions came to be intermingled with long-term judgments and plans regarding the mix and nature of academic programs. Chiefly economic rationales for retrenchment came to be mixed up with academic ones.

As with faculty layoffs, there is little empirical research on academic reorganization. However, a recent national survey indicates that the activity is widespread. Of 406 institutions (124 community colleges, 35 baccalaureate institutions, 123 comprehensive universities, and 124 doctoral institutions) 40 percent had "eliminated academic programs," and 7 percent had terminated faculty.[16] There are some case studies of how restructuring is accomplished.[17] In reviewing such cases, it is clear that academic reorganization is being driven not by normal academic review and traditional criteria of academic quality, but by ad hoc, administratively initiated efforts to reposition the institution given considerations of perceived market pressures and opportunities.[18]

The shift to market-based criteria in programmatic planning has obvious implications for academic involvement in such decision making. As with salaries, so with reorganization. The less decisions are matters of academic judgment, the less powerful faculty's claim to a role in decision making.

Faculty's position in decision making also is undermined by recent scholarship and commentary that is critical of the proliferation of academic courses, programs, and specialties. Faculty are portrayed as self-interested professionals who have successfully gained increased discretionary time by reducing their involvement in teaching.[19] In exercising their expense preferences, faculty have caused indiscriminate expansion and growth by accretion of academic programs. In the current fiscal environment it is left to central administrators to stop this trend, to ensure growth not by accretion, but by substitution.[20] (The argument is ironic: there is little empirical evidence of "academic bloat" in terms of student/faculty ratio—indeed, quite the opposite, the ratio is up; by contrast, there is much evidence of "bureaucratic accretion" and rising administrative costs.[21])

The boundaries between economic and academic rationales for increased managerial flexibility vis-à-vis faculty are blurred in more than just the literature. I serve on my university's Strategic Planning and Budget Advisory Committee. The committee's title itself suggests confusion. It is an oxymoron. Strategic planning and budget neither are similar functional areas nor can they be merged comfortably together. They are competitors. In practice, the effort to academically plan more than three years into the future is generally subsumed to the immediate task of figuring out how to meet this (coming) year's budget contingencies. Planning loses out. Institutions do not budget to plans; more typically, they "plan" to this year's budget.[22] At my institution this past year's budget confronts us with a $5 million "anticipated shortfall."

(That means we got less than we bargained for, and that we already bargained— in committing monies for land and buildings—for more than we will get.) The topic of one meeting was the need for managerial flexibility in dealing with faculty positions. Especially the flexibility to take "vacated" faculty "lines" (positions vacated through retirement, or a faculty member leaving) and reallocate them to other units. One vice-president, noting the need to free up faculty lines by prioritizing and eliminating academic programs that had grown out of control, referred to the "problem" of tenure. Another vice-president suggested that managers needed flexibility in dealing with faculty positions to meet the $5 million goal. "How's that," I asked? "'Sweeping' and reallocating a handful of faculty positions from one unit to another will not save $5 million. You would have to vacuum up and throw out the positions altogether. Even then, you would have to do a lot of vacuuming. We don't get paid *that* much."

That is the irony of much current discussion surrounding retrenchment and reorganization. Increased attention has been devoted to the costs of academic departments and faculty and to cutting those costs, at a time when faculty account for a smaller proportion of the work force and of institutional expenditures than two decades ago. As noted in Chapter 2, faculty account for a decreasing proportion of the professional workforce: in 1989, they accounted for 55 percent of the professional work force, down from 64 percent in 1977; they accounted for 32 percent of all higher education employees, down from 34 percent. Moreover, they are neither the highest paid category of worker in higher education nor the category that has realized the largest increases in wages.

Nevertheless, across the country, there is a hue and cry among academic administrators and some faculty for more managerial flexibility. Such flexibility in moving and dismissing academic personnel is restricted by tenure. It is also restricted by collective bargaining agreements.

What, then, of the contracts? There is limited empirical research on retrenchment clauses in collective bargaining agreements. One recent study analyzed the emergence of retrenchment policies in Texas community colleges. Only 41 percent of the forty-nine public community college districts had policies, and half of these policies had been implemented after 1986.[23] Other studies have analyzed general faculty rights and academic input into decision making in various academic areas in the contracts.[24]

Elsewhere, I built on such work in analyzing forty-five contracts from the 1980s.[25] Here, as there, my general focus is on professional involvement and managerial discretion in various domains of decision making surrounding retrenchment. As before, I examine retrenchment clauses in terms of categories found in the contracts. For example, articles may speak to the conditions that justify retrenchment, the decision-making process (including consultation) as to whether and where to retrench, order of layoff, notice, reassignment of faculty to other positions within the institution, retraining, and faculty's rights to re-employment (recall) in openings that arise for a defined period after layoff. I pay special attention, as before, to financial exigency.

However, I also expand upon my previous analysis. First, I analyze what rationales, if any, are provided for retrenchment. Are they more economic or academic in nature? In my previous analysis I measured how much relative space was devoted to defining conditions that justify retrenchment, and only in the case of exigency did I analyze the character of these conditions. Second, I examine faculty involvement and managerial discretion in the provisions. In particular, to what extent are faculty involved in the decision to retrench? To what extent do managers have discretion not only in whether and where to retrench, but in what order, with what notice, and with what rights for laid off faculty? In my previous analysis, I paid more attention to the size of the various sections of retrenchment clauses. The relatively small size of sections addressing consultation and alternatives was interpreted as evidence of limited faculty involvement in decision making. Here I focus on specific examples of faculty involvement and managerial discretion. Third, I consider what professional conditions and strategies constrain managerial flexibility and provide protections for faculty. Some of these are established structures found in most contracts, such as rules of order for layoff. Others are strategies found in selected contracts that speak in distinctive ways to retrenchment and work force reorganization. Finally, I explore dimensions of professional stratification in retrenchment clauses. To what extent do provisions (for example, for notice) differentiate among various strata of faculty?

Rationales for Retrenchment, Financial Exigency

In a national sample of 45 contracts negotiated in the 1980s, 40 percent (18) utilized the term *financial exigency*, in their retrenchment clauses. By contrast, of 212 HECAS contracts negotiated in the 1990s, only 15 percent (32) refer to financial exigency in their retrenchment clauses (another 8 specify the term in other articles—for example, articles on sabbatical or tenure). There may have been some change over time in contractual use of the term. However, none of the 7 contracts in the previous study that utilized exigency language and that are in HECAS dropped the terminology in their 1990s contracts.

The principal explanation for the differential incidence of exigency provisions lies in the differential nature of the study populations— HECAS has a smaller proportion of contracts in four-year institutions and of AAUP negotiated contracts. As in the previous study population, in the HECAS population exigency provisions are more common in the contracts of four-year institutions than in those of two-year colleges and in AAUP-negotiated contracts than in those negotiated by other agents (see table 3.1). In the HECAS population, there is a dependent association between the incidence of financial exigency mentions and institutional type ($x2=43.78$, significant at the .005 level).

Half of four-year institution contracts mention financial exigency; less than one-tenth (9 percent) of two-year college contracts do so (technical colleges are underrepresented—only one of sixteen contracts). That is comparable to the findings for forty-five contracts in the 1980s: 56 percent of four-year institution and 17 percent of two-year college contracts had exigency clauses. Similarly, in the HECAS population there is a dependent association between the incidence of financial exigency mentions and bargaining agent ($x2=15.41$, significant at the .005 level). Almost two-thirds (62 percent) of AAUP-negotiated contracts mention financial exigency; less than one-fifth of AFT (14 percent) and NEA (18 percent) contracts do so. Again, that is comparable to the findings for forty-five contracts in the 1980s: 61 percent of AAUP, 25 percent of NEA, and 27 percent of AFT, negotiated contracts had financial exigency clauses.[26]

Not many contractual provisions utilize the AAUP definition of financial exigency. Of the forty provisions that mention financial exigency, four refer to it as "demonstrably bona fide" (three four-year institutions and a junior college). Only six define the exigency as applying to the entire institution (four four-year institutions and two two-year colleges). In no case does a contract utilize the terminology of demonstrably bona fide and apply it to the whole institution. One contract (Cuyahoga Community College) refers to "good faith" and "crisis" financial exigency and interprets them as applying to the entire institution. One (Dowling College) refers to "bona fide" and another to "demonstrable" financial exigency as applying to the whole institution.

TABLE 3.1
INCIDENCE OF FINANCIAL EXIGENCY PROVISIONS

	Fin exig	Demonst bona find	Whole insti- tution	Define	Fac involv, react	Fac involv, comm
Two-year	13 (9 %)*	1	2	3	3	2
Tech	1 (6 %)	0	0	0	1	0
Four-year	26 (50 %)	3	4	5	7	4
AAUP	8 (62 %)	x	x	x	x	x
AFT	6 (14 %)	x	x	x	x	x
NEA	22 (18 %)	x	x	x	x	x
Total	40**	4	6	8	11	6

* The percentage of all such contracts in HECAS.
** The bargaining agent numbers do not add up to 40 because some contracts are negotiated by independent agents.

Only eight contracts (five in four-year, three in two-year institutions) define the condition of exigency. Most (six) definitions are short, general statements about current revenues and institutional obligations. Two pairs of clauses are almost identical. Ediston State Community College's provision (see below), negotiated by the NEA, is virtually the same as that of Cuyahoga Community College, negotiated by the AAUP. Both institutions are in Ohio. (The national association does not itself negotiate contracts. Rather, negotiation is by institutional faculty who serve as local, union representatives.) "Financial exigency is defined as that condition when revenues are so limited that the College can no longer continue to fulfill current and/or future financial obligations under the contract without disrupting the administration and program integrity of the College." (Article 21). Who determines (and how) what "administration" and "program integrity" are, and whether they will be "disrupted?" The same question applies to Delaware State College's definition: "When the financial position of the College demonstrates that a financial crisis is imminent and that failure to retrench would seriously jeopardize the College" (Article 10.5.2). The same applies to Hofstra University's definition: "Financial exigency will be declared when it appears that there will be an inability of the University to meet its financial commitments in any fiscal year." (Article 9.16) When it appears to whom? And what particular financial commitments?

Flathead Valley Community College's contract is somewhat more specific: "[W]hen the general fund deficit is of such magnitude that balancing the general fund requires the termination of a Member(s)" (Article 16). Specifying the "general fund" is important. In a public institution such as Flathead it focuses the discussion on certain state appropriations to the exclusion (depending on the local situation) of other monies (sometimes including state support for land, buildings, and improvements) that may not be inconsequential. It addresses neither the total revenues nor the assets of the institution. (That is even more explicit in the definition of the Massachusetts State College System: "Whenever, in any fiscal year, the monies allocated or otherwise made available from or by way of legislative appropriation for all of the operations of such College . . . shall be insufficient for the continuation" Article 10.C). Moreover, it fails to specify who decides what "magnitude" of deficit requires retrenchment rather than a reduction in monies allocated for academic units' operating budgets or a reduction in administrative, nonfaculty professional or other staff.

Two other contracts have more detailed, restrictive definitions. The provision in Portland State University's contract for full-time faculty (AAUP) (see below) is almost the same as that in Southern Oregon State College's contract (independent agent).

a. A condition of financial exigency may be declared if the President
finds that the University's budget has insufficient funds to do all of the
following: 1) maintain all essential programs and services; 2) finance the
full compensation of all tenured faculty; 3) finance the full compensation of faculty on fixed term appointment until the end of the period of
appointment; 4) finance the full compensation of all other faculty until
the end of an appointment, including the providing of timely notice. The
University's Division of Continuing Education is considered to be a separate entity for purposes of financial exigency. b. A condition requiring
the reduction or elimination of a department may be declared if the
President finds that institutional operations within a reduced budget, or
failure to reallocate funds, would result in a serious distortion of the academic or other essential programs and services of the University if
retrenchment procedures were not implemented. (Article 22)

Three important features stand out. Some parts of the curriculum are
exempted (continuing education—and, in case of Southern Oregon,
summer school). There is a distinction between conditions of a general
exigency (a) and that applied to a department (b) (Southern Oregon
State's contract refers more loosely to "an impairment of function").
Finally, the financial obligations are largely those of paying faculty
(although in place of number 3 above, the Southern Oregon State contract specifies "all other employees"). This does not apply to financial
obligations in general. Exigency occurs when you cannot meet the faculty payroll. That leaves less room for managerial discretion. Still, how
to decide whether failure to retrench "would result in a serious distortion"? It is in the hands of managers.

All of the eight contracts that define financial exigency provide for
some faculty involvement in decision making surrounding a declaration of exigency. An additional nine contracts do so as well (six four-
year institutions, two two-year colleges, and one technical college).
Faculty involvement takes one of two principal forms, with some variation. In one scenario, management provides the union and/or faculty
governance bodies with information or data surrounding its intention to
declare an exigency. The association is then given an opportunity to
offer recommendations and/or suggest alternatives. In a second scenario, a formal committee is constituted to develop recommendations
about the exigency. Presumably, a committee provides for the possibility of a more significant level of faculty involvement, particularly if it is

a standing faculty committee rather than an ad hoc committee appointed by the administration.

Most (eleven) of the seventeen contracts providing for faculty involvement follow the first model. The clauses have varying levels of detail.

> There shall be no layoffs due to financial exigency unless the College President, 60 days prior to making his/her recommendation to the Board of Trustees, notifies the Faculty Senate, and the CTC AAUP that a recommendation for such action may be made. The Faculty Senate and the CTC AAUP may offer their advice, recommendations, and alternatives to the College President. The President shall consider those and forward them along with his or her own to the Board of Trustees. (Cincinnati Technical College, Article 7.D.6)

Portland State University's contract for full-time faculty has a similar section, calling for the president to meet with various faculty bodies and association representatives "for the purpose of presenting and discussing a full description and analysis of the financial condition of the University." Faculty groups then have "at least" thirty days to respond with recommendations, "unless the president finds and states that circumstances require a response in a shorter period of time." The provision then calls for the president to give "thoughtful consideration" to this feedback. (Article 22, Section 3) Dowling College's provision extends the deliberation period even further. It first requires the college to notify the union "in writing prior to March 15 [beware the Ides of March?] of the year preceding the academic year in which the reduction is to be implemented." It then gives the union forty-five days to make recommendations, the Board of Trustees thirty days to make a decision, and the union another forty-five days "to make a determination of the disciplines or areas in which the positions are to be eliminated" (Article 8C01).

Perhaps one faculty strategy is to draw the process out. Make it fairly complicated procedurally to declare exigency, forcing management through various steps/processes. In that way, quick, arbitrary actions are prevented. Decisions must be considered, debated, data based, and reconsidered.

The second model of involvement is consistent with academic ideology about shared governance and collegial, committee based decision making. Faculty involvement in decision making surrounding the declaration of exigency in six provisions (four four-year and two two-year institutions) is through formal committees. The names, size, and consistency of the committees vary. But they all consider management's exigency proposals and then make recommendations of their own. For example:

> In the event of retrenchment for reason of financial exigency or decreasing enrollment, a committee composed of 3 faculty selected by the President of the Association and 3 administrators appointed by the President shall be given an opportunity to study the financial exigency and/or decreasing enrollment and make a report to the Board of Trustees with respect to the retrenchment. Upon request of this committee . . . the Board will invite this committee to a meeting to discuss its report with the Executive Committee or a subcommittee thereof. (Rhode Island School of Design, Article 18.B)

The two provisions that most restrict managerial discretion in cases of financial exigency specifically identify alternatives to retrenching faculty. Hofstra University's contract requires consideration of various measures by which to cut costs and/or to increase revenues in lieu of laying off faculty.

> Prior to the reduction of faculty because of bona fide financial exigency, the Administration will consult with the appropriate academic constituencies, including the AAUP, and take steps to attempt to curtail costs in other areas, such as the indirect costs of sustaining non-academic and academic programs. Also, consideration will be given to the reduction in the number of administrative and support lines and the filling of academic and administrative vacancies with qualified members of the Hofstra faculty. Attempts will continue to be made to increase revenue by all feasible means. (Article 9.17)

Delaware State College's provision goes even further. It requires a "statement of the amount of money needed to relieve the exigency." And it calls for a "Financial Exigency Committee" of five faculty and five administrators to "first investigate ways to relieve the exigency by means of exhausting the possibilities of immediately initiating mechanisms for raising funds or of reallocating current funds. The College and the Association agree that unit members should not bear the brunt of financial exigency alone." (Article 10.5.6.a).

The clause prioritizes faculty over other personnel and operations or programs. It also affords them the opportunity to play a direct role in targeting nonacademic units and personnel in the institution for reductions.

However, faculty influence on the declaration of financial exigency should not be overstated. In those twenty-three contracts in which there is no explicit provision for faculty involvement, judgment rests in the hands of managers. Phrasing such as "In the event of" and "Whenever in the judgment of" leaves little question as to where decision-making authority lies. Moreover, in those seventeen contracts that provide for some level of faculty involvement, ultimate authority still rests with the administration. For example:

> Final authority on the need to reduce staff for reasons of bona fide financial exigency rests with the Board of Trustees. (Dowling College, Article 8.C.01)

> Recommendations from faculty shall be reviewed and considered by the President, but such recommendations are advisory, and the final determination of methods to alleviate the financial exigency shall be made by the President and the Board of Trustees. (DuPage College, Article D.12)

> Decisions on the disposition of the recommendations shall rest with the President. (Ediston State Community College, Article 18.2.b)

> It is specifically agreed that the decision as to when a reduction in force is necessary due to . . . financial exigency . . . is reserved to the administration and the Board. (Nebraska State College, Article 13.2)

Some contracts vest authority in management in an even more powerful way, by indicating that decisions about whether there is an exigency are *not* subject to arbitration (the Rhode Island School of Design contract for full-time faculty, the University of Nebraska, Kearney, Southern Oregon State College and Portland State University's contract for full-time faculty). Even in those contracts where such decisions can be grieved, court precedent suggests that outside authorities generally are reluctant to question administrations' declarations of exigency.[27]

Rationales for Retrenchment: Other

Much of the talk surrounding reorganization and retrenchment in higher education refers to present and future financial conditions. It is a rare college or university president or provost who has not invoked the institution's financial situation to justify repositioning its academic resources, to have more managerial "flexibility" vis-à-vis academic personnel and functions, to reorganize academic programs, to reallocate resources, to retrench faculty.

But what of the contracts? Financial exigency is one rationale for retrenchment. Seldom (five contracts) is it the only one. (In two cases that is the only condition for laying off tenured faculty, but nontenured faculty can be laid off for other reasons). What other rationales are provided for retrenchment? Contractual language falls into four general categories: (1) economic rationales other than the mention of financial exigency; (2) rationales that speak to academic programs and missions; (3) rationales that refer to student demand; and (4) a residual category of miscellaneous rationales that do not fit in any of the previous three groupings.

Many contracts identify more than one rationale. Most contracts (sixty) that provide a rationale for retrenchment mention two categories. A smaller number (twenty-seven) mention three. Few mention only one category (nine) or all four (seven).

However, many contracts offer no rationale. Of 178 contracts with retrenchment articles (84 percent of the HECAS population) 103 provide a rationale for retrenchment (see table 3.2). A substantial minority (42 percent) of contracts with retrenchment articles (and a slight majority—51 percent—of all HECAS contracts) offer no justifying condition for laying off faculty.

TABLE 3.2
INCIDENCE OF RATIONALES FOR RETRENCHMENT
IN CONTRACTS WITH RETRENCHMENT CLAUSES

	Any rationale	Economic, other than fin exig	Academic	Student demand
Two-year	63 (54%)*	38	43	38
Technical	2 (14%)	1	2	1
Four-year	38 (81%)	12	32	10
Total	103	51	77	49

* The percentage of all such contracts in HECAS.

There is a dependent association between the incidence of clauses with rationales and institutional type (x2=21.86, significant at the .005 level). The contracts of four-year institutions are overrepresented: 81

percent have language specifying rationales. The contracts of two-year and technical colleges are underrepresented: fifty-four and 14 percent respectively have language specifying rationales.

The most common rationales provided for laying off faculty are economic. Most of these eighty-three contracts do *not* mention financial exigency. Other economic language is found in fifty-one contracts, as compared to thirty-two contracts that mention financial exigency to justify retrenchment. In contrast to exigency language, which is most common in the contracts of four-year institutions, other economic language (thirty-eight of the fifty-one cases) is slightly more common in two-year college contracts (there is not a statistically significant association between incidence and institutional type, $x2=3.17$).

One-third (seventeen) of the clauses invoking economic rationales other than financial exigency utilize the language of crisis. In ten contracts, nine of which are in Washington State, the phrase *declaration of financial emergency* is utilized and defined—as reductions in allotments by the governor and/or legislature.[28] Other crisis language includes "bona fide financial crisis" (Western Michigan University), "fiscal exigency" (University of Hawaii), "extraordinary financial circumstances" (University of Delaware) and "bona fide financial reasons" (Massachusetts Regional Colleges).

However, most of the "other" economic rationales are considerably less restrictive than financial exigency. They do not suggest that the institution must face dire financial straits before laying off faculty. To the contrary. In fourteen cases, the clause simply refers to financial "reasons," "conditions," or "considerations." In twenty other cases, language invokes a sense of deficiency—"lack of funds," "adverse" conditions, or "insufficient" funds. Yet the terms are unspecified. How much of a "lack"? How "adverse"?

Only two contracts refer to or define any sort of pattern over time. Lakeland Faculty Association's contract refers to a "pattern of declining income." That is it. No details on how many years make a "pattern." Is decline over two years a pattern or a random break in a longer term trend? Cloud County Community College's contract provides some clarification, referring to "insufficient funds over a 2 semester period." But how "insufficient"? Does a decline or deficit of 1.5 percent over two semesters really justify retrenchment? The economic rationales provided in the contracts suggest that faculty may be laid off due to short-term economic contingencies. In most cases (thirty-two financial exigency and seventeen clauses utilizing "other" economic language), those contingencies are identified as crises. In many cases (thirty-four) they are not.

Almost as many contracts (seventy-seven) invoke academic rationales to justify the retrenchment of faculty as do those that mention economic rationales. There is a dependent association between the incidence of academic rationales and institutional type ($x2=20.76$, significant at the .005 level). Such language is more likely in the contracts of four-year institutions than of two-year and technical colleges: 62 percent of contracts in four-year schools, as compared to 30 and 12.5 percent in two-year and technical colleges invoke academic rationales.

By far the most common academic language, found in fifty-six contracts, is of program "discontinuation," "curtailment," "elimination," or "reduction." Note the term is *program*, not *department* (sometimes the latter term is included as well). Managers need not eliminate an entire department in order to justify retrenching faculty in a department. They can eliminate a program, which often exists within a department—either a degree program, or a specialization area. (In part, this is what the struggle was over in the recent dispute involving the University of Minnesota faculty's threat to unionize—new policy language that specified the possiblity of such *sub*department elimination as a rationale for retrenchment—although current policy enables administration to retrench faculty if they eliminate entire departments.)

The language in many contracts is even less restrictive. In fifteen cases, reference is to programmatic "changes" or "reasons." In an additional six cases, eliminating courses is enough to justify retrenching faculty.

A smaller number of contracts invoke changes that go beyond individual programs. Six clauses refer to changes in institutional mission or educational policy. Another three refer to changes in degree requirements.

Only a few contracts (seven) use the term *reorganization* to justify faculty layoffs. For example, the contracts of two major systems—SUNY and the Florida State University System—each refer to the "reorganization of administrative or academic structures, programs, or functions." Nevertheless, reorganization is precisely what is being invoked in most cases as a rationale for retrenching faculty.[29] Program curtailment and change have to do with the internal reallocation of resources that is a part of the efforts of managers to reposition institutions in ways that will more closely link them to external markets, improve productivity, and generate revenue. Such efforts are not grounded in traditional conceptions of academic quality. Indeed, of the seventy-seven references to academic rationales, only one invokes quality: "Lack of quality as identified in internal academic program or external accreditation reviews." (Shawnee State University, Article 15.3.C).

The influence of the market is particularly plain in student demand-based rationales for retrenching faculty. Such rationales are somewhat more common in two-year colleges than in four-year institutions and technical colleges, although the differences are not statistically significant ($x2=3.92$). Of forty-nine contracts with student demand language, thirty-eight are in two-year colleges (ten are in four-year institutions, and one is in a technical college).

The most common student demand language, found in twenty-two contracts, is quite general. Reference is simply to "changing," "declining," "inadequate," or "insufficient" enrollments. That vague, sweeping terminology tells us very little. How much change? 20 percent? 10 percent? 5 percent? Does a one or .05 percent decline in enrollment justify laying off faculty?

Many contracts (sixteen) modify general references to enrollment decline. Clauses utilize adjectives and wording such as "a substantial decrease," "significant drop," "significant decreases," "major decline," "a material decrease," and "demonstrable enrollment reduction." Of course, that still begs the question of what constitutes a "significant" or "substantial" decline.

Fourteen other contracts modify the general language in another way. They specify enrollment decline to particular academic units within the college. (In some cases, such as the Massachusetts State College System, when contracts apply to several colleges, the contract specifies the decline to a particular college; similarly, the Wisconsin Indianhead District contract specifies declines to the campus level.) In several cases, reference is to *either* general decline or decline in a specific unit. For example: "declining enrollment either in the College or a particular program" (Alpena Community College, Article 8.A).

Either is a critical choice of words. Faculty may be laid off if the college as a whole is experiencing some enrollment decline, even if in their program enrollments are stable or rising. Level of specification is particularly important when one considers that many institutions now have more than one campus. Should enrollment decline at one campus justify layoffs at another?

A few contracts (three) use language that goes beyond general references to enrollment. For example, Washtenaw Community College's contract refers to "the number of fiscal year equated students." Jackson Community College's contract refers to the level of "credit generating units." In going beyond simple, headcount enrollment, these contracts invoke measures that allow for more focus on matters of productivity. Headcount enrollment might drop without reducing credit hour production and without reducing tuition and fee income coming into the institution. For example, a change in the mix of full- and part-time students, or of students' course loads, could create such an effect. For purposes of academic planning and of analyzing student demand and productivity, headcount enrollment is not a particularly useful index. Yet it is unusual for contracts to specify student demand in this way.

It is also unusual, as with the economic rationales, for contracts to use student demand language that speaks to change over a span of time. Only four contracts allude to time span. For example, Cloud County Community College's contract refers to "substantial and prolonged decrease in student enrollment" (Article 35.2.B). That still begs the question of "How long is prolonged?" (and How much is substantial?) Schoolcraft College's contract provides more specification, defining "insufficient enrollment" as a situation in which for the second consecutive semester, not all faculty in the discipline have a full load. Solano County Community College's contract refers to a decline in average daily attendance for the first six months that is less than either of the previous two years. Hardly a crisis, one would think.

With these modest exceptions, in most cases, retrenchment is justified by short-term shifts in enrollment of an unspecified degree, shifts that most institutions experience in the normal course of operations. The student demand curve is rarely a straight line of steady, year by year increments.

A final category of rationales found in twenty-seven contracts provides a good segue for moving to a discussion of managerial discretion. (Four contracts foreshadow my discussion in chapter 5 of technology, justifying retrenchment by "technological change.") After identifying other rationales for retrenching faculty, eleven contracts close the sentence with the following: "or any other reasons," "or other reasons," "or other good faith reasons." Such phrases are a blanket granting of discretion to managers. Another nine contracts justify layoffs with simple statements about "overstaffing" or "lack of work." In six other cases there is not even a suggestion of too many faculty or too little work. The clause simply states that retrenchment will occur when management decides to "decrease the number of faculty," or words to that effect. The rationale for retrenchment is that management has decided to retrench.

Faculty Involvement and Managerial Discretion

To what extent are faculty involved in the decision making surrounding retrenchment? Do faculty have a voice, other than of righteous indignation and disbelief, in the various matters that have to be decided? Do they have voice in questions ranging from whether it is necessary to retrench, to what units and faculty to retrench, to what order of layoff to follow, to what notice to provide, to whether and where faculty will be reassigned and retrained in lieu of layoff and be recalled from layoff? Moreover, what is the form of faculty involvement? Is there provision for "meet and discuss," "meet and confer" (or as a union colleague calls it, "meet and defer") with the bargaining agent? Are decisions made by committees that have faculty membership? Are these standing or ad hoc committees?

By the same token, to what extent do managers have discretion in these various matters? Must they consult with the union and/or faculty? If they must consult, do they have final authority? Can they make exception to standing rules and procedures—for example, to established rules regarding order of layoff and notice? How much flexibility can managers exercise in the various decision areas surrounding retrenchment?[30]

As noted earlier, only 103 (58 percent) of the 178 contracts with retrenchment clauses specify conditions that justify laying off faculty. Thus, in 42 percent of the contracts with retrenchment clauses managers need not provide a rationale for retrenching faculty. That in itself is an important measure of managerial discretion (as is the vagueness of much of the language that speaks to rationales, as discussed previously).

Such discretion is greater in two-year and technical colleges than in four-year institutions. One example of this lies in the very titles of the articles common in the different sectors. The articles in the former institutions are more likely to be entitled "Reduction in Force" than are those in four-year institutions, which are more likely to use the terminology of retrenchment and layoff. The difference is important. Reduction in force clauses often open with simple declarative statements, such as: "If the Board determines that there is to be a reduction in force . . . the following procedures shall be followed" (Allen County Community College, Article 8.A); or "When at the discretion of the Board, staff reduction is necessary" (Iowa Central Community College, Article 3). Such language explicitly and authoritatively accords extraordinary discretion to managers to reduce and reallocate faculty resources. In short, by this rough but significant measure of whether managers must even justify retrenchment by some rationale, managers have more flexibility in two- than in four-year institutions.

Faculty Involvement

Of the 178 contracts with retrenchment clauses, almost half (46 percent) have some provision for faculty involvement in decision making surrounding faculty layoffs. There is a dependent association between the incidence of such provision and institutional type ($x2=24.71$, significant at the .000 level). As might be expected, four-year institution contracts are overrepresented: about two-thirds (67 percent) of such contracts provide for faculty involvement, compared to just less than one-third (31 percent) of two-year college contracts (and 19 percent of technical college contracts) (see table 3.3). Faculty involvement is more often found in four- than in two-year institutions.

Only a handful of contracts address decisions other than whether and where to retrench. In five contracts, faculty committees are involved in decisions to make exception to established rules of order. For example:

On the recommendation of the appropriate standing committee, the President may retain an employee out of the above order, if he or she is the only employee qualified and prepared to teach a course(s) necessary to the proper functioning of the college. (Broome Community College, Article 48)

If the College decides to retrench Faculty with greater seniority than those with lesser seniority within a program because of the needs of the College and the value of the Faculty member(s) involved, it may do so after serious consideration of the recommendations of the Faculty Affairs Committee. (Franklin Pierce College, Article 17.5)

In 3 other contracts committees are involved in reassignment decisions. One contract provides for a committee to make decisions about retraining.

TABLE 3.3

INCIDENCE OF PROVISIONS FOR FACULTY INVOLVEMENT

	Any mention	*Consult/ reaction*	*Meet/ discuss*	*Committee*
Two-year	44 (31%)*	17	15	13
Technical	3 (19%)	2	0	1
Four-year	35 (67%)	11	10	19
Total	82	30	25	33

* The percentage of all such contracts in HECAS.

In the questions of whether and where to retrench, what is the form of faculty involvement? I code references to involvement into three categories. Some provisions simply call for the bargaining agent to be consulted, often with the expectation that the association will provide some recommendations. A second category is the traditional "meet and confer" or "meet and discuss" provision, which simply indicates that management will meet with the agent and discuss matters. (In Columbia Basin College's contract the provision is called "meet and explain." In another contract, the union is "briefed.") A third type of clause identifies a committee, either ad hoc or standing, that includes faculty.

Keeping in mind that some contracts refer to more than one type of involvement, there is a fairly even distribution among the categories of provision. There are thirty-three contracts with provision for involvement by committees that include faculty members, thirty contracts that call for consultation, and twenty-five that indicate management will meet and discuss matters with the association. The distribution varies somewhat by institutional type. The most common category in four-year institutions is faculty involvement through committees (19 contracts, compared to 11 with consultation and 10 with meet and discuss). Provisions for faculty involvement through committees are the least common of the three in two-year colleges (13 contracts, compared to 17 with consultation and 15 with meet and discuss). There is a dependent association between the incidence of provisions for faculty involvement through committees and institutional type ($x2=23.13$, significant at the .000 level). The contracts of four-year institutions are overrepresented; those of two-year and technical colleges are underrepresented.

I further disaggregate my analysis by determining how many provisions for faculty involvement through committees refer to ad hoc committees, formed by administrators specifically to deal with retrenchment, and how many are standing faculty committees (e.g., of the academic senate). Of thirty-three such provisions, only seven refer to standing faculty senate committees or governance bodies. All but one of these are in the contracts of four-year institutions (the other is in a technical college contract). Another three contracts refer to faculty senate involvement in forming a special committee (two of these are in four-year institutions).

Finally, I gauge the extent of faculty involvement by categorizing the periods of time afforded for consultation. Only twenty-eight contracts specify a particular number of days that the association or the committees has to deliberate before forwarding recommendations to the appropriate administrator. The time periods identified range from five to sixty days. Again, a difference emerges between the contracts of two- and four-year colleges. In 8 contracts, the time for deliberation extends beyond thirty days. All are contracts in four-year institutions. In ten contracts, the period is thirty days. In ten others, it is between five and twenty days. Not a great deal of time for consultation, deliberation, and recommendation. Yet such provisions do serve, if nothing else, to draw out the process of laying off faculty.

Managerial Discretion

Almost all (94 percent) contracts with retrenchment clauses have some provision for managerial discretion. By contrast, slightly less than half of the contracts ensure some form of consultation with the union and/or faculty regarding the decisions about whether and where to retrench. Even in these contracts it is clear in the vast number of cases that final authority rests in the hands of managers. For example:

> It is specifically agreed that whenever a reduction in force is necessary . . . a faculty advisory committee shall be established on the affected campus to provide recommendations to the campus administration. . . . In each instance, the faculty advisory committee shall provide recommendations to the campus administration regarding program viability and within the time limits established by the administration. It is specifically agreed that the faculty advisory committee recommendation shall be advisory only and that any final decisions regarding the necessity of reduction in force shall be reserved to the administration and Board. (Nebraska State College, Article 13.1)

In eight of the contracts, there is provision for the union or faculty body to bring its recommendations directly and independently to the board, along with the president, rather than making recommendations to the president, who then interacts alone with the board. Even then the retrenchment decision is essentially a managerial right.

In most sections of the contract, managerial discretion is extensive. My index of the extent of discretion is the percentage of contracts that explicitly accord managers freedom to exercise judgment in making decisions rather than having to follow a set formula.

In matters of order, managers may break the established rules in 82 percent of the contracts. Generally, there are defined rules of order for laying off faculty. There are also nearly always exceptions to those rules. For example:

> Retrenchment will then be made as circumstances require, providing that the following order be utilized to the extent feasible. . . . Retrenchment shall be made in inverse order of seniority, provided the remaining employees have the necessary qualifications to teach the remaining courses and/or perform the remaining duties. (Clatsop Community College, Article 16.1–2)

> In selecting among bargaining unit members . . . the order of retrenchment shall be in inverse order of seniority, provided that the Employer/University Administration may disregard said order if the Employer/University Administration determines that continued employment of a bargaining unit member(s) is essential to: 1) the mission and purpose of the unit or the University; 2) the integrity or operation of the

unit; or 3) the campus affirmative action goals. (University of Massachusetts, Amherst, Article 22.4.g)

Similarly, in matters of reassignment, managers have extraordinary flexibility. Most reassignment clauses are grounded in assumptions that managers will decide whether to reassign faculty targeted for retrenchment and whether such faculty members are qualified to fill particular positions. In 84 percent of the provisions, managers are explicitly accorded the discretion to make such decisions. In the remaining cases there is no mention of managers having the freedom to exercise their judgment in making decisions about reassignment.

The one section of the contract in which managers lack much discretion is notice. In only 22 percent of these provisions are managers exempted in some cases from following requirements to provide notice within a defined time. More than other contractual structures, notice provisions constrain managers' flexibility. Of course, the level of constraint depends on the extent of notice, which I explore in the subsequent section.

Finally, a significant measure of discretion is the extent to which managers' decisions are subject to appeal, grievance, and/or binding arbitration. Most contracts do not specify such matters in the retrenchment clauses. Of the forty-four that do, seventeen offer some means of appeal, and twenty-seven either deny such appeal or restrict it to certain matters. Of those contracts offering some means of appeal, in seven there is some mechanism for faculty to appeal retrenchment, but the final decision in the appeal is rendered by the board. In another ten, there is provision for grievance and binding arbitration. Of those contracts denying or restricting such appeal, thirteen explicitly state that grievance and arbitration procedures do not apply to retrenchment actions. Another fourteen contracts allow for the grievance of some matters, with thirteen of these specifying that the substantive decision about whether to retrench cannot be grieved. Only procedural matters, such as whether rules of order were followed, may be grieved. Although that suggests that the professional rights of faculty members to challenge layoffs are limited, procedural structures also can be important grounds for them to not just make retrenchment procedurally complicated and time consuming, but to challenge managers' actions.

Professional Constraints and Strategies

If managers have much discretion in a range of decision-making areas surrounding retrenchment, they also confront many constraints. In some cases those constraints are in the form of standard structures found in a large proportion of the contracts. Most contracts define rules of order, notice, and recall, and many define reassignment and retraining rights of faculty targeted for layoff. As noted in the previous section, managers often have considerable discretion to make exceptions to these rules. Still, they must address those rules and justify exceptions. Similarly, in choosing to reassign faculty or provide them with retraining, managers have much discretion. Yet there are procedures that must be followed, and there is the constraint of having to decide whether and how to exercise discretion when faculty apply for reassignment or retraining. Moreover, in matters of notice and recall there is far less often provision for discretion.

In addition to established structures that are negotiated constraints on managerial discretion, there are other professional strategies less widely found in the contracts. Some are slight variations on established structures. Others represent distinctive efforts to inhibit and/or block faculty layoffs.

Rules of Order

More than any other structure of constraint, articles of retrenchment define rules of order. There are 150 such provisions, 84 percent of the retrenchment articles. Their incidence is dependent on institutional type ($x2=6.67$, significant at .05 level): they are more likely to be found in the contracts of four-year institutions and technical colleges than those of community colleges: 77 and 94 percent of the former have rules of order, compared to 66 percent of the latter (see table 3.4).

The rules of order define priority by categories of faculty— tenured/untenured, full/part-time, probationary/temporary. In almost all of these provisions, the order is within the layoff unit, not within the institution. Moreover, in almost all of them, the order is by seniority within each category, within the layoff unit. For example, untenured faculty will be laid off before tenured faculty. Untenured faculty in the layoff unit will be laid off in inverse order of seniority. "Within the layoff unit" is a critical modifying phrase, for it means that managers can specify units smaller than a department and thereby lay off faculty who are more senior than some others in the department or college who are not within the affected area.

TABLE 3.4
INCIDENCE OF PROVISIONS FOR PROFESSIONAL CONSTRAINT

	Order	Notice	Reassignmt	Recall
Two-year	95 (66%)*	57	39	78
Technical	15 (94%)	10	6	12
Four-year	40 (77%)	29	29	38
Total	150	96	74	128

* The percentage of all such contracts in HECAS.

The definition of seniority is more organizational than professional. That is, with a few exceptions, seniority is measured from date of hire, not from time of entry into, or rank within, the profession. A full professor hired three years ago by this definition is less senior than an assistant professor hired five years ago. A faculty member who has been teaching for twenty-five years, but has worked at the present institution for only six years, is defined as less senior than one who has been teaching for only seven years, but started at the present institution. In a few cases—for example, Southern Oregon State College—seniority is defined by time in the department. "Within these categories, termination shall be in inverse order of seniority by academic year, length of service in the department which has been identified for reduction or elimination" (Article 11.E.6). Regardless of how long a faculty member has been in the institution, the seniority clock starts ticking when he or she entered his or her current department.

Several criteria other than seniority are utilized to define rules of order. Most refer to the contractual status of faculty. The most common distinction is between full- and part-time faculty, found in seventy-one provisions. Tenure status is part of the defined rules of order in forty-five contracts. Finally, thirty-four contracts speak to "probationary" or "temporary" categories of faculty, and twenty refer to "continuing" status. Generally, if tenure status is mentioned, it takes priority over any other categories. (Tenure status does not distinguish between full and associate professors—academic rank does not figure in contractual rules of order.)

Very few contracts list other criteria for defining order. Generally, such criteria give managers more discretion than the criteria that are grounded in categories of faculty. For example, North Central Michigan College District's contract defines order according to "abilities," academic qualifications, and "professional versatility." Hawkeye Community College's contract specifies "instructional needs," training, experience, ability, and performance. Southern State Community College's contract identifies criteria such as skill, performance, ability, and programmatic need.

In each of these and a few other such exceptional cases managers make the judgments about faculty's abilities and versatility. Of course, managers enjoy much discretion in following rules of order, as there are typically exceptions to any set order. Nevertheless, the established structure represents something of a constraint on managerial flexibility. It could also be argued that such rules represent something of a protection of professional position. However, the predominant protection is of seniority, organizational and academic. And, as I note below in discussing professional stratification, such protections may have unintended effects.

Notice

Only 54 percent of contracts with retrenchment clauses specify a period of notice for faculty who will be laid off. (This is distinct from notice to the association that retrenchment is being planned.) That in itself indicates that managers enjoy considerable contractual discretion in the timing of layoffs. There is a dependent association between the incidence of such provisions and institutional type ($x2=6.21$, significant at .05 level). Community colleges are underrepresented: only 40 percent of their contracts speak to notice. Four-year institutions and technical colleges are overrepresented: 56 and 62.5 percent of their contracts, respectively, speak to notice (see table 3.4).

Of the ninety-six contracts that address notice, how much notice is required? Does the time period constrain managerial flexibility? The answers to those two questions are, not much, and not really.

I code notice into five categories: one month or less; two to six months; seven to eleven months; one year; and more than a year. For all institutions combined, and for each type of institution, the modal period of notice is two to six months. For all institutions, two to six months notice is more than three times as common as any other time period. For two- and four-year institutions it is more than twice as common. (In technical colleges it is almost the only time period mentioned.)

My coding is based on a liberal calculation of how much notice is given. In many provisions, a specific date is provided. I calculate months from the beginning of the next academic year, *not* months from the end of the current academic year. For example, if faculty must be notified by May 1, that can be read in one of two ways. First, as I read it, it provides the faculty member with 4 months notice (assuming that most academic years start around September 1). However, it could also be read as providing only 1 month's notice. Most academic years end by early June, and most faculty are not on contracts that run through the summer (they may teach during the summer, but not as part of a yearly contract). If anything, then, my interpretation of the dates *under*estimates managers' flexibility. (Yet another interpretation of the dates is that the particular choices of days are ironic. I understand that there are accounting/budgeting logistics and rationales, but I could not help noticing with amusement that the most common days were the Ides of March [March 15], April Fools Day [April 1], and tax day [April 15].)

In the contracts of eleven institutions (seven community colleges, three four-year institutions, and one technical college) the required notice is only one month or less. In two cases (Danville Area Community College and Northern Michigan University—for faculty with one to two years of service) the requirement is for only two weeks' notice. Hardly what would be expected for professional workers.

At the other end of the continuum are fifteen contracts (four in community colleges and eleven in four-year institutions) in which managers are required to give faculty one year's notice. In nearly half of these cases (seven) the provision applies only to tenured faculty. Only three contracts call for more than a year's notice, stipulating time periods of sixteen and eighteen months, in all three cases for tenured faculty. Such provisions constrain relatively quick managerial actions, taking layoffs out of the current budget year cycle.

Reassignment/Retraining

Almost half (49 percent) of the retrenchment clauses provide for the possibility of faculty targeted for layoff being reassigned to another position or being retrained. Such provision is distinct from clauses that allow targeted faculty to "displace" or "bump" other faculty to avoid being laid off. I explore those practices in closing this section with a discussion of various professional strategies for protecting faculty jobs.

Most of the reassignment or retraining provisions deal with reassignment, although some contracts address both. Of the eighty-seven provisions, seventy-four speak to reassignment and twenty-three speak to retraining. (Of the seventy-four provisions that speak to reassignment, ten also address retraining.) Over half of the retraining provisions (thirteen of twenty-three) are in contracts that do not address reassignment. There is a dependent association between the incidence of reassignment provisions and institutional type ($x2=14.01$, significant at .000 level). Such clauses are more likely to be found in the contracts of four-year institutions than of two-year colleges: 56 percent of contracts in four-year institutions have such provision, compared to 27 and 37 percent respectively of two-year and technical college contracts (see table 3.4). There is no dependent association between the incidence of retraining provisions and institutional type. The distribution virtually mirrors the distribution of contracts in HECAS.

Reassignment provisions take various forms. Two of the most detailed provisions give a sense of a range of possibilities.

When there is a demonstrable need to terminate unit members, the [Financial Exigency] committee, in consultation with the affected Departments and the appropriate Vice-President shall first pursue and if possible recommend alternatives that would allow such unit members to remain employed at the College. . . . Other specific measures taken may include, but not be limited to, each of the following: 1. Provide an opportunity for affected unit members to apply for vacant positions for which they may be qualified. 2. Provide an opportunity for full-time faculty to complete a full-time teaching load in another discipline in which they are qualified. 3. Provide an opportunity for full-time faculty without a full-time teaching load to apply for part-time non-teaching or administrative duties where vacancies exist in order to complete a full-time workload, provided that they are qualified for the position. 4. Give serious consideration to transferring an affected tenured faculty member to a vacant non-faculty position for which she/he is qualified. (Delaware State College, Article 10.5.6.c)

When there is a demonstrable need to terminate faculty, as specified above, the Administration, in consultation with the departments involved, will pursue alternatives that will allow such faculty to remain employed at the University. Specified measures taken may include, but will not be limited to, each of the following: a) Provide an opportunity for full-time and adjunct faculty to apply for vacant teaching positions for which they are qualified, in other areas of the University. b) Provide an opportunity for full-time faculty to complete full-time teaching loads in another area of the University in which they are qualified. c) Provide an opportunity for full-time faculty without full-time teaching loads to apply for part-time, non-teaching or administrative duties where vacancies exist in order to complete full-time work loads, provided that they are qualified for such positions. d) Other options which may be considered are: 1. Joint teaching assignments at other institutions while retaining tenure, seniority, and fringe benefits. . . . 3. Transfer to vacant non-teaching positions for which he/she is qualified. . . . (Hofstra University, Article 9.2)

The two cases above are exceptional in two regards. First, they provide a much broader range of reassignment options than is typically the case. Second, they provide for collective faculty involvement in the decision making surrounding reassignment, either through a special committee or through the departments.

Most reassignment provisions are much less detailed and do not provide for collective faculty involvement. They are phrased in ways that allow for broader managerial discretion. For example, they indicate that the administration will make "every reasonable effort" to place targeted faculty in other positions. Or they state that the college "may" decide to reassign targeted faculty. Or they may consider faculty applications for vacant positions. In any case, the vast majority of such provisions address reassignment by one of the means identified in the above contracts: by filling a vacant position in another department, by transferring to another unit, or by filling out a full-time load with part-time courses.

Whatever the options specified in reassignment provisions, managers have considerable discretion in the placement of targeted faculty in other positions. Nevertheless, such reassignment provisions are an important constraint on managerial discretion. Managers who wish to lay off faculty are forced to consider certain options. If nothing else, such provisions make the process of laying off faculty more involved and difficult and more subject to challenge in appeals, grievances, or court cases.

In some respects, retraining provisions are even more constraining for managers. They generally involve some outlay of resources. As with reassignment, there is much variation in form. The most common provision is for a retraining sabbatical (see Ferris State University). Some contracts (for example, North Country Community College) provide tuition benefits to faculty who are laid off. In some cases, there is provision for paid retraining leaves or for release time.

> Any unlimited faculty member . . . who has received a written notice of layoff shall be granted up to 3 quarters or the equivalent of release time for the purpose of retraining. . . . The arrangements and schedules for such release time shall be subject to the mutual agreement of the faculty member and the college president. (Minnesota Community College, Article 19.4)

Generally, there is not even an implicit quid pro quo, let alone a guarantee, that the retrained faculty member will be hired in another department.

As with reassignment decisions, few contracts provide for collective faculty involvement in retraining decisions. Managerial discretion is broad, though normally it is not so explicitly stated as follows:

> At the sole discretion of the President, and subject to the agreement of the retrenched unit member and the President, a program of retraining may be undertaken for a period of up to two-years . . . provided, however, that the college shall not thereby be obligated to continue to employ such unit member following the completion of the approved program of retraining. (Massachusetts State College System, Article 10.G.7)

This is not exactly a lifetime commitment to retraining and retention of employees.

Two contracts that *do* involve faculty collectively in retraining decisions, and that presume the ongoing retention of retrained faculty, are in community colleges. Ironically, one of them is in the same state as the contract quoted above from a four-year school as exemplifying lack of commitment.

> Any unit member facing retrenchment shall be eligible for consideration for sabbatical leave regardless of his/her length of service and, if recom-

mended by the president of the College or his/her designee to retrain for a suitable position which would be available concurrent with the date of retrenchment, such sabbatical leave shall be granted subject to the approval of the Board. No later than 60 days after the execution and ratification of this Agreement, the Joint Study Committee shall establish a retrenchment retraining subcommittee which shall study and report on the feasibility of providing retraining opportunities for retrenched unit members. A unit member who is retrenched or who shall forseeably be retrenched may request the approval of the President or his/her designee to enter a retraining program without cost to the College and if such approval is granted he/she shall be extended priority of consideration for any position which the president of the College or his/her designee deems the unit member is qualified for subject to the availability of a position. (Article 19.08, Massachusetts Regional Community Colleges)

Full-time faculty members who are subject to retrenchment affecting their program, teaching, or academic support service shall be given the opportunity to retrain in lieu of layoff. . . . Affected faculty members shall be given an opportunity to meet with the appropriate Vice-President to establish a retraining plan based upon program, teaching, and academic support needs of the College. The agreed upon retraining plan will then be submitted to the Training/Retraining Committee for approval. (Lake Land College, Article 2.F.9)

Few retraining provisions detail this level of faculty involvement in decision making and of college commitment to the employment of the faculty member. Nevertheless, all retraining provisions establish a range of procedures to follow and decisions to be made before faculty can be finally laid off.

Recall

Nearly three-quarters (72 percent) of contracts with retrenchment clauses provide for laid off faculty's recall or re-employment. As a professional strategy, recall rights are an effort to prevent faculty being laid off and replaced by cheaper personnel. Recall rights establish some claim for retrenched faculty on the positions they have lost. The limitation of the strategy is that it might be more appropriate to layoffs stemming from economic rather than academic considerations. Recall rights do not mean as much when they attach to programs that have been curtailed or eliminated because the direction of the institution is moving elsewhere and resources are being reallocated accordingly. Nevertheless, recall rights make it procedurally more complicated for management to downsize and eliminate some units and then quickly recreate new, related units.

The incidence of recall provisions is dependent on institutional type ($x2=7.24$, significant at .05 level). Four-year institutions and technical colleges are overrepresented: 73 and 75 percent of contracts in these institutions have recall provisions, as compared to only 54 percent of two-year college contracts.

However, there is not much difference among institutional types in the extent of recall rights that are provided. That is, the length of time after layoff that faculty must be considered for new jobs in the layoff or related units does not vary that widely among institutions. In very few cases (seven, all in two-year colleges) recall rights extend for only one year. The modal time period in each institutional sector is two years, found in sixty-five contracts. The second most common time period in two- and four-year institutions is three years, found in thirty-four contracts. Only a handful of contracts extend recall rights to four (four cases), five (five cases), or six (one case) years.

Summation of Constraints

In short, the established structures of order of layoff, notice, reassignment or retraining, and recall all serve to make the retrenchment of faculty more complicated. Apart from procedural complexity, the time period involved in retrenching faculty is considerable. Factoring in time for consultation on the front end, provision of notice to the individual faculty member, provision of reassignment and/or retraining opportunities, and then the recall period after layoff, draws the process out. Notwithstanding a genuine faculty commitment to due process and faculty involvement in decision making, it is likely that one of the strategies of unions is simply to make retrenchment more difficult, to extend the constraints, demands, and time required for managers to lay off faculty.

Professional Strategies

In addition to the widespread, established structures discussed above, there are other professional strategies for protecting faculty positions and/or constraining managerial discretion to retrench faculty.

These various measures are significant, not for their numbers, but for the insight they offer about the politics of professional work. In addition, they point to possibilities for addressing not just faculty layoffs, but the restructuring of higher education's professional work force.

The most widespread of the distinctive professional strategies are twenty provisions that give senior faculty the right to "displace" or "bump" less senior faculty rather than be laid off themselves. A typical clause reads much like Northern Michigan University's contract, though often in less detail.

> Within 10 working days of issuing layoff notices to a bargaining unit member, any affected bargaining unit member must request, in writing, an opportunity to exercise the bargaining unit member's seniority rights under this Agreement or the right will be deemed to be waived. Within 15 working days of issuing layoff notices, the Employer shall convene a meeting to afford each bargaining unit member who has so requested the opportunity to exercise the bargaining unit member's seniority rights. In the event the bargaining unit member has qualifications and experience at least equal to another less senior bargaining unit member, the bargaining unit member shall be allowed to displace the less senior bargaining unit member. . . . [T]he University shall determine whether a bumping bargaining unit member has qualifications and experience at least equal to another less senior bargaining unit member by reviewing the full range of duties to which the less senior bargaining unit member may be assigned. The University academic administrator making such a determination is strongly encouraged to consult with other department faculty when reviewing the qualifications and experience of the bumping bargaining unit member. (Article 6.3.1)

Such a practice can hardly be expected to contribute to good, collegial feelings. More than reassignment provisions, displacement and bumping clauses place the onus of responsibility on the individual faculty member to "exercise their seniority rights." One can only suspect that what is "displaced" is not only the bumped faculty member's job, but his or her anger, redirected from the administration to his or her senior colleague.

From the faculty's perspective, perhaps the most serious shortcoming of bumping is that it does not protect faculty positions. It protects the jobs of current senior faculty. But someone still gets laid off. Again, though, such provisions make layoffs procedurally more complicated.

A variation on bumping colleagues is to prohibit administrators or other non-bargaining unit members from bumping faculty. There are 6 such provisions.

The right of a person employed in an administrative position to become a first year probationary faculty member once his or her administrative assignment expires or is terminated shall not result in the termination or failure to re-employ any contract or regular faculty member. (San Joaquin Delta Community College, Article 31)

The assignment of an individual serving in an administrative position to full-time duties within the bargaining unit shall not be cause for layoff of any full-time employee in that department or equivalent unit. (California State University System, Article 38.43)

No tenured employee shall be laid off for the purpose of creating a vacancy to be filled by an administrator entering the bargaining unit. (Illinois Board of Governors, Article 15.3)

Such provisions read like reactions to past cases of the practice in question.

Far more significant in terms of a professional strategy to prevent the reconfiguration of the professional work force are two provisions that speak to the ratio of faculty to other staff.

In the case of a substantial reduction in funds available to the State Board for Community Colleges every effort shall be made to equalize the effect of the reduction on all staff classifications in the System. (Minnesota Community Colleges, Article 19.5)

The College and the Association agree that should tenured faculty be issued layoff notices . . . layoff notices will be sent to classified staff and administrative/exempt staff to make proportional the reduction equal to or greater than the reduction in full-time faculty. (Highline Community College, Section 502.2)

Such provisions look to maintain the current profile of the higher education work force, which as noted in chapter 2 has seen a reduction in the proportion of professional personnel that are faculty. (Along these same lines, some contracts speak to the use of part-time faculty in the layoff unit or even in related fields. Others speak to the ratio of full- to part-timers. I examine such provisions in chapter 4 on the use of part-time academic labor.)

At the level of work force issues, two other provisions on subcontracting speak to professionals' response to a managerial strategy to reduce costs.

> Existing employees will not be retrenched in the event of the Employer's contracting out work previously performed by employees in the bargaining unit. (Jefferson Community College, Article 12.4)

> For the duration of this contract there will be no subcontracting of bargaining unit work, when bargaining unit members are available to teach, which would result in the layoff of a bargaining unit faculty member. (Lakeshore Technical College, Article 10.7)

It is common in many unionized work forces, to find negotiation between managers and workers over such matters of jurisdiction. Unionization and the collective bargaining agreements clarify a process whereby management seeks to restructure the work force, replacing unit members with (cheaper) workers outside the bargaining unit. (Again, this is a matter that I pursue in chapter 4, focusing on management's use of part-time faculty and the restructuring of the academic profession to an increasingly part-time work force.)

One other work force focused provision related to the use of part-time faculty is found in the University of Lowell's contract. "Before implementing retrenchment under this Article, and where it becomes completely necessary to stabilize enrollments and prevent retrenchment, the University shall incorporate courses then currently being given under the auspices of the Division of Continuing Education into the regular work assignments of regular faculty" (Article 13.A). Core academic faculty are to be protected by bringing courses that are outside the control of regular full-time faculty back under the purview and assignment of bargaining unit faculty.

Several measures speak to a professional strategy of seeking to minimize the cuts or negotiate adjustments that cushion the effects of layoffs. For example, Jackson Community College's contract "limits" layoffs to "not more than 5 percent of the number of continuing contract and continuing contract track faculty and laboratory assistant positions existing on the first day of the previous winter semester." (Article 12.K) Dowling College's contract forbids program curtailment induced retrenchment in the contract's first year. Several contracts provide for severance pay. Western Michigan University's contract calls for alternate academic year appointments—in effect, job sharing: "In departments where faculty have agreed to alternate-academic-year appointments as an alternative to layoff, Western agrees, where programs and qualifications permit, to rotate such assignments" (Article 14.7.1).

The strategy of professionals voluntarily sacrificing to preserve their colleagues' positions calls to mind actions of some faculty during the Great Depression. In the face of financial duress senior faculty took pay cuts so that junior colleagues would get paid or receive raises. That speaks to a context of collegiality, a sense that we are all in this together. Not an uncommon sentiment during the Depression, in which job loss was seen less as a matter of personal deserts than of misfortune.[31] Not so evident today. Faculty are stratified and divided in ways that lead them to believe that other faculty and units should be cut. Some justify such sentiments with the claim that some units are consumers rather than generators of revenue. Other faculty believe that rather than all units sharing across-the-board cuts and supposedly declining to a common mediocre status, some units should be cut so that others can thrive.[32] Not exactly a collegial sentiment but one that suggests the strength of stratification and hierarchy in academe.

Professional Stratification

The structures discussed above are not just constraints on managers' discretion in decision making. They are also mechanisms that reveal and perpetuate pre-existing patterns of professional stratification. As such, they limit change in the established professional order, with some significant unexplored and perhaps unintended dimensions.

Order

Defined rules of order not only protect professional and organizational standing, but they also perpetuate existing professional and organizational hierarchies. In these most common of retrenchment provisions, each of the major categorical criteria for defining order privilege some faculty over others in their claims on their jobs. By definition they privilege senior over junior, tenured over untenured, continuing over temporary, and full- over part-time faculty.

Such mechanisms protect faculty's position as a professional work force. In seeking to reduce personnel costs, managers would like the flexibility to lay off more expensive senior, tenured, and full-time faculty, replacing them with cheaper junior, untenured, and part-time faculty. It is not in the interests of the profession as a whole to allow such downgrading to occur.

However, such mechanisms (which are found not just in collective bargaining agreements, but in the retrenchment policies of nonunionized colleges and universities) are unmeritocratic and discriminatory in their effects. In giving priority to senior, tenured, and full-time faculty, rules of order violate the dominant academic value of merit as the principal selection criteria. Moreover, the criteria embedded in order clauses give priority in a collective sense to men over women. Larger proportions of senior versus junior faculty are male. Larger proportions of male tenure-track faculty are tenured (71 percent) than are female (50 percent). And larger proportions of full- versus part-time faculty are male (72.1 versus 59.9 percent).[33] As a generalization, to follow such a pattern of layoff means to disproportionately retrench faculty from the underrepresented group.[34] Not only does it perpetuate professional hierarchy, but also it heightens the gender gap in faculty positions.

Notice

Of the ninety-six contracts that identify required periods of notice, nearly one-third (thirty-three) differentiate those required periods for different strata of faculty. In the overwhelming proportion of cases, such differentials are found in the contracts of four-year institutions. There is a dependent association between the incidence of differentials and institutional type ($x2=29.63$, significant at the .000 level). In twenty of the twenty-nine contracts in four-year institutions that have notice provisions, and in 38 percent of all contracts in four-year institutions, there are differentials; only eleven of the fifty-seven contracts in two-year institutions that have notice provisions, and only 7 percent of all contracts in two-year institutions, have such differentials. Professional stratification is greater in four- than in two-year institutions.

The principal basis of differentiation is tenure status, found in twenty-one of the thirty-three provisions (and in four community college contracts that use the terminology of probationary/nonprobationary instead of tenure). The length of the differential varies. For example, the University of Hawaii and Rhode Island College contracts call for 1 year's notice for tenured faculty and 4 months' notice for term contract faculty. Adrian College's contract requires 1 year's notice for tenured faculty, and 8 months for faculty in their third to sixth years (no notice is defined for others). The California State University System contract calls for 45 days' notice for term faculty, 90 days' for probationary faculty, and 120 days' for tenured faculty.

Another seven contracts differentiate by years of service. For example, Beaver County Community College's contract specifies notice of February 1 for first- and second-year faculty, and October 15 for those with more than two years of service. Dutchess Community College's contract specifies April 1 for faculty in their first year, February 1 for those in their second year, and one year's notice for faculty with more than two years of service.

Several contracts combine differentials for tenure and years of service. For example, the Massachusetts State College System contract requires fifty-two weeks' notice for tenured faculty with ten or more years of service, thirty-seven weeks for tenured faculty with less than ten years of service, and sixteen weeks to all other faculty. The professional hierarchy is even steeper in the Pennsylvania State University System contract, which specifies notice of March 1 for faculty in their first year of service, December 15 for those in their second year, December 1 for probationary faculty with more than two years of service, and October 30 for tenured faculty. Western Michigan University's contract calls for sixty days' notice for term faculty, four months' notice for untenured with less than three years of service, and one year's notice for tenured faculty with more than three years of service. The differences by status can be considerable.

In this most basic condition of employment—how much notice one receives of layoff—then, there is considerable professional stratification. In one sense, the principal basis of stratification is professional—tenure status. Yet if tenure is not simply a proxy of seniority, it is certainly highly correlated with it. It is also correlated with gender. As a generalization, differential treatment by tenure status means differential treatment of male and female faculty in a collective sense.

Reassignment/Retraining

Of the eighty-seven provisions for reassignment or retraining, only four differentiate among categories of faculty. In two cases of reassignment, and one case of retraining, the provision applies only to tenured faculty. In a fourth case (Muskegon Community College) the provision for retraining applies only to faculty with ten or more years of service.

Of course, these numbers vastly underestimate the role of professional status in shaping reassignment. As discussed earlier, one of the principal professional strategies for protecting tenured and full-time faculty from layoff is to provide for the possibility of displacement or bumping. That is, tenured and/or full-time senior members of the faculty can apply to displace or bump their untenured and/or part-time junior colleagues.

Such practices speak not of a collegium of equals but of a highly stratified occupation in which job rights are defined not by merit but by seniority and full-time status (of course, seniors can only bump their juniors if they are qualified to teach and/or perform their duties). Again, such practices must be placed in context. Managers, for their part, are retrenching and reorganizing academe according not to merit but to perceived markets and costs. Some fields may be downsized not because they are of low quality but because they are not seen as potential revenue generators. And some faculty may be laid off not because they are of low quality but because they are expensive. Professional strategies of displacing and bumping, then, can be read as perpetuating (or sharpening) academic hierarchy. They also can be read as protecting the profession against efforts to downgrade fields/positions.

Recall

In 22 percent of those contracts defining recall periods, professional stratification is evident in the length of recall periods accorded different strata of faculty. There are two principal bases of differentiation—tenure (in twenty contracts) and length of service (in seven contracts) (in the other contract the basis of differentiation is full- or part-time status). In nine contracts, recall rights are provided only for tenured faculty. In eleven others, differential time periods are extended to tenured and nontenured faculty. For example, in Ferris State and Western Michigan University's contracts, tenured faculty's recall period is three years, compared to two years for non-tenured faculty. Several contracts differentiate recall time periods by the faculty member's length of service. That does not mean that faculty with fifteen years of service get a fifteen-year recall period. The longest recall period is six years. Contracts give differential recall periods to faculty with more or less than a certain number of years of service at the institution. For example, in the contracts of Dyke College and Hawkeye Community College, faculty with two or more years of service have a two-year recall period. Those with less than two years of service get either one year (Hawkeye) of recall or a period equal to their time in service (Dyke).

Most of the contracts that differentiate by tenure are in four-year institutions (five of the eight that give rights only to tenured faculty, and nine of the eleven that give differential rights to tenured and non-tenured). In fact, the incidence of differential recall rights is dependent on institutional type ($x2=22.62$, significant at .005 level). Gradations of professional status are more likely to differentiate faculty in four-year than in two-year institutions.

Discussion

Academic managers commonly invoke fiscal considerations in justifying restructuring. It is surprising, then, that relatively few contracts identify financial exigency as a condition justifying retrenchment. Perhaps, though, it is not so surprising. There is a public relations cost to declaring that an institution confronts financial exigency. There is also some legal risk—the term carries much political and legal baggage. And institutions prefer to stay out of court. Finally, financial exigency is a concrete condition, the terms of which are difficult to establish and easy to dispute. Invoking financial exigency invites dispute. Faculty may demand to see the books. They may point to alternative means for saving money. Indeed, the prominent strategies for constraining managerial discretion appear to be to define the conditions that justify retrenchment and to provide for faculty review of (and challenge to) relevant data so that they may suggest alternatives. Better, then, from a managerial perspective, to not raise the issue, and instead to talk generally about fiscal constraints.

The broad scope of managerial discretion is evident in the incidence, range, and generality of provisions that define conditions which justify retrenchment. Many contracts do not even identify rationales (and in some contracts, the rationale is that managers have decided to retrench). Moreover, as I concluded in 1993, "conditions justifying retrenchment went well beyond and fell far short of financial exigency, including fiscal, programmatic, and enrollment-related conditions."[35] HECAS data enables me to elaborate on that point. Financial exigency is not even the only economic rationale. There are others, and they provide managers with far more flexibility than exigency. Most other economic rationales do not identify conditions of crisis. Nearly as many contracts identify academic rationales for retrenchment. Retrenchment is justified by institutions' academic program reorganization. Managers may also invoke "the market" to justify retrenchment, as forty-eight contracts refer to shifts in student demand. Such market and academic program-based conditions, along with "other" economic conditions, are far less restrictive and crisis based than the condition of financial exigency. Moreover, although retrenchment is justified by the need to strategically reorganize and to reallocate resources internally, the changes are not based on any long- or even medium-term patterns of change either in finances or in student enrollment. The varied rationales provide managers with extensive discretion.

What is the balance between faculty involvement and managerial discretion in decision making surrounding retrenchment? Again, as I concluded in 1993, "The contracts gave faculty a limited and reactive role in decision making surrounding retrenchment and gave administrators broad discretion."[36] Here, I offer a slight variation on that theme. Faculty involvement is limited and advisory and is focused almost exclusively on decisions about whether and where to retrench. Such involvement is more likely to take the traditional, committee based form in four-year than in two-year institution contracts (as with the definition of restrictive conditions justifying retrenchment). In all institutions, however, managers enjoy broad contractual discretion, particularly in making exceptions to the layoff order and in reassignment. That discretion to steer the educational direction and academic configuration of colleges and universities calls into serious question the belief that faculty exercise collegial governance of the curriculum.

At the same time, in this chapter I have also examined various structures and professional strategies that work to constrain managerial discretion. Several established structures found in most contracts work to draw out the process of laying off faculty and make it more procedurally complicated. Rules of order for layoff (and for recall) are one example. Required notice is another.

Two stories define the extremes of notice periods. As I was writing this book, I got a phone call from a faculty member who had recently received notice of layoff. He had been referred to me as someone who was knowledgeable about faculty's rights in retrenchment. He was furious. Employed at a small, private, nonunionized institution, he had been given two weeks' notice. "They don't realize that they can't treat me like a day laborer," he stated. As do most faculty, he had a clear sense that as a professional he was entitled to certain rights, certainly more than those accorded "day laborers." Although I believe that two weeks' notice is outrageous for any employee, there was little encouragement or advice that I could offer. Indeed, a few HECAS contracts have two-week notice periods defined for their faculty. Several others define periods of thirty days or less. Most of those contracts that even define a period—and 46 percent do not—require notice of only six months or less.

At the other extreme are those contracts that define periods of notice longer than one year. There are only 3 of them in HECAS. In talking with an AAUP official who helped negotiate one of those provisions some years ago at Wayne State University, he indicated that he believed the union's "greatest victory" was negotiating eighteen months' notice for layoff (for tenured faculty). In his view, it took the layoff decision out of the immediate budget cycle.[37] At the time, I was struck by how small a "victory" that seemed. Having read through the retrenchment provisions of 178 contracts, I no longer feel that way. Nor do I any longer regard such provisions as reactive, defensive, after-the-fact strategies that represent minor efforts to cushion the effects of layoff. Instead, I believe that such structures are also proactive professional strategies that make managers' efforts to lay off faculty more difficult. By extending the process, such a strategy may effectively subvert retrenchment.

However, in the context of retrenchment that is grounded less in current budget cycles than in ongoing academic reorganization, the effectiveness of such a strategy is reduced. The contracts reveal a few professional strategies aimed at controlling the configuration of higher education's professional work force. For example, some provisions require retrenchment of nonfaculty personnel in proportions equal to those of faculty layoffs. And some, as I explore in the next chapter, speak to the ratios of full- to part-time faculty.

In addition to exploring the constraining effects of structures and professional strategies on managerial discretion, I consider how they also reveal and perpetuate pre-existing patterns of professional stratification. In particular, I point to the relatively unexamined dimension of gender. What is clear in the contracts is the privileging of tenured, senior, and full-time over untenured, junior, and part-time faculty. As with so much language (and literature) regarding professions and occupations, these categories of faculty are disembodied abstractions. The reader gets no sense of the people who fill these categories. The contract analyst generally would not consider that the underprivileged categories are disproportionately female and the privileged categories are disproportionately male. The work force effects of prioritizing personnel actions according to these abstract, seemingly universalistic categories are discriminatory toward women (and toward other categories of faculty who have disproportionately large numbers of junior and part-time members). That is not to say that in this regard, among individual faculty of equal tenure, seniority, and full-time status, males are privileged over females. In the collective sense, however, that is the case.

Much, then, is undefined in the contracts. Not only is gender missing (except in he/she, and his or her language), but there is virtually no attention devoted to matters of productivity and revenue generation beyond the front end choice of where to retrench. That is remarkable, for those are major drivers of decisions about where to retrench and how to reorganize. Yet there are no contracts that build in any evaluation of retrenchment actions along these lines. Nor do any contracts call for any cost or benefit analysis of particular programs, or of plans to reallocate resources internally.

Managers, then, have much discretion in retrenchment and reorganization. But there is also much in the contracts that makes retrenchment difficult. Can managers lay off tenured faculty? They *can*. But they *may not* (or they may do so to a much lesser extent) because of various costs/obstacles and because it requires a great deal of political will and persistence. As a result, managers may choose less drastic measures for restructuring the academic work force.

Reorganizing the Faculty Work Force for Flexibility: Part-Time Professional Labor

The last quarter of the nineteenth century saw the rise of an academic profession, along with other professions, in the United States. That rise was marked by the establishment of faculty as full-time employees of colleges and universities, with career tracks in their fields.[1] The last quarter of the twentieth century has seen the decline of the academic profession's prestige, along with that of other liberal professions. That decline has been marked by an erosion of the position of faculty members as full-time employees in the professional work force of colleges and universities. Faculty salaries have declined, in absolute terms and relative to the salaries of their managers. Faculty numbers have declined as a proportion of higher education's professional work force, down from 64 percent in 1977 to 55 percent by 1989, and falling. And the proportion of faculty who are full-time has declined, from slightly over 78 percent of the senior instructional work force in 1970 to about 57 percent in 1994.[2]

There are more subtle ways of reorganizing the academic work force, of reallocating and reducing faculty resources, than by retrenching faculty. There are more efficient and less politically problematic ways that have more dramatic results. Hire more part-time faculty. They are cheaper. They make it easier to shift faculty resources from one unit to another, for they are easier to hire and to release. In hiring larger proportions of part-time faculty, managers are renegotiating the position of faculty as a full-time professional work force.

In the late 1960s Jencks and Riesman wrote of an "academic revolution."[3] By that they meant the triumph of a national academic profession and its norms of meritocracy and professionalism, the triumph

131

over control by society, by boards of trustees composed of nonacademics, of laypersons. They meant the triumph over the demands of "special interest" groups that had established colleges to serve their particular, parochial needs—each religious, ethnic, and gender group with its own colleges. They meant triumph over administrators, in the selection of colleagues, the determination of the curriculum, and much more. Jencks and Riesman celebrated the increased power of faculty within and beyond the university, gained in part by virtue of increased federal support of the research or faculty through grants.

How times have changed. The 1970s, 1980s and 1990s brought increased critique of and challenge to academics' norms, autonomy, and job security. Faculty have been criticized for norms that focus more on their peers than on serving undergraduate clients, more on research than on teaching, and more on career self-interest than on the public interest.[4] Many state legislatures have sought to legislate how much time faculty spend in classrooms. Many academic managers have sought greater flexibility over a work force said to be unresponsive to student, employer, and societal markets and demands. In this environment, the "problem" of tenure is debated. In this environment, greater numbers and percentages of part-time faculty are employed.

The increased use of part-time faculty is ironic given current criticism of full-timers. If many full-time faculty are not in their offices on Fridays, part-timers do not even have offices. If full-time faculty do not spend enough time with their students outside of class and office hours, part-timers may not have defined duties outside of classroom teaching and office hours. If full-time faculty do not care enough about the quality of their teaching, part-timers may not have their teaching evaluated by peers.

Using more part-time faculty enhances managers' flexibility in directing the academic work force. It also has implications for faculty's conditions of employment. Therein lie my dual interests in analyzing contractual language about part-time faculty. I am interested in the extent of professional involvement and control and of managerial discretion or constraint regarding the use of part-time faculty. I am interested as well in the conditions of employment of part-time faculty and what they tell us about academic stratification.

The higher education literature on part-time faculty is largely taxonomic and/or functionalist.[5] It offers insights into the unmapped terrain of part-time faculty by classifying types of part-timers. It provides an overview of employment conditions and use of part-timers. It focuses on issues such as motivation (of employers and part-timers) and quality.[6] It recommends planned, rational use of part-time faculty, incorporating them into the life of the organization, improving their practice and enhancing educational and institutional performance.[7] It promotes "effective policies and practices."

Generally sympathetic to part-timers, the literature accepts managers' stated need for increasing numbers of such faculty. Many problems experienced by part-timers are attributed to full-time faculty more interested in protecting their professional privileges than in ensuring educational quality or employment equity.[8] That critique has been extended to the tenure system, portrayed as inhibiting managerial flexibility and as contributing to the exploitation of part-time faculty. "Are [full-time faculty] willing to preserve tenure and the associated privileges at the expense of exploited nontenure-track academic workers? . . . We question . . . the viability of the existing tenure system because it requires that tenured faculty be subsidized with a work force that carries heavy loads at low pay."[9]

By contrast, I work out of a modified professionalization theory. My analytical interest is in how faculty are being reorganized as a managed, stratified professional work force. I do not study the use and condition of part-timers to make policies and practices more "rational" or organizations more "effective." Rather, I seek to understand the politics of professional work. I see these politics as involving more than full-time faculty pursuing their interests. In focusing on collective bargaining agreements, I foreground the organizational politics of professionals and their managers that is overlooked in most professionalization studies.[10] I analyze the conditions of academic work negotiated between management and professional labor (faculty). These parties' strategies and positions are embedded in contractual provisions that enhance managerial discretion or ensure professional control in the use of part-time faculty. I am also interested in professional stratification, a topic pursued in recent sociological work that goes beyond professionalization studies.[11] The divide between full- and part-time faculty highlighted in the literature is a key fault line in the academic profession. I focus on part-timers' conditions of employment to provide insight into the gradations of faculty—between full- and part-timers, and among types of part-timers.

Professions are monopolies of expertise. They are groups that establish "closure" by controlling entry into, and the definition and practice of, a domain of work.[12] The growing number of part-time faculty is a challenge to the academic profession's closure. It is a challenge most plainly to the profession's definition of faculty positions as full-time, as careers, not jobs, with a secure future. It is a challenge to tenure as *the* professional structure defining faculty's terms of employment, for part-time faculty have no chance to gain tenure. Finally, it is a challenge to full-time faculty's job security, for cheaper part-time faculty may be used to replace them.

In the private sector of the economy the threat of part-time workers to full-timers is clear. From the "temping of America" to "the end of work," scholars have documented, in various sectors of the economy, the substantial growth of a contingent, part-time work force, to the detriment of full-time—and unionized—jobs (part-timers are far less likely to be unionized).[13] The largest category of new jobs in America is part-time positions.

What of academe? One of the greatest threats posed by part-time faculty is that they will reduce the numbers (and proportions) of full-time faculty positions. It is not that current full-timers will be retrenched en masse and replaced by part-time faculty. Instead, it is a matter of foregone full-time faculty positions. Full-time positions are declining proportionately, and in some cases in absolute numbers (for example, in some states and institutions, such as the California State University System), because of the increased use of part-time faculty. Whether through the filling of vacancies caused by current full-time faculty leaving or retiring or through the filling of new positions, part-time faculty numbers have increased in absolute and proportional terms, and the trend continues.

Foregoing Full-Time Positions for Part-Time Faculty

Consider the national data. From 1970 to 1993, the proportion of part-time faculty nearly doubled, from 21.9 percent of the senior instructional work force to 40.1 percent (these numbers exclude teaching assistants). In that time period, the number of full-time faculty did increase. However, the number of part-time faculty increased by more than fourfold that number.[14] Converting those part-time faculty to full-time positions would have resulted in a substantial number of new full-time faculty positions.

Does that apply to the recent past? In times of financial stress, would we not expect managers to fire larger proportions of part-timers, protecting and thereby raising the percentages of full-time faculty? Is that not one of the reasons for employing part-timers—they are easier to release?

Perhaps in some places and at some times. However, at the national level, from 1972 through 1977, a time of one of higher education's most serious financial crises in history, there occurred the greatest increase of part-time faculty in the last twenty-five years: the proportion of part-time faculty increased from 24 to 33.9 percent of the total faculty work force.

But what of the recent, and by all accounts ongoing, financial crisis in higher education? As of the writing of this book, published data of the National Survey of Postsecondary Faculty are incomplete, based on numbers from the "faculty," not the "institutional" survey.[15] Numbers of part-time faculty identified in the faculty survey are somewhat lower than estimates derived from the institutional survey. Preliminary analysis of other data suggests that the proportion of part-timers has grown to 43 percent of the faculty. Yet even these conservative estimates of part-time faculty numbers suggest that overall, the percentage of part-time faculty has increased from 1991 to the present. And data from 1989 through 1991 indicate that numbers of full-time faculty declined by .7 percent. A slight increase in full-time faculty numbers from 1991 through 1993 is overshadowed by major increases in part-time faculty during this time.[16]

The data are even more plain in looking at a couple of large, industrial states in which large numbers of faculty are unionized. In Michigan, between 1976 and 1991, part-time faculty numbers in public institutions grew by 97.7 percent in terms of full-time equivalent faculty. At the same time, tenure track faculty numbers declined by 11 percent. In New York, the proportion of part-time faculty members in all public institutions increased from 41 percent in 1977-78 to 51 percent in 1989-1990. During this time, as part-time faculty numbers increased by 7,903, the number of full-time faculty slightly decreased, by 418.[17]

The trend is even more dramatic in looking at two-year colleges. The use of part-time faculty is most widespread in these institutions, where part-timers now account for 65 percent of the faculty (in public and private institutions respectively, part-timers account for 24 and 38 percent of the faculty). The ten largest states in total numbers of community college faculty (California, Florida, Illinois, Michigan, New York, North Carolina, Ohio, Pennsylvania, Texas, and Wisconsin) each have *at least* twice as many (66 percent) part-time faculty as they do full-timers. And the numbers are increasing. In Illinois, part-time faculty numbers went from 72 percent of all two-year college faculty in 1981 to 74 percent by 1991. During this time, the number of full-time faculty decreased by 6 percent.[18]

The numbers and proportions of part-time faculty are greatest in two-year colleges. But they are a significant part of the academic work force in every sector of American higher education: 16 percent of research university, 24 percent of doctoral granting, 30 percent of comprehensive university, and 31 percent of liberal arts college faculty. As such, and as their numbers grow, part-time faculty are a threat to the growth of full-time faculty numbers.

Retrenching Full-Time and Hiring Part-Time Faculty

Full-time faculty may not be retrenched en masse, only to be replaced by part-timers. However, there is much precedent for managers restructuring the work force by laying off full-time faculty and hiring part-timers in their place. A few examples are suggestive of managerial strategies being practiced.

For decades, in its national bulletin, the AAUP has reported selected retrenchment cases that it has investigated. Such cases are significant in that the association has targeted them as indicators of trends in managerial actions that threaten the academic profession. In analyzing retrenchment cases reported by the AAUP in the 1980s, Slaughter finds that "the major mechanisms that administrators used for retrenchment were program restructuring, strategic planning, and increased use of part-time labor."[19] No financial exigency cases reported by the AAUP in the 1970s involved the (mis)-use of part-time faculty. However, "In the 1980s, six of the seventeen financial exigency cases involved explicit discussions of substitution of part-time for full-time faculty labor."[20] The pattern continues. Following up on Slaughter's work, I briefly review five cases in the 1990s that reveal managerial strategies for substituting part- for full-time faculty.

At the University of Bridgeport, two tenured professors (the senior faculty in the Psychology Department), were terminated with thirty days notice. Some of the courses which one of them taught were subsequently assigned to a part-time instructor.[21] A (cheaper) part-time faculty member was retained to do the work previously done by a tenured, full-time faculty member. That speaks to the order of layoff sections typically found in retrenchment clauses, discussed in chapter 3. It violates the typical provision for an order that prioritizes tenured faculty, full-timers, and seniority.

A variation of the strategy at Bridgeport is evident in a case settled in court in 1991. In Vandever v. Junior College District of Metropolitan Kansas City, Missouri, a jury awarded $267,000 to a faculty member who had been "furloughed" from her position in 1979. Under the institution's layoff policy, a faculty member has recall rights to teaching positions for which she is qualified. However, the administration appointed several new part-time instructors to such positions without offering the plaintiff the opportunity to return to full-time service. Such "replacements" were found to constitute a "breach of contract."[22]

Alaska Pacific University provides another twist on replacing retrenched full-time faculty with part-timers.[23] Its administration was explicit about replacing "expensive teachers who regularly teach extremely small classes" with part-timers to teach service courses offered by the affected departments that fulfill the university's general education requirements. The departments of Humanities and Social Sciences were replaced by Liberal Studies, which relied on part-timers. Retrenched faculty were not offered reassignment in that unit, nor were they offered the opportunity to displace less senior faculty. Full-timers were retrenched at the same time that part-time faculty doing similar work, for which the full-timers were qualified, were retained.

St. Bonaventure University provides an example of the conversion of full to part-time positions.[24] With the institution confronting financial exigency the president met with faculty to encourage voluntary reductions in status. He obtained twenty-one "separations from full-time status"—three transfers to administration and seven to part-time status. Subsequently, an additional eighteen tenured faculty were released, the principal subject of the AAUP investigation.

Finally, Essex Community College provides a case of replacing full-time faculty by redefining work.[25] The administration discontinued for-credit occupational programs, including Hotel-Motel/Restaurant-Club Management. Similar courses were then offered on a noncredit basis, through the Continuing Education Department, which had only part-time and/or nontenured instructors. Laid off tenured faculty were offered renewable one-year appointments without tenure.

The above concrete examples of managerial practice inform my contract analysis. I look for contractual provisions that accord managers the flexibility to pursue the strategies noted above. I also look for contractual constraints on such discretionary actions.

The National Unions on Part-Time Faculty

The AAUP's reporting of these and other retrenchment cases involving the (mis)use of part-time academic labor speaks to their concern about the issue. So does their featuring "The Use and Abuse of Part-Time Faculty" in the November/December 1992 issue of *Academe*. The AAUP's official position is set forth in that issue in a report by Committee G, "On the Status of Non-Tenure Track Faculty."[26] The themes and rhetoric of the report are strong. Using part-timers "undercuts the tenure system, severs the connection between control of the curriculum and the faculty who teach it, and diminishes the professional status of all faculty members."[27] Throughout are words such as, *erosion, exploitative, alarming*, and *deleterious*. Committee G decries the treatment of part-time faculty, an "underclass" that is denied the "professional conditions" they deserve. Their treatment is a "barometer" by which to gauge the general status of the profession. As the use of part-time faculty reduces employment opportunities for those seeking full-time careers, the report recommends that institutions reduce and limit their reliance upon nontenure-track and part-time faculty members to 15 percent of total instruction, a number well below current practice. In the meantime, part-timers should be accorded the conditions of employment enjoyed by full-time members of the profession. For example, part-timers should be evaluated regularly, eligible for promotion, receive fringe benefits, given a full term's notice of non-reappointment, have a role in governance, and given access to positions that are converted to full-time.

The AFT also recently has published a report on part-time faculty, *Part-Time Faculty Issues*, updating a 1979 "Statement on Part-Time Faculty Employment."[28] The rhetoric of this report, and of the 1979 statement, is strong. References throughout are to the "rising tide," "misuse and abuse," and the "exploitation" of part-time faculty. Perhaps reflecting the different histories and strategies of the two organizations and the constituencies that they represent (the AFT represents more than 30,000 part-time faculty), there are also some important differences from the AAUP report.

> The heavy dependence upon part-time faculty, which may once have had 'innocent' beginnings, is becoming more and more obviously a form of administrative resistance to faculty unionism. A reserve army of unorganized, noncontract teachers can destroy the rights and prerogatives which faculty have fought for and have gained through collective bargaining. . . . Part-time faculty must be protected by the same regulations and granted the same rewards and dignity as those enjoyed by their full-time colleagues.[29]

The AFT report focuses on organizing part-time faculty, including them in the same bargaining unit with full-timers. It also calls for upgrading their conditions of employment—according them benefits, improved pay, and professional due process in hiring, evaluation, and release.

The NEA also views the "misuse" of part-time faculty as an important issue. In a report analyzing reform in higher education and "Defining Our Stance," the NEA refers to "invidious patterns" of "widespread and excessive use of part-time faculty" that are "undermining tenure" as well as academic and intellectual freedom and educational quality. In 1992 the NEA amended a 1976 resolution regarding part-timers.

> The National Education Association believes that part-time education employees should receive the same salary and benefits as full-time education employees prorated according to the workload. The Association deplores the practice of employing part-time education employees for the primary purpose of reducing instructional budgets or for the purpose of reducing the number of full-time education positions.[30]

As of this book's writing, the NEA has formed a task force on "contingent faculty" to explore issues surrounding part-time and other contingent faculty. The national unions, then, are critical of the use and treatment of part-time faculty. As representatives primarily of full-time faculty (although they also include part-time faculty and units), they do not seek simply to maintain the current position of full-timers at the expense and through the exploitation of part-time faculty.[31] Indeed they see the fates of these bifurcated halves (haves and have-nots) of the academic profession as being intertwined. They see the current use and treatment of part faculty as a direct threat to full-timers and to the profession as a whole. Faculty unions seek to restrict managerial discretion in using part-time faculty. They also seek better, more professional conditions of employment for part-timers.

Methods

In this chapter, I address two questions: (1) To what extent do collectively bargained agreements provide for managerial discretion/constraint and professional involvement/control regarding the use of part-time faculty? and (2) To what extent do part-time faculty's conditions of employment suggest gradations of faculty among part-timers, and between them and full-timers? I pursue these questions in an analysis of 183 contracts in the 1990s that address part-time faculty.[32] The vast majority of the HECAS contracts have provisions regarding part-timers. (The overrepresentation of NEA contracts in HECAS is suited to the analysis here. Part-time faculty are most numerous in two-year colleges, where the NEA is strongest, and research suggests the NEA is the union most receptive to part-timers.[33]) The clauses are not concentrated in one article, as with the salary structures and retrenchment clauses analyzed in chapters 2 and 3; they are dispersed throughout the contract.

In addressing my first research question I examine references to part-time faculty that relate to personnel and special work-force actions (that is, to appointment or release and retrenchment) or to the work force's makeup (that is, the number or proportion of full- and part-time faculty). References to general hiring and firing are coded as "appointment/release."[34] References are coded as "individual workforce" when they apply to conditions surrounding layoff, with language referring to the rights of individual workers in the action. Such rights do not necessarily impact the overall number of part-timers, or their ratio to full-timers. References are coded as "collective workforce" when the language explicitly invokes the total or proportional numbers of part-time faculty *or* when language implicitly refers to work-force makeup by addressing contingencies surrounding the hiring of additional part-time faculty. Last, I code language that (dis)allows conversion of full- to part-time positions or that provides for conversion of part to full-time lines as "conversion."

For each coding, I look for evidence of managerial discretion and professional constraint, involvement, and/or control. Evidence of managerial discretion takes three forms: (a) absence of conditions—for example, if conditions of layoff are not specified, greater discretion lies in managers' hands; (b) statements of management rights regarding work-force matters; and/or (c) exceptions to particular rules—for example, order of layoff—with managers having discretion to determine whether exceptions apply. Evidence of professional constraint, involvement, and/or control consists of (a) explicit and/or absolute conditions inhibiting managerial discretion, and/or (b) language providing faculty and/or the union involvement in determining the application of conditions or exceptions.

In addressing my second research question, I examine part-time faculty's conditions of work and look for explicit ranking of professional privileges by faculty status. In identifying such conditions, I am guided by the structure of contracts. I examine part-timers' rights and perquisites to gauge the extent to which they are extended the privileges enjoyed by full-timers and whether part-time faculty have opportunities for professional development. I investigate part-timers' duties, to find if they are responsible for having office hours, being evaluated, and participating in the academic life of their units. I code the extent to which experience as a part-time teacher is even credited by the institution in a range of contractual considerations (for example, seniority, time towards some professional right or perquisite). Finally, I code any contractual conditions in which full-time faculty were explicitly given priority over part-time faculty (or vice-versa) as "priority."

I supplement my textual content analysis with chi-square analyses of two contexts—type of institution and unit membership. I compare the incidence of contractual terms/conditions of academic labor in the relevant populations (four-year institutions, and two-year and technical colleges; units covering only full-time faculty and those including at least some part-timer faculty). Past studies of higher education institutions and of contractual conditions suggest the likelihood of significant variation between two- and four-year institutions.[35] In addition, the different legal boundaries of contracts covering only full-time faculty versus those covering at least some part-time faculty and the different interests of these constituencies suggest the likelihood of significant variations between contracts with different unit membership.

Roughly one-third (36 percent) of the 183 contracts I analyze cover only full-time faculty. Thus, 118 contracts cover at least some part-time faculty. Different definitions of unit membership carry varying legal limitations in what the agent can bargain. For example, a unit that represents only full-time faculty cannot bargain salaries for part-time faculty. Moreover, a unit that represents some part-time faculty often defines part-time in such a way as to exclude large numbers of part-time faculty. Such a unit cannot bargain some matters for excluded part-timers. The scope of membership affects the scope of what can be bargained. Nevertheless, *any* unit may negotiate conditions that directly and indirectly affect part-time faculty. For example, contracts that cover only full-timers may speak to personnel and work-force matters, the focus of my first research question. They may ensure the involvement of full-timers in the hiring of part-time faculty, institute an order of layoff that gives priority to full- over part-time faculty, and establish staffing ratios to limit the proportion of part-time faculty. In fact, every condition of work that I study is addressed in some contracts covering only full-timers.

Managerial Discretion and Professional Constraint, Involvement, and Control: Part-Time Faculty in Personnel and Work-Force Actions

Appointment/Release

The absence of provisions about general personnel actions is striking. No conditions of appointment/release for part-time faculty are specified in 145 (79 percent) of the 183 contracts in which part-timers are mentioned. There are few contractual constraints on managerial discretion in this area.

The incidence of appointment/release provisions is independent of institutional type.[36] That is somewhat surprising. Part-time faculty are more common in two-year than in four-year institutions. Thus, one might expect two-year colleges to be more likely to have provisions about hiring/firing such faculty. Or, by contrast, one might expect the proportionately larger and stronger faculty in four-year institutions to be more likely to negotiate clauses ensuring their involvement in hiring part-time faculty and ensuring due process constraints in releasing them. Neither expectation is met. Managers are relatively free contractually in both sectors to hire and fire part-time faculty (see table 4.1).

TABLE 4.1
INCIDENCE OF PERSONNEL PROVISIONS

	Appointment/ Release	Appointment	Release
Two-year	29	27	4
Technical	0	0	0
Four-year	14	13	2
Full time only	9	9	0
Full & part time	34	31	6
Total	43	40*	6

*Of these, only nine provide for full-time faculty's involvement in hiring part-time faculty.

However, there is a dependent association between the incidence of appointment/release provisions and unit membership ($x2=5.26$, significant at the .025 level). Contracts for full-time faculty only are *under*represented. They account for 21 percent of the provisions, as compared to 36 percent of the contracts that mention part-time faculty. In one respect, that makes sense. Contracts that cover some part-time faculty are more likely to deal with conditions of their appointment/release. In another respect, the finding is surprising. One might expect full-time only contracts to seek some control over the hiring of part-timers by ensuring full-timers' involvement in the process. Yet, only two of the nine contracts with such clauses are in full-time only units. (Of course, it is likely to be harder for such units to negotiate matters regarding nonunit members. Union bargaining agents can more easily justify negotiating "impact" matters such as layoff order because it clearly has an impact on members of the unit. Yet, so too do hiring and quality.) All but three of the forty-three contracts with appointment/release conditions deal with appointment. One union negotiator told me,

"Analysis of appointment and release should be separated; the latter is much easier to bargain."[37] Perhaps in general, release *is* easier to bargain than appointment. The findings of the salary and retrenchment chapters (2 and 3) certainly point to that conclusion. Apparently, in the case of part-time faculty, however, the reverse is the case in relative terms. Yet in absolute terms, appointment is not so easy to negotiate. There are few such provisions. Most are brief references to postings or listings of jobs and to the logistics of the appointment process. Only nine contracts provide for full-time faculty's involvement in hiring part-timers. In those few cases in which faculty are involved, their role is limited and advisory. Thus, Western Michigan University's contract provides faculty "the right to make timely recommendations to the appropriate administrator" but follows that line with a "deem clause" according full discretion to managers: "Nothing in this article, however, shall prevent Western from hiring part-time instructors at its sole discretion when the need to hire a part-time faculty member is unexpected and there is insufficient time to consult with departmental faculty" (Article 14.1). The clause ensures managerial flexibility. That is one of the chief reasons managers utilize part-time faculty: they can move quickly to add (and reduce) them, unhampered by extensive due process procedures.

Managerial discretion is even greater in *releasing* part-time faculty. Release is dealt with in only six contracts. SUNY's contract defines a period of notice (minimum of forty-five days before the end of the appointment), which varies depending on years of service. Two contracts provide due process constraints on the release of part-time faculty. Shasta-Tehama-Trinity College's contract establishes part-time faculty members' right to appeal, but the appeal is processed "through the administrative chain to the Vice President for Instruction, whose decision shall be final" (Article 1.6.1.1.a), not through an external arbitrator. By contrast, Schoolcraft College's contract ensures that the grievance procedure (which includes arbitration) applies to part-time faculty. Yet these exceptions prove the rule of limited contractual protections and professional due process for part-time faculty in routine personnel actions.

In sum, contractually, full-time faculty have very little involvement in and control over the hiring and firing of part-time faculty. That bodes ill not just for full-time faculty's control over the selection of their colleagues, but for the incorporation of part-time faculty into the life and community of the academic units in which they teach. Moreover, few part-timers have contractual protections in hiring and firing processes. They are more a contingent than a professional work force in this regard, subject to the inclinations and discretionary actions of managers.

Individual Work Force

Just less than half (eighty-seven) of contracts mentioning part-timers do so in regard to work-force actions affecting individuals—that is, layoff. In 52 percent of my sample, managerial discretion is not contractually constrained by provisions for full- relative to part-time faculty's job rights in retrenchment.[38] Nor is managerial discretion constrained by contractually defined rights of part-time faculty.

Four types of individual work force conditions are identified. By far the most common (59 contracts) is order of layoff. Contracts provide that *within the layoff unit*, part-time faculty will be laid off prior to full-time faculty. However, such provisions virtually always include the condition that administrators can violate that order if they determine that the remaining full-time faculty cannot fulfill the program's academic needs. Only four clauses call for a faculty body to make or be consulted about such a decision: discretion is almost entirely in the hands of the administrators. That discretion is contractually unconstrained in the 152 HECAS contracts that lack any reference to layoff order of full- and part-timers in retrenchment (see table 4.2).

Overwhelmingly, references to part-time faculty in individual work-force actions do *not* have to do with part-timers' rights. They merely establish the priority of full- relative to part-time faculty. Determining layoff order by job status clearly supports status differences between these faculty.

Such differences are also evident in displacement or reassignment rights given to full-time faculty who are to be laid off. If a full-time faculty member can fill out or construct a full-time load from current part-timers' duties, the full-timer will displace the part-timer and/or will be reassigned those duties. Full-time faculty have displacement rights in nineteen contracts, *if* they are judged qualified to teach classes taught by current part-time faculty. Managers make this judgment. Managers have similar discretion in reassigning full-time faculty. Of fourteen contracts, five provide that full-timers can be reassigned to part-time jobs. In other words, managers can convert full- to part-time positions.

TABLE 4.2
INCIDENCE OF INDIVIDUAL WORK FORCE PROVISIONS

	Clauses	Order of Layoff	Displace- ment	Reassign- ment	Recall
Two-year	53	30	12	10	14
Tech	7	4	4	0	3
Four-year	27	25	3	4	5
FTO	31	23	10	9	1
F & PT	56	36	9	5	21
Total	87	59	19	14*	22**

* In five cases, the clauses enable managers to reassign full-time faculty to part-time jobs.
** In four cases, the clauses provide for the recall rights *of part-time faculty.*

The fourth type of individual work force category is recall, providing laid off faculty the right within a defined time period to claim new jobs for which they are qualified in the layoff unit. References to part-timers in this context give laid off full-time faculty the right to new part-time positions in the layoff unit (and the right to turn them down), normally without sacrificing their claim within the given time period to a full-time position. Of twenty-two contracts, four provide recall rights *of* part-timers to such positions. These are the *only* examples of individual work-force provisions that accord professional rights to part-time faculty. In the absence of such contractual constraints, managerial discretion in dealing with part-timers in special individual work-force actions is extensive.

In short, the professional claims of full-time relative to part-time faculty are defined in order, displacement, reassignment, and recall clauses. Yet managers enjoy much discretion even in clauses that seek to protect the jobs of full-time faculty—for example, in exceptions defined in order of layoff provisions. Finally, the rights of part-timers of any sort are overlooked even in those contracts that cover at least some part-timers. Of fifty-six contracts that cover at least some part-time faculty and have individual work-force provisions only four define rights for any group of part-timers. Managerial discretion, then, in regard to part-time faculty professional rights, is virtually unconstrained in the contracts.

Individual work-force clauses are slightly underrepresented in the contracts of two-year institutions. However, chi-square analysis reveals that institutional type is independent of incidence of individual work-force clauses ($x2=3.98$; collapsing technical and two-year colleges yields a chi-square of 3.71, significant at the .1, but not the .05 level). The incidence of such clauses by unit membership mirrors the distribution of sample contracts, revealing no relationship between incidence of provisions and type of unit.

However, disaggregating such clauses, the incidence of particular types of individual work force provisions *is* dependent on institutional type and/or unit membership. Order of layoff is dependent on institutional type ($x2=14.6$, significant at the .005 level). Contracts in two-year colleges are underrepresented; those in four-year institutions are overrepresented. That finding is consistent with earlier research on the differential nature of retrenchment clauses in two- and four-year institutions.[39] Yet institutional type is independent of displacement, reassignment, and recall provisions ($x2=5.42$, .5, and 1.23 respectively).

There are dependent associations between unit membership and the incidence of reassignment ($x2=4.35$, significant at the .05 level) and recall clauses ($x2=10.46$, significant at the .005 level), but not for order or for displacement provisions ($x2=.63$, and 2.81, significant at .1, but not .05 level). In reassignment clauses, nine of the fifteen provisions are in full-time only contracts. In recall clauses, contracts covering only full-time faculty are underrepresented: twenty-one of twenty-two provisions are in contracts that cover full- and part-timers. There is no clear pattern of faculty in full-time only units being the most aggressive in asserting the priority of full- over part-time faculty's rights.

Collective Work Force

Collective work-force provisions constitute the clearest constraints on managerial discretion in hiring part-time faculty. Individual work-force provisions offer some protection for current full-time faculty. They do not protect full-time positions that may be foregone in the future. Managers may increase the number of part-time faculty by filling vacated full-time lines with part-timers, or by hiring more part-time faculty. Collective work-force provisions limit the number or ratio of part-timers. Of the 183 contracts that refer to part-time faculty, 29 percent have such provisions.

The negotiating positions of faculty unions and of administration are evidenced in two contracts discussed below. Each contains provisions limiting the use of part-time faculty and clauses granting managerial discretion in the use of part-timers. The first contract speaks to the proportion of part-time faculty's collective instructional load:

> The total number of contact hours generated by part-time faculty members during the Fall and Winter semesters shall not exceed 37 percent of the total number of credit hours generated within the college during the Fall, Winter, and Spring/Summer semesters. Non-credit contact hours shall not be subject to this provision. [Section 0107.5] The College shall have the unrestricted right to use part-time and/or full-time adjunct faculty notwithstanding the provisions of 0107.5 of the Agreement. [Section 0108.1] (Washtenaw Community College)

The association position is to cap part-time faculty use by limiting the ratio of total credit hours that part-timers generate; the administration position is unrestricted rights to use part-timers. The last line of section 0107.5 is an important exclusion to the credit hour cap, restricting the scope of full-time faculty's curricular control to *credit* courses. Managers may do as they wish with noncredit courses.

The second contract captures the struggle surrounding part-timers' use in case of retrenchment.

> A faculty member on recall shall have the first right of refusal to any part-time assignments in her/his reduction-in-force unit(s); provided, failure to accept such assignment shall not alter recall rights to full-time vacancies otherwise established; and further provided nothing herein shall require the District to consolidate part-time positions into a full-time position. In the instances where a full-time faculty member is on recall status, the number of part-time assignments, if any, made in the applicable reduction-in-force unit shall not be increased over the number in existence at the time of reduction-in-force by more than the equivalent of one-half of a full-time load. (Columbia Basin College, Article F.9)

The association position is to fight the conversion of full- to part-time lines in retrenchment; the administration position is to have a free hand, with no requirement to save full-time lines by consolidating part-time jobs.

Of course, the replacement of full-time lines with part-time faculty can take place not just with retrenchment, but with attrition. Western Michigan University's contract addresses this as a matter for study. The chapter and university will meet to discuss the distribution and number of tenure-track positions by department over time; the credit-hour generation of different categories of faculty by department; and the number of vacated lines that have been filled by tenure-track versus nonunit, renewable-term instructors. At issue is whether full-time faculty will retain their overall share of positions and curricular responsibility (for example, in credit-hour generation).

Of the fifty-three contracts with collective work-force provisions, eleven have clauses that in various ways ensure managerial discretion in determining the total numbers and proportions of full- and part-time faculty. For example:

> Full-time faculty members shall be given employment preference over part-time faculty members; however, the College reserves the right to determine the number of full and part-time faculty. (Baker College, Section 2.1.G)

> The district reserves the right to establish the number of full-time and part-time faculty to be employed. (Skagit Valley College, Article 9.8.b)

Each of the above clauses establishes that it is solely the responsibility of the administration to determine the configuration of the faculty work force. In fact, responsibility regarding "the number of full and part-time faculty required to operate the educational program" is defined in Baker College's contract as a management right (Section 1.5). A clause in Kirtland Community College's contract extends that "exclusive right" to reorganization actions.

> The board has the exclusive right to initiate, eliminate, or modify college programs to meet the changing needs of the college and its constituents. It is recognized by both parties that all college programs are under continuing critical review and there is a possibility that current staffing needs and staffing configuration could change. Enrollment factors may also cause adjustment to part-time status. (Article 16.M)

In the forty-two contracts that limit managerial discretion in collective work-force issues there is much variation in the provisions. Most common are clauses speaking to retrenchment (fourteen), the ratio of part- to full-time faculty (fifteen), or to restricting the use of part-time faculty to replace full-timers (twelve). Relatedly, eight references deal with the legitimate uses of part-timers.

Collective work-force clauses regarding retrenchment generally focus on order of layoff in a collective sense or on hiring part-timers during layoff.

> The University in its discretion may renew and retain Lecturers provided that it is agreed that in case of retrenchment or imminent retrenchment in the faculty bargaining unit, Lecturers and Adjuncts are and remain part-time faculty; and it is understood and agreed that in accordance with the Order of Retrenchment, and without exception regardless of other rights or entitlements claimed, NO FULL-TIME UNITS FACULTY, TENURED OR UNTENURED, MAY BE RETRENCHED AHEAD OF PART-TIME (LESS THAN FULL-TIME) FACULTY, said order being "absolute in any retrenchment situation, anything in the contrary notwithstanding." (Caps in original, University of Lowell, Article 10.B.5)

Such collective-order provisions are an exception to the contractual rule. McHenry Community College's administrative deem clause makes explicit what holds true overwhelmingly for contracts with order clauses. "The order of layoff set forth in paragraphs 3–5 above shall not require the Board to dismiss all part-time, probationary, or less senior faculty members prior to any layoff of a full-time tenured faculty member" (Article 9.6). Priority of full-time faculty in layoff order is far from absolute. Managers are free to retain part-time faculty even as they lay off full-timers.

Several contracts speak to hiring part-time faculty during layoff: the restriction may apply to the layoff unit or to the institution as a whole.

> In the instances where a full-time faculty member is on recall status, the number of part-time assignments, if any, made in the applicable reduction-in-force unit shall not be increased over the number in existence at

the time of reduction-in-force by more than the equivalent of one-half of a full-time load. (Columbia Basin College, Article F.9)

If there is to be a reduction in force at the College involving layoff of full-time members . . . the College will, in consultation with the RCCEA and FAMAT, maintain the subsequent annual general fund budget for part-time faculty positions at a level no higher than the increase needed to provide for any negotiated part-time salary increase. (Rogue Community College, Article 9.B.2)

Some work-force clauses limit the conversion of full to part-time lines more generally. These clauses nevertheless afford managers much discretion.

The Board shall not seek the employment of part-time teachers for the purpose of reducing the number of professorial staff, replacing full-time teachers. (Macomb Community College, Appendix G)

The College will attempt to employ qualified full-time faculty for full-time positions in preference to part-time personnel, where qualified, provided, however, that full-time faculty are reasonably available and interested in such employment (Clinton Community College, Article 10)

The College will attempt to employ qualified full-time staff members for full-time positions in preference to part-time personnel where qualified full-time staff members are reasonably available and interested in such employment, and such full-time employment is consistent with the long range educational objectives of the College. (Schenectady County Community College, Article 5.A)

Phrases such as *for the purpose of, will attempt, where qualified*, or *reasonably available*, give managers considerable flexibility. By contrast, some contracts' language prohibits the replacement of full- with part-timers.

The Board shall not use part-time employees to replace full-time members presently employed. (Washtenaw Community College, Section 0107.3)

Adjunct faculty will not be used in combination with one or more part-time employees as a replacement for a full-time faculty member who vacates a bargaining unit position. (Lakeland Faculty Association, Article 1.1.b)

The strongest restrictions on managerial discretion lie in clauses that call for reduced numbers of part-time faculty or that lock institutions into particular ratios (or delimit parameters) of full- to part-time faculty, in this way shaping the academic work force. Various levels of specificity are built into these provisions—overall numbers or workload (for example, credit hours), departmental ratios, and procedures for when the prescribed ratio is exceeded.

The University, in consultation with the Association, shall develop a plan to reduce dependence on part-time faculty. (Shawnee State University, Article 2.B.1)

The current practice generally shall prevail with full-time instructors assigned to teach approximately two-thirds of all on-campus classes. Exclusions to the ratio shall continue for community education classes, EMD classes, apprenticeship classes, sabbatical replacement classes, and fee generated classes. . . . The College President and the Association President will meet at least once annually to compare base salary budgets of full-time to part-time faculty (excluding fringes and fees) to make certain the current 4.4 to 1 ratio has not changed significantly. If the budgeted dollar ratio moves to a position of 4.1 to 1 or under, the College agrees to correct the ratio to not less than 4.4 to 1 for the following budget year. (Clackamas Community College, Article 3.2)

The College will maintain 162 full-time district funded faculty positions on an institutional basis as long as the annual student full-time equivalency remains between 5,000 and 7,000. If the student full-time equivalency drops below 5,000 or rises above 7,000 the college will maintain a fiscal year instruction ratio of sixty percent full-time to forty percent part-time. (Mt. Hood Community College, Appendix G)

The part-time faculty to full-time faculty ratio based on credit hours taught will not exceed a 1:4 ratio on an annual basis. . . . Whenever the part-time to full-time ratio in a department exceeds 1:3, the department, the dean, and the Vice President for Academic Affairs will meet to address the excessive reliance upon part-time faculty and to design a plan to rectify this excessive reliance. (Saginaw Valley State University, Article D.13)

Except at the Massachusetts College of Art, not more than fifteen percent of an academic department's total number of three credit courses and sections shall be taught by part-time employees during an academic year. (Massachusetts State College System, Article XX.C.9)

There may be no more than 1 nine hour part-time assignment in any department. In the case of new programs, there may be 2 nine credit hour part-time assignments. This cannot continue beyond the fourth semester of the program's operation. (Joliet Junior College, Section 1.1.4.b, c)

What is evident in all of the above provisions is that faculty union strategies involve seeking to control not the hiring/firing and quality, but the numbers and use of part-timers. One exception to this rule— Ferris State University's contract—illustrates that the strategies could go hand in hand.

Commencing winter quarter 1988, no course shall be taught by a non-bargaining unit member for more than one quarter unless the credentials of the non-bargaining unit member have been made available for review to the bargaining unit members in the seniority unit in which the class is offered. Unless two-thirds of the bargaining unit members reviewing the aforementioned credentials recommend against hiring the non-bargaining unit member for the specified class(es), the non-bargaining unit member may be hired for that class(es). The recommendation, however, must come from more than one reviewing bargaining unit member. (Article 17)

Overwhelmingly, they do not. Instead, bargaining agents aim to restrict the use of part-time faculty to delimited realms and ratios.[40]

What is also evident in the provisions regarding ratios is that broad areas of the curriculum—particularly for community colleges—are exempted from professional controls. That leaves much room for managerial discretion. The ratio restrictions in Saginaw Valley State's contract do not apply to off-campus programs in two areas or to noncredit continuing education programs. Ratio limits in Roger Williams University and Shasta-Tehama-Trinity College contracts apply only to day courses. The Lincoln University contract's ratio limit does not apply to graduate programs or to summer sessions. (Along the same lines, Ferris State University's contract provides for the creation of full-time positions from continuing part-time loads, but excepts part-time clinical faculty and cooperative education.) Such exclusions are particularly significant in that the excepted areas of the curriculum are growth areas.

Only one collective work-force provision protects the rights of part-timers. The University of Massachusetts at Amherst's contract provides for the increased job security of various grades of part-time faculty, ensuring longer contracts for larger numbers of part-time faculty. "A minimum of 40 percent of bargaining unit faculty shall be offered one-year contracts (current—35 percent) and 15 percent shall be offered two-year contracts" (Article 21).

In short, 53 contracts have collective work-force provisions. In 21 percent of those contracts, managers are given authority to determine the configuration of the work force. In the remaining contracts (23 percent of all contracts that mention part-time faculty), various professional controls are established on the use and the numbers/proportion of part-time faculty.[41] However, in most cases, provisions still afford managers much discretion. Only one contract, of the 118 that cover at least some part-timers, limits managerial discretion through the establishment of part-time faculty's professional rights (see table 4.3).

TABLE 4.3
INCIDENCE OF COLLECTIVE WORK-FORCE PROVISIONS

	Clauses	Managmt right	Order	Ratio	Replace-ment	Conver-sion
Two-year	30	10	9	7	6	7
Tech	5	0	3	1	1	1
Four-year	18	1	2	7	5	2
FTO	22	4	6	5	7	3
F & PT	31	7	8	10	5	7
Total	53	11	14	15	12	10*

* In four other contracts, there are clauses that call for "reverse conversion," the translation of existing part-time assignments into full-time positions.

The incidence of collective work-force provisions in general is *not* dependent on unit membership ($x2=1.14$). Neither are the three main categories of collective work-force provision—order, ratio, and replacement ($x2$'s$=.34$, 2.84, and $.03$ respectively). In other words, the 65 contracts covering only full-time faculty are statistically no more likely to have such clauses than the 118 contracts that cover at least some part-timers. That is surprising. (That is not to say that unit membership does not matter. Unit membership may predict specific professional protections for part-time faculty, at least in particular cases. For example, Wayne State University's contract has a small number of "fractional time" faculty legally ruled in the unit and provides special protection to them, with fractional tenure.[42])

Including only those contracts that offer some professional controls on managerial discretion, the incidence of collective work-force provisions is dependent on institutional type (x2=9.66, significant at .01 level). Contracts in four-year institutions are overrepresented: they account for 40.5 percent of contracts with such clauses, although they represent only 24 percent of the contracts in the sample. However, the incidence of order, ratio, and replacement is not dependent on institutional type (x2's of 4.22, 2.01, and 4.29 respectively).[43]

Conversion

Perhaps the most dramatic example of managers' discretion to shape the faculty work-force profile consists of clauses that explicitly grant managers the right to convert full- to part-time positions. Ten contracts have such clauses (by contrast, four clauses in the collective work-force category call for "reverse conversion"—the translation of part-time assignments into new full-time positions). Some apply to retrenchment: full-time faculty can accept a part-time position in lieu of layoff. The blanket deem clause of Lehigh County Community College dramatizes managers' degrees of freedom. "The College's decision to retrench and the resulting layoff of faculty or reduction to part-time status shall not be subject to the grievance/arbitration procedure by either the Association or the faculty member(s) so effected" (Appendix A). Some conversion clauses are general provisions enabling managers to reduce full- to part-time positions. A few others refer to voluntary adjustments, or to reduced work-load programs (these do not include voluntary retirement clauses, found in thirty-three contracts).

Overall, then, managerial discretion is extensive. Of 183 contracts that address part-time faculty, 117 speak to work-force issues in individual and/or collective terms (including conversion). Of those 117, 64 deal only with individual work-force matters, 27 deal only with collective work-force matters, and 26 deal with both. Only 53 contracts, then, constrain managerial discretion in shaping the faculty work-force profile as a collectivity. Only 42 do so in a restrictive way.

Professional Stratification:
Part-Time Faculty's Conditions of Employment

Gradations of Part-Time Status

As is emphasized in the literature, "part-time faculty" is far from a monolithic category. Part-timers are defined in various ways in the contracts. Even those contracts that include some part-time faculty in the bargaining unit generally exclude some others. There are numerous gradations in job status, with strata typically related to course load. Nearly two-thirds (64 percent) of the contracts in HECAS cover at least some part-timers. About half of those specify restrictions on what part-timers are included in the bargaining unit. The restrictions are defined by number of course hours (ranging from four credit hours per week to eight or more hours to nineteen hours to thirty hours or more), or by percentage of full-time load (ranging from 20 percent or more to three-quarters or more and all points in between). In three contracts, hourly faculty are included. In a few cases, inclusion is defined by type of course taught: credit courses are included; continuing education or night courses are not.

The clearest classes of part-time faculty defined in the literature and in surveys are "regular" and "temporary." But even these classifications lack definitive national standards. In fact, the latter category was so problematic that it was not used in reports of the 1993 National Survey of Postsecondary Faculty. Generally, the former category refers to those part-time faculty with a substantial course load and some continuity of service in the institution. "Regular" part-time faculty are the most likely to be covered in contracts, and they account for roughly 69 percent of part-time faculty. Of course, far fewer part- than full-time faculty—10 versus 23 percent—are unionized.[44]

As was noted earlier, the scope of the bargaining unit affects what can be negotiated. It may also affect what is likely to be negotiated and what management regards as negotiable. There are limits to what units covering only full-time faculty can negotiate. Full-time only units have negotiated each of the provisions I consider in this section of the chapter. However, in each case I look for a possible association between unit membership and the incidence of each of these provisions regarding conditions of work.

Contractual Conditions of Employment: Rights/Perquisites

By far the most common conditions of employment defined for part-time faculty in the contracts are rights/perquisites. Such conditions are found in seventy-four contracts. Thus nearly two-thirds of HECAS contracts do *not* accord part-time faculty *any* of the rights/perquisites accorded full-time faculty. Only 39 percent of the 183 contracts that address part-timers in some respect speak to such rights.

Of the seventy-four contracts that define some rights/perquisites for part-time faculty, eight involve negative references, explicitly denying part-timers certain rights/perquisites. For example, part-timers are excluded from basic work provisions such as sick leaves, insurance, retraining, and due process rights to grievance and arbitration. Such negative references simply explicate what is in fact the case in most contracts by virtue of omission.[45]

As one would expect, the contracts least likely to provide part-timers with rights/perquisites are those that cover only full-time faculty. There is a dependent association between these clauses and unit membership ($x2=31.31$, significant at the .000 level). Of sixty-five contracts that mention part-timers but cover only full-timers, only six have provisions that provide part-time faculty with rights/perquisites. Another three such contracts explicitly deny professional privileges to part-time faculty (of eight such negative references, then, five are in contracts that cover full- and part-time faculty) (see Table 4.4).

Yet, there is a striking absence of defined privileges even in the 118 contracts that cover at least some part-time faculty. Of seventy-four references, nine are in full-time only contracts, and five others that are in contracts covering at least some part-timers explicitly deny such faculty these privileges. Thus, nearly half (49 percent) of the contracts covering at least some part-timers do *not* speak to *any* of these faculty members' rights/perquisites.

As in the case of work-force provisions, there is evidence of gradations among part-time faculty, in addition to the distinction between them and full-timers. For example, the Jackson Community College contract indicates that there is some insurance coverage for part-time faculty, but not for those who are not on annual and continuing contracts. That makes explicit what is true for virtually all contracts that cover only certain categories of part-time faculty—some grades of part-time faculty are excluded.

TABLE 4.4
INCIDENCE OF PROVISIONS DEFINING CONDITIONS OF EMPLOYMENT

	Rights/ Perks	Duties	Experience	Priority
Two-year	48	28	41	22
Technical	5	1	4	3
Four-year	13	10	13	6
FTO	6	2	14	13
F & PT	60	37	44	18
Total	66*	39**	58***`	31****

* In another eight contracts, the provisions explicitly deny part-time faculty certain rights/perquisites.
** In three of these contracts, the provisions are negative references.
*** Over one-fourth of the ninety-five references in these contracts are negative, explicitly indicating that faculty are *not* credited for part-time teaching experience.
**** Only three of these contracts protect the rights of part-time faculty.

The most common categories of rights/perquisites are the 146 references in seventy-four contracts regarding leaves (39), insurance/benefits (38), professional development (10), tuition waivers (9) and work space (8). The extent of omission with respect to particular rights/perquisites is striking. Moreover, part-timers' access to certain rights/perquisites apparently has declined relative to earlier findings that nearly two-thirds of contracts give part-time faculty sick leave and nearly one-half provide insurance benefits.[46] The literature on improving the use of part-time faculty so as to enhance the quality of educational programs emphasizes integrating such faculty into the lives of the units in which they teach. But only ten contracts provide any professional development opportunity or support to part-time faculty. Only eight ensure the provision of work space. None enfranchise part-time faculty in the academic decision making of their units.

The incidence of rights/perquisites provisions overall is independent of institutional type ($x2=1.36$). Yet there is a dependent association between provisions for leaves and institutional type. Collapsing two-year and technical colleges into one category, the association is significant at the .1 level ($x2=3.71$).[47] Two-year colleges and technical colleges are overrepresented: 79 percent of such provisions are in two-year and 11 percent percent in technical college contracts, whereas 68 and 8 percent of the sample population contracts are in these institutional types. Four-year institutions are underrepresented, accounting for only 11 percent of leave clauses, as compared to 24 percent of the sample population. That finding runs counter to prevailing assumptions about conditions of work and professional privileges in two- versus in four-year institutions.

Contractual Conditions of Employment: Duties

What is expected of part-time faculty? As another indicator of such faculty's integration into units in which they teach, I code contractual provisions regarding their duties. Only 39 contracts have such provisions—three of these are negative references. What is explicit for those 3 contracts, which do *not* require part-time faculty to hold office hours and do *not* require them to be evaluated, holds true for the great majority (83 percent) of HECAS contracts. It holds true for 80 percent of the 183 contracts that mention part-timers. It holds true for 69 percent of the contracts that cover at least some part-time faculty (only two full-time only contracts define duties).

The incidence of duties provisions is independent of institutional type ($x2=1.87$). This runs counter to assumptions and expectations about conditions of employment and faculty responsibilities in four- versus two-year institutions. Duties are relatively undefined in either sector—32.5 percent of contracts in two-year colleges that cover full and part-timers, and 34.5 percent of contracts in four-year institutions that cover full- and part-timers.

By far the most commonly mentioned duties in the contracts are that part-time faculty be evaluated (twenty-one contracts) and that they hold office hours (fourteen contracts). (Being evaluated is classified as a duty—or professional responsibility—rather than a right because the provisions do not offer part-timers the right of evaluation as a means to ensure salary increases or reappointment.) Only five of the thirty-nine contracts that speak to part-timers' duties fail to mention either being evaluated or holding office hours. A few duties provisions speak to noninstructional matters such as attending orientation, graduation, and parents weekend and participating in faculty meetings.

Yet there is not much detail in the definition of duties, even when they are mentioned. For example, most of the references to being evalu-

ated are made in a sentence or two. Two exceptions point to the significance of this pattern, for there is much about evaluation that could or
should be defined.

In conjunction with the department personnel committee or, where one
does not exist, any other appropriate mechanism, the department chair-
person/head and academic administrative officials, as appropriate shall
evaluate part-time faculty at least once annually on an appropriate form.
The form will provide an appropriate space for the evaluation of any
assigned duties other than teaching. During a part-time faculty member's annual review, the departmental personnel committee or, where
one does not exist, any other appropriate mechanism shall examine the
part-time faculty member's performance in teaching, including student
evaluations. Each department shall develop or adopt one of several
forms appropriate to the evaluation of part-time teaching in that department, as well as procedures for the administration of student evaluations
of part-time teaching. Upon the request of a part-time faculty member,
the chair of the departmental personnel committee or, where one does
not exist, any other appropriate mechanism, or the chairperson/head
shall meet once with the part-time faculty member to discuss or obtain
information with regard to the faculty member's performance and/or the
written comments already provided. Each part-time faculty member
retains the right to respond in writing to any written comments by any
individual or group of individuals on his/her evaluation form and to have
the response affixed to the evaluation. (University of Massachusetts,
Amherst, Sections 21.5–21.7)

While administrators will strive to evaluate part-time faculty as often as
possible, the frequency of the evaluation will be determined by the divisional dean or his/her designee. During the first teaching assignment,
each new part-time faculty member will be observed in the classroom by
his/her immediate supervisor or other individual(s) designated by the
divisional dean. It is expressly understood that this first observation is
for the purpose of assisting the faculty member and is not valuative [sic].
The supervisor may recommend additional supportive resources to promote teaching excellence and enhance student success. Part-time faculty
members to be evaluated will be given reasonable advance notice. The
criteria and methodology to be used in the evaluation will be determined
and published by the divisional dean or his/her designee as early in the
academic year as possible. Before earning associate continuing status,
each part-time faculty member must have at least one formal evaluation.
(Lansing Community College, Article 5.F.2)

The detail in the two contracts above clarifies the significance of what is missing in other contracts. It also points to the existence of considerable managerial discretion even in the context of such detailed provisions. From the standpoint of part-time faculty it is desirable to have various conditions surrounding evaluation well defined, as a matter of due process protection. From the standpoint of the profession, some definition of regular review of part-time faculty is desirable in order to ensure professional treatment of instructors and to maintain professional standards. As contracts stand, however, they leave managers broad discretion to decide whether, by whom, how, and to what ends evaluation of part-time faculty will be done. There are few professional obligations of or constraints on managers in the contracts.

The relative absence in the contracts of defined duties for part-timers highlights the fact that with the exception of holding office hours (12 percent of the 118 contracts that cover full and part-time faculty) such faculty have virtually no noninstructional obligations. Part-timers' work duties are delimited more narrowly than are those of full-timers. As increasing numbers of part-timers are hired, the faculty work force is being deskilled, in terms not only of certification, but of the nature of work being performed. Part-time faculty simply deliver instruction (and contracts do not ensure much guidance or review of this by managers or by full-time faculty). Such a pattern offers little room for professional growth and development.

Conditions of Employment: Experience

As a more direct measure of whether part-time teaching is regarded as professional work, I consider whether such experience is credited in calculating eligibility for any of a range of contractual considerations (for example, salary scale, time toward sabbatical). Such experience is mentioned in less than one-third (31 percent) of the contracts that mention part-timers. In the fifty-eight contracts in which it is mentioned, over one-fourth (27 percent) of the 95 references are negative, explicitly indicating that faculty are not credited for time spent teaching part-time.[48]

As might be expected, part-time experience is most likely to be ignored in contracts that cover full-time faculty only. There is a dependent association between such clauses and unit membership ($x2=4.79$, significant at the .05 level). Full-time faculty only contracts represent

36 percent of agreements that mention part-timers, but only 24 percent of those that have experience clauses. However, such contracts are no more likely than are contracts covering full- and part-time faculty to have *negative* references to experience ($x2=1.91$). Incidence of experience provisions, or of negative references to experience, are independent of institutional type ($x2$'s$=.34, .735$ respectively).

Conditions of Employment: Priority

The provisions described above make explicit what holds true for virtually all of the contracts: full-time faculty take priority over part-timers, whose terms of labor are qualitatively different than those of full-time faculty. To underscore the extent of that priority, I examine contractual references that explicitly accord full-time faculty priority over part-timers. One would expect that the contracts of full-time faculty only would be the most likely to have priority clauses. But chi-square analysis reveals that there is no dependent association between the incidence of these clauses and unit membership ($x2=.67$). Nor is there a dependent association between the clauses and institutional type ($x2=.65$).

Of the thirty-one contracts speaking to priority, only three protect the rights of part-timers. For example, two contracts give part-time faculty priority in the filling of full-time positions, though the clauses vary in their strength.

> Part-time faculty members of the bargaining unit shall be given consideration in the filling of teaching vacancies within the university which may occur within their fields of competence. (Roger Williams University, Article K.2)

> Preferential consideration for new appointments to the rank of full-time faculty shall be given to the most senior part-time faculty member who applies. (Erie Community College, Article 19.4)

A third contract (Franklin Pierce College) protects the course assignments of part-time faculty with at least six years of experience, excluding their courses from the overload list of courses that can be claimed by full-timers.

Virtually all of the priority references are to some dimension of course assignment. (Priority in the makeup of the work force, in layoff order, and in terms of rights/perquisites and experience have already been discussed.) The most common provisions have to do with course assignment in general (eighteen of fifty-five total references) and overload assignments (thirteen references). Full-time faculty are given ownership of their regular courses or the right to claim overload courses before part-time faculty are assigned. Some provisions relate to course assignments that lie outside the mainstream, regular academic curriculum. For example, five references are to summer session courses, three are to continuing education courses, two to evening courses, and one each to adult education and off-contract courses. These curricular areas are where part-time faculty are most likely to be found.

Such provisions might be read as pointing to areas of the curriculum in which part-timers and full-timers compete for courses. Given that all but one of the thirty-one contracts give priority in these matters to full-time faculty, such provisions also might be read as pointing to full-timers' ownership of the curriculum. However, 83 percent of the contracts that mention part-timers, and 85 percent of all HECAS contracts, do *not* establish such course priority. The percentages are even higher with respect to summer session, continuing education, evening, adult education, and off contract courses. In other words, full-timers lack contractual claims on a wide range of curricula. To the extent that there is a contest over curricular realms, it has been decided. Contractually, the formal decision lies in the hands of managers.

(Of course, one might point out that curriculum is one of those "educational matters" that is largely outside the typical scope of bargaining. Moreover, many might argue that faculty have typically exercised a great deal of influence over such matters through collegial, committee-based control of the curriculum. Certainly, faculty do have much de facto, effective influence on decision making in colleges and universities. However, just as certainly, with the rising tide of criticism regarding faculty, such influence is increasingly being questioned and challenged. Moreover, through the increased discretionary use of part-time faculty, and through the increased use of ad hoc committees to undertake strategic planning, restructuring, and reorganization exercises above and beyond the traditional channels of faculty influence, managers are negotiating greater discretion and control in regards to "educational matters." Indeed, chapter 3 speaks directly to that point, as does chapter 5.)

In sum, one powerful indicator of part-time faculty's professional position is the extent to which conditions of employment are *un*defined for *any* categories of part-timers, despite the inclusion of at least some part-time faculty in 118 contracts. Managerial discretion is extensive, for few professional controls are built into the contracts. Part-time faculty's conditions of employment contrast significantly with conditions that attach to full-time faculty's employment. Finally, the rights/perquisites and duties clauses in particular point to divisions and gradations among part-timers.

Discussion

Restructuring activities in American higher education involve more than retrenching individual faculty. Strategic decisions about institutions' academic directions are also consequential choices about the distribution and nature of the faculty work force, and of the professional work force in general in academe.[49] A significant dimension of restructuring that work force is the increased ratio of part- to full-time faculty. In this chapter, I have addressed two questions about contractual conditions applying to part-timers. Both speak to the politics of professional work, to negotiated conditions that affect the use and stratification of part-time faculty in unionized academe.

First, I ask, To what extent do collectively bargained contracts provide for managerial discretion/constraint or professional involvement/control regarding the use of part-time faculty? The focus is on the formal negotiation between managers and faculty over the shape and control of the professional work force. Yet I also gain insight into the stratification of full and part-time faculty, as evidenced in their rights and claims in work-force actions.

In answer to the first research question, I find that there is extensive managerial discretion, contractually. A major source of discretion is the lack of defined conditions regarding part-time faculty in appointment/release and work-force actions. Over three-quarters (80 percent) of HECAS contracts (and 77 percent of the 183 contracts that address part-timers) do not define conditions of appointment/release for part-time faculty. In 59 percent of HECAS contracts (and 52 percent of contracts that address part-timers) the job rights of part-timers, and of full relative to part-timers, in individual work-force actions (layoffs) are undefined. Over three-quarters (80 percent) of HECAS contracts (and 77 percent of contracts that address part-timers) do not have collective work-force provisions that limit managerial discretion in relation to part-time faculty.

Managerial discretion is further evidenced contractually in clauses that explicitly accord administration full decision-making authority—in 21 percent of the collective work-force provisions and in the 10 contracts that allow for the conversion of full to part-time lines. Discretion is also explicit in the granting of exceptions to defined conditions. For example, virtually all of the individual work force provisions regarding order of layoff—the most common conditions—give managers the right to violate that order. Finally, a major source of discretion is explicit in many collective work-force provisions that except particular, and growing, areas of the curriculum.

By contrast, I find only limited professional involvement or controls built into the contracts. Individual and collective work-force provisions are generally not absolute conditions that prevent managerial discretion without exception. Only a handful of provisions define ratios that expressly delimit the numbers and/or proportion of part-time faculty. Virtually no conditions provide faculty or the union involvement in determining the application of conditions or exceptions. Fewer than 5 percent define rights of part-time faculty, contractually protecting them from managers' arbitrary actions.

For all the talk, then, of the need for greater managerial flexibility, and of unions' restrictive effects on managerial discretion, it is hard to imagine managers having more freedom contractually in utilizing part-time faculty than they do at present. If the national unions have called for reduced reliance on part-time faculty, only a few units have successfully negotiated clauses that define and delimit the institution's reliance on part-time faculty. If such clauses were more widespread, the strategy might effectively restrict and even reduce the number of part-time faculty.

The strategy of restricting numbers makes for an interesting contrast with the union strategy that is most contractually apparent in regard to retrenchment—making decisions procedurally complicated. As discussed in chapter 3, managers have broad legal and contractual rights to lay off faculty. They have much discretion. But the most common contractual obstacle to the exercise of that discretion is due process, which draws out the process. Consult with faculty about the action, notify faculty, follow a particular order of layoff, provide for the possibility of reassignment, with its own time lines, and give recall rights with attendant procedures after the layoff has taken place. That appears to be the union strategy. At least it is the most widespread sort of constraint on managerial flexibility in retrenching faculty. No such strategy is evident in the use of part-time faculty. Due process is very limited in the appointment and almost nonexistent in the release of part-time faculty. Full-time faculty have no involvement in the process. And in layoff actions, part-time faculty are accorded virtually no due-process rights.

Over time, managers have increased the number and proportion of part-time faculty, over whom managers have almost total discretion and full-time faculty have almost no control. The relative lack of standard professional processes and job rights for hiring and firing part-time faculty, and their subordinate position as defined in work-force actions, suggests that this growing category of faculty is less professionalized than full-timers.

Chi-square analyses reveal that the incidence of some work-force provisions is associated with institutional type and unit membership. There are dependent associations between institutional type and three work-force provisions—appointment/release, individual work-force, and collective work-force provisions that provide professional constraints. Technical colleges are underrepresented (in fact, missing) in appointment/release clauses. Four-year institutions are overrepresented in individual and collective work-force provisions (although not for the specific categories *within* these two types— e.g., order, ratio). That suggests somewhat stronger professional limitations on managerial discretion exist in four- than in two-year institutions. There are also dependent associations between unit membership and appointment/release, individual work-force recall, and individual work-force reassignment clauses. In the first two cases, contracts including only full-time faculty are underrepresented. In the latter case, such contracts are overrepresented. No clear pattern emerges.

My second research question is, To what extent do part-time faculty's conditions of employment suggest gradations among part-timers and between them and full-time faculty? The analytical focus is on professional stratification. However, I also gain insight into managerial discretion in utilizing part-timers, evidenced in part-timers' limited professional privileges.

In answer to the second research question, I find that the conditions of employment for part-time faculty are relatively undefined. The most common condition is rights/perquisites. Yet it is undefined in 65 percent of HECAS contracts (and 60 percent of contracts that address part-timers), and the rights/perquisites that are defined are very limited. Only 17 percent of HECAS contracts (and 20 percent of contracts that address part-timers) define part-timers' duties outside the classroom—generally, holding office hours and being evaluated. Part-timers' work is typically delimited to instruction. That is a major dimension of deprofessionalization, augmented by managers' extensive discretion in whether and how to evaluate part-timers. Professional processes for evaluating quality and rewarding merit and professional control of such processes are lacking.

The low status of part-time instruction is explicit in the failure of over two-thirds (68 percent) of contracts that address part-timers to mention part-time teaching experience in calculating eligibility for a range of contractual considerations. It is also dramatized by the fact that over one-quarter (27 percent) of the references to experience are negative. Teaching part-time is *not* credited as professional experience.

The professionally subordinate position of part-time faculty is defined in the 15 percent of HECAS contracts (and 17 percent of contracts that address part-timers) that give priority to full over part-time faculty in course assignment. In short, the contracts point to the deprofessionalized conditions of part-time relative to full-time faculty's employment and to managers' broad discretion contractually in dealing with part-timers. The contracts also point to various gradations of part-time faculty.

Chi-square analyses reveal a dependent association between three of the four conditions of employment and unit membership. Provisions that address part-timers' rights/perquisites, duties, and experience are dependent on unit membership, with contracts covering only full-time faculty underrepresented. That is as one would expect. However, contrary to expectations, priority provisions are *not* dependent on unit membership. Units covering full- and at least some part-time faculty are as likely as units covering only full-time faculty to define full-timers' priority over all part-time faculty.

Only one type of clause—leaves—has a dependent association with institutional type. Such clauses are more likely in two-year and technical colleges than in four-year institutions. That runs contrary to prevailing views about working conditions in the different higher education sectors.

In the literature, the subordinate position of part-time faculty has been attributed to full-time faculty seeking to protect their professional position(s).[50] The above findings, individual and collective work-force provisions that establish full-timers' priority in work force actions and collective work-force provisions that set limits on the numbers and/or proportion of part-time faculty might be read as confirming that view. Yet faculty unions nationally promote the improved treatment of part-time faculty. Moreover, institutions nationally are reducing the benefits of all faculty. Further, part-time faculty are often used by managers precisely because such faculty are cheaper and because managers have more flexibility in hiring and releasing part- relative to full-time faculty. Currently, academic managers are seeking to further reduce professional constraints on work-force actions. For example, in the eight state colleges in New Jersey, management is taking the position that part-time faculty are not employees, thereby arguing to the Public Employment Relations Committee that they are ineligible to organize.

Management shares much of the responsibility for part-time faculty's conditions of employment. Indeed, in the negotiation process managers could grant enhanced conditions of employment without requiring some concession from full-timers. Some such conditions are "revenue neutral." It would not cost managers any money, for example, to involve full-time faculty in hiring and evaluating part-timers. What it would cost is time. And establishing professional (due) processes that involve full-time faculty would come at the expense of managerial flexibility. It is in managers' own interests to maintain discretion in utilizing part-timers. By contrast, it is in the public's interest (and the long-term educational and economic interests of the institutions) if both parties to negotiations addressed issues of quality and of incorporating part-timers into the academic community in which they work.

Quality- and community-oriented provisions for the use of part-time faculty are equally in the interests of full-time faculty, who in fact have a direct interest in the conditions and quality of work of part-time faculty. Full-timers' best hedge against management's increased exploitation of cheaper part-time faculty is to negotiate for the better treatment and pay of part-time faculty. There is an important point to be made here about managerial flexibility. Such flexibility is not simply a matter of finances. It is a political economic matter that shapes various social relations. It shapes relations between employer and employee as well as among employees. It also speaks to relations between management and the state. Thus, the example of New Jersey's state colleges, noted above, points to the fact that managers seek to gain flexibility *through* the state (to define part-time faculty as nonemployees) and *from* the state. If part-time faculty are not employees, then managers are free from all sorts of state-based requirements in personnel matters, from unemployment compensation to affirmative action guidelines.

There is still much empirical detail about part-time faculty that is lacking and that is required in order to more fully explore the politics of professional work. Past typologies of part-timers have provided some useful insight into categories of part-timers. Similar work is required to further disaggregate the work and experience of part-time faculty.

For example, we need to disaggregate by institutional type so that we can explore yet another facet of deskilling and intraprofessional hierarchy. There is evidence of an association between institutional type and the incidence of various sorts of provisions. Moreover, a comparison of 1988 NCES data with 1993 National Survey of Postsecondary Faculty data reveals that in some institutional sectors (private research, public doctoral, private comprehensive, and public two-year) the proportion of part-time faculty has increased (3.3, 1.8, 7.4, and 1.3 percentage points respectively, representing increases of 15, 10.5, 23, and 2.5 percent). In other sectors (public research, private doctoral, and private liberal arts) the proportion of part-timers has decreased (1.4, 9.8, and 1.6 percentage points respectively, representing increases of 10, 23, and 5 percent).[51] At this point the results are preliminary and suggestive, but they raise interesting questions. Why the differences by sector? Why have the numbers of part-time faculty increased in some sectors but not in others, particularly as the variations cut across public/private institutions and within the research and doctoral institution sectors?

We also need to disaggregate by field of study. At present, there are tabular data on aggregated numbers of part-time faculty in particular fields. As one might expect, there are higher percentages of part-time faculty in some career oriented fields such as business (38 percent), education (37 percent), law (54 percent) and occupationally specific programs (43 percent) than in the natural sciences (30 percent) and social sciences (29 percent).[52] (However, there are other professional fields that have relatively low numbers of part-time faculty, such as engineering [24 percent] and nursing [26 percent].) There are also relatively high percentages of part-timers in arts and science departments that bear heavy general education, service course responsibilities, such as English (41 percent) and math (41 percent). The point is that restructuring the faculty work force is a disaggregated phenomenon.

A further dimension of disaggregation among part-time faculty is gender, which further enhances our understanding of professional stratification. As indicated in chapter 2, the gender gap in salaries persists. The concentration of women faculty in the lowest levels of the institutional hierarchy (for example, community colleges) and in the lowest paid fields of academe (for example, education) certainly contributes to that gap. Layered on top of those dimensions of stratification is the fact that the largest representation of women among faculty is in the ranks of part-time faculty (and in the nontenure-track categories of instructor and lecturer, the lowest academic ranks in the hierarchy of full-time faculty). That has obvious implications for salaries. It also has implications for job security. As noted in chapter 3, retrenchment actions (and reorganization) have taken place disproportionately in fields with relatively large numbers of women faculty and students. Layered on top of that source of restructuring is the fact that the largest proportion of women faculty are part of the contingent academic labor force. The differential representation of women in the full- and part-time faculty work forces should be factored into any analysis of relations between these groups, and between part-time faculty and full-time administrators.

Taken together with my findings about managerial discretion being especially broad in certain excepted areas of the curriculum (for example, continuing education), the above patterns raise some interesting questions. To what extent is the extensive use of part-time faculty in particular curricular areas a threat to faculty's control of the curriculum? In other words, to what extent are managers gaining increased control over certain parts of the curriculum through the increased use of part-timers in these areas? To what extent are part-timers simply delivering a curriculum that has been developed elsewhere? Who controls the definition and development and even the form of delivery of these curricular areas? These questions should be kept in mind as one moves into the next chapter on the use/control of instructional technologies.

In closing, reorganization should be analyzed not simply in the context of the faculty work force, but of higher education's professional work force in general. Faculty members are not the only professionals in the academy. In fact, at the same time that American colleges and universities are increasing their numbers and proportion of part-time faculty and decreasing their proportions of full-time faculty, they are increasing the numbers and proportion of full-time administrators and nonfaculty professionals. Most administrative and nonfaculty professional positions in academe are full-time (94.6 and 83.7 percent)—far higher percentages than the percentage of full-time faculty (57 percent). The number of nonfaculty-support professionals has mushroomed, not only in central administration but in academic colleges.[53] We are witnessing a shift in the configuration of professional and production work in higher education. As colleges and universities hire more and more support professionals—for example, in computing and technology—to assist in the "production," in the processing and graduating of students, they are also hiring more and more part-time faculty to teach these students. This point should be kept in mind as I move on to an analysis of instructional technology. We are witnessing a substantial challenge to the professional position of the academic profession. Full-time academics are no longer as central as they once were. The increased use of part-time faculty is a central part of that challenge.

The Production Politics of Teaching and Technology: Deskilling, Enskilling, and Managerial Extension

New technologies may ease the burden of labor. They may increase quality. They may increase productivity. They may require existing workers to develop new skills. They may require new workers who have more, or different, skills. They may reduce the number of workers, replacing people with machines.

It is clear that such effects apply to blue-collar workers. Consider the auto industry.[1] It is also clear that these effects apply to clerical workers. Consider telecommunications services.[2] But could such effects apply to professionals? Could they apply to a labor-intensive professional enterprise such as higher education, and particularly to the most labor intensive part of that enterprise—teaching? Could professors be replaced by machines?

Certainly, most faculty are skeptical about the effects of new instructional technologies, if they are even aware of such technologies. At a recent professional conference, a presenter, who was an administrator, suggested that new instructional technologies will dramatically impact the delivery of instruction in higher education. A close faculty colleague of mine leaned over from his adjacent seat, shaking his head, and whispered, "I've been around too long. I've lived through a lot of so-called 'revolutions' in my time. I remember when people said that TV was going to fundamentally change education. Never happened."

If we are talking about the effects of instructional technology on the quality of education, then I agree with my colleague. If we are talking about the work lives and instructional practices of most current faculty, then, again, I agree. In their classrooms, at least, faculty are, for the

173

most part, technologically "challenged," stuck in the age of black-boards and overheads.

But if we are talking about the social relations of work between faculty and administrators, then I do not agree. Those social relations are the focus of this book—the balance of managerial discretion and professional control and the internal stratification of the academic profession. In this chapter, I examine how the use of new instructional technologies is linked to what I call the "production politics of teaching and technology." I focus on how the use of new instructional technologies is affected by, and in turn affects, the social relations of work in the academy.

First, I explore how pre-existing social relations of power affect the use of new technology. To what extent do faculty have input and managers have discretion regarding the general decision to introduce teaching technologies and the specific choice of which technology to utilize? Such decisions express pre-existing patterns of managerial prerogative and professional power that are embedded in contractual provisions. They also foreshadow future patterns of faculty control over academic work.

Second, I explore teaching technologies' effects on social relations. To what extent does the use of teaching technologies suggest the possible enskilling or deskilling of faculty, and to what extent does it involve extending managerial discretion over pedagogy (in shaping how instruction is delivered), over the curriculum (in creating a curricular arena outside the realm of traditional faculty controls), and over faculty? Using such technologies may involve faculty developing new skills. It may involve hiring new professionals with special technological skills, employees who do not become part of the collective bargaining unit. It may involve using more part-time faculty, personnel over whom managers have more control. In any of these scenarios, it may further stratify the professional work force—between full-time faculty with and without technological skills, between full and part-time faculty, and between faculty and new professionals.

Yet I hesitated to undertake a contractual analysis of provisions regarding instructional technology. It was not just the skeptical academic voice of my colleague, and of myself, that gave me pause. It was the passive academic voice and stance into which I have been socialized. Academics tend to write in a "passive" voice, and to study rather than try to effect change. Moreover, to study change properly tends to involve studying it from a distance, after it has happened. Thus, I wondered, are new instructional technologies so new that it is too soon to determine how they will affect the terms of academic labor? One reader of an early version of this chapter thought so, stating, "This paper is about five years before its time. The technologies are now developed, but not yet installed in enough places and the social relationships have not yet been worked out such that one can draw any conclusions about the effects on the professional work force."[3]

To some extent, I agree with that reader. Many colleges and universities are beginning to address, or currently working through, the issues I am analyzing. Any conclusions about the effects of new instructional technologies on the social relations of work must be provisional. It is simply too early to tell what the "ultimate" effects will be.

However, a study at this point is useful. It provides a baseline of what terms of work are found (and are absent) in the first institutions to establish provisions surrounding the use of new instructional technology. The number of contracts (seventy-eight) that have such provisions is not negligible—over one-third (37 percent) of the HECAS population. It is a larger sample than is generally available for studying terms of academic labor.

Moreover, for all of the HECAS contracts, it is possible to draw conclusions about how pre-existing social relations of power will affect the selection of new instructional technologies. Those relevant terms of labor are already in place, available for study. Indeed, recognizing the weakness of those contractual terms currently, the national faculty unions are encouraging units to negotiate more faculty involvement in decision making surrounding the decision to use, and the purchase of, new instructional technologies.

The latter point speaks to another possible reason for pause. Nearly two-thirds of HECAS contracts lack specific provisions regarding the use of instructional technology. Does that suggest the issue is not important, either for administrators or for faculty? I think not.

It is often in managers' interest to keep matters out of the contract—that generally increases their discretion. Absence from a large number of contracts does not necessarily mean lack of managerial interest in the issue. Indeed, managerial interest is strong.[4]

Managerial interest in new instructional technologies is not surprising. As institutions of higher education seek to increase their efficiency, expand their services, and minimize labor costs, new technologies for delivering instruction become more and more attractive. Moreover, if public institutions do not move in this direction of their own accord, they may be encouraged to do so by state legislatures. A recent NEA commissioned survey of education committee chairs in forty-nine states found that these key legislators were virtually unanimous in their endorsement of the expanded use of technology as a means for delivering educational instruction in higher education.[5]

Public institutions are also being encouraged to move in this direction by governors and boards. One example of this is the Western Virtual University, a venture initiated in 1995 by the Western Governors Association. The goal of the Virtual University is to offer distance (virtual?) degrees, with the aim of enrolling twenty thousand new students. The educational delivery model fits the managerial (and political) ideal—a university with no faculty, just students and administrators (to be contrasted with the faculty ideal of no administrators or students, just faculty).

Of course, distance education—for example, courses delivered through television—has been around for some time. New technologies (new to higher education and to instructional use) such as e-mail, the Internet (with the World Wide Web), fiber optic networks, and various telecommunications means for audio/video conferencing offer a broader range of possibilities not only to reach more students but also to provide for interaction between faculty and students. Yet much of the managerial and legislative enthusiasm for new instructional technologies derives from economic and enrollment contingencies. In a time of fiscal stringency, institutional managers see such technologies as a means by which to increase productivity—to increase student numbers (and tuition revenues) with current or reduced faculty numbers. State legislators see such technologies as a cost-effective means by which to meet enrollment needs and ensure access for constituents—far cheaper than building new campuses. Analysts have cautioned against the "rapture of technology," noting that such productivity gains are illusory, at least in the near future, more "potential than performance." They stress that the costs of technology have been vastly underestimated.[6]

However, the strength of their cautionary notes speaks to the extent of managerial interest.

Absence from many of the contracts, likewise, does not necessarily mean lack of union interest in the issue. Quite the contrary. From the standpoint of the national faculty unions, technology is an issue that should be negotiated. For example, in addition to focusing one of its annual higher education meetings (in 1996) on instructional technology, the NEA has adopted resolutions about such technology. One outlines various terms of work: "Education employees, including representatives of the local association, must be involved in all aspects of technology utilization, including planning, materials selection, implementation, and evaluation. . . . [N]o reduction of positions, hours, or compensation should occur as a direct or indirect result of any technological programs."[7]

The issues at hand are professional control of pedagogy and curriculum, work load, training and skills, jobs, salaries, and professional evaluation. The resolution calls for faculty involvement at each stage of decision making. Managers should not make decisions about instructional technologies without faculty counsel. The resolution calls for preparation time to plan programs or courses and to develop materials for training and for open evaluation of instructors. In other words, the institution should ensure that employees are given extra time to perform the additional work involved in planning and delivering instruction with technology. Faculty should not have to incorporate such activities on top of their current course and work load. Moreover, current faculty should be provided training to utilize new technologies. Institutions should organize and underwrite this professional development, this learning of new skills. In addition, courses and programs delivered with instructional technology should be staffed by current faculty and should be voluntary. The use of new technology should not adversely impact the number of faculty or faculty salaries. Finally, technology should not be used covertly to evaluate unsuspecting faculty. Any use of technology to evaluate faculty must be open.

A similar set of issues was addressed in the AFT's 1996 Higher Education Issues conference, the theme of which was Technology and the Changing Nature of Work. They are also identified in a 1996 report of an AFT task force on technology, *How Unions Can Harness the Technology Revolution on Campus*. The report emphasizes that technology is "changing basic employment rights" and that "the key problem is the decision making process itself. As long as the purchase and utilization of technology on campus is left primarily to management, bad decisions are sure to result."[8] The report recommends faculty and union involvement in the following areas: "Assessing the costs and benefits of major technology purchases; Providing access and training in new technologies; Maintaining educational quality; Controlling workload, compensation, jurisdiction and staff levels; and Protecting intellectual property rights in cyberspace."[9] The principles underlying these recommendations are that decisions surrounding instructional technology are academic decisions, that academics should maintain the involvement and control over course approval and staffing of distance education that they have over traditionally delivered curricula, and that distance education should be a limited source of credit hour generation. In discussing the protection of faculty and staff rights, the union's position is to resist layoffs and/or reduced staffing due to instructional technology; reduce reliance on part-time faculty in delivering distance education; ensure institutional support of training; protect faculty's privacy rights (for example, against administrative monitoring of e-mail); and provide for faculty's intellectual property rights, including control over use and rebroadcast of telecourses.

The national unions, then, firmly believe that instructional technology and the expansion of distance education have profound implications for the academic work force. They are encouraging locals to negotiate contractual language, for they believe that managers should not be left to make technology decisions without faculty involvement, outside the normal channels and processes that structure decision making regarding the mainstream curriculum. The national unions are convinced that instructional technologies are changing the social relations of professional work. Faculty unions are engaged in a production politics of teaching and technology.

Local faculty who are union representatives negotiating the contracts are already overworked, burdened by various responsibilities. In the current fiscal environment, they are fighting against reduced benefits, inadequate wage increases, and layoffs. There are only so many contractual battles that they can wage at once. In many cases they may not have devoted much thought or time to negotiating contractual provisions regarding instructional technology. In other cases they may have attempted to negotiate them, unsuccessfully. At any rate, 63 percent of contracts lack provisions about instructional technology.

Nevertheless, some locals are successfully negotiating technology issues along with a wide range of salary issues. For example, in spring 1996 Temple faculty (Temple Association of University Professionals/AFT) settled with the administration on a contract that in the area of wages provided a 12 percent salary increase over the course of the five-year contract; funds to redress salary compression for senior faculty; and 80 percent salary and compensation for participants in the 1990 strike. In the area of technology, the settlement affords the association two seats on the committee that recommends technology policy to the provost and board. In other words, faculty gained a role in developing plans and programs surrounding technology. However, work load and compensation issues for faculty involved in delivering distance education were left open for the union to negotiate as needed.[10] Some local faculty unions, then, as well as the national unions, are currently engaged in the production politics of teaching and technology.

The Literature on Production Technologies and the Social Relations of Work

The literature on technology and work is extensive. Many scholars have studied how new technologies of production impact the social relations of work and are themselves mediated by those relations. These patterns have been examined in various organizational contexts, ranging from manufacturing and retail firms, to accounting and financial services companies, to social services in governmental agencies and hospitals.[11]

Research has identified competing patterns of technology's effect on social relations and contrasting effects of different patterns of social relations on the introduction and implementation of new technologies.[12] Several schools of research theorize the interaction between technology and the social relations of work. Two polar positions are defined by deskilling and enskilling theories. In between lie socio-technical and contingency theories that dispute other theories' "technological determinism," which posits direct correlations among technology, job skills, and social relations of work. Recent work shifts the debate, challenging the field's central assumption about the link between job skills and control of the work process.

Deskilling theory holds that new technologies lead to more routinized jobs with downgraded skill requirements. Workers experience reduced degrees of freedom in exercising discretion in their work, which is increasingly defined and controlled by managers. Indeed, the aim of managers in introducing new technologies is to extend their power in the work place by reducing labor's skills and costs.[13] Technology is used by dominant classes to subjugate the working class. Pre-existing structures of social relations are reinforced and reproduced through the use of technology.[14]

By contrast, enskilling theory holds that new technologies lead to the reduction of low-skill jobs and the creation of jobs requiring greater skill and worker autonomy. Workers enjoy increased degrees of freedom and decision-making responsibilities in a postindustrial workplace with more decentralized and less hierarchical patterns of worker-manager relations. Managers may be reluctant adopters of process technologies that transform the structure of authority in the workplace, but they are ultimately unable to resist the economic advantages that come with technological advance.[15] Technology emerges and filters into organizations in ways that lie beyond the control of a particular group or class. Pre-existing power structures are transformed.

Some scholars have argued that deskilling and enskilling theories share a technological determinism: technology's introduction and its effects on job skills and social relations follow an inexorable logic.[16] Yet empirical evidence of technology's influence on organizational structure "is at best, confusing and contradictory."[17] Such discrepant findings suggest that technology's effects may be contingent.[18] Thus, socio-technical and contingency theories have been advanced. The former points to managers' strategic choices regarding technology, which are shaped by characteristics of the market, such as the extent of product standardization, production volume, and type of competition.[19] It posits a fit between environment, technology, and work organization. Contingency theory points to contingencies in the organizational and institutional context that shape the choice of technology and its effects on social relations of work.[20] In other words, technology not only can affect organizational and social structure, but also it can be structured by pre-existing social relations. The choice of technology, and the effects of technology are negotiated, in a process of "structuration." Sometimes technological change is an "occasion for [re]structuring"; sometimes not.[21]

One set of contingencies is unions, their strategies, and industrial relations. Scholars have noted unions' strategy of negotiating not choice and control of technology, but its application, hoping to ameliorate its effects and thereby focusing on matters such as retraining, job protection, and rights of displaced workers.[22] By contrast, turning labor market segmentation theory on its head, Kelley has found an inverse correlation between unionized, industrial-type internal labor markets and enskilling.[23] It may be that collective bargaining's highly codified arrangements impede reorganization of blue-collar work roles. It may also be that managers wish to create new occupations outside the bargaining unit to undermine the union's strength and for this reason will not retrain and/or enskill unionized workers.

Some recent work challenges the presumed link between job skills and control of the work process. Empirical studies of information systems' impact on the workplace suggest the rise of an "algorithmic regime" which requires an increasingly skilled work force but which also reduces workers' decision-making discretion. Workers are increasingly monitored and regulated. Their activities are reduced to Tayloristic regimens and to rules implemented and stored by computers.[24] Workers are more skilled. But they are more controlled by central managers, who by virtue of technology extend their control over workers (and mid- and low-level managers).[25]

Another dimension of what I call "managerial extension" is that managers may not acknowledge or reward existing skills. They may also impose new skill requirements on jobs that are otherwise downgraded and compartmentalized.[26] Workers have and develop many skills that are not rewarded. Job skills are neither defined nor rewarded objectively. Their definition and the connection between that definition and a reward system are socially constructed and politically negotiated. So, too, with workers' skills and their connection to autonomy. There may not be a direct, positive relationship between them. An understanding of both requires an analysis of the negotiated terms of labor.

Most work on technology and the social relations of work focus on manufacturing establishments and blue-collar occupations. There are also many studies of service operations and of clerical and white-collar jobs.[27] For the most part, however, professionals are overlooked. There is little research on the formally negotiated terms of employment between managers and professionals.[28]

Most work on technology and the social relations of work also overlooks higher education, perhaps because it is seen as a labor-intensive industry. Technology is not believed to play the same role in the production process that it does in other organizational arenas. Indeed, the labor intensive character of higher education, which inhibits technology-driven increases in productivity has been labeled its "cost disease."[29] Notwithstanding this presumed affliction, some academic services in higher education—such as libraries—have incorporated much technology into their production process and do not suffer from this condition. And many academic managers are investing in the hope that advances in communications and computer technologies will increase the institution's instructional productivity.

Deskilling, Enskilling, Managerial Extension, and Faculty

I focus on instructional technologies, in part because teaching is the principal activity of most faculty in most higher education institutions.[30] It is especially the principal activity of most faculty in unionized colleges and universities. The institutions most likely to be unionized—community colleges, comprehensive state colleges and universities, and public doctoral granting universities—are the most teaching oriented and the most disposed to reaching out to students with new technologies for course delivery.

Can theories generated by research on largely blue-collar and clerical workers be applied to professionals? Do conceptions of deskilling, enskilling, and managerial extension make sense in analyzing faculty? Faculty unions certainly believe that they do. I do as well.

Consider my first research question: To what extent do faculty have input and managers have discretion regarding the general decision to introduce teaching technologies and the specific choice of which technology to utilize? The recent history of higher education is one of managers initiating the reshaping of colleges and universities' missions, organization, and instructional programs and activities. That is precisely what restructuring is about. Recent history also provides a context in which academic managers are critical of faculty's narrow self-interest in curricular matters and of their resistance to change of any sort. Deskilling theory's thesis that managers introduce new technologies to increase their control over workers makes sense in this context. Managers will not be particularly inclined to involve faculty in choices about instructional technology.[31]

In contrast to deskilling theory, much higher education literature about governance suggests that there is "shared governance" in colleges and universities. Higher education is different. Faculty have substantial decision-making responsibilities regarding curricular matters; administrators are largely responsible for financial matters.[32] The use of instructional technology involves and implicates academic/curricular matters. Thus, managers will not have complete discretion to decide whether and which technology to use. (The tradition, if not the reality, of "shared governance" declines as one moves "down" the institutional hierarchy of higher education: faculty involvement is more likely in four- than two-year institutions.[33] Moreover, managers are likely to claim responsibility for the specific choice of technology, framing it as a financial, not an academic, matter.) Faculty will be inclined to exercise a significant role in such decisions.

Faculty unions agree, invoking traditional academic ideology to support their claim to a role in decision making surrounding instructional technology. Here lies a distinctive feature of professional settings. Faculty are as likely as any other workers to believe that unchecked, managers will make not just poor decisions about technology, but decisions that do not serve the interests of employees or clients. Unlike other workers, professionals can call upon a well-developed ideology and set of professional practices to support their claim to involvement in decision making. (Moreover, professional knowledge/ ideology provides them with arguments against the effectiveness of new technology. Contact with faculty has been found to be critical to learning, and research calls into question the effects of technology on learning.)

Now consider my second research question: To what extent does the use of teaching technologies suggest the possible enskilling or deskilling of faculty, and to what extent does it involve extending managerial discretion over pedagogy, curriculum, and faculty? What new skills are involved in utilizing instructional technology? The most obvious are skills related to the operation and maintenance of the technologies. The Internet and e-mail, for example, have many instructional functions and possibilities of which faculty are unaware or in which they are inexperienced (students are generally far more advanced "surfers" of the net than are faculty). Moreover, there are various communication skills specific to the new technologies that many if not most faculty presently lack, or need experience to develop. In addition, faculty need training, time, and assistance in developing materials for classes to be delivered with instructional technology. Such a course is not simply a new preparation, but a different kind of preparation than developing new lectures and reviewing new readings for discussion.

Enskilling theory would suggest that such skills would serve as one criteria for selecting and assigning faculty to deliver courses with instructional technology. Faculty would be (re)trained to develop new skills. Faculty with such skills would receive remuneration reflecting their professional growth, a salary increase prorated on their current salary. In effect, upgraded faculty positions would be created.

By contrast, deskilling theory would suggest that faculty delivering courses with new technology will actually be less skilled. Faculty selection will have less to do with their abilities than with managers' ability to control them. For example, managers may hire less-certified part-time teachers or uncertified teaching assistants to simply deliver pre-prepared curricula. No training for utilizing new technologies will be provided. If faculty receive additional remuneration for such work, it will be at a piece rate, comparable to remuneration for less-skilled work. Rather than upgrading faculty positions, managers will seek to reduce faculty numbers and to retain the flexibility to do so through the use of technology. For example, a taped course may be utilized again and again without utilizing the same faculty member—less-certified instructors may be employed to deliver the material and interact with students. In effect, faculty as a work force will be downgraded.

Enskilling theory makes sense in professional settings. Professions are based on expertise, on knowledge bases that expand and require new skills. By contrast, deskilling theory is less obviously relevant to professional workers. Yet colleges and universities are ripe for deskilling. Managers may utilize increasing numbers of less-certified faculty—for example, part-time faculty, who are more likely than full-timers to have bachelor's and master's rather than doctoral degrees. Managers may hire reduced numbers of fully certified professionals.

They may diminish faculty's role and the scope of their expertise, delimiting instructors to classroom teaching and challenging and supplanting their expertise in curriculum planning, development, and delivery systems. In each of the above respects, deskilling is a concept relevant to faculty as a work force.

Consider, now, the second half of the second question, the issue of faculty autonomy and of managerial control over pedagogy, curriculum, and faculty. How can new instructional technologies affect faculty's autonomy and managers' control over pedagogy, curriculum, and faculty? If pedagogy is in large part a matter of how instruction is delivered, then obviously choices about whether to utilize instructional technology and about which technology to utilize, impact pedagogy. Faculty's collective input and control regarding these decisions is in part a proxy of their autonomous control of the curriculum. So, too, is their individual choice about whether to use new instructional technologies. To the extent that managers may direct faculty to utilize such technology in delivering courses, they have reduced faculty's autonomy. Similarly, the use of instructional technology raises the possibility of a range of new duties. For example, consultation with students may no longer be solely through office hours. It may take place through e-mail. And as technology opens up the potential for increased numbers of students per course, at a distance, there may be need for faculty to visit various sites. To the extent that managers identify special duties for faculty utilizing instructional technology, that are above and beyond those normally required, faculty autonomy has decreased. Technology also raises the possibility of increased oversight of faculty. Managers may monitor e-mail communications, the amount of time devoted to technologically supported interactions. Technology enables managers to observe course delivery itself without notifying faculty (for example, viewing tapes and/or transmissions). Shutting the classroom door may no longer mean that faculty are alone with their classes.

Deskilling theory would suggest that new technology will increase managerial control of the work process, of faculty and of the curriculum, reducing faculty autonomy. In these matters, managerial extension theory is consistent with deskilling theory, By contrast, enskilling theory would suggest that new technology expands workers' job autonomy and their discretionary control of the curriculum.

But what of the ownership and use of the materials that are developed? Who decides whether the tape will be (re)broadcast, how many times it can be used, and by whom (that is, who is the instructor of record)? In these regards, faculty may be somewhat different from other workers. They want control not only over their work process but over their work product. That makes for an interesting amendment to deskilling, enskilling, and managerial extension theories, when they are applied to professional settings.

These are not merely abstract academic suppositions or extrapolations. They are the subject of concrete negotiation. For example, in fall 1996, most such matters were negotiated in a contract that in many ways sets the standard for national unions' positions regarding distance education—that of Belleville Area Community College (the previous contract—1993–1996—of which is featured in subsequent pages of this chapter). The new contract ensures that instruction will be live and interactive; use will be voluntary (the college wanted to make it involuntary and to make new hires subject to dismissal if they refused to use it); use will not result in reduced numbers of full-time faculty; training will be provided and paid for; no extra duties will be assigned for distance-learning courses; courses will not be taped without the faculty member's consent; and intellectual property belongs to the faculty member.

At any rate, I pursue the issues of deskilling, enskilling, and managerial extension in an analysis of contractual provisions surrounding instructional technology. Instructional technology matters are only recently beginning to be addressed in many contracts.[34] The findings must be read as provisional, as providing a useful baseline. Nevertheless, the seventy-eight clauses in HECAS offer useful insights into the contractual parameters of managerial control and faculty autonomy in the area of instructional technology.

The Contracts

In order to identify contractual provisions, I searched HECAS for references to technology, to courses using telecommunications, to distance education, and to intellectual property such as tapes, which are products of instructional technology.[35] There are seventy-eight contracts that have provisions speaking to instructional technology. There is not a dependent association between the incidence of such provisions and institutional type (x2=2.8): 51 clauses are in the contracts of two-year colleges, eighteen in those of four-year institutions, and nine in those of technical colleges (see table 5).

TABLE 5.1
INSTRUCTIONAL TECHNOLOGY IN THE CONTRACTS

	Two-year	Tech	Four-year	Total
Provision	51	9	18	78
Deciding to use	3	6	3	12*
Training	7	0	2	9
Skills/hiring	2	0	0	2
Prorated pay	0	1	1	2
Piece-rate pay	20	2	4	26
Displacement	11	2	3	16**
New duties	9	1	1	11***
Course scheduling	10	1	2	13****
Intell property	13	1	3	17

* In eight cases (five of which are in technical college contracts), these provisions are in the management rights section of the contracts.
** In five of these sixteen cases (all in community college contracts) technological change is a justification for displacement.
*** In two of these cases the provision indicates that there will be no additional duties.
**** In three of these cases the provisions indicate that normal procedures will be followed; in eight other cases there is provision for considerable faculty input.

Deciding to Use, and Selecting Specific Technology

Of the seventy-eight contracts that refer in some way to instructional technology, twelve have clauses regarding the general decision to utilize instructional technology or the particular choice of technology. Of the twelve, eight are phrases in the "management-rights" section of the contracts, according managers complete discretion to determine, among other things, "utilization of technology" (five of these provisions are in the contracts of technical colleges). The four contracts that provide for faculty involvement all speak to the general decision to utilize. For example:

> The District shall consult with the Association, upon request, on any proposed changes in the use of electronic and technological devices if the use impacts on working conditions. Such consultation shall occur during the decision making process at a time that will allow the

Association input into the eventual District decision. (San Joaquin Delta Community College, Article 6.9.13.b)

The Guild shall be advised of changes in the telecourse delivery system adopted by the District which will result in work load increases. Such increases will not be implemented until negotiated between the Guild and the District. (Glendale Community College, Appendix H)

In two cases, provisions also address the specific choice of technology, but through different mechanisms. One contract maintains collective faculty control over the use of technology for the delivery of particular courses.

Utilization of technology for established courses as defined in subsection 1.a. above and its impact on each course offering as it relates to bargaining unit work shall be presented to local and State Meet and Discuss for its approval. Unless approved by local and State Meet and Discuss, the proposed utilization of technology will not occur. New courses to be offered by utilization of technology must have the course approved through the University curriculum process prior to submission to the procedure identified in subsection 3.a. above. (Pennsylvania State System of Higher Education, Article 7.H.3)

A second contract provides for departmental control of decision making.

As state funding for higher education continues to be reduced, it is ever more critical that new ways be found to carry out teaching and scholarly activities in ways that make best possible use of available resources. In our judgment, decisions regarding new instructional formats, curricular reforms, and new ways of using technology for instructional and scholarly purposes are best made at the school and departmental level. . . . For the 1994–95 academic year, there shall be established for each member of the collective bargaining unit a sum of $1400 to support undergraduate instruction. These monies, held in a separate departmental account, may be used for such purposes as the purchase of equipment, software, instructional materials. . . . Annually, each department shall forward to the Provost, through the appropriate dean, a report of expenditures from this account. . . . In addition the Instructional Equipment Fund, administered by the Provost, $136,000 shall be available for the 1994–1995 academic year for the purchase of equipment to support teaching and scholarship. The total of these monies shall be expended according to established procedures whereby departments prepare their requests, these are reviewed and put in priority order by the deans and directors, and allocations made by the Provost. (Southern Oregon State College, Letter of Agreement)

Southern Oregon State College's provision is particularly notable in at least two regards. First, it refers explicitly to the financial impetus for utilizing instructional technology. Second, it decentralizes the choice process to the production unit (department) level, and even to the individual faculty member. That is an extremely strong example of extending faculty's control over their work—as enskilling theory suggests. Of course, it is also an extremely rare provision.

In short, traditional academic ideology has not been translated into the contracts. There is very little evidence of contractual provision for faculty involvement either in the general decision to utilize instructional technology or in the specific decision of which technology to purchase. Only 5 percent of those contracts that speak to instructional technology have any provision for faculty involvement in decisions to utilize and purchase new technologies. Although nine other contracts refer to future study/negotiation of instructional technology issues, only one of them (Belleville Area Community College) refers to the choice to utilize instructional technology.

The Telecommunications Committee shall be formed consisting of 5 faculty members appointed by the BAC AAUP/AFT President, and 5 administrators appointed by the College President. The charge of the Telecommunications Committee is to research and explore the development of telecommunications such as video tapes and disks, television broadcasting (other than that now included in the Memorandum of Understanding as [sic] Telecourses), fiber optics and other modes of electronic image and/or information transfer as they relate to instructional and educational uses. The Committee shall specifically investigate matters of instructors' rights and the academic quality of such methods of instruction using electronic image and/or information transfer in higher education classrooms. (Section 3.16)

The eight other provisions (which refer to existing committees studying technology issues or to the future negotiation of such issues) address the displacing effects of technological changes (SUNY), class size and work-load credit (Los Angeles Community College System, Northcentral Technical College, and Youngstown State University), pay and ownership (Oakland Community College, Oakland University), and general contractual language (Kirtland Community College, Pennsylvania State System of Higher Education).

It might be argued that for those seventy-eight contracts with provisions regarding instructional technology there is no need for clauses about the utilization and selection of technology. The choices have already been made. Technologies have already been adopted. Perhaps. However, there are decisions to be made beyond the original adoption choices. Maintenance, the need to upgrade, and the emergence of new products all make investment in and selection of technology ongoing decision-making processes.

For those contracts that do not mention instructional technology, it might be argued that in the absence of contractual language, past-practices clauses may apply. Such clauses invoke the precedent of all past policies and activities not covered in the contract. However, as noted in chapter 1, these clauses are limited in number (48) and especially in scope. More relevant is contractual language that establishes "management rights." Simply searching on the terms *management rights, board rights*, and *rights of the board* yields 128 provisions. Many of these are general, sweeping statements. Many others specify areas of management rights as well as advancing management's general claims. A common reference is to "means and methods of instruction." Such blanket provisions reserve broad rights to management.

Faculty Job Skills and Autonomy: Training

There is little evidence that institutions are contractually committed to offer training in instructional technology so that faculty may upgrade their skills. Only nine such clauses are in HECAS (seven community colleges and two four-year institutions). That is but 12 percent of those contracts that mention instructional technology. Not very strong support for the idea that technology leads to enskilling.

Provisions range from in-services on television presentation (Western Michigan University) to more general orientations and training programs.

> Prior to receiving an assignment of a television course, a mandatory orientation session must be attended by the faculty member. (Schoolcraft College, Appendix R)

During each of the three years of this Agreement, the College shall provide $10,000 to be used for educating faculty members and librarians in the use of new technology in their disciplines. (Rhode Island School of Design, Article 14)

The administration agrees to be mindful and supportive of the faculty's professional development needs and to review those areas faculty may from time to time indicate and in which changing technology necessitates an upgrade of faculty skills and techniques. (Belleville Area Community College, Section 5.1).[36]

The College will develop or adopt a formal training program, which will include an evaluation component, to prepare selected faculty to become competent in offering instruction in a telecommunications mode. The first three faculty seeking to teach in this mode, The Dean of Academic Affairs, and the Media Specialist shall form a committee to develop this program; the program shall be reviewed and updated periodically. Successful completion of this training shall qualify a faculty member to teach a telecommunications course and shall count toward regular vertical and horizontal salary advancement. A faculty member will have an option under the College's existing faculty continuing education program of enrolling in other institutions to obtain additional knowledge or training in telecommunications. (Spoon River College, Article 4,H)

An Employee who, at the request of the District, undertakes and completes the appropriate training, as determined by the District, to utilize the new state fiber optics system and who designs course curriculum suitable for such technique of instruction, will be paid the sum of $500.00 upon the successful completion of such training and course design. (Iowa Valley Community College, Article 11.C.6)

Only two contracts designate monies for such activities (there may, of course, be campuses that provide such support for training but do not lock themselves into such a financial commitment with a contractual clause). Yet the financial commitment is minimal compared to the technology's purchase and maintenance. Moreover, many training activities would be virtually revenue neutral, simply taking the time of technology professionals who are already employed.

There are a large number (144) of *general* training provisions in the contracts, for professional development leaves and activities.[37] Such provisions perpetuate some professional perquisites that predate faculty unions. That may partially explain the relative absence of training provisions specific to instructional technology, for faculty could take professional development leaves and during that time gain some expertise in the use of instructional technology. Yet this possibility is virtually never mentioned in the contracts, even in those contracts that address other issues surrounding instructional technology.

Faculty Job Skills and Autonomy: Skills and Hiring

In selecting and/or screening faculty to deliver courses with instructional technology, is any consideration given to faculty's skills? If current faculty are utilized, are they selected on the basis of whether they have certain skills or certification? If new faculty are hired, are their skill levels and certification lower, similar to, or higher than current faculty?

Only two contracts mention any selection or screening criteria (those few contracts that accord current faculty priority in teaching such courses make no mention of qualifications of any kind). In one case (Gogebic Community College), seniority is the basis upon which selection is determined. In the other case (Belleville Area Community College) the contract invokes standards in a professional, peer-review sense.

Changes in minimum standards for instructional areas will be made in consultation with the faculty in the affected area of instruction. Proposed changes, or a request to review current standards will first be given to the faculty of the affected instructional area by the appropriate Dean. The faculty will have 10 working days to respond in writing to the appropriate Dean. This 10 day review process shall be repeated in the event that the original proposal is revised as a result of the comments received from faculty during the review period. Such written response will accompany the recommendation of the administration. The proposed minimum Standards shall then be reviewed by the Executive Committee of the AAUP/IFT Chapter and the Executive Committee's recommendations shall then be taken into consideration by the administration. If there is disagreement between the administration and the AAUP/IFT Executive Committee regarding the proposed minimum standards, the Board of Trustees shall be informed of the AAUP/IFT Executive Committee's objections. Final authority for minimum standards rests with the Board of Trustees. (Section 3.15)

The minimum standards clause is in the general section of the contract dealing with instructional technology. It is followed by a clause discussing a telecommunications committee (discussed earlier in this chapter), charged, among other things, to investigate the academic quality of instructional technology methods, one of the few such references in any of the seventy-eight contracts.

Upgraded skills, then, are not contractually inscribed in college and universities' personnel practices and systems. Indeed, to the extent that managers use (less-certified) part-time faculty to deliver courses with instructional technology, they are "deskilling" the faculty work force, for part-time faculty have lower levels of degree certification than full-timers.

The findings also speak to the increased discretion that managers enjoy in this emergent and growing area of the curriculum. As with the hiring and firing of part-time faculty, discussed in chapter 4, there are virtually no contractual limits on managerial discretion having to do with hiring criteria. Technology expands managers' flexibility not by enhancing their control over faculty in traditional curricula, but by enabling them to develop new curricular areas and hire new faculty outside the purview of traditional contractual and academic/faculty constraints.

Faculty Job Skills and Autonomy: Remuneration

The largest number of provisions (twenty-eight) regarding instructional technology deal with pay. That is 36 percent of contracts that speak to instructional technology. Still, if faculty are being enskilled as employees, they are not, for the most part, being rewarded for it as professionals.

Of the twenty-eight provisions that specify some remuneration, only one provides pay that is prorated according to the faculty member's salary. And in that case, the calculation serves only as an upper limit on compensation.

> Additional compensation for the development of courses offered via technology will be locally determined, but shall not exceed 1/24 of the FACULTY MEMBER'S academic year salary per credit hour. Additional compensation for the delivery of courses offered via technology will be locally determined, but shall not exceed 1/24 of the FAC-

ULTY MEMBER'S academic year salary per credit hour per selection/site/linkup per semester. (Pennsylvania State System of Higher Education, Article 7.H)

One other contract (North Central Technical College) offers first time ITV instructors "an additional 2 percent per period per week" (Article 3.E,8).

The remaining twenty-six provisions offer faculty variations of piece and flat rates, comparable to pay scales for part-time faculty. Most commonly, the contracts provide a flat rate per student or per credit hour: in other words, the prorating is by student, not by faculty member's salary. If faculty are being professionally enskilled, in two-thirds (66 percent) of the contracts that specify additional remuneration, faculty are being paid at piece rates.

Of the twenty-eight provisions, twenty are in two-year, five in four-year, and three in technical institutions. That pretty much mirrors the HECAS distribution of institutional type. There is *not* a dependent association between the incidence of salary provisions and institutional type ($x2=1.11$). That is surprising. The prevailing view is that conditions are more professionalized in four- than in two-year settings.

Faculty Job Skills and Autonomy: Displacement

About one-fifth (20.5 percent) of contracts that address instructional technology have provisions regarding the displacement of faculty by technology. Yet, nearly one-third (five) of these sixteen contracts mention displacement caused by the use of new technology—"technological change"—as a *justification* for reductions in faculty numbers and retrenchment of faculty. Can faculty be replaced by technology? In these contracts, the answer is yes. Indeed, to do so is a managerial prerogative.

> The parties recognize reduction of faculty positions may become necessary as a result of major decline in enrollments, technological changes, or lack of financial resources. These conditions may result in curtailments or elimination of departments, programs, disciplines or courses as determined by the Board. (Linn-Benton Community College, Article 10)

All of these provisions are in the contracts of community colleges, where full-time faculty positions appear to be most vulnerable.

Only eleven contracts, then, have clauses that in some way protect faculty from displacement caused by the use of new technology. Such protections take various forms and are of differential force: limits on course type or numbers, or on class size for curriculum using instructional technology (five contracts); statements forbidding layoff due to use of instructional technology (four contracts); limits on the use of instructors other than bargaining unit members (three contracts); and in one case (Alexandria Technical College, Article 6, Section 11) a ban on the use of instructional technology to deliver courses during a strike (the numbers add up to more than eleven because some contracts had more than one condition).

Several of the conditions I have coded as limiting the use of technology actually provide managers with considerable discretion. Consider Jackson Community College's contractual provision: "The college may operate temporary (defined as 12 months or less) or experimental courses or programs outside the terms of this Agreement when a regular instructional faculty member is not involved. In such cases, however, the President of the Association will be notified before new programs are implemented" (Article 13).

Managers can bypass the agreement and the unit, utilizing nonunit, part-time faculty. They need only notify the association that they are running such "temporary" programs.

Two other contracts that address instructors (Alexandria Technical College, Los Angeles Community College System) take the restriction one step further. They indicate that the college may utilize part-time, nonunit faculty *only* if no regular (unit member) faculty will perform the work. The union aim is to keep the work within the bargaining unit. Yet if such work expands beyond the capacity of current bargaining unit faculty to staff such courses on overload, then there is no restriction on hiring increased percentages of part-time faculty. Future full-time positions may be foregone.

Similarly, the conditions forbidding layoff due to use of instructional technology provide managers with considerable flexibility. The strongest of the clauses (Pennsylvania State System of Higher Education) indicates that technology will not be used to reduce, consolidate, or eliminate faculty positions. Yet that does not prevent managers from investing resources in the expansion of instructional delivery through technology in ways that inhibit the future hiring of regular faculty and reduce regular faculty members' proportion of instructional personnel. Two other clauses (Alexandria Technical College, Gogebic Community College) indicate that telecommunications systems shall not cause a current faculty member to lose work. Of course, such cause is difficult to demonstrate and again does not address future personnel patterns. Indeed, Gogebic's clause, from Article 17, reads: "A telecommunications system shall not cause the layoff, replacement, displacement, or reduction of any faculty member's work hours. This provision shall not be construed to prohibit replacement or reduction through attrition, nor will this provision have any bearing on layoffs or reductions not related to the operation of the system." The fourth clause forbidding layoff (Spoon River College, Article 4,H) states that it is "[T]he College's current intention that the new telecommunications program not result in any layoffs of bargaining unit members." Intentions, of course, are often different than outcomes and are more difficult to demonstrate. Such provisions, then, are limited in their limitations on managerial flexibility. They speak of the unions' concern that faculty will be replaced by technology. At the same time, they point to management's ability to reconfigure the work force through the introduction of technology.

The strongest professional constraints lie in clauses limiting course type, numbers, or class size for instructional technology curricula.

Faculty members who agree to have their course(s) taped on College premises shall: 1) be the instructor of record whenever the tape is used for off-campus instruction; . . . 3) have the tape used for off-campus instruction only; 4) use the tape for no more than 2 overload credit sections in any given semester; 5) be able to utilize the tape for off-campus instruction for a maximum period of two-years. (Oakland Community College, Article 2.1,G)

Up to three computer-based and/or media-based courses may be developed and/or taught on an experimental basis during each academic year of this Agreement, providing the faculty member who teaches each course receives regular workload credit for it the first time it is offered, and providing further that the Administration and the Association reach agreement on workload credit for the course prior to it being offered a second time. . . . With the exception of the courses provided for above, there shall be no media-based or computer-based courses offered at the University for academic credit during the term of this agreement. (Youngstown State University, Article 13.1)

In fact, NEA officials have recommended addressing displacement concerns "through specific language and articles relating to class size."[38] In other words, do not allow instructional technology to expand to such an extent that it becomes a threat to the traditionally delivered curriculum. Belleville Area Community College's contract sets a maximum of seventy-five students (Alexandria Technical College's contract notes that instructional television can be used to increase class size, but that more than three sites cannot be used).[39] Jackson Community College's contract takes restrictions much further:

No credit-bearing courses taught by non-traditional methods (television, computer aided instruction, video tape lecture, or any other electronic or other media) will be offered without the approval of the department members involved in teaching in that subject area in consultation with the Department Chairperson. . . . Class size in such courses will be limited to the class size for a regularly taught section of the course unless the instructor(s) and the dean agree otherwise. (Article 5)

Departmental faculty are accorded discretion to control what courses in which instructional technology can be used. As with the Southern Oregon State College contract cited earlier in the decision to use technology, the Jackson contract is distinctive for a unionized setting in decentralizing control to the departmental level. A mechanism more common to unionized settings is found in the contract of the Pennsylvania State System of Higher Education, which lodges the decision in local and state meet and discuss processes.

Faculty Autonomy and Managerial Control: Job Autonomy

One dimension of faculty's job autonomy is that managers only define in a limited way what faculty's responsibilities are—for example, number of classes and office hours. If more duties are defined for faculty utilizing instructional technology, *and* if those duties are layered on top of existing duties, I take that to be evidence of reduced faculty autonomy. (It is also "speeding up" faculty, asking them to do more without reducing their responsibilities in some other domain.)

Only eleven provisions—14 percent of those provisions that deal with instructional technology—address the duties of instructors who utilize such technology. All but two of these detail special responsibilities that lie above and beyond those of all faculty (one contract indicates that there are no duties above and beyond the norm for regular faculty; another specifies that instructors are not responsible for maintaining the equipment). In two cases, the extra duty is simply to keep up to date with or to utilize available technology in the field. A third contract offers much more detail along these lines. "The instructor shall keep well informed with particular attention to the latest developments of his [sic] subject area and teaching technology. . . . Each instructor shall prepare yearly an up-to-date outline reflecting changes, if any, for the Dean of Instruction's office" (Kirtland Community College, Article 10).

In six cases the extra duties include more consultation with students. In other cases, further responsibilities refer to syllabi, exams, review sessions, and the offices that run the telecourse programs. For example:

> Instructors are expected to maintain one student conference hour per week for each hour of credit in the telecourse. These Telecourse student conference hours are in addition to the normal office hours and are in addition to the regularly scheduled mid-term and final examinations for telecourses. (Belleville Area Community College, Section 3.14)

> Office hours posted pursuant to Article IX, Paragraph D, shall be noted in the Telecourse syllabi. Faculty members teaching telecourses further agree that they will make themselves available by other appropriate means, at times other than the stated office hours, to telecourse students who have difficulty contacting their instructor, such as by returning phone calls to students who contact the department office. (County College of Morris, Letter of Intent)

> A special format syllabus shall be developed for course use. . . . The instructor must communicate with the students by telephone or mail at least twice monthly (costs shall be borne by the College). A minimum of three review sessions shall be scheduled during the semester. . . . Tests will be made available within one week following the review session. The student shall have the next week to take the test. Grades must be available to the student (through the Learning Resource Center) within one week after tests have been taken. (Schoolcraft College, Appendix R)

Responsibilities include: ... Assisting in the development and application of appropriate support, e.g., roll-ins, graphics, computers, telephone, FAX, etc. Conducting pre- and post-class consultation with the media production staff. Establishing schedule times for office hours, site visits (if needed), student consultation, testing, grading, course evaluation and continuous contact with the offices of Telecourse Programs and Media Services. (Western Michigan University, Article 30)

The detail of the above provisions points to faculty's reduced autonomy when they utilize new instructional technology. Such use is accompanied by a range of additional responsibilities. It is true that only a limited number of contracts specify additional duties. Yet those few clauses highlight demands on faculty time that will materialize whether or not managers and contracts detail them. Using instructional technology does *not* decrease the burden of faculty labor, as enskilling theory suggests. Quite the contrary, technology increases faculty's burden. It may also, as in these cases, reduce faculty's autonomy, further subjecting them to managerial control, as deskilling and managerial extension theory suggest.

A second dimension of faculty's job autonomy has to do with faculty's freedom in the classroom. Faculty define what goes on behind closed doors. Moreover, when faculty close the classroom doors, they are on their own. New technologies can pose a threat to that freedom, enabling detailed monitoring and/or surveillance of workers' activities. Indeed, the NEA has passed a resolution that speaks to such concerns: "The evaluation of education employees in any technological program should be conducted openly."[40]

Four contracts have provisions regarding surveillance. For example:

The presence of cameras, tape recorders or similar recording devices during the meeting of a class shall be subject to the permission of the instructor . . . (Schoolcraft College, Article 3, Section 10)

All monitoring or observation of the work performance of an instructor shall be conducted openly with his/her full cooperation. The use of eavesdropping, closed circuit television, public address, or audio systems, and similar surveillance devices shall be strictly prohibited. (Jackson Community College, Article 10)

These contracts articulate the unions' concerns about technology. They point to what is possible in terms of managers' use of technology. The relative absence of such provisions means that management has contractual discretion in using technology to monitor and evaluate faculty more closely. Obviously, it is not evidence that managers are technologically watching or spying on faculty. Yet the very nature of the technology means that it is easier for managers to gather and review data regarding faculty's teaching activities. That is precisely the argument of managerial extension theory.

Faculty Autonomy and Managerial Control: Discretionary Control of the Curriculum

I operationalize "discretionary control of the curriculum" as control of course approval and assignment/scheduling (hiring and other personnel matters were discussed earlier). To what extent are faculty involved and to what extent do managers have discretion to act as they wish?

Such provisions are found in thirteen contracts. In three cases, clauses indicate that "normal" or "regular" procedures are to be used for course approval or scheduling. Those procedures are not specified. But the point is that in these cases technologically delivered curricula are neutral in terms of faculty involvement and managerial discretion in curricular matters.

Two contracts have "deem clauses" that accord management full discretion in these (and other) matters. What is most important about each of these clauses is the particular managerial office that is accorded authority. For the University of Northern Iowa, authority is vested in the university's continuing education program. For Moraine Valley Community College, authority lies with the Division of Alternative Learning. Both cases foreshadow the emergence of offices outside the purview of traditionally faculty governance, or at least the existence of such offices that will house the emergent activity of delivering curriculum with instructional technology.

In eight contracts, there is provision for substantial faculty input. In four cases, that input extends to review and even control. The strongest of these are provisions discussed in the subsection on displacement: union efforts to limit the number of instructional technology courses, particularly in existing areas of the curriculum and union efforts to ensure that technologically delivered courses are staffed by bargaining-unit members. (Yet these are the exceptions to the rule of managerial discretion by default in the contracts. Against these few examples of faculty maintaining their discretion over technologically delivered curriculum are the overwhelming proportion of contracts—83 percent of contracts that deal with instructional technology—in which such provision is lacking.)

There are few examples of managers explicitly expanding their discretion over the curriculum in the area of instructional technology. Technologically delivered curriculum does not impinge much on current faculty's discretionary control of the curriculum that they currently teach. Rather, managerial discretion is extended to a curricular realm in which current faculty are in some sense peripheral.

Another dimension of curricular control explored here has to do with the development versus the delivery of curricula. Traditionally, faculty have had responsibility for developing as well as delivering curricula. Are these roles separated in technologically delivered curriculum? Is faculty's function reduced to the delivery of curriculum that by virtue of its technological dimensions or complexity is developed elsewhere, by others who are outside the bargaining unit? There is no contractual evidence of such separation. Of six contracts that speak to course design and development, two suggest no separation of roles and four point to additional time or pay for developing a course. There is no indication that these faculty will not also teach the course.

The one type of provision that foreshadows such separation (supporting the deskilling thesis) is found in only a few contracts in clauses regarding ownership (see my ensuing discussion on ownership). A couple of such clauses, as in the case of Cuyahoga Community College, indicate that faculty who develop a course which is taped are guaranteed to be the instructors of record for that course for a certain amount of time (in the case of the Cuyahoga contract, it is the first two summers). After that period, and in the case of all other contracts, the college can utilize any other faculty, including part-timers, to deliver curriculum developed by someone else—that is, current full-time faculty. In such cases, instruction is deskilled to consist simply of delivering a course developed by someone else. Current full-time faculty are not being "deskilled," but the faculty work force is as a collectivity.

Faculty Autonomy and Managerial Control: Ownership

Thus far, I have analyzed faculty autonomy and managerial control in regards to the work process. In this section, I focus on the work product. In this regard, professional settings may be distinctive. There is an expectation on the part of faculty that their creative insight and effort are essential to producing intellectual property and that they should therefore own the product. The emergence of new technologies complicate an already complicated issue. Faculty claims to royalties for intellectual products such as textbooks are relatively clear, but sometimes there are limitations on whether faculty can use such texts in their own classes, directly profiting from the use of their curricular materials.[41] Moreover, faculty generally cannot make money from the curricula they deliver if it is in the form of class notes or collections of readings that they require (such matters are governed not by contract but by legal rulings). New technology introduces a different sort of intellectual property and curricular possibility—software and tapes of faculty lectures and courses. Ownership claims are far less clear in these areas.

There are seventeen contracts with provisions related to ownership. Only remuneration is the subject of more references in the seventy-eight contracts that address instructional technology. Nevertheless, that still represents less than one-quarter (22 percent) of such contracts.

All but three of the seventeen references to ownership address the specific issue of whether and to what extent the faculty member or the institution owns the rights to curricular materials created for technologically delivered curricula (typically, tapes). In those three cases, contracts speak only to issues of rebroadcast and use. In addition to the Cuyahoga Community College contract provision noted above, Oakland Community College's contract indicates that tapes may be utilized for off-campus instruction for a maximum of two years. The contract for Minnesota Community Colleges states that tapes may be reused only with the instructor's permission. Such limits not only protect faculty's right to control the use of their intellectual products, but they represent a measure of discretionary control over the curriculum and an effort to restrict the expansion of technologically delivered curriculum in ways that could lead to the displacement or reduction of current/future faculty numbers. With these ownership provisions, unions seek to minimize and marginalize technologically delivered curriculum. Yet the clauses are few. And even in these few cases managers retain the discretion to utilize part-time, nonbargaining-unit faculty to tape and deliver such courses on the "periphery," beyond the control of current faculty, and beyond the scope of most contracts.

Of the fourteen contracts that speak to who owns the intellectual property of technologically delivered curriculum, four include provisions about use similar to those discussed above. Alexandria Technical College's contract requires that the faculty member consent to rebroadcast of their tapes and gives them "the authority to erase or to have erased any video tape of his or her telecast instruction." (Article 6,9.3) The Florida State University System's contract states that any use of instructional technology materials "outside of the employee's assignment" "shall be the subject of a written agreement between the employee and the university" (Article 9.8.d). The Pennsylvania State System of Higher Education's contract indicates that the future use and disposition of taped materials shall be subject to an agreement by the faculty member and the university. Western Michigan University's contract is quite detailed, offering the initial instructor "first consideration to administer the re-broadcast of this course," or if he or she declines, "a royalty of 10% of the total tuition received from all students based on the continuing education tuition rate" (Articles 30.2.5.1, 30.2.5.2). The contract also ensures the instructor the right to "request that the course be reviewed by the Office of Telecourse Programs for either substantial revision or removal from circulation" and that they have first right of revision (Article 30.2.5.4).[42]

Most of the ownership provisions (ten) deal with "tapes" as part of separate intellectual property articles (rather than being discussed along with other aspects of instructional technology). Two considerations are significant in determining ownership and in governing use and reuse of telecourse tapes. The first is whether the product of instructional technology was created with institutional resources. In all ten cases, if materials were created without substantial institutional resources or release time, the copyright belongs to the faculty member. There is variation among contracts in cases when substantial institutional resources were utilized: in three of the ten contracts, the college is given joint ownership. If the materials were created as specific "work for hire" (at the institution's direct request), then in eight of ten contracts the college owns (at least jointly) the copyright.

The two exceptions to this pattern point to a second consideration regarding use, evidenced in the contract provision that follows:

> If such above described books, teaching aids, or other material [tapes are specified in the previous clause] is developed by a unit member or members in conjunction with and while participating in College assigned or undertaken projects authorized or directed by the College, or using College staff or facilities, the said unit member or members shall retain the ownership of the material, subject to the following rights and privileges of the College: (1) the College shall have the right to use the said material in connection with its academic programs or in an exchange program in return for the use of academic material from other academic institutions; (2) the College shall be reimbursed to the extent of its contribution in salaries paid, laboratory or other equipment used, space provided, secretarial or other services. Any profits, royalties, or commissions accruing for said material shall, after the aforesaid reimbursement to the College, remain the property of the unit member or members, exclusively. (Salem Community College, Article 7)

Northampton County Area Community College's contract has a similar clause. Two additional contracts (those of Brookdale Community College and Flathead Valley Community College) have reimbursement clauses. Three have provisions enabling Colleges to review and utilize materials copyrighted to faculty. For example:

> Intellectual property created by the employee in the fulfillment of the employee's normal duties and responsibilities under this collective bargaining agreement is presumed to belong to the employee for proprietary or marketing purposes outside of the college but is available to the college for internal review and for review by external agencies regulating the college. (Belleville Area Community College, Section 17.3)

> The College shall have non-transferable rights, in perpetuity, to unrestricted use within the College of all inventions, discoveries or writings made or authored by members of the staff or faculty while under contract to the College. (Brookdale Community College, Article 5.4)

In other words, the negotiation concerns not only the ownership but also the use of the instructional materials. Managers seek to retain the college's right to use faculty's property within the institution.

In those contracts with ownership clauses, faculty simply have extended existing property claims to include instructional technology materials.[43] It is not that faculty have greater ownership claims over instructional technology products than over other forms of intellectual property. For the most part, however, such terms of ownership are undefined—over three-quarters (78 percent) of those contracts that speak to instructional technology do *not* define property claims to instructional technology materials. And, surprisingly, they are no more likely to be found in the contracts of four- than of two-year schools (x2=.67). (Prevailing assumptions about expertise and employment rights in the two sectors would suggest that intellectual property provisions would be more prominent in the contracts of universities than of community colleges.)

Discussion

Instructional technology is a relatively new area of negotiation. Still, a little more than one-third of the HECAS contracts have provisions regarding instructional technology. These provisions offer insight into how pre-existing social relations are shaping the use and choice of technology. They also offer a baseline for understanding how instructional technology in turn is shaping social relations in the academy between faculty and managers.

Overall, I found far more support for deskilling than for enskilling theory. However, the strongest findings are that the contracts do *not* suggest that enskilling is taking place. Contractual evidence of deskilling was more indirect. I did not find support for managerial extension theory—which posits that workers gain skills, but managers gain control. I interpret the contracts to suggest that faculty are being professionally "marginalized" (or that they are contributing to their own marginalization), bypassed by technological developments in the production process. For example, there is little contractual provision for decision making surrounding the general determination to utilize instructional technology and the specific choice of technology. Of those few clauses, more provide discretion to managers than accord input to faculty. In this curricular area of increasing importance, contracts do not ensure that current faculty will be consulted.

Among the provisions that address training and skill requirements, there is virtually no support for enskilling theory. There are few contracts with training provisions. Only one addresses skill requirements for faculty selection. Only one provides prorated pay for faculty who utilize instructional technology. There is no contractual evidence that faculty positions are being upgraded, that new skills are being built into various personnel and incentive structures.

However, to the extent that there is *de*skilling, it is *not* primarily of current faculty. For the most part, use of instructional technology is not an involuntary assignment. Thus, training may not be provided, new skills may not be required, and additional pay may be at piece rate. But current faculty are not required to endure these deskilled conditions of work. Instead, contracts allow for part-time faculty to be hired, leading to the deskilling of the instructional work force in a collective sense.

Among the provisions that address faculty autonomy and managerial control there is again no support for enskilling, although there is some support for deskilling. There is no evidence of faculty's increased job autonomy in utilizing instructional technology. Quite the contrary. There is some contractual evidence that additional duties are associated with such work. There is little evidence that faculty gain increased discretionary control of the curriculum, shaping work load and course assignment. Neither is there much direct evidence of managers increasing their discretionary control. Instead, managers' increased span of control is realized by virtue of the absence of provisions in the contracts and by virtue of the fact that part-timers may be utilized to deliver curriculum with instructional technology. That does not impinge on or reduce current full-time faculty's discretionary control of the curriculum they currently teach. The discretionary shift applies to the curricular periphery, to curriculum delivered with instructional technology. Finally, there is some evidence that some faculty extend existing ownership rights to include the curricular materials developed for technologically delivered courses. Yet, in the overwhelming proportion of contracts, such ownership rights are not found.

Managerial extension theory, then, as articulated by Vallas in studying clerical and skilled manual laborers, does not appear to apply to the particular professional workers I am studying.[44] There is little evidence of enskilling in terms of training and skill requirements. Nor is there much evidence of deskilling in terms of job autonomy and managerial control.

Yet I do find evidence of managerial extension of another sort. Managers have the contractual discretion to extend their control over the instructional process through what I call professional "marginalization." As with Vallas' managerial extension, there is a separation between job skills and control of the work process. However, in the case of professional marginalization the job skills of *current* workers neither increase nor decrease. Instead, they remain largely the same. Managers extend their discretionary control neither by deskilling professionals nor by gaining greater control through technology over enskilled professionals, but by bypassing existing full-time faculty. This managerial strategy in the production politics of teaching and technology is to establish new processes of student production on the periphery of the organization over which they have greater control. This periphery, which is largely outside the purview of traditional professionals and faculty input, is currently a marginal means by which to deliver curriculum and generate credit hours. However, that marginal activity, like the number of part-time faculty, many of whom will staff such courses, is likely to become increasingly central in coming years. To the extent that the use of instructional technology does grow, and to the extent that the use of part-time and/or nonbargaining-unit faculty to staff such course delivery grows, the position of full-time, traditional faculty will become increasingly marginal.

There is another dimension to that increasing marginalization. As I have discussed in earlier chapters, there are increasing numbers of nonfaculty professionals in the higher education work force. To what extent do some personnel in instructional technology become professionalized? That is, to what extent do categories of workers in instructional technology begin to develop technical bodies of knowledge, associations, codes of ethics, and the like in the way that other nonfaculty professional groups have emerged in the academy in recent decades? And if such professionals do emerge in instructional technology, what social relations develop between them and traditional professionals on campus—that is, faculty?[45] As these new production workers emerge, participating in the delivery of more of higher education's instructional work, traditional faculty are likely to be further decentered.

In the case of instructional technology, I believe that faculty unions are contributing to a bypassing and marginalization of current faculty. In the face of new production technologies, a strategy of unions in any sector is to protect the current work force. It is interesting that faculty unions have not followed the general union strategy of bargaining "adjustment" to technology, cushioning workers from technology's worst effects.[46] To the extent that faculty unions negotiate protections from instructional technology, it appears that the goal is to minimize such technology's use, or to marginalize its use to a periphery of nonacademic, noncredit, nondaytime curricula delivered by part-time faculty. One problem with this strategy is that part-time faculty and nontraditional curricula are becoming increasingly central parts of the production process in higher education. There is little evidence of faculty negotiating active control over decisions surrounding the choice, purchase, and use of instructional technology. Nor is there evidence of faculty unions actively promoting the collective enskilling of the faculty work force. That would suggest the negotiation of different provisions from those that protect current faculty by making the use of instructional technology voluntary. The alternative is not to make it involuntary, but to ensure that current faculty develop expertise and become collectively involved in the implementation of instructional technology's use.

There is much that is missing from the contracts. It is not just that 63 percent of the contracts make no mention of instructional technology. Nor that the provisions are limited in the seventy-eight contracts that do address technology: only one of the categories of clauses that I analyzed—pay—is found in more than one-quarter of all the contracts. Rather, the point is that many issues are overlooked entirely.

One major rationale for utilizing new instructional technologies is to increase productivity and to generate more tuition revenues. Yet none of the contracts speak to productivity issues. For example, there are no incentives to units or to individuals to increase their productivity through the use of instructional technology. Nothing like revenue sharing, awarding employees a share of increased revenues generated by increased productivity, although such a provision would seem to serve the interests of *both* management and faculty.

Neither are there provisions that involve evaluating instructional technology purchases, courses, and programs. I do not mean the evaluation of individual faculty utilizing instructional technology—three clauses speak to that sort of evaluation. Instead, I mean the evaluation of the efficiency of using technology to deliver instruction. Is it cost effective? Given the current managerial concern with cost containment, and the union concern to protect faculty from cost cutting measures, it would make sense to provide for an evaluation of instructional technology's costs and benefits. Similarly, given the current public concern with the quality of education, it would make sense to provide for evaluation of the quality of courses, curricula, and programs delivered with particular instructional technologies (or to compare student evaluations of such courses with the evaluations of traditionally delivered courses). I do not mean to suggest that technology should be sold if it does not "pay off" immediately in terms of increased productivity/revenues or quality gains that outweigh its costs. I simply mean that institutions and faculties should have a data-based sense of the economic and human resource investment and the economic and educational yields of decisions about instructional technology.

As it is, the politics of production in higher education has focused on managerial control and professional autonomy. Managers seek more discretion in decision making, and more control over faculty. Faculty seek to maintain control of their time and their work and independence from the organization and its managers, areas explored in more depth in chapter 6.

Managerial Domain and Academic Employees: Outside Employment, Intellectual Property, and Faculty's Own Time

What claims do faculty have on the time that they devote to their intellectual labor and on the products of that labor? For decades, faculty have negotiated with their colleges or universities over control of their time. Faculty's claims to a professional domain, to having their own time separate from the claims and responsibilities of the employing organization, have been widely recognized in formal conditions of work that allow faculty outside employment. Although they are full-time employees of one organization, faculty can still use their "own time" as independent professionals to do consulting with other organizations. To what extent in recent years have institutions' claims on faculty as employees been renegotiated? For decades, too, faculty have negotiated independently with organizations outside the employing college or university over intellectual property rights. Faculty's claims to a professional domain in controlling the products of their academic labor have been widely accepted in institutions' terms of employment. Although they are full-time employees of one organization, faculty can still act as independent professionals who create their own intellectual property, the rights to which they negotiate in agreements with publishing companies (for book copyrights), federal agencies, and businesses (for patents). To what extent in recent years have institutions' claims on the products of intellectual labor been renegotiated?

In legal terms, faculty are salaried employees. Yet in practice they have hardly been quintessential "organization men" and women who work endless hours and days devoting themselves to the organization.[1]

For example, a central condition of academic employment is the nine-to ten-month contract. Indeed, that contractual reality is part of an institutional and scholarly calculus in converting and comparing faculty and administrator salaries.[2] Faculty's vacations are extended; their summers are their own. Summer employment and salaries for faculty are generally supplemental to their base academic year salary. Moreover, sabbaticals and teaching loads well under a forty-hour work week have long established academics' claims to and control over their "own time."[3] Employment conditions have included faculty's right to spend some of their own time engaging in professional activities for pay outside the employing organization—in short, to sell their services as independent professionals during the academic year.

A widespread term of academic labor has been the so-called "one day a week" rule concerning outside employment.[4] That rule can be interpreted and applied in various ways. It may mean no more than one day per week. It may mean no more than fifteen days per academic semester, in which case faculty could consult for a week (or all fifteen days) straight. It may mean no more than fifty-two days per year. Policy discussions in many institutions have focused on precisely this question. What does one day a week mean? Whatever the particular interpretation, it means generally that many colleges and universities have effectively recognized faculty's right to work for pay elsewhere for one-fifth of the time during the academic year.

However, recent years have witnessed increased external and internal criticism of faculty's allocation of effort and use of time. Popular and scholarly authors depict faculty as self-interested careerists who ignore students and exploit institutions to serve their own narrow purposes.[5] As in the 1970s, some state legislatures have discussed legislating class contact hours and increasing faculty teaching loads. In this context, managers have tried, at least publicly, to redirect faculty's work, orienting it more toward lower division, undergraduate education. Deans and Provosts have pushed faculty to spend more time with students. In short, colleges and universities are renegotiating faculty's claims on their time, with obvious implications for faculty's right to engage in outside employment. As institutions increasingly emphasize productivity and efficiency, and as they increasingly move toward a market orientation, they lay greater claim to faculty's time as full-time employees. In some cases, particularly in selected professional schools (for example, business, engineering, and medicine), institutions have laid claim to a share of the proceeds of faculty consulting.

So, too, with the products of faculty labor. In the past, employing colleges or universities advanced relatively few, if any, claims on copyrights, inventions, and patents that were the products of faculty labor. However, legal and technological developments have reopened the negotiation of faculty's intellectual property rights. With the 1980 federal patent law allowing colleges and universities to hold patents, institutions became potential claimants to and direct economic beneficiaries of inventions created by faculty. In institutional policy and in the courts, institutions began renegotiating faculty's intellectual property rights, energetically advancing their claims to the products of academics' intellectual labors.[6] The actions of public institutions have been supported and encouraged by many state boards, which have established policies to ensure institutional ownership of scientific discoveries made by faculty in public institutions. Many states have passed legislation that revises or establishes exceptions to conflict-of-interest statutes, thereby enabling and encouraging faculty and university involvement in technology transfer and its attendant commercial activities.[7] The creation of marketable intellectual property has been defined as part of institutions' service function to the state and the public.

The scramble of not-for-profit higher education institutions and states to stake new claims on the products of faculty labor has also been spurred by scientific and technological developments in biotechnology, microcomputing, and educational technology. In biotechnology, not only has the distance between basic research and product development (which is considerable in most fields) been drastically reduced, but the marketability of the products has become expansive, holding out the possibility of direct and enormous profits from faculty's intellectual labor. (In this case, such developments are more relevant to research universities, very few of which are unionized, than they are to comprehensive state colleges and universities and community colleges, where most unionized faculty work.) Moreover, with the explosion of technological advances in microcomputing, the individual faculty member at her desktop with her personal computer has become a potential producer of valuable intellectual property—software. And that applies to faculty in all types of institutions and to products focused on instructional use as well as on use in the private marketplace. Finally, technological developments in communications have enhanced the potential of delivering high quality, interactive educational experiences to dramatically larger numbers of students than in the past. The expanded use and extraordinary course delivery potential of educational technology in distance education opens up another domain of faculty's intellectual property that holds much revenue potential for the institution. That particularly holds true in colleges and universities that are more oriented to teaching than to research—in unionized institutions.

In short, the rules and technologies have changed, the opportunities have expanded, the stakes have gone up, and higher education institutions have become more aggressive claimants to the products of faculty's intellectual labor. A key issue in the renegotiation of intellectual property rights between universities and colleges and faculty members is faculty's time. Can faculty claim ownership to the products of their intellectual labor by claiming that such products were created on their "own time"?

In the late 1980s and early 1990s, I studied the renegotiation process firsthand, sitting on and observing a public research university's technology transfer committee as it developed and revised institutional policies surrounding intellectual property.[8] Composed of faculty and administrators, the committee's discussions made the competing claims of faculty and of the institution quite clear. Faculty repeatedly invoked Stanford University's intellectual property policy as the ideal, for faculty members were given ownership rights to their intellectual products in many circumstances, and the institution had limited claims on royalties stemming from inventions. Such an incentive system was seen as wise and just: it acknowledged that faculty were the sole creators of intellectual property, and it rewarded them accordingly. Institutional representatives on the Technology Transfer Committee articulated a somewhat different position. The Stanford model was said to be "not realistic" because the board of trustees of the public university had insisted that the institution owned faculty's patentable intellectual property (they laid no claim to faculty's copyrightable products—such as, books—and were unclear about software products). However, the need for an incentive system that rewarded faculty's intellectual labor was recognized: the struggle was over the size of faculty's share and the distribution of shares among department, college, and central administration.

It is interesting that both faculty and administrators contrasted university settings to those of private business, in which employees have no claim to the proceeds of their intellectual labor. As people said, the organization owns the employee's time and mind. By contrast, in universities, faculty are professionals who merit and require independence and incentives. Indeed, they have the principal claim on the proceeds of their intellectual labor.

Yet one of the outcomes of the renegotiation of property rights at this institution was the elimination of a clause that accorded faculty ownership of property if it was created "on their own time." The new policy has an incentive system that rewards faculty with a share of the proceeds of their intellectual labor. But the university owns faculty's time and work. In the renegotiated terms of work faculty are less independent professionals than they are salaried employees. The notion of employee is taking on a more inclusive definition. Faculty are losing claim to their own time, their independent professional and personal space.

Of course, this book is about the terms of work for faculty in unionized colleges and universities. The public research university discussed above is not unionized. Most research universities are not, which is precisely the point. The trend in the institutions where faculty have been believed to enjoy the greatest measure of autonomy—research universities—is toward the reduction of faculty claims to their "own time." Thus one might expect to find a similar and even stronger trend in sectors where managers have been believed to exercise more control over faculty as employees. (A counterargument here would be that in unionized institutions management might be less likely to extend its domain over faculty's intellectual property because there is little property of value being created by faculty in these settings. I address this and other points in the conclusion of this chapter.)

Methods

There is little research on the terms of academic labor in unionized institutions on the issues described above. In fact, there is limited research on such terms in any kind of postsecondary education institution, particularly if one is interested in the state-of-the-art in a large number of colleges and universities. This chapter fills that gap with a thorough reading of contractual provisions regarding outside employment and intellectual property in a national sample of collective bargaining agreements. My analytical focus is on the extent of managerial claims on faculty's time and work products, and on professional independence or autonomy.

Outside Employment

I coded all references in the contracts to outside employment. Of course, *outside employment* is not always the term used. In reading through the contracts I identified various terms that were used instead—for example, *other* or *additional* employment, *outside activities, commitments,* and *consult**. Some references are in separate articles devoted entirely to outside employment. More commonly, they are found in sections within broader articles on faculty rights (and responsibilities), conditions of work, and leaves (many references are to outside employment while on one of various sorts of leave). The contractual provisions deal with various issues, discussed below, around which I have organized the data analysis and presentation in this chapter.

What is the *context* of outside employment? Some provisions specify that the contract applies only during the academic year or during normal working hours, giving faculty the professional freedom to pursue independent work outside those times. Many apply only to outside employment while faculty are on leave—sabbatical, sick leave, leave of absence. For example, contracts may limit the amount of outside compensation a faculty member may receive while on sabbatical and receiving compensation from the institution.

Does outside employment create a *conflict of commitment?* Many contracts speak to faculty's primary commitment to the institution, indicating that outside employment should not adversely affect faculty's performance of their duties. In some cases, provisions include a statement about the value of outside professional activities and/or about faculty's right to such employment, explicitly validating faculty's professional autonomy. Some other clauses accord managers the discretion to require faculty to reduce or stop outside employment if it is adversely affecting their performance (the managers decide whether the employment is a conflict of commitment).

Does outside employment create a *conflict of interest?* Such concerns are distinct from conflicting time commitments. Some contracts invoke legal conceptions of conflicts of interest that may accompany outside employment. Often such references simply invoke institutions' conflict of interest policy.

Is *prior approval* required? Such clauses accord managers the discretion to determine whether faculty may engage in outside employment. Yet the level of constraint varies and is affected by the context. In some cases, the approval must be written; in others, it need not be. Some provisions apply generally; others apply only to the use of institutional facilities.

Is *notice* required? Many provisions require notice but not approval. Of course, in some cases the clause allows for managers to take action in regard to a faculty member's outside employment about which they have been notified. The level of managerial constraint on faculty autonomy varies in terms of whether notice must be prior and/or written.

Are there limits on the *use of institutional facilities or resources*? Many contracts restrict faculty's use of institutional facilities or resources in the course of outside employment. Some prohibit such use outright or make it contingent on administrative approval. Other clauses provide that the institution be reimbursed for such use.

Are there limits on the *time* faculty can devote to outside employment? Given the literature's finding that the one-day-a-week rule is prevalent in nonunionized institutions, this enables a direct comparison of constraints on faculty claims to their "own time" in the two sectors of higher education—unionized and nonunionized. It also represents a clear indicator of the extent to which faculty are constrained in pursuing outside employment.

Two remaining provisions are found in only a few contracts: (a) *outright prohibition* of outside employment; and (b) reference to *conflict resolution* in cases where disputes may arise between faculty and the administration over the faculty member's outside employment. (Absent from all the discussion in this chapter is the issue of outside employment of nonbargaining-unit members.)

Intellectual Property

I coded all contractual references to intellectual property. Of course, *intellectual property* is not always the term used. In reading through the contracts, I identified various terms that were used instead of intellectual property—*patents, copyright, inventions, tapes* (as in distance learning), *materials, royalties, ownership*, and *property rights*. Many references are in separate articles that detail intellectual property rights. More often, property rights are detailed in sections that are subsumed within broader articles that address faculty rights or conditions of work or other, more general topics. My data analysis and presentation follow the considerations that are dealt with in the contractual provisions.

What *property* is mentioned? Contracts are varied in their levels of specificity and inclusion. Some provisions refer only to copyrights (for example, of books). Some refer to patents and/or copyrights. Some refer only to tapes. Some refer only to materials. Some refer to various types of property.

Who *owns* the property? Provisions may accord sole ownership to faculty or to the institution. Ownership may be joint. Provisions may accord ownership to faculty in some situations and to the institution in others.

What *conditions of production* affect ownership? In most contracts, ownership depends on whether faculty did the work "on their own time," whether they utilized institutional resources/facilities, and/or whether it was "work for hire." A key condition affording professional autonomy is explicit recognition of faculty having their own time.

What is the *process* for determining ownership and profit shares? The process may be more or less defined and/or detailed. Decision making may be joint negotiation between the individual faculty member and the designee of the president; it may involve faculty collectively, or it may lie entirely with managers' discretion. Procedures may be more or less detailed. And there may be various mechanisms for dispute resolution—for example, binding arbitration.

Who gets the *profits*? Provisions may detail profit shares (for example, of royalties) for various parties. Even if the institution owns the property, a provision may be more or less generous in according a share of the proceeds to faculty. It may also define rules governing shares. Or disbursement of profits, as with determination of owership, may be identified as a matter for negotiation between the individual faculty member and the institution.

What controls or limits are there on the *use of the product*? A key point here is who exercises such control. For example, in the case of tapes for distance education, does the individual faculty member or the union have control over whether and how the institution can use the tape in the future? In the case of teaching materials, does the institution place limits on faculty's commercial use of these materials within the institution—that is, on whether they can sell them (or sell them at full price) to students?

Apart from analyzing the contractual provisions in their own terms, I analyze the incidence of provisions and conditions by institutional type. Are outside employment and intellectual property clauses more likely to be found in the contracts of one institutional type than another? Does any such pattern hold for specific conditions within these provisions?

There is some basis in the literature for making predictions along these lines. As noted in chapter 5, studies of occupations and professions tend to presume a positive relationship between workers' expertise and their autonomy. That presumption especially holds for professionals. The greater the expertise the greater the autonomy. The higher education literature on faculty presumes a positive relationship between an institution's prestige and the expertise and autonomy of its faculty. The greater the prestige and faculty expertise, the greater the autonomy. It is widely accepted that institutional type can serve as a proxy measure of the institution's prestige and its faculty's expertise. As one moves up the hierarchy of institutional types in higher education, from two-year to four-year colleges, and from comprehensive to doctoral granting to research universities, institutional prestige and faculty expertise increases. As a first step in analyzing institutional differences, then, I compare the incidence of provisions and of conditions within provisions in four-year institutions and in two-year and technical colleges. The literature suggests that professional autonomy will be greater in four-year institutions and that managerial discretion will be greater in two-year institutions. Of course, chapter 5's findings call into question the presumed positive correlation between workers' expertise and job autonomy.

It is tempting to invoke policies in nonunionized settings as a foil for my study of collective bargaining agreements. Unfortunately, there is no comparable data base of policies in such settings. The one exception is the research on the one-day-a-week rule regarding outside employment. There is not a national data base that I can consult. However, there is research based on a national study of consulting policies. Given those findings, I would expect to find that unionized faculty's outside employment will be no less and probably more restricted than that of faculty in nonunionized settings. Why? Because of the presumed positive correlation between institutional prestige and faculty expertise, on the one hand, and professional autonomy, on the other hand. Few research universities and elite private colleges and universities are unionized. A large proportion of community colleges and public comprehensive colleges and universities are unionized. On balance, then, unionized institutions are less prestigious institutions in which faculty are less likely to have doctorates, to be engaged in research, and to receive external research support. Thus, I would expect to find that faculty in unionized institutions have less autonomous control over their own time.

Outside Employment

How regulated are faculty in unionized colleges and universities when it comes to outside employment? Relatively loosely. Only 42 percent of HECAS contracts have provisions that speak to outside employment. Moreover, most provisions in these eighty-nine contracts are fairly limited in their scope and in the discretion they afford managers. Contractually, faculty in unionized settings enjoy considerable professional autonomy to engage in outside employment.

There is no "typical" outside employment provision. Rather, there is great variety in the conditions that are covered. My analysis concentrates on nine such conditions: context, conflict of commitment, conflict of interest, prior approval, notice, use of institutional facilities or resources, time limits, prohibitions, and conflict resolution. In the eighty-nine contracts that have outside employment provisions (three of these refer to institutional policies but do not describe the conditions), there is not one that covers all nine conditions. Two contracts cover eight conditions. One covers seven, two cover six, and five cover five conditions. In thirty-two contracts only one condition is dealt with (in twenty-one cases, that one condition is sabbatical or leaves; in eight cases, conflict of commitment): seventeen address two, fourteen address three, and ten address four, conditions. There are also different combinations of conditions dealt with in different provisions. That variation makes it misleading to speak of a "typical" outside employment contractual provision. It also underscores the limited scope of contractual provisions.

A clear sense of the limitations of these provisions comes with exploring in detail each condition covered by the provisions. To what extent do faculty have autonomy in pursuing outside employment? To what extent are there constraints on faculty's outside employment? And to what extent do managers have discretionary authority in regard to such employment?

Conflict of Commitment

The most common contractual provision speaks to conflict of commitment: 62 percent of provisions that speak to outside employment address conflict of commitment. In some way, each of these fifty-five clauses constrains faculty's outside activities. Such constraint takes various forms.

All of the provisions have language that relates to outside employment's impact on faculty's work responsibilities at the employing institution—that is, conflict of commitment. The terminology varies. For example:

> Educators may engage in outside compensated activities provided such activities do not interfere with their teaching effectiveness or College duties and responsibilities. (Atlantic Community College, Article 3.Q)

> Therefore, the College expects that no faculty member will engage in any outside consultation or teaching activity which may prevent him/her from fulfilling that obligation. (Rhode Island College, Article 11.C)

> Under no circumstances shall any outside employment infringe upon the employee's ability to perform his/her contracted duties with the College. (Treasure Valley Community College, Article 18.F)

Some of the language is declarative—"under no circumstance," or "shall not." In other cases the language is conditional—"provided that." In both types of clauses, much still is left unsaid—for example, who determines (and how do they determine) whether the faculty member is performing his "contracted duties" or his "obligation." Nevertheless, the provisions establish an initial level of constraint on faculty's freedom to pursue outside employment.

At the same time, by identifying situations in which outside employment is *not* allowed, conflict of commitment clauses implicitly identify other conditions in which it *is* allowed—for example, when it does not interfere with faculty members' other duties. In effect, the provisions acknowledge faculty's general right to engage in such employment. This point is made explicit in ten contracts with a phrase/sentence that values or accepts faculty's right to outside employment.

> The personal life of a professional employee, especially concerning outside employment and activities, is not an appropriate concern of the Board except as it may directly prevent the professional employee from properly performing his/her assigned functions. (Dodge City Community College, Article 3.B)

> A faculty member has the right to determine the amount and character of the work and other activities he/she pursues outside the College provided such work and other activities do not interfere with the discharge of his/her responsibilities under the terms of this Agreement. (Massachusetts State College System, Article 5.A)

> Full-time teaching faculty members shall be encouraged to engage in professional activities (other than Central Community College employment) as a means of broadening their experience and keeping them abreast of the latest developments in their specialized fields, provided such activities do not interfere with their regular duties with the college. (Central Community College, Article 16)

Statements about professional autonomy are generally combined with phrases about conflict of commitment. In four other cases faculty's independence as professionals is explicitly recognized with language specifying that limits on outside employment apply only to the academic year or work week.

> Nothing shall prevent a faculty member employed on an academic year basis from being employed during the remainder of a fiscal year, in the summer sessions, or in other service. (Southwestern Oregon Community College, Article 13.5)

> No full-time staff member of the College shall engage in outside employment which interferes with his/her regular College duties within the College work week as defined in this policy. (Big Bend Community College, Article 17.A)

In either of the previous two types of contractual provisions it is acknowledged that faculty have their own time, independent of the employing organization. About one-quarter (25.5 percent) of the fifty-five conflict of commitment provisions, then, are explicit about faculty being more than salaried employees whose time is owned entirely by the institution.

Nevertheless, conflict of commitment clauses indicate that the responsibilities assigned by the employing organization have priority. The institution has first claim on the faculty member's time. It also has claim to a job completed and well done. In eight contracts, such claims are explicit, as in the first part of the sentence cited above from Rhode Island College's contract: "A faculty member's professional responsibility is to perform fully all of his/her College duties and assignments; therefore, . . . " Elsewhere:

> An employee's performance of professional obligations to the university as specified in Article 6.1.a shall be given priority over any outside employment. (Illinois Board of Governors, Article 6.10)

> Faculty members owe primary responsibility to their College duties. (Clinton Community College, Article 6.C.1)

> Full-time employment by the College shall be considered the basic full-time employment of all educators. In the performance of his/her specific and individual duties and obligations to the College, the educator shall be regarded as an employee of the College. (Dutchess Community College, Article 6.1)

In eight other contracts, there are outright prohibitions of outside employment. Yet most of these are fairly limited. For example, they prohibit "other major employment" (Jackson Community College, Article 8.4.e), "other full-time employment during the official academic year" (University of Lowell, Article 16.A.2), a "full-time appointment to the faculty" of another institution (Youngstown State University, Article 25.4), or the teaching of regularly scheduled or similar courses at other institutions (Saginaw Valley State University, Article D. 15, Rhode Island School of Design, Article 9.C).

Another point that is tacit in conflict of commitment provisions concerns who decides if outside employment is interfering with a faculty member's assigned responsibilities who decides what to do in this situation? In some cases (33 percent of the conflict of commitment clauses) the answer is explicit—administrators decide.

> An employee may have outside employment as long as it does not impair his/her effectiveness as a professional staff member as determined by the appropriate Dean. (North County Community College, Article 11.8)

> Upon written request directed to an individual full-time faculty unit employee by the appropriate administrator, the faculty unit employee shall provide a written statement of the amount and approximate distribution of time devoted to continuous outside employment during the academic term in which he/she has been appointed. Such requests may be made when the appropriate administrator has determined that such information is necessary to ascertain compliance with provision 35.1 of this Article ["shall not conflict with normal work assignments"]. (California State University, Article 35.2)

> Should the College subsequently determine that such employment interferes with the faculty member's performance of his/her professional responsibilities, or conflicts with College services or programs, then such employment shall be terminated within two weeks of written notice from the President that such employment must be terminated. (Terra Technical College, Article 10)

> Provided such activities do not interfere with their regular duties with the college or represent a conflict of interest or shall not prevent contractual duties from being performed satisfactorily. Satisfactory performance is to be determined by the administration. (Central Community College, Article 16)

In most cases the answer is implicit—and thereby rests in the hands of administrators. In no case is there provision for a faculty body to decide.

The scope of managerial discretion in such clauses varies considerably. In some cases, managers may ask the faculty member for information. In other cases, managers may require faculty members to terminate outside employment. In a couple of cases managers may terminate faculty if they do not discontinue their outside employment. Whatever the scope, the criteria by which managers determine that there is a conflict of commitment and the due process procedures that are to be followed are limited or vague at best. That further extends managers' discretion. (In three contracts, specific mechanisms for conflict resolution are identified. For example: "Faculty members contesting such determination [an institution's judgment that a conflict of commitment exists and that outside employment must cease] may file a grievance regarding Oakland's action before severing the outside relationship or ceasing such work" (Oakland University, Article 10.72).

Context of Outside Employment: Sabbaticals/Leaves

The second most common outside employment provision (51 percent of such clauses) addresses employment in the context of sabbaticals and other leaves. Of these forty-five provisions, thirty speak to sabbaticals, ten to leaves of absence, three each to sick and personal leaves, and one each to child-rearing, paid educational, and professional leaves (some contracts address more than one context).

In one respect, these provisions underscore the limited nature of contractual constraints on faculty's outside employment. In nearly half (47 percent) of the contracts with sabbatical or leave provisions on outside employment, that is the sole condition of such employment that is addressed. In other words, the scope of these provisions' limitations on outside employment does not extend beyond the context of some sort of leave. These twenty-one contracts are nearly one-quarter (24 percent) of all the contracts that address outside employment.

Several sorts of restrictions on outside employment are embedded in sabbatical or leave provisions. By far the most common is a restriction on the amount of income that can be earned from outside employment while on leave.

> Staff members granted sabbaticals may not receive other salary remuneration in excess of one half of that individual's base salary for the leave period. Where compensation is in direct relationship to the leave project, the total earnings from the College and an outside agency will not exceed the individual's base salary for the leave period. (DuPage Community College, Article 1.9)

> In addition to sabbatical leave pay, the faculty member may accept a scholarship, fellowship, grant-in-aid, or other similar assistance, but may not accept compensation for employment which added to his/her sabbatical leave payments equals an amount greater than that he/she would have received had he/she not been on sabbatical leave. (Southwestern Oregon Community College, Appendix C)

Such restrictions are aimed at preventing faculty from utilizing sabbaticals (and other paid leaves) to increase their incomes. In seven of twenty such contracts that restriction includes the institution's discretion to reduce or eliminate its payments or to approve such outside employment during the leave period.

> Part-time faculty members shall not accept teaching appointments at any other institution or otherwise be employed for remuneration, other than outside professional employment to no greater extent than the part-time faculty member had engaged while teaching full-time, during the terms of the sabbatical leave, without permission from the President. (Rhode Island School of Design, Part-Time, Article 10)

> Faculty members on sabbatical leave may accept part-time employment but remuneration for such employment plus sabbatical leave pay shall not exceed the regular salary for the period except by special arrangement with the President. (Lincoln University, Article 5.5)

Stronger restrictions are found in eight contracts that prohibit other full-time employment while on leave and nine that prohibit any outside employment while on leave.

> Recipients of sabbaticals may avail themselves of fellowships, assistantships, or other sources of limited means, to offset travel and displacement cost; however, this policy shall not permit full-time employment for any person while on sabbatical. (Nebraska State College, Article 7)

> Such personal leave days may not be used for recreation, to engage in other employment, or to extend a holiday or vacation period. (Nicolet Area Technical College, Article 11)

> Faculty on paid leave should not engage in employment outside the scope and purpose of the leave proposal. (Mt. Hood Community College, Full-Time, Appendix B)

The aim is to prevent faculty from drawing pay from the institution for one purpose and then utilizing the time for other employment.

Seven other contracts prohibit faculty members from utilizing a leave to seek or gain other employment. Many such clauses apply to leaves of absence.

Under no circumstances shall leave be available for purposes of personal convenience, or for the extension of a holiday or a vacation period, or to seek other outside employment. (Mt. San Antonio Community College District, Article 2.C.3)

No leaves whatsoever shall be granted for the taking of employment for pecuniary advantage elsewhere. (Lansing Community College, Article 7.A.3.k)

Institutions do not want to subsidize faculty members' job searches.

Notice

The third most common outside employment provision is also relatively limited in the constraints it provides on such employment. In thirty contracts faculty are required to provide some notice or report of outside employment. Notice is distinct from approval, although in some cases managers may take restrictive action based on the information provided. To be required to notify managers of outside activities is quite different from having to ask their permission to engage in such activity. It suggests considerable professional autonomy.

Two contracts exemplify perhaps the ultimate minimalism in a reporting requirement: notice is termed a matter of "professional courtesy."

As a matter of professional courtesy, notice of such outside employment or commitment should be given to the President. (Adirondack Community College, Article 13.C)

Any faculty member who engages in outside teaching, counseling, or library services should have the professional courtesy to notify the Dean of Academic Services regarding such outside employment prior to his/her commitment to work. (Luzerne County Community College, Article 29.1)

Even the choice of auxiliary verbs is minimally restrictive. It is not that faculty "shall" have professional courtesy, it is that they "should" have it.

Eleven other provisions explicitly accord professional autonomy in one of two ways. Some leave it up to the faculty member to report activity that they believe might constitute a conflict of commitment. Others specify that the notice requirement only applies during the contract year or week.

> Reporting outside employment according to this Article applies only to the academic year when the College is in regular session. (Adrian College, Article 15.C)

> The provisions of the above paragraph which require notification shall not apply during any summer term in which the faculty member has not contracted to teach for the college. (Pensacola Junior College, Article 6.11)

Faculty have their own time outside the purview of the employing institution.

The extent of managerial constraint varies some, according to whether notice must be written and whether it must be prior to engaging in outside employment. Well over half (60 percent) of the provisions require written notice, in some cases on a standard reporting form. All but five of the thirty provisions require that notice be either prior to the activity or "in a timely fashion" (Kishwaukee College, Article 8.5). A few provisions require faculty members to report outside activity in much detail.

> An employee who proposes to engage in any outside activity which the employee should reasonably conclude may create a conflict of interest, or in any outside compensated professional activity, shall report to the employee's supervisor, in writing, the details of such proposed activity prior to engaging therein. The report . . . shall include, where applicable, the name of the employer or other recipient of services; the funding source; the location where such activity shall be performed; the nature and extent of the activity; and any intended use of university facilities, equipment, or services. A new report shall be submitted for outside activity previously reported at: the beginning of each academic year for outside activity of a continuing nature; and such time as there is a significant change in an activity (nature, extent, funding, etc.). (Florida State University System, Article 19.4)

> Prior to accepting any outside work assignment or consultation, during a term in which the faculty member is scheduled to teach, a faculty member shall advise the department chairperson and dean in writing of the scope and duration of the assignment to be undertaken and the employer or agency to be served. Such notification shall be provided on an annual

basis for assignments or work agreements which exceed one year. (Saginaw Valley State University, Article D 15.1)

Few notice provisions afford managers discretion in utilizing the information that is reported by faculty. Of thirty such provisions, six give managers the right to act on information faculty provide. For example, they can require faculty to reduce or terminate their outside employment. In one case (Lincoln Land Community College) that oversight is accorded to the president of the Faculty Association. A rare case of peer regulation.

Prior Approval

Prior approval represents a greater degree of constraint than does notice. It is, by definition, a contractual provision of managerial discretion (to approve or not to approve). Fewer contracts have prior approval than have notice provisions. Of the eighty-nine contracts that speak to outside employment, a little over a quarter (27 percent) have such provisions.

Yet the constraint on professional autonomy is in many ways limited even in these provisions. Only fourteen of the twenty-four require written approval. Only three require specification of the nature and duration of the outside employment.

What is more important, in many clauses the scope of the approval requirement, and thus of managerial discretion, is limited. Approval often is required only for specific domains of outside employment: seven provisions speak to approval for outside employment during sabbaticals or leaves; twelve others speak only to that employment that involves use of institutional facilities and/or resources.

Outside employment during the period of sabbatical leave must be approved by the faculty member's college or division president. (San Diego Community College, Article 11.6.5.7)

In the event that faculty engage in outside employment it is understood that any and all use of College personnel, facilities, services, or equipment in conjunction with a faculty member's outside consulting must be approved by the College in writing in advance of such use. (Community Colleges of Rhode Island, Article 15.F)

In these provisions managerial domain in controlling faculty's outside employment is limited to particular circumstances.

Ten approval provisions cover faculty's outside employment in general. Yet there is much variation in the extent to which faculty's freedom to pursue outside employment as independent professionals is delimited.

> Prior to acceptance of employment involving substantial time, the individual concerned shall obtain the approval of the President, but such approval shall not be arbitrarily withheld and shall be given or withheld in a timely manner. (Rogue Community College, Article 3.C.2)

> A full-time faculty member shall not, during the academic year, be employed for remuneration by employers other than the District, except with the approval of the Chancellor and the Board. Anyone who wants approval must make written application to the Board through the Chancellor on the standard form entitled "Request for Approval of Proposed Non-College Employment." . . . Activities will be reported at the end of the year on the standard form entitled "Report of Non-College Employment Performed." (Illinois Eastern Community College, Article 2.3)

In Rogue Community College's clause, managerial discretion is mitigated by a sentence about arbitrary managerial action and by limiting the approval requirement to only those situations "involving substantial time." Even Illinois Eastern Community College's clause, which is filled with the authoritative language of commands—"shall not," "must," "will be"—is limited to employment "during the academic year."

In short, even the most constraining of the prior approval provisions implicitly grants faculty control over their own time, apart from their obligations to the institution. At the same time that contractual provisions accord managers discretion, they may also recognize professional autonomy. In five of the twenty-four prior approval provisions, such acknowledgement is explicit.

(In three other conflict resolution provisions faculty are provided with recourse to challenge managerial judgments. The Florida State University System contracts provide for an "Expedited Grievance Procedure" in those situations in which "the employee disagrees with that [the manager's] determination" (Article 19.5). In Lincoln

University's contract, "If the decision of the President is adverse, the faculty member may appeal through the President to the Board of Trustees." (Article 3.7) Western Michigan University's contract provides "Faculty Recourse" to appeal the institution's judgment regarding outside employment "through the grievance procedure set forth herein" (Article 29.3.2).

Use of Institutional Facilities or Resources

As noted in discussing prior approval, some outside employment provisions address faculty's use of institutional facilities and resources. Of eighty-nine contracts mentioning faculty's outside employment, twenty (23 percent) speak to such use. The issue is not *whether* faculty can pursue outside employment, but *under what conditions*, if any, they can draw on institutional facilities or resources in doing so.

The most restrictive provisions are those that establish a constraint without exception. Eight of the twenty clauses prohibit use of institutional facilities or resources. They are simple, declarative sentences.

> A faculty member should not use college property for outside employment activities. (Lakeland Faculty Association, Article 3.B.3)

> Any outside employment engaged in by a faculty member must: . . . Not involve the use of facilities, equipment, or materials of the College. (Michael J. Owens Technical College, Article 8.D)

> Except for incidental use of one's office and telephone, a member engaging in any outside employment shall not use the offices, telephones, facilities, equipment, supplies, or other services of the College in connection with such outside employment. (Western Oregon State College, Article 19.4)

In the twelve other clauses the provisions accord managerial discretion in dealing with the issue. In all twelve, faculty may only use institutional facilities/resources if they obtain prior approval. Conditions and/or qualifications surrounding such constraint and approval vary somewhat.

> No faculty member shall use the University facilities, supplies, or equipment other than in the course of University duties, except with prior approval of the President. (University of Hawaii, Article 3.B.d)

> If such consulting or outside employment involves the use of institutional facilities, the institution name or personnel, the faculty member shall obtain prior approval from the Administration. (Western Montana College, Article 7.300)

Some clauses read as if the presumption is that outside employment will involve the use of institutional facilities and that it simply requires prior approval. Other clauses have more restrictive or prohibitive language.

An additional condition applies in seven of the twelve clauses that require prior approval. The contract specifies that the institution may or will receive some remuneration for the approved use of facilities or resources.

> Approval for the use of University facilities, equipment, or services may be conditioned upon reimbursement for the use thereof. (Florida State University System, Article 19.6)

> That any and all use by the involved faculty member or the client of the University's personnel, facilities, services, or equipment be approved in advance; and That arrangements for the use of University personnel, facilities, services, or equipment shall provide for reimbursement of costs and overhead to the University. (Western Michigan University, Articles 29.3.1.5, 29.3.1.6)

> Faculty members may engage in professionally relevant outside consulting or teaching activity provided: . . . that arrangements for the use of College personnel, facilities, and services, or equipment shall provide for reimbursement of costs and overhead to the College as determined by the appropriate Dean in consultation with the department chairperson, unless specifically authorized by the Vice-President for Academic Affairs. (Rhode Island State College, Article 11.5.d)

The mechanism for determining remuneration is generally quite vague. There is little specification of the process or criteria surrounding such judgment.

Conflict of Interest

Some contracts address conflict of interest issues that are distinct from conflict of commitment. They reference legal and pecuniary conflicts of interest that may compromise the institution or the faculty member's professional judgments, as opposed to time conflicts that detract from the faculty member's ability to adequately fulfill her responsibilities. One-third as many contracts (eighteen) have conflict of interest as have conflict of commitment (fifty-five) provisions.

Many such provisions (ten of the eighteen) offer some specification of what is meant by conflict of interest. For example, both of the technical college contracts that have conflict of interest provisions prohibit the use of information that is not available to the public.

> Any outside employment engaged in by a faculty member must: Not involve the use of official information of the College which is not available to the public. (Michael J. Owens Technical College, Article 8.02.A)

> Such activities must: Not involve the use of information obtained from College sources which is not available to members of the general public pursuant to the Ohio Public Records Law. (Cincinnati Technical College, Article 14.A)

Cincinnati Technical College's contract further indicates that faculty must "Not take advantage of a bargaining unit member's position with the College to sell goods or services to students of the College" (Article 14.D). Two provisions refer to institutional policy (Big Bend Community College, Article 17.D) or state statutes (Northern Montana College, Article 3.12) on conflict of interest. Still other provisions broadly prohibit faculty's use of their professional position for personal gain.

> To engage in no outside employment that will impair the effectiveness of professional service and permit no commercial exploitation of his/her professional position. (Joliet Junior College, Article 11.3.3)

> Under no circumstances shall a faculty member have direct business dealings with students in the sale of textbooks, instruments, lecture notes, or similar materials or use his/her position in the COLLEGE to promote or solicit sales of any kind for any organization in which he/she has a vested interest of a pecuniary nature. (Luzerne County Community College, Article 29.1)

In the above and six other cases, provisions mention both conflicts of interest and of commitment, distinguishing between the two (yet not detailing procedures by which conflicts will be addressed). The definition of conflict of interest is classic—prohibition against corrupting professionals' position, relations with clients, and judgment with the influence of commercial gain. Given the recent rise of a market orientation among professionals and not-for-profit entities such as colleges/universities, such a definition may seem surprising. Surprising perhaps, but not prevalent. Conflict of interest provisions are found in only 20 percent of contracts speaking to outside employment.

Limits on Time

Surprisingly, one of the most common policies found in nonunionized universities as a condition of outside employment is *not* found in the contracts of most unionized higher education institutions. Only five of the eighty-nine contracts that mention outside employment have provisions that limit the amount of time that faculty can devote to such employment. The limit in these five exceptions is some variation of the so-called one day a week rule.

> Such nonconflicting outside activities for compensation normally should be limited to an average of one day per week per semester. (Central Michigan University, Article 23.1)

> It is expected that all faculty members will be on campus a minimum of four days per week to fulfill their responsibilities as full-time members of the faculty. (Dowling College, Article 4A02)

> Generally, consulting and/or outside employment shall not exceed the equivalent of one workday per week. (Youngstown State University, Article 25.4)

Two clauses provide for some managerial discretion in approving employment for more than one day a week and for specifying how to interpret one day a week.

> If outside work involves more than one day per academic week, prior approval of the respective dean is required. (Saginaw Valley State University, Article D 15.3)

> Faculty members who engage in consulting, contact, or private employment during the duty period shall not exceed one day or an accumulation of 8 hours per calendar week excluding Sundays and holidays. Up to six working days per academic year may be accumulated, from time not uti-

lized for consulting, contract, or private employment during weeks within the duty period, for consecutive days of professional consultancy. Days not used during the academic year will not carry forward to the next academic year. Plans for consecutive days of professional consulting shall be submitted in advance to the appropriate Dean, Director, or Provost for prior written approval. (University of Hawaii, Article 3.4, 5)

The University of Hawaii provision addresses a central question in the general debate surrounding the one day a week rule: is it only one day per week, or can days be accumulated over time? Hawaii's clause accords managers discretion to (dis)approve the use of such accumulated hours. Nevertheless, limitations on the specific amount of time faculty may devote to outside professional employment are the exception, not the rule, in unionized settings.

Effect of Institutional Type and Unit Membership

In what types of institutions is faculty's freedom to undertake outside employment as independent professionals most likely to be constrained by contractual provisions or by managerial discretion? The results run counter to prevailing assumptions about hierarchies of prestige and autonomy in higher education and among faculty. The incidence of outside employment provisions in general is dependent on institutional type ($x2=10.72$, significant at .005), but not in the direction suggested by the literature. Four-year institutions are overrepresented: they account for 24 percent of HECAS contracts but 36 percent of outside employment provisions. Two-year colleges and technical institutions are underrepresented: they account for 68 and 8 percent of HECAS contracts, but 58 and 6 percent of outside employment provisions (see table 6.1). In short, contracts in the more prestigious institutions—four- versus two-year and technical—are more likely to have provisions impinging on faculty's autonomy to pursue outside employment.

Could the difference be due to greater numbers of part-time faculty in two-year institutions, and thus the greater likelihood of contracts covering full and part-time faculty? It might be less likely for such contracts to advance claims on unit members' time, when a proportion of them are part-time. Neither possibility holds. The proportions of full-time only and of full- and part-time contracts in two- and four-year institutions mirror the proportions of these contracts in HECAS. And the incidence of outside employment provisions is not dependent on unit membership.

TABLE 6.1
INCIDENCE OF OUTSIDE EMPLOYMENT PROVISIONS

	Two-year	Tech	Four-year	Total
Clauses	52	5	32	89
Conflict commitment	28	3	24	55
Sabbatic/ leave	27	2	16	45*
Notice	11	1	18	30**
Prior Approval	10	0	14	24***
Use of facilities	4	2	14	20****
Conflict interest	7	2	9	18
Limits on time	0	0	5	5

* In thirty of these cases the provision speaks to sabbaticals.
** In eighteen of these cases the notice is written; in twenty-five cases it is defined as prior or timely notice.
*** In fourteen of these cases the provision requires written approval.
**** In eight of these cases the provision prohibits such use.

The findings for the incidence of specific conditions surrounding outside employment essentially mirror the findings for the incidence of outside employment provisions in general. (Sabbatical or leave clauses are an exception: their incidence is dependent neither on institutional type—$x2=4.12$—nor on unit membership—$x2=3.22$.) The incidence of conflict of commitment provisions is dependent on institutional type ($x2=14.42$, significant at .005), but not unit membership ($x2=.9$). Four-year institutions are overrepresented, and two-year colleges are underrepresented. More surprising, four-year institutions are overrepresented in those clauses that provide for managerial discretion ($x2=7.93$, significant at .025).

Notice provisions are dependent on institutional type ($x2=23.51$, significant at .000), but not unit membership ($x2=1.01$). Four-year institutions are overrepresented, accounting for 60 percent of the provisions, although they represent only 25 percent of HECAS contracts. It is hard to understand why this would be the case. There is no reason to believe that faculty in four-year institutions are that much more likely than faculty in two-year colleges to be engaged in outside employment and thus require more regulation. In fact, variations within the academy are due more to field of work (for example, business versus history) than to institutional type.[9]

Likewise, prior approval provisions are dependent on institutional type (x2=14.03, significant at .000) but not on unit membership (x2=1.82). Four-year institutions are overrepresented, accounting for 58 percent of the approval provisions, more than twice their representation among HECAS contracts. Such a finding is particularly surprising in a condition that by definition accords managers considerable discretion over professional employees' lives.

Use provisions, too, are dependent on institutional type (x2=25.62, significant at .000) but not unit membership (x2=1.4). Four-year institutions are greatly overrepresented, accounting for 70 percent of these provisions, almost three times their representation among HECAS contracts. Professional autonomy is more likely to be constrained by prohibitions on use of facilities and by managerial discretion in (dis)approving and determining reimbursement for such use, in four-year as compared to two-year institutions of higher education.

Similarly, conflict of interest clauses are dependent on institutional type (x2=7.96, significant at .025) but not on unit membership (x2=.29). Four-year institutions account for one-half of these provisions. Two-year colleges are underrepresented, accounting for 39 percent of such provisions, although they represent 68 percent of HECAS contracts.

Finally, all five of the time provisions are in the contracts of four-year institutions. Two of the five contracts with time provisions cover full-time faculty only units (the numbers are too small for a chi-square analysis).

Intellectual Property Rights

How extensive are managerial claims on intellectual property created by faculty? Not very extensive. One-third of HECAS contracts have provisions that speak to intellectual property rights. Moreover, a substantial majority of the seventy-one contracts grant surprisingly extensive faculty claims to the ownership and proceeds of the property they create. Faculty in unionized institutions enjoy considerable professional claims on their time and the products of their work.

Most of the intellectual property provisions deal with most of the conditions analyzed. Of the seventy-one contracts, sixty speak to who owns the property, fifty-eight to conditions of production that determine ownership, forty-nine to process, fifty-nine to profits, and twenty-seven to controls or limits on the use of the property. There is more consistency, then, across intellectual property provisions than is found with outside employment. Moreover, intellectual property provisions tend to be broader in scope and more detailed than are outside employment provisions.

What Property is Mentioned?

The presumption of many scholars would be that different types of intellectual property would be more or less prominent in the provisions of collective bargaining agreements. The presumption would also be that the contracts of four-year versus two-year institutions would be more likely to have provisions dealing with certain types of intellectual property. Consider the case of patents. Many would presume that patenting is not a widespread activity among unionized faculty and thus would not be mentioned in intellectual property provisions. So, too, many would presume that to the extent patenting is mentioned in intellectual property provisions, it would be in the contracts of four-year institutions.

It may be that patenting is not a widespread activity among unionized faculty. (Of course, neither is it a widespread activity among nonunionized faculty, even in elite research universities.) However, over two-thirds (69 percent) of the collective bargaining agreements that have intellectual property provisions address patents. Equally remarkable, of those forty-nine provisions, thirty-five are in two-year colleges' contracts. The incidence of such provisions is *not* associated with institutional type ($x2=2.825$) (see table 6.2).

Similarly with the case of copyrighting. That type of intellectual property is addressed in 83 percent of the provisions. Of these fifty-nine provisions, forty-five are in two-year colleges' contracts. Again, the

incidence of such provisions is *not* associated with institutional type
(x2=4.8)

TABLE 6.2
INCIDENCE OF INTELLECTUAL PROPERTY PROVISIONS

	Two-year	Tech	Four-year	Total
Clauses	51	2	18	71
Property/ patent	35	1	13	49
Property/ copyright	45	1	13	59
Property/ tapes	14	1	6	21
Ownership	46	2	12	60*
Faculty produce on own	45	2	8	55
Faculty use instl resources	43	2	8	53
Faculty produce for inst	37	0	6	43
Process	38	1	10	49**
Profits	46	2	11	59***
Limits on use	9	1	0	10

* In fifty-five of these cases the provision identifies some situation in which the faculty has out-right ownership.
** In only two cases do the provisions indicate that committees are involved in the process.
*** In forty-nine cases the provision is for faculty to get a share of the profits.

Almost one-third (30 percent) of the provisions speak to tapes or
other electronically produced materials. One might expect such provisions to be more likely in the contracts of two-year colleges. Of these
twenty-one provisions, fourteen are in two-year colleges' contracts. Yet
again, the incidence of such provisions is *not* associated with institutional type (x2=.44).

In short, contrary to expectations, intellectual property provisions
that address patents are no more likely in the contracts of four- than of
two-year institutions. Neither are provisions that address tapes (dis-

tance learning) any more likely in the contracts of two- than of four-year institutions.

There are types of intellectual property other than copyrights, patents, and tapes that are mentioned in the provisions. At least different language is utilized to refer to the intellectual property. For example, thirty provisions refer to "materials" (twenty-six are in two-year colleges' contracts). In some cases, materials are specified as "instructional," "teaching," or "course" materials. More often, they are simply referred to as "materials." Other property language includes "inventions" and "processes."

Keep in mind, of course, that for all the types of property that are mentioned in the 71 contracts that have intellectual property provisions, there are 141 contracts in which there is no contractual provision regarding property rights. Faculty claims and managerial domain in regard to intellectual property are relatively undefined contractually.

Who Owns the Property?

In those sixty contracts that explicitly define ownership of intellectual property, there is surprisingly extensive provision for faculty ownership. In fifty-five cases, there is provision under some conditions for faculty's outright ownership of property that they create. Fifty-one clauses define conditions in which the institution owns the property outright. In eleven cases, joint ownership is established under some conditions.

Most of the contracts define more than one condition of ownership. There are three contracts that only define ownership for the institution. In two contracts only faculty ownership is defined (and two contracts simply provide for negotiation). The fifty-three other contracts speak to two or more conditions of ownership. Generally, they identify conditions under which faculty or the institution have outright ownership. In another twenty-six provisions, one of the conditions identified involves a case by case negotiation of ownership.

> The ownership of any materials or processes developed on an individual's own time, off-campus, and at no expense to the College shall vest and be copyrighted or patented, if at all, in the faculty member's name. The ownership of materials or processes produced solely for the College

and at the College expense shall vest in the College and be copyrighted or patented, if at all, in its name. . . . In those instances where materials or processes are produced by a faculty member with College support, by way of use of significant personnel time, facilities or other College resources, the ownership of the materials or processes shall vest in (and be copyrighted or patented by, if at all) the party designated by written agreement between the parties entered into prior to the production. (Clackamas Community College, Article 14)

In other words, the answer to who owns the property depends on the conditions in which it was produced. In 95 percent of those contracts with intellectual property provisions, faculty's ownership claims either are ensured in some situations (fifty-five cases) or are defined as a possible result of negotiation (two cases).

It is surprising that four-year institutions are *not* overrepresented in defining ownership (indeed, there is not a dependent association between incidence and institutional type—$x2=3.55$). Nor are they overrepresented in those contracts that provide for faculty ownership. Quite the contrary. There is a dependent association between the incidence of such contracts and institutional type ($x2=8.46$, significant at .025 level), but not in the expected direction. Four-year institutions are *under*represented, accounting for 13 percent of such contracts, compared to 25 percent of HECAS contracts. Put in other terms, almost one-third (32 percent) of HECAS contracts in two-year colleges provide for faculty ownership. Only 13 percent of HECAS contracts in four-year institutions have such provision. Managerial domain is greater in four- than in two-year institutions. Faculty claims to their intellectual property are greater in two- than in four-year institutions.

(Twelve contracts speak to intellectual property issues but do not define ownership. In five cases—all in four-year institutions—the contracts simply refer to board policy. In five of the seven other cases, the property mentioned is tapes. That is significant given the discussion in chapter 5 of the emergent area of instructional technology, for the presumption in these contracts is that tapes belong to the institution.)

What Conditions of Production Affect Ownership?

The key factors that determine who owns intellectual property are fairly consistent across the fifty-eight contracts that specify such conditions. The language varies, but the conditions fall into three general categories. The most common condition, found in fifty-five contracts, refers to property independently produced by faculty. An equally common condition is found in fifty-three contracts that refer to faculty's use of institutional resources and/or personnel time to produce the property. Finally, forty-three contracts refer to property that is commissioned by the institution—"work for hire."

There is surprisingly extensive provision for conditions in which faculty independently produce intellectual property. In fifty-five contracts faculty are recognized as professionals who have time and work that is independent and outside the control of their employer. All but three of the contracts that address conditions of production accept the possibility that faculty might produce intellectual property on their own and thereby own the property outright. (Four contracts indicate that faculty own property developed while on sabbatical, another dimension of independence; three others address production during consulting.) In thirty-seven of these contracts, reference to faculty's *own time* is implicit. Language refers to property produced by faculty's "independent efforts," "individual effort and expense," "independent labors without the use of paid time," or "own individual initiative." An additional eighteen contracts explicitly refer to faculty's "own time," a surprising finding given that managers appear to be dropping such language from nonunionized research universities' policies.

It is also surprising that the provision of professional independence in property rights is more commonly found in the contracts of two-year colleges than those of four-year institutions. There is a dependent association between institutional type and the incidence of clauses that either implicitly or explicitly accord faculty their own time ($x2=6.56$, significant at the .05 level). Such language is found in almost one-third (31 percent) of HECAS contracts in two-year colleges, compared to only 15 percent of contracts in four-year institutions (and 4.5 percent of those in technical colleges). (However, no such dependent association is found between institutional type and the incidence of explicit "own time" language—$x2=2$.)

At the other conditional extreme are those situations in which property is produced by faculty specifically for the institution, addressed in forty-three contracts. The language surrounding such "work for hire" varies. In fact, only two provisions use that phrase. In addition to DuPage Community College's contract, Black Hawk Community

College's contract identifies the term in defining one condition in which the college owns the property: "The product is assigned duty or a 'work for hire' as defined in the Copyright Act (17 U.S. Code 101)" (Article 5.2.c.2). The most common phrase refers to property that is "produced solely for the College and at College expense." Other phrasing also points to the institution's sponsorship: "paid by the College specifically for the work," "commissioned projects," and "as part of a faculty member's duties, responsibilities, or assignments" (Baker College, Article 3.2). In other words, it is not just a matter of using college resources. The work must be assigned. For example, the contract of the County College of Morris defines distinct ownership claims for the two conditions.

> Institutional Ownership. If a faculty member produces materials in the performance of assigned duties, then the College shall own such materials . . . Joint Ownership. If the College funds creation of a work by means of released time, or through the assistance of other employees, or with equipment to which the faculty member would not normally have unrestricted access, then the College shall have joint ownership with the faculty member. (Article 24.B)

(The institution does not always claim ownership even when the product is a work for hire. In three contracts, faculty still own the property, with one condition of ownership being reimbursement for college investment. In two cases, ownership is left to individual negotiation.)

In between faculty's independent production and their production for the institution is the less clearly defined middle ground identified in fifty-three contracts. These are situations in which faculty use institutional resources and/or time in the production of property. A few contracts (such as, Washtenaw Community College) specifically define the amount of institutional resources or time that must be used by the faculty member for the provision to apply.

> Those materials developed by a faculty member with major support from a College department will be reviewed to determine ownership and residual rights. . . . The requirements or criteria which constitute major or substantial support from the College and require that the proposal be brought before the Intellectual Property Rights Committee are any one of the following: a) The faculty member has been provided, or it is estimated that the project will require, the equivalent of 30 or more hours of

support from a College department. b) An administrator from the supporting department estimates that the expertise, skill, or creativity that will or is being provided is a very significant part of the collaboration. c) The faculty member has been granted release time to work on the project. d) The faculty member has received extra compensation to work on the project. (Article 29.2)

For the most part, however, the contractual language is relatively vague. Olympic College's contract uses the phrasing most commonly found.

In those instances where materials, processes or inventions are produced by an employee with College support, by way of use of significant personnel, time, facilities, or other College resources, the ownership . . . shall vest in (and be copyrighted or patented by, if at all) the person designated by written agreement between the parties entered into prior to production. (Article 5, Section 13.c)

The term *significant* is undefined. How much use is "insignificant"? Similarly, in other contracts phrases such as *on district time or at district expense*, *at College expense and on College time*, and *use of the resources of both faculty member and the College*, are undefined.

Whatever the particular language, it is this middle ground condition of production in which ownership is most likely to be negotiated. As in Olympic College's contract above, the negotiation is between the individual faculty member and the institution. It is interesting that contractual language assumes that intellectual property is produced by individuals. Only three contracts (those of Highline Community College, San Diego Community College, and Washtenaw Community College) speak to property that is created by a group of faculty.

What is the Process for Determining Ownership and Profits?

In matters of intellectual property, the process for determining ownership and profits generally follows a case by case, individualistic negotiation. That is, the faculty member negotiates with the institution, as an individual, independent professional. In only two cases are committees involved in decision making surrounding intellectual property rights. Procedures are generally relatively undefined. And there is little contractual definition of a process by which to arbitrate negotiations that break down.

Of the forty-nine contractual provisions that speak to process, forty-seven refer only to negotiations between the faculty member and the institution. In only two cases are committees part of the process. At first blush, that arrangement appears to give broad discretion both to faculty members and to institutional managers to negotiate a deal appropriate to each case. Consider, however, that many contracts have a clause regarding negotiations that reads as follows: "In the event there is no such written agreement entered into, the ownership shall vest in the College" (Mt. Hood Community College, Article 9.N.3). Management enters any such negotiations not only with more in the way of resources, legal expertise, and experience. Negotiations begin with the understanding that if the faculty member does not agree to a deal that is acceptable to management, ownership vests in the institution. Moreover, only four contracts define any appeal process in a situation in which negotiations break down.

In each of the two contracts with committees involved in the process, the committees' role is to make judgments regarding the conditions of production, ownership, and distribution of profits.[10]

To ascertain whether any inventions or materials members of the bargaining unit are planning to prepare, preparing, or have prepared, will be considered college supported, as set forth in this policy, a bargaining unit member initiates an inquiry to the college committee on Copyrights and Patents, hereafter called the "Committee" to which inquiry the Committee will respond. (Johnson County Community College, Article 7.3)

The [Intellectual Property Rights] Committee will be responsible for developing an agreement between the College and the author(s) as to ownership and residual rights. The Committee will review the proposal and estimate the costs of the project and the extent of College support involved. The Committee will deliberate and decide on right to royalties and royalty percentages or other methods of cost reimbursement if the product is to be marketed. The Committee will decide on other options related to ownership and usage rights such as the methods of distribution and marketing, if that is the intent, and the methods of revision of the material in the future. (Washtenaw Community College, Article 29.2)

The existence of such committees, particularly when they include faculty, establishes some collective professional constraint on managerial discretion.

There are relatively few contractual constraints on managerial discretion surrounding the disposition of intellectual property. Instead of establishing a specified and/or detailed set of procedures and processes, most clauses have but a sentence or two regarding negotiations.

Of the forty-nine provisions, five have some detail. For example, Rogue Community College's contract speaks to the faculty member providing "prompt notice" to the college about his activities. In turn, the college is enjoined to bargain "in good faith." Along the same lines, Tompkins Cortland Community College's contract indicates that faculty shall provide the college with written notice and that the college shall respond within twenty days defining any restrictions on the faculty member's work. The contract also indicates a time limit (six months) within which the college must apply for copyrights or patents on a faculty member's work, after which time the college's rights are waived.

Another thirteen contracts provide more extensive detail regarding the process for determining property rights. Some clauses are several paragraphs; others are as long as several pages. For example, the contract of the Florida State University System has three pages on "Inventions and Works" and another full page on "Instructional Technology." The provision has detailed definitions of the property; of independent effort; and of procedures surrounding disclosure, university review of property and declaration of interest, and release of rights. Highline Community College's provision details the property to be covered, the conditions surrounding the written agreement negotiated between the faculty member and the institution (for example, timing and content), the conditions applying to a faculty member's infringement or violation of other persons' property rights, and the sale of materials to college students.

The few examples cited above illustrate just how complicated the decision-making processes regarding intellectual property can be. At present, most provisions define little in the way of "process" surrounding decision making in such matters. Only 37 percent of those provisions that speak to process provide even limited detail. That represents only 25 percent of all intellectual property provisions and only 8.5 percent of HECAS contracts. In short, managerial discretion in this regard is extensive. Contrary to what might be expected, such discretion does not vary by institutional type: there is no dependent association between institutional type and process provisions ($x2=2.62$).

Who Gets the Profits?

Ownership is one matter. Distribution of the proceeds is quite another. For example, although research universities own the inventions developed by their employees (faculty), intellectual property policies generally provide for a distribution of royalties and proceeds to the faculty member and sometimes to their lab and/or to intermediate academic levels such as the department or college.

In contracts' intellectual property provisions, the profits generally follow ownership. Yet there are some interesting exceptions to this rule. In addition, there are situations in which profits are shared or reimbursements are required, in spite of ownership. However, even in these exceptional cases the sole claimants to the proceeds of intellectual property are the two sole claimants to ownership—the individual faculty member and the institution.

Profits are addressed in fifty-nine contracts. In forty-nine cases there is provision for faculty retaining attendant benefits. Generally, such profits accompany faculty's outright ownership of the property. The incidence of such provision is dependent on institutional type, but not in the expected direction ($x2=11.59$, significant at .005 level). Provision for faculty profits is *under*represented in four-year institutions, which account for only 8 percent of such provisions, as compared to 88 percent for two-year colleges, which are *over*represented (technical colleges are slightly underrepresented, at 4 percent).

As with the faculty claimant, so with the institution. Generally (with some exceptions), profits accompany the institution's outright ownership. There are thirty-six such provisions.

Some provisions leave the question of ownership to be negotiated between the faculty member and the institution. In these cases, profits are also left undefined. Thus, in twenty-five contracts, the distribution of profits is determined by negotiated agreement between the faculty member and the institution.

Finally, in another nineteen contracts there is provision for shared ownership and claims on profits. The precise proportion of shares is specified in eleven of these cases. For example, the University of Lowell contract calls for a fifty-fifty split, as does the County College of Morris contract, even when the College funded the creation of the work. Jackson Community College's contract calls for a twenty-five–seventy-five split when the faculty member is compensated by the College to develop the work (the smaller share going to the faculty member). So, too, with the Johnson Community College contract, with a slight variation. The split is twenty-five–seventy-five in favor of the college when the supported property is recorded materials and inventions; the shares are reversed for written materials. By contrast, in Illinois Eastern Community Colleges' contract, the eighty-twenty split favors faculty when the property is inventions and/or written materials—it favors the institution when the property is recorded materials. In Cuyahoga Community College's contract faculty receive 80 percent of the royalties of property developed with substantial use of college personnel or facilities. Youngstown State University's contract sets a 25 percent limit on the institution's share, even when the research is subsidized by the institution.

> Research is considered to be subsidized by YSU only if the faculty member receives a reduction in teaching load, a Research Professorship, a Faculty Improvement Leave, or a University Research Council grant, for the purpose of conducting the research. Under no circumstances shall YSU's share exceed 25 percent of the proceeds after the recovery by YSU of the cost of subsidy specified in the contract. The signing of a specific contract with YSU for subsidized research cannot be a stipulated condition of employment. This policy shall not apply to royalties, which go exclusively to the author. (Article 24.3)

In short, there is considerable provision for faculty sharing in the proceeds of the intellectual property they create. The extent of faculty claims is evident in the following: six contracts (all in two-year colleges) have provisions that speak *only* to faculty profits; six other contracts (four community colleges, a technical college and a four-year institution) have provisions that speak *only* to faculty shares and negotiation; and seven contracts (four community colleges and three four-year institutions) have provisions that speak *only* to faculty profits and joint shares.

What Controls/Limits are There on the Use of the Product?

The principal contractual control/limit on faculty's use of intellectual property relates to selling materials to students and to institutions' internal use of materials. Such provisions are found in ten contracts. All are in two-year institutions (nine community colleges and one technical college).

The language and particular conditions vary. Several contracts deal with college use. For example, Cloud County Community College, Cuyahoga Community College, Brookdale Community College, Illinois Eastern Community College, and Schoolcraft College's contracts accord the institution the right to use materials internally without charge.

Several other contracts deal with sales to students. The contracts of Hudson Valley Community College and Jackson Community College require college permission to sell materials to students. In the contract of Kern Community College there is provision that any materials sold to students must be sold at cost. Northeast Wisconsin Technical College's contract extends this limit to other Wisconsin vocational schools. Highline Community College's contract stipulates that materials must be sold through the college bookstore and that there must be a conflict of interest waiver.

The specific language varies, then, but the general principle is pervasive. Faculty should not profit commercially from instructional materials they develop by utilizing them within the institution that employs them (and by generating revenue from the students whose tuition pays their salaries). In the words of Northampton County Area Community College's contract:

> An Employee shall not realize a pecuniary gain from students of the College or from the College itself on any books, teaching aids, or equipment required or recommended for his classes except for royalties, commissions, or profits from commercial or university presses or production companies but excluding subsidy (vanity) presses, duplicating or printing companies and self-production. Any books or teaching aids authored, edited, invented, or produced by the Employee and published, printed, or produced by the Employee himself or through subsidy publishing or production shall be made available to the students or the College at cost. (Article 15.E)

In the end, the faculty member is an employee.

(The principal contractual control that faculty have on the institution's use of intellectual property created by faculty relates to the (re)broadcast of tapes or other materials in distance education. This ownership issue was addressed in chapter 5. Suffice it to say here that there are very few contracts that require faculty members' permission for the reuse of such materials.)

Institutional Type and Unit Membership

There is *not* a dependent association between the incidence of intellectual property provisions in general and institutional type ($x2=3.5$). That is surprising. It runs counter to expectations given prestige hierarchies among institutions and faculty. Intellectual property provisions are no more likely in the contracts of four- than of two-year institutions, despite a presumption in the literature that faculty in two-year insitutions do not produce intellectual property. Equally surprising is the fact that in those specific conditions in which there *is* a dependent association—faculty ownership, conditions recognizing faculty's autonomy, faculty profits—it is *not* in the expected direction. Faculty's claims on their property, on professional autonomy as independent professionals who create intellectual property on their own, and on profits are greater in two- than in four-year colleges and universities.

In no case, either of intellectual property provisions in general, or in the specific conditions analyzed, is there a dependent association between the incidence of such provisions and unit membership.[11] The contracts of units that cover only full-time faculty are no more or less likely to have intellectual property provisions in general or to have particular conditions addressed than are those contracts that cover some part-timers.

Discussion

The findings of this chapter are the most counterintuitive of the book. It is not just that contractual provisions in unionized institutions regarding outside employment and intellectual property are less restrictive of faculty autonomy than are comparable policies in research universities. It is that among unionized institutions, the provisions in two-year institution contracts are less restrictive than those in four-year institution contracts. Institutional prestige does *not* translate into more "professional" conditions of employment in the cases of outside employment and intellectual property. In these matters managerial domain is less extensive and faculty claims on their own time are more expansive in less prestigious higher education settings.

In regard to outside employment, the prevailing standard in research universities has been the "one-day-a-week" rule. Only five contracts set such a time limit on unionized faculty's consulting activities. Most (58 percent) HECAS contracts do not have outside employment provisions. Of the eighty-nine contracts that do have provisions, twenty-one deal only with sabbaticals or other leaves. Although many contracts accord managers the discretion to intervene and require faculty members to discontinue activity that has been determined to interfere with their assigned responsibilities, only thirty contracts require faculty to provide notice of their activities, and only twenty-four require them to gain prior approval. Those are far smaller numbers than what has been found for samples of ninety-eight major universities, or of 236 public universities: in these studies 70 and 48 percent of the institutions, respectively, had time allocation limits; 78 and 61 percent had prior approval requirements.[12]

Faculty in unionized settings do not appear to be subject to the same constraints on their professional outside employment activities as have been found in research universities (largely nonunionized). If they are employees, faculty in unionized colleges and universities are given much freedom to pursue consulting activities as independent professionals. They have much time of their own.

Disaggregating between two- and four-year institutions, faculty's independence is greater in the former than in the latter, at least when it comes to outside employment. Four-year institutions are overrepresented in contracts that have conflict of commitment clauses (and that provide for managerial discretion) as well as notice, prior approval, use of resources (and managerial discretion in such use), and time limits. In no case can the differences be attributed to the presence of part-time faculty in the unit, who might be less regulated in this regard. There are no provisions for which incidence is associated with unit membership.

In regard to intellectual property, the results are similar. Literature on research universities suggests that faculty's claims to their intellectual property have been increasingly circumscribed. Faculty are losing claim to "their own time" during which they may create intellectual property. Yet most intellectual property clauses in unionized settings afford faculty a claim to have produced intellectual property independently. A significant minority of provisions refer explicitly to faculty's "own time." In several contracts, even when the institution has supported the development of the property, faculty retain ownership and/or claims to profits. There is surprisingly extensive provision for faculty claims to ownership and to profits. Moreover, there are no intervening organizational levels in the institution—for example, departments, colleges—that lay claim to the proceeds of property. Faculty negotiate their claims independently with management. Contractually, they are treated as entrepreneurial, salaried professionals. In unionized settings, employment does not equal employer ownership of faculty's time and expertise.

Contrary to what might be expected, faculty's claims to the products and proceeds of their labors are not greater in four- than in two-year institutions. If anything, the reverse is true. Two-year college contracts are overrepresented among those provisions that accord faculty ownership rights and claims to profits. As in the case of outside employment provisions, in no case can the differences be attributed to the presence of part-time faculty in the unit, who might be less regulated in this regard. There are no provisions for which incidence is associated with unit membership.

These findings are so counterintuitive that many readers will find them hard to accept. Particularly readers who are more personally invested in research and who are located in more prestigious settings—four-year and/or research universities. How might these findings be explained?

I have presented these findings at professional meetings. I have also circulated this chapter to colleagues for their review. The most common response I have received focuses on intellectual property and goes something like the following. Of course faculty's claims on their intellectual property are more regulated in nonunionized settings. Faculty in unionized settings do not produce any intellectual property of value. Similarly, of course, faculty's claims on their intellectual property are more regulated in four- versus two-year institutions. Faculty in community and technical colleges do not produce any intellectual property of value. Intellectual property regulation is a function of the value of faculty's intellectual labors. The more valuable the property generated by faculty labor, the more likely that institutions will move to regulate and/or harness that labor.

There is certainly some plausibility to the above argument and proposition, particularly if we equate the award of federal research grants and contracts with valuable intellectual property. Yet the argument presumes that unionized institutions cannot be counted among those institutions that successfully compete for federal research grants and contracts. As a broad generalization, that is largely true. However, it overlooks some important exceptional cases among unionized institutions. It also suffers from some basic assumptions that overlook some significant domains of intellectual property. Of the top one hundred institutions in terms of share of federal funds for academic research, eleven are unionized; of the next ninety-four institutions, seven others are unionized.[13] These are exceptions to be sure. But a significant number nonetheless (although the total—eighteen—falls far short of the number of contracts with intellectual property provisions).

Perhaps what is more important, equating valuable intellectual property with federal grants and contracts for research overlooks the enormous value of intellectual property oriented to teaching. In research universities we tend to conflate intellectual property with high technology products that stem from research grants in science, medicine, and engineering (just as we conflate productivity with number of research publications and research grants). As a result, we overlook the extensive amount of valuable and revenue-generating intellectual property produced by faculty in fields such as nursing and education (for example, various tests, diagnostic instruments, and curricular materials). And we overlook the value of intellectual products that are geared to instruction. Computer software programs are a particularly significant example of such products. If we consider these sorts of intellectual products, then we begin to see that faculty in various fields and types of institutions may produce intellectual property that has much value, including marketplace value.

At any rate, the argument that there is a positive relationship between the value and the regulation of intellectual property may seem plausible in principle. But in practice it does not explain a curious finding regarding intellectual property provisions. There is *not* a dependent association between type of property covered by the contract (for example, patents, distance education tapes, copyright) and institutional type, a point that runs directly counter to the preceding proposition.

Of course, none of this speaks to the findings in regard to outside employment. An argument about the differential value of faculty's work in different higher education sectors is far less plausible when it comes to consulting. For example, in community colleges and comprehensive state colleges and universities large numbers of faculty work in technical fields. The consulting activities of these faculty are grounded not solely or even primarily in their expertise as members of the academic profession, but in their expertise in a profession other than academe. Moreover, the consulting activities of faculty are widespread throughout the higher education system. There is no reason to believe there is any great differential between the two- and four-year sectors in this regard. Thus, how are we to explain the greater freedom that faculty have in unionized institutions in general, and in two-year versus in four-year institutions, among unionized colleges and universities?

We are left with a couple of ironies. First, the most elite segments of professions may be the most monitored and controlled. Recent and current scholars of professions overlook this possibility, whether in talking of "academic revolution," the increasing importance of markets, or the growth of "academic capitalism."[14] Too often, scholars presume that by generating significant external revenues, professions or occupations (or segments of them) enhance their independence. It may be, as one reader suggested to me, that research universities provide more time, facilities, and support to faculty for research than do community colleges, and that it is therefore neither surprising nor unreasonable that they have more claim to the products of that research. Perhaps not. However, it runs directly counter to our assumptions and theories about a positive relationship between faculty expertise and faculty autonomy.

Notwithstanding the literature on academics, expertise, and autonomy, scholars might consider the possibility that commercial value, connection to external revenue sources, and connection to capital all bring with them increased regulation of activity. A classic example is a study of Chicago lawyers which found that criminal attorneys who defended working- and lower-class offenders had more control over their time and work than did attorneys in law firms that had big corporate clients.[15] A current example is a study of "experts" which suggests that professionals are increasingly oriented to the market and increasingly defined by their market and organizational position. The result may be more private sector models of organizational claims on employees, professional or otherwise.[16] At the very least, we should consider the possibility that the relationship between the economic value of one's work and one's autonomy is more complex than the current literature allows.

A second irony surrounding my findings is that the very settings that are more likely to control faculty more at their place of employment actually regulate them less in their outside employment and in their own time spent generating intellectual property. In unionized institutions, the most contractually regulated dimension of a faculty member's work is instruction. Course load assignments and office hours are far more common subjects of contractual provisions than are research activities. And such provisions are more detailed, extensive, and restrictive in two-year colleges than in four-year institutions, sometimes involving the regulation of clock hours on campus.[17] (Such "regulated" time is still far less than a forty hour week. Contact hours for teaching are generally no more than fifteen, with specified office hours beyond that bringing the total to around twenty hours per week. That leaves faculty in even the most regulated situations with much time of their own.)

Too much should not be made of unionized faculty's control of their time and work. Managers' contractual discretion is extensive in matters of outside employment and intellectual property rights. Outside employment provisions accord managers much discretion—for example, in determining whether there is conflict of commitment between the outside employment and the faculty member's principal employment activity and in approving use of institutional resources and facilities. Managerial discretion is even broader in intellectual property matters. For the most part, decision making in this arena consists of individual negotiations and discretionary determinations about faculty's use of institutional personnel, facilities, and time, among other matters. There is very little provision in either situation for due process or appeal.

Nevertheless, if faculty are salaried employees, they are also more than that. Unionized faculty are professionals who enjoy much claim contractually on the time they devote to their labor and to the products of that labor.

(Of course, they are also more than "professionals"; they are people. In analyzing outside employment and intellectual property rights clauses, I have addressed the "public," "professional" domains of faculty time. Although I did not pursue the issue in this chapter, I want to close by noting that groups of faculty (women's groups in particular) have contributed to the introduction of various sorts of leaves—for example, family, maternity, child-bearing/rearing—that effectively protect or extend the "private" domain of faculty's lives, thereby challenging managerial efforts to gain increased control of employees' time. It is worth exploring the extent to which such provisions have been incorporated into unionized faculty's collective bargaining agreements.)

Unionized Faculty: Managing the Restructuring of Professionals and Production Work in Colleges and Universities

My conclusion is my title. Unionized faculty are managed, stratified professionals. The contractual terms of faculty employment are such that managers have considerable flexibility to restructure academic labor. The exercise of that discretion is contributing to increased stratification among categories of faculty.

Of course, it is more complicated than that. The politics of professional work, in this case the bargaining between unionized faculty and management, is not one-sided. Administrators' contractual discretion to manage faculty is extensive. Yet unionized faculty have established professional structures, constraints, and rights in the contractual terms of their labor that restrict managerial prerogatives and discretion. They have negotiated important safeguards for professional autonomy and independence.

So, too, the politics of professional stratification is not one-sided. Administrators' contractual discretion enables them to differentially treat and utilize categories of faculty, contributing to increased stratification among them. Yet the structures, constraints, and professional rights that unionized faculty have embedded in the contracts also serve to perpetuate and sharpen stratification among faculty. Unions have negotiated mechanisms that (pre)serve the professional position of tenured, senior, and full-time faculty.

Neither is the politics of professional stratification one-dimensional. In many matters, such as salary structure and retrenchment, the traditional institutional differentiation of faculty's working conditions

257

prevails. Conditions tend to be more "professional" and more restrictive of managerial flexibility in four- than in two-year institutions. Yet
that division does not prevail within or throughout the contractual terms
of employment examined here. Moreover, in some matters, such as outside employment and intellectual property rights, the hierarchy is
reversed, with unionized faculty in two-year colleges enjoying more
"professional" working conditions than those in four-year settings.

In summarizing my findings in the first section of this chapter, I
come back again and again to these variegated themes. I also extend
these themes to the context of nonunionized higher education. This
study's data are on unionized colleges and universities. However, the
implications and relevance of the findings extend to higher education as
a whole.

In the next section of this chapter I return to the literatures on which
I have drawn. I suggest the principal implications of my work analytically and substantively for sociological research on professions and for
higher education research on college and university faculty.

Finally, I move on to discuss the theme that runs throughout the
entire book—the restructuring of faculty as a work force, indeed the
restructuring of the professional work force as a whole and of production work in higher education. I organize this section around four major
pieces of work in the last quarter of a century regarding academe. The
collective bargaining agreements I analyzed are limited in what they
can tell us directly about restructuring. They cannot tell us how many
faculty have been retrenched, and in what fields. They cannot tell us
how many academic programs have been reorganized out of existence.
They cannot tell us how many part-time faculty are utilized. They cannot tell us the amount of money that institutions have invested in educational technologies and the extent to which these technologies have
been utilized to deliver distance education. They cannot tell us the
extent to which faculty are engaged in outside employment, or the
amount of intellectual property that colleges and universities own
which was created by faculty. But the contracts do offer insight into the
mechanisms and strategies that suggest and facilitate patterns of
restructuring. Thus, in discussing restructuring and production work, I
also speak to major issues and challenges confronting unions in particular and faculty in general.

Summary of Contractual Findings

Salary Structures

Nowhere is the complexity of the politics of professional work in unionized institutions clearer than in collective bargaining agreements' salary structures. So, too, nowhere are the patterns of restructuring and stratification in academe as a whole clearer.

Unions promote the collective interests of faculty as professionals. The most basic salary structure is across-the-board percentage raises. In a profession that is built on the ideology of individual meritocracy, that might seem anomalous, even anathema. However, in a profession that in practice has not realized a real increase in salaries from wage levels two decades ago, that is arguably a useful strategy to promote faculty's collective interests. Too often, in nonunionized settings so-called merit monies do not even equal cost-of-living increases. They may be called "merit." In fact, they often constitute a reduction in pay in real terms.

So, too, with set salary structures and salary minimums and ranges. In a profession built on the ideology of individual performance, such scales might seem strange. However, in a profession that in practice rewards seniority and (administrative) experience, and in which salaries are increasingly differentiated by market-driven adjustments, that is arguably a reasonable strategy to promote the profession's collective interests. In the profession at large, rewards are increasingly shaped more by market than by merit.

Unions are not antithetical to merit or to market, particularly not in the four-year sector. Merit and market mechanisms are built into the salary structures of most collective bargaining agreements in four-year institutions. Although they are less evident in the contracts of two-year colleges, they also have a significant presence there as well. Moreover, over two-thirds of the contracts accord managers discretion to set initial salaries.

At the same time, the existence of equity provisions in a little less than half of four-year institutions' contracts (and just under one-tenth of two-year colleges' contracts) speaks again to unions' efforts to promote faculty's collective interests. The provisions speak far more to general and market-induced than to gender based inequity. Gender issues do not figure prominently in the salary provisions of contracts. That relative absence is remarkable given the continued and expanded gender gap in faculty salaries.

Despite union efforts to constrain managerial flexibility in differentially setting and shaping faculty salaries, and to restrain salary inequities among faculty, the prevailing trend in salaries over two decades is increased salary dispersion. Measured by average salaries in various academic fields there is much stratification among faculty salaries. Moreover, the gap between fields at the top and bottom of the salary hierarchy has increased over time, as has the gap between men and women.

Such patterns point to a reallocation of resources among fields and among faculty. In other words, restructuring is in evidence not simply in recent dramatic efforts to eliminate academic programs and terminate faculty. Restructuring has been taking place gradually, over the course of decades, in the increasingly differentiated structure of academic salaries.[1] College and university managers are differentially investing and allocating their monies across academic fields, restricting growth in some areas even as they accelerate growth in others.

Retrenchment

Retrenchment clauses, too, point to the complexity of the politics of professional work. The rationales justifying retrenchment suggest a shift from financially and crisis-driven layoffs to programmatically and enrollment-driven medium- and long-term reallocations of faculty resources. Few contracts utilize the language of financial exigency in their retrenchment provisions. Many do not even identify conditions to justify faculty layoffs. Of those that do, most invoke a range of vague, noncrisis conditions that afford managers extensive discretion. Most such conditions are grounded in program curtailment that stems from planned reorganization or shifting student demand. That speaks to the salary trends noted above. Managers have the flexibility not just to pay faculty in some fields more than similarly qualified, experienced, and productive peers in other fields. They can also retrench faculty in some fields, even as they increase faculty numbers in others.

The contractual provisions are not unlike the policies and procedures found in any research university's faculty handbook. Retrenchment generally is justified either by financial difficulties or by programmatic changes, or both. Notwithstanding the dispute at the

University of Minnesota, which centered partly on whether faculty could be retrenched when subunits within departments are reorganized, in most public research universities (including Minnesota) tenured faculty can be retrenched due to departmental "reorganization."

Unions have negotiated a range of structures and provisions that discourage managers from exercising their flexibility in laying off faculty. Retrenching faculty, even tenured faculty, is *not* illegal. However, due to the efforts of faculty unions it *is* more procedurally (and politically) difficult than most managers would like. From provision for consultation about retrenchment to a defined order for laying off faculty, to required periods of notice, to procedures surrounding the reassignment, retraining, and or recall of targeted or laid off faculty, provisions are filled with structures that draw out the time and energy required to lay off faculty. You can find similar policies/procedures in most research universities' faculty handbooks.

Contractually, in most matters, managers retain final authority and/or extraordinary discretion to make exception to established procedures. They can, for example, violate the order of layoff. They can choose not to reassign or retrain faculty. They can wait to recreate new positions in layoff units until after the recall period, or they can define newly created units and positions in ways that reduce or eliminate laid off faculty's claims on positions. And for all the consultation in which they engage faculty, it is the managers who determine whether and where to retrench.

A considerable number of contracts provide for some consultation with the unions and/or faculty prior to effecting a layoff. In many cases it is simply an agreement to give the union information and consider the union's recommendations. In many other cases, it is an agreement to meet and discuss. In either case, the union and/or faculty are in a reactive position. They must react to plans that already have been drafted. Even in those contracts that call for committees to be formed or consulted, faculty are reacting to managers' plans. Nevertheless, faculty play at least some role in the process. And again, it establishes a process that takes time, that involves dispute and challenge, and that extends and to some extent constrains managers.

Professional stratification is evidenced in two ways in the retrenchment provisions. First, there is variation by institutional type in the various types of provisions. For example, contracts in four-year institutions are more likely than those in two-year colleges to define rationales for retrenchment. Faculty consultation is more likely in four- than in two-year institutions. The findings support prevailing views in the literature regarding the greater degree of managerial flexibility vis-à-vis faculty. Yet reality and discretion are multilayered and complex. As noted in chapter 2, these same managers enjoy less flexibility than do their counterparts in four-year institutions in matters of setting salaries, for the contracts of community colleges often have set salary schedules. Moreover, the salary structures of four-year institutions are more likely to have merit and market mechanisms, which afford managers more discretion in setting faculty salaries.

A second dimension of professional stratification evidenced in retrenchment provisions is in the consistent professional strategy of preserving professional privilege and the position of those who benefit from such structures. Established structures such as order of layoff (and recall) by definition give priority to tenured, senior, and full-time faculty, who as a collective are more likely to be Anglo males. So, too, with the practice of displacement/bumping through the exercise of "seniority rights." Moreover, in matters of notice, retraining, and recall, the provisions often vary according to faculty members' contractual status. Of course, the aim of this professional strategy is to prevent managers from downgrading the profession by targeting its most senior and expensive members for layoff. However, the effect of such a strategy is not just to preserve, but also to heighten the divisions among categories of faculty.

Part-Time Faculty

Provisions regarding the use of part-time faculty provide an interesting contrast by way of professional strategy. There is, of course, the prioritizing of full- over part-time faculty in layoffs. However, there is little evidence of complicated and varied procedures that have the effect if not the design of drawing out the process of utilizing part-timers.

Consider the hiring and firing of part-time faculty. There is very little by way of process that has been negotiated. At least, not much got into the contracts. Certainly, one of the main attractions of using part-time faculty for managers is the flexibility they can exercise in (re)allocating these faculty resources. It is surprising, then, that unions have not more actively (or successfully) negotiated standard professional procedures that would make it more complicated for managers to utilize part-time faculty, thereby discouraging them from utilizing as many as they increasingly do. Indeed, part-time faculty lack basic professional rights that would set parameters on their use. Contracts that speak to their rights in personnel and work-force actions are few and far between.

There are some provisions that seek to control the configuration of the work force. They establish or delimit ratios of full- to part-time faculty, seeking to contain the growth of such faculty. However, these are exceptional cases. And most contracts lack provision for full-time faculty's involvement in and control over the use of part-timers when they are used. Whether in selecting or in reviewing faculty, full-timers are largely absent.

What is also absent are basic employment perquisites and professional duties for part-time faculty. They enjoy little by way of leaves and benefits, speaking to the sharp stratification of full- and part-timers. What little they enjoy is influenced by the makeup of the bargaining unit. Most of the units in HECAS include at least some part-timers, and these are, as one would expect, the most likely contracts to define some perquisites for part-time faculty. Yet, large numbers of part-time faculty are excluded from these units, speaking to the various gradations within the part-time work force. And most of these contracts lack provision for perquisites for any part-time faculty. As with established procedures, then, there is little by way of perquisites that would discourage managers from extensively utilizing part-time faculty. Obviously, part of the attraction to managers of utilizing part-timers is that they are cheaper than full-timers, not just in terms of salaries but in terms of benefits. One hedge against their increased use would be to substantially improve their terms of labor in these regards.

Another strategy that is little in evidence is to bargain the quality of working condition issues that would integrate part-time faculty more fully into the life of the departments in which they work. Involving full-time faculty in the hiring process would be one means of achieving this. So, too, would negotiating a range of conditions that would expand part-time faculty's role (and thus their pay).

The marginal professional position of part-time faculty is further evident in the few provisions that exist regarding duties and part-time experience. Part-time faculty simply deliver instruction. The wide range of duties that characterize faculty work is reduced in scope to the classroom (and sometimes to office hours). The contractual status of that work is clarified by the fact that of the minority of agreements that speak to whether (previous) experience teaching part-time is credited in salary and seniority calculations, one-quarter are negative references. Part-time teaching is discredited not just by omission, but by stark statements that such work is not credited as professional experience.

In sum, the professional strategy of unionized faculty appears to be to simply contain the use of part-time faculty to the margins. Increasingly, however, it is full-time faculty who are being marginalized in much of American higher education, as managers hire greater and greater numbers and percentages of part-time faculty. Of course, part-time faculty's terms of employment are a function of more than the professional strategies of unionized faculty. They are also a function of managerial strategy, which is to maximize flexibility vis-à-vis all faculty.

The exercise of that managerial flexibility has contributed to various dimensions of professionals' stratification. The most obvious dimension is the gap between the working conditions of full- and part-time faculty in general. That is layered on top of the differentiation among various institutional types and among various academic fields in the use of part-time faculty. Some institutions are becoming largely part-time, further heightening the hierarchy among institutions. So, too, some fields are becoming largely part-time, contributing to sharper stratification within institutions. Finally, hidden within the previous dimensions is gender stratification. In proportional terms women are most highly concentrated in the ranks of part-time faculty, and in the lower status institutions and fields that have the highest percentages of part-time faculty.

Instructional Technology

Contractual provisions regarding the use of instructional technology are few. And, as with provisions regarding the use of part-time faculty, they are quite limited in scope. The eventual outcome may also be similar. Contractual provisions will have little effect in blocking managerial discretion to reduce full-time faculty's centrality in generating student credit hours.

Some observers might suggest that it is at least five years too early to determine what the effects of instructional technology will be. We should wait to appraise the impact on the social relations and character of professional work in higher education. By contrast, I would suggest that it is five years too late for bargaining agents to negotiate faculty involvement and rights in the use of instructional technology. Social relations in the academy are already shaping decisions about whether to invest in new instructional technologies and about what specific technologies to utilize. In the process, the professional work force that "produces" instruction is being reshaped.

Instructional technologies are more than just new methods of delivering instruction. They are means by which managers can bypass full-time faculty's influence and claims on the curriculum. Utilizing instructional technology to provide courses and programs of study potentially represents a variation on subcontracting bargaining-unit work. It is electronic subcontracting.

Managers are constructing a curricular realm over which they have more discretion and control. For example, they have more control over what courses will be offered and when. They have more influence over the form and delivery of curriculum. They may staff the courses with larger numbers of part-time faculty. Instructional technology may be utilized and controlled in a relatively separate curricular enclave that may be more insulated (some would say protected) from the control of full-time faculty. Moreover, new positions and occupations are emerging to technically support and direct the implementation of instructional technology in the curriculum (not only in separate course delivery, on which I have focused, but also in supporting faculty in the traditional curriculum who utilize new technologies in their courses). In short, more and more personnel other than traditional, full-time faculty are coming to be involved in the delivery of instruction.

The national faculty unions are encouraging local bargaining agents to negotiate a range of issues surrounding the use of instructional technology. Yet only a little over one-third of HECAS contracts have any provisions related to instructional technology. And the provisions that exist are limited in scope. The professional strategy appears to be more of a defensive reaction against some of threats posed by technology than a proactive effort to gain involvement in a range of decisions surrounding its purchase and use. As with the use of part-time faculty, so with the use of instructional technology: the contracts do not reveal structures/procedures that make it more complicated and difficult for managers to deliver instruction with new technologies.

If faculty unions aim to marginalize the use of instructional technology, they run the risk of being themselves marginalized. To dismiss technology's importance, or to believe that its use can be contained, may be as fruitless and misguided as the efforts of Luddites in early nineteenth-century England to smash the machines that threatened their jobs. New technology offers new opportunities for establishing broader faculty control of instructional delivery. If faculty do not take advantage of this opportunity, other groups will step in to fill the void. Indeed, I believe that is already happening with the development of yet another nonfaculty, nonbargaining-unit technical/professional group—support professionals and staff involved in the use of instructional technology. In the absence of contractual provisions that afford full-time faculty a major role in the utilization of new instructional technologies, managers will likely increasingly utilize these technologies to deliver an increasing proportion of the curriculum beyond the purview of bargaining-unit faculty. They are likely to appoint and rely upon new categories of nonfaculty, nonbargaining-unit members to support and oversee the delivery of such coursework. And they are likely to increasingly utilize part-time faculty (especially those who are outside the bargaining unit) to deliver instruction with technology.

Outside Employment and Intellectual Property Rights

My analysis of outside employment and intellectual property rights provides probably the most counterintuitive findings of the book, counterintuitive in terms of academic hierarchy. The presumption is that as one moves up the hierarchy of higher education institutions the prestige and expertise, and thus the professional autonomy, of the faculty increases. My findings are that among unionized faculty, those who are in two-year colleges enjoy more autonomy in their outside employment and more claim on their intellectual property than do faculty in four-year institutions. Moreover, my findings suggest that unionized faculty may enjoy greater professional claims in such matters (particularly in outside employment) than do nonunionized faculty who are in research universities.

Outside employment and intellectual property policies and provisions rest in part on the determination of how much claim the employing organization has on a faculty member's time. Faculty like to believe that their colleges and universities do not own all their time and expertise. Faculty claim the privilege of selling their professional services to outside employers. They claim the right to the products of their labors. They justify such claims in part in terms of having their "own time," distinct from the load— instructional and otherwise—that the institution assigns them.

Surprisingly few contracts have provisions that delimit the time faculty can devote to outside employment. Relatively few require faculty to even give notice of their outside activities. Even fewer require prior approval. In their outside employment, unionized faculty are relatively unregulated.

The situation is similar with intellectual property rights provisions. Only one-third of the contracts have provisions. Of those, the vast majority grant faculty quite extensive claims not just on the proceeds but on the ownership of the products of their labors. On occasion such claims are granted even when that work was commissioned by the institution. Throughout, there is acknowledgement that faculty can create inventions independently, on their own time.

And yet, again it is more complicated than that. Unionized faculty may be more autonomous than nonunionized faculty in their freedom to pursue outside employment. However, they are less autonomous than nonunionized faculty in research universities in the regulation of their teaching work load. In the contracts, teaching is the principal work-load activity that is regulated.[2] And there are differences between the contracts of two- and four-year institutions that follow the higher education hierarchy. Faculty in two-year institutions not only have more contact hours in the classroom with students, but their time outside class is more regulated. For example, contracts often specify not just office hours, but the number of days per week and sometimes even the hours per day that faculty must be on campus. By contrast, faculty in four-year institutions have fewer contact hours in the classroom with students, and their contracts, if they mention time on campus at all, refer only to the need for faculty to "maintain a significant presence on campus."[3] It is interesting that contrary to popular mythology, between 1987 and 1992, in every category of institution other than liberal arts colleges, those contact hours increased. And in yet another twist that points to the complexity of professional autonomy, as one moves up the institutional hierarchy, faculty report spending more time at the institution, with the most hours being spent by public research university faculty. These hours have declined from 1987 to 1992. Perhaps the more that external bodies try to regulate faculty's time—for example, in class—the less time faculty spend "at work."

At any rate, autonomy in this individualistic sense is not the be all and end all of professional work. Collective control of decisions that affect entry into and configuration of the professional work force, as well as of the content and evaluation of professional work, is also critical and can be considered an aspect of faculty's collective autonomy. It may be that faculty unions are best at negotiating freedom, professional autonomy, and insulation from managerial control. After all, that is what most unions seek to do for workers, to increase their autonomy at work. As indicated in the opening chapter of this book, that is a defining issue in labor history, the efforts of employees to attain some control over their working lives and the efforts of employers to gain managerial prerogatives over those employee's lives. However, in the current context of restructuring, autonomy may not be enough. Bargaining agents need to address more proactively and gain some measure of faculty input in major work-force and programmatic developments. They need to extend faculty's traditional purview over course and program content to professional involvement in shaping the strategic programmatic choices and the technical production activities and personnel that are part of restructuring.

Renewing the Literature

For all the complexity of the contractual findings, the collective bargaining agreements also serve to clarify some significant points in the analysis of professionals and faculty. In framing my analysis I have drawn on sociological studies of professions, on higher education scholarship, and somewhat less so on labor relations studies of workers. In concluding my study, what can I give back to these fields?

What are the implications of my findings? First, by grounding my analysis of the politics of professional work in collective bargaining agreements I clarify and make more concrete some abstract concepts in the sociology of professions literature—for example, "jurisdiction." Second, the defined range of those agreements directs our attention to the significance of an organizational level between the campus and the state, a level that is often overlooked in the sociological and higher education literatures. Third, the negotiations underscore the expansion of less-certified categories of faculty and the emergence of new production workers, both of whom are challenging full-time faculty's control of the curriculum. Moreover, the contracts make clear that in the current context it makes little sense to distinguish between financial and curricular decisions, as is so often found in the higher education literature. Finally, the agreements clarify that restructuring is shaped not just by abstract "markets," but by the negotiated politics of professional work.

Scholars of professions in recent years have analyzed competition among professions. Abbott has employed a concept of 'jurisdiction' to sharpen our understanding of competition among professions.[4] Studying unionized faculty makes the concept of jurisdiction quite clear, though probably not in a way that Abbott would have anticipated. For faculty unions, jurisdiction is about the province of the bargaining unit. Does the reorganization of departments or reclassification of units rearrange members and sectors out of the unit? Does the unit lose membership (and control over emerging areas of work)?

More than simply clarifying the concept, my analysis of collective bargaining agreements raises new issues about challenges to professionals' jurisdiction. The formalized union issues of membership and scope of control clarify that the struggle is not simply among professionals, but is between professionals and their managers. There are various objects of struggle. One obvious one is remuneration, which affects the standing of the profession as a whole. Another object of struggle is over control of the work force. Managers seek to replace expensive full-time professionals with cheap, nonbargaining-unit, part-time labor. Professionals' domain is challenged not just by other established professions, but by less highly certified (and paid) workers to whom work is essentially subcontracted. In large organizations increasingly sensitive to costs, professionals compete for jurisdictional control with nonbargaining-unit faculty and paraprofessionals, although the direct negotiation is between unit faculty and their managers over the use of such employees.

In addition, in analyzing contractual limits on the use of part-time faculty, for example, I have attended to different mechanisms for controlling a domain of work than are typically examined in the sociology of professions. Sociological research tends to focus on "the profession" and "society," on professions seeking broad legitimacy and seeking control through the state. Such an analytic also applies to unions, which seek broad legitimacy and work through various levels and branches of the state to enable, protect, and expand union activity and the scope of collective bargaining. However, the collective bargaining agreements in higher education also point us to an intervening organizational level that is too often overlooked in the literature, not just in sociology, but in higher education. Contracts extend our sociological gaze beyond "the organization." The individual enterprise is valorized in most organization theory and higher education literature that focuses on decision making and leadership. Scholars of higher education too often focus on a college or university as if it were an independent firm. The fact that it is a part of larger organizational systems, formal or otherwise, is typically ignored. (Sociologists of organizations attend to organizational systems, but not in the sense of being arenas in which groups negotiate work-force and work-place control.) Unionized institutions clarify this intervening level. Multiple campuses or colleges in a district or system all reach well beyond the organization, yet they fall below the state. Here lies an intervening level between the individual organization and the state that is important to determining how professionals negotiate control over their work.

Yet another struggle for jurisdictional control is occasioned by the rise of new occupational groupings (noted above). As suggested in chapter 5, in the case of new instructional technologies, we are witnessing the rise of nonfaculty professionals who are increasingly central to the production work of higher education. Again, the analysis of collective bargaining agreements clarifies what is at stake. The struggle is over control of the production work of the unit and the products of professional workers' labor. There are a range of new occupations (professional and paraprofessional) of growing importance—from instructional technology and curriculum specialists to lab technicians, to tutoring and assessment personnel, to computer professionals, to grants and sponsored projects officers, to research and technology transfer administrators. Scholars have yet to fully explore the relationship between these occupational groups and the principal professionals on campus—faculty.

I found the literature on unionized workers particularly useful in thinking generally about the transformation of the work force and in this particular case, technology's impact on the transformation of social relations in the work place. Concepts that have been developed in the study of blue-collar and clerical workers need to be adapted somewhat to the context of professional workers. But there is a large degree of overlap. That should not be so surprising. Professionals pursue what all workers and unions pursue, autonomy in work. If that union goal is achieved anywhere, it ought to be with unionized faculty.

However, as my analysis of the production politics of teaching and technology suggests, the pursuit of autonomy may be far from effective when the work force and production work is in the midst of being transformed. Existing faculty maintained autonomy vis-à-vis the new production technology—use of technology is largely voluntary. The jobs of current faculty are for the most part not at risk. Yet faculty as a work force are to some extent being marginalized, for they have not sought to negotiate control over the use of new instructional technology. Theirs has been a narrow, defensive action. As a result, a considerable portion of the curriculum is being delivered through means and processes that are outside full-time faculty's control.

The case of unions' negotiation of new technology, and relatedly of part-time faculty, underscores the connection between matters that in the higher education literature are generally separated. Traditional models of shared governance in the academy have separated budgetary, fiduciary, and even strategic decision-making matters—the realm of administrators—from academic and curricular matters—the realm of faculty. As a recent study of "strategic governance" indicates, such a model makes little sense in the current context: "Dual models which once suggested that budgetary matters are purely administrative while leaving academic matters primarily to the faculty are clearly inadequate when a scarcity of resources requires decisions that squarely impact academic programs."[5] Given my contractual analysis, I would go a step further. A range of work-force matters impact not just the profession's configuration and control over a domain of work, but the form, content, and delivery of academic programs. Unions (and faculty generally) need to more actively negotiate not just wages, benefits, and working conditions, but control over work force and forms and products of work (technology). Such provisions critically impact institutions' current and future academic direction and functioning.

Contractual analysis clarifies that restructuring is a negotiated process. Recent sociological research has addressed internal divisions among professions and, somewhat less, divisions within professions. It traces those divisions to "market position" and to broad systems of competing professional jurisdictions. So, too, with higher education research on the academic profession. Studies have addressed the rise of a national academic profession, systemic stratification within the academy, changing and challenging demographic patterns, and, most recently, broad, national patterns of changing resource dependencies that shift incentive systems at the national and academic unit level.[6] The various contractual provisions I have studied highlight the fact that the (re)configuration of the faculty work force is not a simple function of invisible hands and disembodied markets, of national economic, demographic trends and of systemic patterns of differentiation and integration. It is also a complex and variegated product of conscious political negotiation between competing parties, enacted in a politics of professional work. Such negotiations are certainly influenced by broad political economic, demographic, and other "external" forces. They are just as certainly central themselves in shaping the restructuring of academic labor.

Restructuring Professionals and Production Work
and Union Work

As a work force, faculty are being restructured. On that, most scholars are agreed. Depending on one's analytical and conceptual choices, the nature of that restructuring varies. For the most part, the concepts are grounded in an academic ideology of merit, and in a presumption of academe's preeminent position in higher education as professionals and as production workers. My analysis complements, yet extends, this body of work. I underscore the extent to which faculty are managed and stratified professionals. And I suggest the potential decentering of traditional, full-time faculty as the sole professionals and production workers on campus.

Classic and recent studies of academe's re-formation see faculty as being empowered and stratified by their expertise, which in the last half of the twentieth century has become increasingly marketable. For Jencks and Riesman, the value of academic research has enhanced the power and facilitated the triumph of a national academic profession and its universalistic norms, what they term an "academic revolution."[7] The result is a stratified, national higher education system, in which position in the hierarchy is a function of ascendant academic meritocracy. For Slaughter and Leslie, the commercial value of academic work has enhanced the position of certain segments of faculty, which have parlayed commercial relevance into preeminent organizational position, amidst a trend toward "academic capitalism."[8] The result is universities that are increasingly stratified internally by the market more than by merit. In both cases, expertise and professional marketability are connected to elite faculty's increased independence and position.

Perhaps because they take a broader view of academe, analyzing a cross-section of the entire profession, Bowen and Schuster see faculty not as empowered, but as imperilled.[9] For them, the principal challenge is to replace an aging work force while maintaining the quality and traditions of the academic profession. Their work is grounded in a long and important tradition of analyzing the demographics and quality of faculty as a work force.[10] Their focus is less on stratification of the profession by merit than on maintaining the merit of the faculty work force, in the face of working conditions and compensation patterns that are not attractive to the most able graduates.

From Clark's systemic, sociological perspective, faculty are stratified into "different worlds."[11] That stratified structure is functional. It enables those who are the meritocratic, at the top, to thrive. At the same time, it provides access to the many at the middle and bottom levels of the system. For Clark, the principal dynamic is the tension between such differentiation and integration, not only between institutions, but between functions, such as teaching and research. The challenge, for these "places of inquiry" is to maintain the creative synthesis of functions at the top of the system, in a "nexus" of research, teaching, and learning.[12] The challenge to academe is to maintain this distinctive American professional structure that is the touchstone of academic merit.

Although my analysis has been of unionized faculty, it is relevant to a broad analysis of academe's structure and restructuring. The processes that are influencing unionized institutions and employees are also impacting nonunionized higher education. Salary dispersion, programmatic reorganization and faculty retrenchment, increased use of part-time faculty, use of instructional technology, and increased organizational claims on employees' time are found within all of higher education. The specific terms of employment may vary, but the broad trends and forces that are (re)shaping academe are similar.

My work supports and extends the analyses described above. Unionized faculty are experiencing the effects of academic capitalism, not simply as Slaughter and Leslie suggest, but in the struggle over their terms of employment. Collective bargaining agreements represent a more formal and collective negotiation of capitalism's effects than is found in nonunionized settings. But they clarify various subjects of negotiation that are relevant throughout higher education. To what extent is salary structure shaped by merit and market considerations? To what extent are institutions increasingly utilizing technology to deliver instruction to students at a distance? To what extent are institutions seeking to expand their domain and claim on faculty's time and work products? Negotiation of such matters is currently taking place. As colleges and universities seek to streamline products, services, and employees to increase productivity and efficiency, and to contain personnel costs, the negotiations accompanying academic capitalism are intensified.

Unionized faculty are also imperilled by demographic patterns, not simply as Bowen and Schuster suggest, but in the profile of the professional work force on campus. As with each of the studies above, Bowen and Schuster focus on full-time faculty as the center and core of the academy. Over the past two decades, however, the profile of higher education's professional work force has become increasingly complex. Academe's reign is declining. New professions are emerging. And the collective bargaining agreements reveal some of the mechanisms by which the change is being effected. Provisions that speak to the restructuring and reorganization of faculty and programs, to the use of part-time faculty, and to the use of instructional technology point to the strategies that unions and management utilize to resist and promote the reconfiguration of the work force on campus. It grounds the demographic patterns in the ongoing politics of professional work.

Finally, unionized faculty are also stratified, and steeply so. They are stratified not only, as Clark analyzes, by institutional sector and disciplinary field, but within institutions, by work-force status (full/part-time). Yet, it is hard to interpret the stratification as functional.

Contractual analysis along with analysis of salary dispersion by field over time indicate that differentiated categories of academe are separate, but hardly equal. Various mechanisms within the contracts work to delimit such differentiation and inequality. And salary data suggests that at least in terms of dispersion among fields, and the gender gap, differentials are reduced in unionized settings. Yet the pressure of market forces, and of managerial efforts to position institutions more closely to particular markets, promise to only heighten such hierarchy.

Each of the points developed above poses a challenge for faculty unions. Several questions come to mind. Have unions benefitted faculty? What is the future of unions in higher education? What strategies and goals should unions pursue? Each of these questions takes me well beyond contractual data. Yet they are also embedded in the agreements I studied.

Clearly, faculty unions have advanced and protected members' interests in wages and benefits. They also have negotiated provisions that make it more difficult for managers to retrench faculty and that grant faculty extensive claims on their time in matters of outside employment and intellectual property rights. At the same time, the contracts suggest that agents have been less successful in negotiating provisions regarding the distribution and configuration of the work force, that effectively restrict managerial discretion and promote faculty involvement in reorganizing the academic work force and in utilizing part-time faculty and instructional technology.

What of the future? In the face of patterns of academic capitalism, faculty unions face the challenge of negotiating not only protections for current unit members and their jobs, but preservation of future full-time faculty members' positions and their central role in the institution. Much is missing not just from the contracts, but from the larger debate about the form and functions of higher education institutions. Colleges and universities are differentially investing in different academic arenas, as evidenced in part by the salary data reviewed at the end of chapter 2. If we are increasingly stratifying academe and the academy, what interests are being served? There is a lot of talk about "tough choices" that managers must make in restructuring their institutions. But there is little discussion in the institution, state, or nation of what the options are. From what future directions can we choose? There is little discussion of what the "right choices" are and little deliberation about how colleges and universities might evaluate choices that have been made in order to determine whether to continue on that path.

How can unions address such issues? They could cultivate and develop a broad alliance of constituencies within and beyond the academy that would shape decision making regarding the future direction of higher education. The biggest challenge facing faculty unions (and management) is to enhance the enterprise's legitimacy in the eyes of clients, employers, politicians, and "the public." (Indeed, this is a challenge that faces academe as a whole.) As Johnston has demonstrated, community political support is absolutely essential to the success of public sector unions.[13] In the case of public higher education, that essential public support extends to the statewide community. Faculty must address a public interest agenda.

The route to success as a union (and as a profession that is under fire) is to tap into the key public interest issues that define state and community politics. The specifics will likely vary from one community and state to the next. But some of the basic themes can be traced throughout the country: costs have escalated too rapidly; quality of service has declined; there is inadequate contribution of the academy to society. There is a widespread sense not only that tuition increases have outpaced inflation, but that they have not been matched by a proportional improvement in the quality of service. In short, consumers believe that they are being gouged. There is also a widespread sense that colleges and universities are not fully responsive to the needs of society, that they do not focus enough on providing education and services that benefit the community and economy. In short, the public is increasingly tired of subsidizing inwardly focused institutions that are insulated from society.

I am suggesting that faculty unions must reorient themselves (as must the academic profession as a whole). A defining issue in the past has been the negotiation of professional autonomy vis-à-vis institutional managers (and on management's part, the negotiation of greater flexibility vis-à-vis professional personnel). In future, faculty unions also should look to address the sorts of issues identified above, to speak to public interest issues that are articulated in local and state communities. That means moving beyond a more narrowly economic and defensive posture to a broader, more proactive effort to shape the future direction of the institution in question.

What does that mean in terms of contractual provisions? One thing it means is to negotiate broader involvement in and deliberation surrounding important strategic choices in the institution. For example, various voices should be heard in any process involving retrenchment and reorganization, for restructuring generally entails certain strategic directions expressed in programmatic change. Not only should more voices be heard, but also criteria should be specified for guiding decisions, and these criteria should speak directly to public interest concerns, such as the educational and economic needs of a broad range of students. Similarly, decisions regarding the purchase and use of instructional technology should entail wider involvement and deliberation. And the decisions should be guided by criteria that speaks to concerns of public interest, such as quality.

Contractual provisions, then, should focus not only on constraining and containing managerial discretion but on guiding and shaping (and on faculty participation in) decision making. They should also focus on evaluating in an ongoing way the costs and benefits of particular choices, decisions, investments, and allocations of resources and personnel. Whether in reviewing programmatic reorganization (and retrenchment) or the use of instructional technology, bargaining agents should negotiate more follow-through and evaluation of managerial decisions. In an era when managers seek more and more flexibility, those will certainly not be easy points to negotiate. Yet they should not be easily conceded. If old programs are to be eliminated to make way for new ones, there should be a process for analyzing the full cost and yield of these new investments. Similarly, if the use of instructional technologies is to be expanded, there should be independent review and assessment of how economically efficient such delivery systems are and how students evaluate their quality (at present, the only evaluation language in the contracts refers to individual instructors).

How can unions address the challenge of emerging and growing categories of employees that represent a challenge to faculty's preeminent position in academic organizations? A wide variety of new production workers are emerging in higher education—paraprofessionals and nonfaculty professionals who are more directly under the control of managers. I call these employees "managerial professionals."[14] They are increasingly involved in delivering instruction, service, and research. In addition, of course, increasing numbers and proportions of part-time faculty are responsible for delivering instruction in higher education. Contractually, there are various strategies that faculty unions could pursue in negotiating provisions to address these challenges to their position. In the case of part-time faculty, unions need to negotiate more clauses that speak to ratio of full- to part-time faculty, protecting future full-time positions. In addition, as noted earlier, bargaining agents should negotiate provisions that enhance the working conditions and role of part-time faculty as full-fledged members of the institution, speaking to public interest concern with quality and service.

Beyond the contracts, a major organizational challenge to faculty unions is to organize/unionize part-time faculty and nonfaculty professionals. As the number of nonfaculty units grows, that will pose the additional challenge of achieving some coordination among these various professionals on campus. Certainly, the potential is there to organize these employees. If unions are to grow in higher education they must organize and mobilize these emergent and expanding categories of employees.

There are costs to pursuing these measures and opportunities, but there are greater opportunity costs to not pursuing them. For I believe there is a broad shift at work in the demographics of professional work in higher education. What is happening in higher education speaks of what is happening in the general work force. In comparison to Western European countries, the United States has long had an occupational structure that is more heavily weighted to white collar, professional occupations, and more lightly weighted toward unionized, skilled labor.[15] The shift to a service-based economy has heightened that occupational distribution, with an important variation. It has contributed to the growth of new middle-class occupations as opposed to skilled, unionized jobs, but it has also contributed to the proliferation of part-time and contingent jobs.

In the face of such developments in some parts of the academy, some individual faculty have recognized the change at work and have pursued the opportunity structures presented by the new production work and emerging nonfaculty professional occupations. I see these as different moves than the traditional pattern of moving into "academic administration." (Of the latter, I am reminded of a couplet I heard years ago at a conference, articulated by a well known British sociologist in good Oxford English: "The working class can kiss my ass. I've made the foreman's job at last.") In my view, faculty unions should take a clue from these individuals. That does not mean they should abandon the ranks of faculty en masse. It means that they should not ignore the changes at work in higher education, seeking merely to protect their current ranks from the effects of such change. Instead, they should move in various ways to define and gain control over these emerging domains of work.

In work and occupations, two defining developments of the turn of the twentieth century were the emergence of professions not only to rationalize and serve capitalism, but also to mitigate its excesses. As well, unions grew to protect employees against the discretion and excess of managers. The defining developments of the turn of the twenty-first century are the increased subordination of skilled and professional workers to managerial control, emulating the excesses of capitalism, and the increased use of contingent, part-time employees.

Unionized faculty, and indeed all faculty, are faced with such patterns. These employees are highly managed professionals. They are experiencing a reorganization that involves managers in more highly stratifying professionals and directing their work. Faculty are witnessing the development of forms of production and service delivery that are being staffed by emergent occupations of nonunion, nonfaculty skilled and professional workers. They also are witnessing the increased delegation of their work to part-time employees. For some years, faculty and their unions have worked to protect their autonomy, to insulate faculty as independent professionals from managers' discretion, to maintain degrees of freedom at the margins, for example in outside employment.

Yet Jencks and Riesman's "academic revolution" and unions' revolutionary rise in organizing faculty are increasingly being eclipsed by the revolutionary rise of nonfaculty, managerial professionals and by a long-term managerial revolution focused on "reduction, reallocation, and retrenchment," on "academic strategy," and on "academic capitalism."[16] The challenge faculty and faculty unions now face is whether they can manage to work in concert as a collectivity to more proactively redirect the academy and whether they can reorganize themselves with other production workers who are currently at the margins of the organization, before faculty themselves are increasingly reorganized to the margins of the academic enterprise.

Notes

Chapter 1. Academics as an Organizationally Managed, Stratified Professional Work Force

1. See Burton Bledstein, *The Culture of Professionalism: The Middle Class and the Development of Higher Education in America* (New York: Norton, 1976); Walter Metzger, "The Academic Profession in the United States," in *The Academic Profession: National, Disciplinary, and Institutional Settings*, ed. Burton R. Clark (Los Angeles: University of California Press, 1987); Edward T. Silva and Sheila Slaughter, *Serving Power: The Making of a Social Science Expert, 1865–1921* (Westport, Connecticut: Greenwood Press, 1984).

2. See Paul Starr, *The Social Transformation of American Medicine* (New York: Basic Books, 1982).

3. See Jane Erikson, "Doctor Sues HMO for Sending Clients to Low-Cost Docs," *Arizona Daily Star March 15*; 1997, Section B, pp. 1–2.

4. See Guy Neave and Gary Rhoades, "The Academic Estate in Western Europe," in *The Academic Profession: National, Disciplinary, and Institutional Settings* ed. Burton R. Clark (Los Angeles: University of California Press, 1987). The academic profession and academic institutions in the United States did not follow a European model of bottom-up institution building, of groups of faculty forming independent guilds and offering classes on their own.

5. See Ernest L. Boyer, *Scholarship Reconsidered: Priorities of the Professoriate* (Princeton, New Jersey: Carnegie Foundation for the Advancement of Teaching, 1990); and William F. Massy and Robert Zemsky, "Faculty Discretionary Time: Departments and the 'Academic Ratchet,' " *The Journal of Higher Education* 65,1(1994):1–22.

6. See Alan Bloom, *The Closing of the American Mind* (New York: Simon and Schuster, 1987); Dinesh d'Souza, *Illiberal Education: The Politics of Race and Sex on Campus* (New York: Free Press, 1991); and R. Kimball,

Tenured Radicals: How Politics Has Corrupted Our Higher Education (New York: Harper and Row, 1990).

7. I used the 1994 version of HECAS. In spring 1996 a more recent version, with more contracts, was produced. As I was in the process of completing this manuscript, I chose not to utilize the later version. All contracts in the 1994 version of HECAS were from the 1990s. The 212 contracts I analyzed included 3 contracts for graduate assistants and one that covers two- and four-year institutions in the same system.

8. See Gary Rhoades, "Retrenchment Clauses in Faculty Union Contracts: Faculty Rights and Administrative Discretion," *The Journal of Higher Education* 64,3(1993):312–47.

9. See Frank Annunziato, *Directory of Faculty Contracts and Bargaining Agents in Institutions of Higher Education, v.21, January 1995* (The National Center for the Study of Collective Bargaining in Higher Education and the Professions, School of Public Affairs, Baruch College, The City University of New York, 1995).

10. See Richard Freeman, "What Does the Future Hold for U.S. Unionism?" in *The Challenge of Restructuring: North American Labor Movements Respond*, ed. Jane Jenson and Rianne Mahon (Philadelphia: Temple University Press, 1993).

11. See J. Victor Baldridge and Frank Kemerer, "Academic Senates and Faculty Collective Bargaining," The *Journal of Higher Education* 47(1976):391–441; Robert Birnbaum, "Unionization and Faculty Compensation," *Educational Record* 51(1970):405–9; Frank Kemerer and J. Victor Baldridge, "Senates and Unions: Unexpected Peaceful Coexistence," *The Journal of Higher Education* 52(1981):256–64, and *Unions on Campus* (San Francisco: Jossey-Bass, 1975); Barbara A. Lee, "Contractually Protected Governance Systems at Unionized Colleges," *Review of Higher Education* 5(1982):69–85, and "Governance at Unionized Four-Year Colleges: Effect on Decision Making Structures," *The Journal of Higher Education* 50(1979):565–84; David W. Leslie, *Conflict and Collective Bargaining*, AAHE-ERIC Higher Education Research Report No.9 (Washington, D.C.: American Association for Higher Education, 1975); Tei-Wei Hu and Larry L. Leslie, "The Effects of Collective Bargaining on College Faculty Salaries and Compensation," *Applied Economics* 14(1982):269–77; D. R. Morgan and R. C. Kearney, "Collective Bargaining and Faculty Compensation," *Sociology of Education* 50(1977):28–39; Kenneth P. Mortimer and T. R. McConnell, *Sharing Authority Effectively* (San Francisco: Jossey-Bass, 1978); and Gary L.

Riley and J. Victor Baldridge, eds., *Governing Academic Organizations* (Berkeley, California: McCutchan, 1978).

12. See Patricia Gumport, "The Contested Terrain of Academic Program Reduction," *The Journal of Higher Education* 64,3(1993):283–311.

13. See Sheila Slaughter, "Retrenchment in the 1980s: The Politics of Gender," *The Journal of Higher Education* 64,3(1993):250–82.

14. See Rhoades, "Retrenchment Clauses in Faculty Union Contracts."

15. See ibid. A comparably sized data set for nonunionized institutions would be enormously time-consuming to gather.

16. For important exceptions, see Howard B. London, *The Culture of a Community College* (New York: Praeger Publishers, 1978); Dorothy E. Finnegan, "Segmentation in the Academic Labor Market: Hiring Cohorts in Comprehensive Universities," *The Journal of Higher Education* 64,6(1993):621–56; and Lois Weis, *Between Two Worlds: Black Students in an Urban Community College* (Boston: Routledge and Kegan Paul, 1985).

17. The largely unstudied and often unacknowledged proprietary sector in higher education has no unionized institutions.

18. See William Zumeta and Janet Looney, "State Policy and Budget Development," in *The NEA 1994 Almanac of Higher Education* (Washington, D.C.: National Education Association, 1994).

19. See Gary Rhoades, "Negotiating the Restructuring of Academic Labor," paper presented at the American Association for Higher Education meetings, Atlanta, January 1996.

20. My thanks to Ernst Benjamin of the AAUP, and to other union negotiators, for emphasizing this point to me.

21. See the various volumes of the *Directory of Faculty Contracts and Bargaining Agents in Institutions of Higher Education* (New York, CUNY: The National Center for the Study of Collective Bargaining in Higher Education and the Professions, School of Public Affairs, Baruch College).

22. The numbers of contracts with termination language are too small for meaningful statistical analysis.

23. See Norman Swenson, "The Unions and Change," paper presented at NEA Higher Education Conference, Phoenix, 1996.

24. See Norman Swenson, "The Unions and Change," paper presented at NEA Higher Education Conference, Phoenix, 1996. That political route

included lobbying the Chicago City Council to pass an ordinance restoring the rights taken away by the state legislature (Chicago's home rule laws enables the city council to do that).

25. See David W. Leslie, Samuel E. Kellams, and G. M. Gunne, *Part-Time Faculty in American Higher Education* (New York: Praeger, 1982); and Kenneth P. Mortimer, M. Bagshaw, and Andrew T. Masland, *Flexibility in Academic Staffing: Effective Policies and Practices*, ASHE-ERIC Higher Education Report No.1 (Washington, D.C.: Association for the Study of Higher Education, 1985).

26. See Rhoades, "Retrenchment Clauses in Faculty Union Contracts."

27. See Melvyn Dubofsky, *The State and Labor in Modern America* (Chapel Hill: University of North Carolina Press, 1994).

28. For the classic statement of professionalization theory see Magali Sarfatti Larson, *The Rise of Professionalism: A Sociological Analysis* (Los Angeles: University of California Press, 1977).

29. See M. Carr-Saunders and P. A. Wilson, *The Professions* (London: Oxford University Press, 1933); William J. Goode, "Community within a Community: The Professions," *American Sociological Review* 22(1957):194–200; Walter Metzger, "A Spectre Haunts the Professions," *Educational Researcher* 16,6(1987):10–19; Talcott Parsons, "The Professions and Social Structure," in *Essays in Sociological Theory*, ed. Talcott Parsons (New York: Free Press, 1954); and Emile Durkheim, *Professional Ethics and Civic Morals* (London: Routledge and Kegan Paul, 1957).

30. See Anne Witz, *Professions and Patriarchy* (London and New York: Routledge, 1992); Edward T. Silva and Sheila Slaughter, *Serving Power*; Magali Sarfatti Larson, *The Rise of Professionalism: A Sociological Analysis*; and Barbara Ehrenreich and John Ehrenreich, "The Professional-Managerial Class," in *Between Labor and Capital*, ed. Pat Walker (Boston: South End Press, 1979).

31. See Gary Rhoades and Sheila Slaughter, "Professors, Administrators, and Patents: The Negotiation of Technology Transfer," *Sociology of Education* 64(1991):65–77.

32. On reform movements, see Lily M. Hoffman, *The Politics of Knowledge: Activist Movements in Medicine and Planning* (Albany: State University of New York Press, 1989). On competition among professions, see Andrew Abbott, *The System of Professions: An Essay on the Division of Expert Labor* (Chicago: University of Chicago Press, 1988); and Witz, *Professions and Patriarchy*. On changing modes and ideologies of profession-

als, see Steven Brint, *In an Age of Experts: The Changing Role of Professionals in Politics and Public Life* (Princeton: Princeton University Press, 1994); and Harold Perkin, *The Rise of Professional Society: England since 1880* (London and New York: Routledge, 1989).

33. See Abbott, *The System of Professions.*

34. See Brint, *In an Age of Experts.*

35. See Henry Etzkowitz, "Entrepreneurial Science in the Academy: A Case of the Transformation of Norms," *Social Problems* 36(1989):14–19; Michael Gibbons, et al, *The New Production of Knowledge: The Dynamics of Science and Research in Contemporary Societies* (London: Sage, 1994); Gary Rhoades and Sheila Slaughter, "Professors, Administrators, and Patents," and "The Public Interest and Professional Labor: Research Universities," in *Culture and Ideology in Higher Education: Advancing a Critical Agenda,* ed. William G. Tierney (New York: Praeger, 1991b); Sheila Slaughter, *The Higher Learning and High Technology: Dynamics of Higher Education Policy Formation* (Albany: State University of New York Press, 1990); Sheila Slaughter and Larry L. Leslie, *Academic Capitalism: Politics, Policies, and the Entrepreneurial University* (Baltimore, Maryland: Johns Hopkins University Press, 1997); and Sheila Slaughter and Gary Rhoades, "The Emergence of a Competitiveness Research and Development Policy Coalition and the Commercialization of Academic Science and Technology," *Science, Technology, and Human Values* 21,3(1996):303–39.

36. See Sheila Slaughter and Gary Rhoades, "Changes in Intellectual Property Statutes and Policies at a Public University," *Higher Education* 26(1993):287–312.

37. On academic recruitment, see Theodore Caplow and Reece McGee, *The Academic Marketplace* (New York: Basic Books, 1958). On self-censorship and the McCarthy Era, see Logan Wilson, *The Academic Man* (New York: Oxford University Press, 1942), and Lionel Lewis, *Cold War on Campus: A Study of the Politics of Organizational Control* (New Brunswick, New Jersey: Transaction Books, 1988). On meritocracy, see Lionel Lewis, *Scaling the Ivory Tower: Merit and Its Limits in Academic Careers* (Baltimore: Johns Hopkins Press, 1975). On academic values in education, see David Riesman, Joseph Gusfield, and Zelda Gamson, *Academic Values and Mass Education* (New York: McGraw-Hill, 1970). On the divided academy see Everett C. Ladd and S.M. Lipset, *The Divided Academy: Professors and Politics* (New York: McGraw-Hill, 1975). On faculty's allocation of effort, see Martin Trow and Oliver Fulton, *Teachers and Students* (New York: McGraw-Hill, 1975). On the increased power of faculty, see Christopher Jencks and David Riesman, *The Academic Revolution* (New York: Doubleday, 1969).

38. See Howard R. Bowen and Jack H. Schuster, *American Professors: A National Resource Imperiled* (New York: Oxford University Press, 1986); Burton R. Clark, *Academic Life: Small Worlds, Different Worlds* (Princeton: Carnegie Foundation for the Advancement of Teaching, 1987); Gail P. Kelly and Sheila Slaughter eds., *Women's Higher Education in Comparative Perspective* (Dordrecht: Kluwer Academic Publishers, 1991); Michelle M. Tokarczyk and Elizabeth A. Fay, *Working Class Women in the Academy: Laborers in the Knowledge Factory* (Amherst: University of Massachusetts Press, 1993); and Slaughter and Leslie, *Academic Capitalism.*

39. On the "snakelike procession," as a subset of the "Academic Procession," see David Riesman, *Constraint and Variety in American Education* (Garden City, New York: Doubleday Anchor, 1958).

40. See Arthur M. Cohen and Florence B. Brawer, *The American Community College* (San Francisco: Jossey-Bass, 1982); London, *The Culture of a Community College*; Weis, *Between Two Worlds*; and Finnegan, "Segmentation in the Academic Labor Market."

41. See Everett C. Hughes, *Men and Their Work* (Glencoe: The Free Press, 1958).

42. See Larry L. Leslie and Tei-Weh Hu, "The Financial Implications of Collective Bargaining," *Journal of Educational Finance* 3(1977):32–53. Also see Richard B. Freeman and James C. Medoff, *What Do Unions Do?* (New York: Basic Books, 1984).

43. See, for example, some historical analyses, such as Sheila Slaughter, "The 'Danger Zone': Academic Freedom and Civil Liberties," *The Annals of the American Academy of Political and Social Science* 448(1980):46–61. Yet such historical work does not, for the most part, address collective bargaining, which is a relatively recent development in the association's history. Moreover, one important study that directly deals with the AAUP and collective bargaining is explicitly hostile to the concept of collective bargaining, regarding it as a threat to both the association and the profession. See Walter P. Metzger, "The Academic Profession in the United States," in *The Academic Profession: National, Disciplinary, and Institutional Settings*, ed. Burton R. Clark (Los Angeles: University of California Press, 1987).

44. See Jack H. Schuster, Daryl G. Smith, et al, *Strategic Governance: How to Make Big Decisions Better* (Phoenix: American Council on Education, Oryx Press, 1994). Also see Robert O. Berdahl, Statewide Coordination of Higher Education (Washington, D.C.: American Council on Education, 1971); James Mingle and Associates, Challenges of Retrenchment: Strategies for

Consolidating Programs, Cutting Costs, and Reallocating Resources (San Francisco: Jossy-Bass, 1981); and Mortimer and McConnell, *Sharing Authority Effectively.*

45. For example, see the volume 23, number 2 issue (March 1994) of *Contemporary Sociology*, which has a symposium on the labor movement.

46. See Paul Johnston, *Success While Others Fail: Social Movement Unionism and the Public Workplace* (Cornell: ILR Press, 1994).

47. See Dorothy Sue Cobble, ed., *Women and Unions: Forging a Partnership* (Ithaca: ILR Press, 1993); and Teresa L. Smith, "The Impact of University Faculty Unionization on the Male-Female Wage Differential," *Journal of Collective Negotiations in the Public Sector* 21,2(1992):101–10.

48. See Marjorie Murphy, *Blackboard Unions: The AFT and the NEA, 1900–1980* (Ithaca: Cornell University Press, 1990).

49. See Robert Michels, *Political Parties* (Gloucester, Massachusetts: P. Smith, 1978); and Philip Selznick, *TVA and the Grass Roots: A Study in the Sociology of Formal Organization* (New York: Harper and Row, 1966).

50. See David Brody, *Workers in Industrial America* (New York: Oxford University Press, 1980, viii), in Melvyn Dubofsky, *The State and Labor in Modern America*, xvii.

Chapter 2. Restructuring Professional Rewards:
The Structue, Stratification, and Centrality of Faculty Salaries

1. That is true for full-time faculty. The greatest salary stratification overall is that between full- and part-time faculty. Comparisons are extraordinarily complicated in that part-timers are paid according to a diverse range of criteria and scales, generally on some sort of piece-rate basis. There is some national data on the reported income of part-time faculty, which dramatizes the salary differentials between them and full-time faculty. See John B. Lee, "Faculty Salaries, 1994–95," *The NEA 1996 Almanac of Higher Education* (Washington, D.C.: National Education Association, 1996). However, thus far, no national survey has captured and detailed the structure of part-timers' salaries. Due to that complexity, in this chapter I concentrate on full-time faculty's salary structures and salary stratification.

2. On comparable worth see Marcia Bellas, "Comparable Worth in Academia: The Effects on Faculty Salaries of the Sex Composition and Labor Market Conditions of Academic Disciplines," *American Sociological Review*

59,6(1994):807–21; and Paula England, *Comparable Worth: Theories and Evidence* (New York: Aldine de Gruyter, 1992). Bellas' data indicates that field-based effects are experienced by males as well as by females in fields with relatively large numbers of female faculty. Of course, field-based differences do not eliminate within-field discrimination.

3. Those faculty receiving counteroffers may consider themselves more meritorious, although other, equally meritorious faculty may choose not to pursue the "get a letter (of offer) get a raise" strategy. On another dimension of market-based variation—among different types of higher education institutions—the market may be seen as coterminous with meritocracy. Of course, one's perspective depends on one's position within the institutional hierarchy running from elite research universities to community colleges. Faculty at the "top" of the institutional ladder believe that prestige (and Ph.D.s) and scholarly merit should be rewarded. Faculty at the lower rungs of the ladder (where somewhat smaller percentages of faculty hold Ph.D.s) believe that teaching and instructional merit should be rewarded.

4. See Christine Maitland, Rachel Hendrickson, and Gary Rhoades, "Bargaining: Restructuring and Labor," *The NEA 1995 Almanac of Higher Education* (Washington, D.C.: National Education Association, 1995).

5. See D. R. Morgan and R. C. Kearney, "Collective Bargaining and Faculty Compensation," *Sociology of Education* 50(1977):28–39, and Robert Birnbaum, "Unionization and Faculty Compensation," *Educational Record* 55(1974):29–33, for findings of unions' positive effects. For studies that found no significant impact, see W. W. Brown and C. C. Stone, "Academic Unions in Higher Education: Impacts on Faculty Salary, Compensation, and Promotions," *Economic Inquiry* 15(1977):385–96, and J. L. Marshall, "The Effects of Collective Bargaining on Faculty Salaries in Higher Education," *Journal of Higher Education* 50,3(1979):310–22. For studies that refine the previous findings, see Tei-Wei Hu and Larry L. Leslie, "The Effects of Collective Bargaining on College Faculty Salaries and Compensation," *Applied Economics* 14(1982):269–77, Larry L. Leslie and Tei-Weh Hu, "The Financial Implications of Collective Bargaining," *Journal of Educational Finance* 3(1977):32–53, and Barbara Guthrie-Morse, Larry L. Leslie, and Teh-Wei Hu, "Assessing the Impact of Faculty Unions: The Financial Implications of Collective Bargaining," *Journal of Higher Education* 52,3(1981):237-55. Finally, see Leslie and Hu, "The Financial Implications of Collective Bargaining," p. 53, for a closing note on spill-over effects. "Aside from what the data show explicitly, little has been said about the spill-over effects of bargaining in nonunion sister institutions. Many long term observers of collective bargaining in this country would acknowledge that salaries and

wage gains in industrial unions have spilled over to non-union employees. Likewise, within higher education—at least within those half dozen states with favorable collective bargaining legislation—the prospect of bargaining probably has had a similar inflationary effect on faculty salaries."

6. See Kenneth P. Mortimer, "A Decade of Campus Bargaining: An Overview," in *Campus Bargaining at the Crossroads*, ed. J. M. Douglas, Proceedings of the Tenth Annual Conference, National Center for the Study of Collective Bargaining in Higher Education and the Professions, Baruch College-City University of New York, April 1982.

7. See J. M. Douglas and N. B. Goldsmith, "Analytical Survey of Contractual Salary and Compensation Methodology in Higher Education Collective Bargaining," in Monograph No.4, National Center for the Study of Collective Bargaining in Higher Education and the Professions, Baruch College-City University of New York, 1981. Also see W. Lee Hansen, "Merit Pay in Higher Education," in *Academic Labor Markets and Careers*, ed. David W. Breneman and Ted I. K. Youn (New York: The Falmer Press, 1988). As Hansen noted, however, it is hard to tell what this means about other collective bargaining agreements, partly because the AAUP tends to be the bargaining agent at private institutions and at single universities, in contrast to the AFT and NEA, which are more commonly bargaining agents at community colleges and large public comprehensive state systems.

8. For an exception, see John B. Lee's "Faculty Salaries" analyses in the 1994, 1995, and 1996 NEA Almanacs of Higher Education.

9. See notes 5, 6, and 7. Also see Martin Finkelstein, *The American Academic Profession* (Columbus: Ohio State University Press, 1984); and Howard R. Bowen and Jack H. Schuster, *American Professors: A National Resource Imperiled* (New York: Oxford University Press, 1986).

10. See Steven Brint, *In an Age of Experts: The Changing Role of Professionals in Politics and Public Life* (Princeton: Princeton University Press, 1994). A similar point would hold with respect to Harold Perkin's conception of "private-sector" professionalism. See *The Rise of Professional Society: England Since 1880* (London and New York: Routledge, 1989).

11. See Patricia Gumport, "The Contested Terrain of Academic Program Reduction," *Journal of Higher Education* 64,3(1993):283–311; Sheila Slaughter, "Retrenchment in the 1980s: The Politics of Gender," *Journal of Higher Education* 64,3(1993):250–82; and Sheila Slaughter, *The Higher Learning and High Technology: Dynamics of Higher Education Policy Formation* (Albany: State University of New York Press, 1990).

12. See Anne Witz, *Professions and Patriarchy* (London and New York: Routledge, 1992).

13. See Paul Johnston, *Success While Others Fail: Social Movement Unionism and the Public Workplace* (Cornell: ILR Press, 1994).

14. The asterisk at the end of the terms allows for inclusion of various suffixes—for example, inequit* identifies inequity, inequities, and inequitable.

15. In postsecondary settings, expecially four-year institutions, the degree itself does not differentiate among many faculty: however, the prestige of doctoral degree has a significant impact. For example, see Barbara Reskin, "Academic Sponsorship and Scientist Careers," *Sociology of Education* 52(1979):129–46.

16. See Hansen, "Merit Pay in Higher Education." Of course, Hansen's sample is solely of AAUP contracts. In my population, AAUP contracts are underrepresented and NEA contracts are overrepresented. What is more important, my sample includes a large representation of two-year institutions, whereas Hansen's sample is of contracts in four-year institutions.

17. The reader will note that the first sentence of the provision refers to "merit/equity salary increases." I have coded this and other such dual references as one reference to merit and one reference to equity.

18. See Douglas and Goldsmith, "Analytical Survey of Contractual Salary and Compensation Methodology in Higher Education Collective Bargaining," and Hansen, "Merit Pay in Higher Education."

19. The large difference in contracts with salary adjustments for degrees probably reflects the fact that a higher percentage of faculty in four-year institutions already have a terminal degree.

20. "Institutional" theorists call this a logic of confidence, confidence and faith in the professionals' certification structures. See John W. Meyer and Brian Rowan, "The Structure of Educational Organizations," in *Environments and Organizations*, ed. Marshall Meyer and Associates (San Francisco: Jossey-Bass, 1978); and John W. Meyer and W. Richard Scott, *Organizational Environments: Ritual and Rationality* (Beverly Hills: Sage Publications, 1983).

21. See Bowen and Schuster, *American Professors*. Also see Hansen, "Merit Pay in Higher Education." Such conventional models could be interpreted as professional "piecework." Merit pay may provide at least the possibility of professional input into the decision-making process. But merit is

ultimately decided by managers. We are all, it would seem, managed professionals.

22. Of course, the difference in four-year institutions is that rather than level or amount of certification, what is important is the source or prestige of the certifying institutions, because essentially all university faculty have the same level of certification.

23. One of the two exceptions is Temple University's contract, which has the same provision for "counteroffers" in the earlier contract that it does for the current contract.

24. Provisions regarding student markets can be seen as exceptions to the more common focus on faculty labor markets. Yet for the institutional sectors that are most likely to be unionized—comprehensive state university systems and community colleges—the two markets are related. In particular, managers are looking to gain flexibility in shifting their faculty resources to those fields that are believed to have the most potential to attract students, thereby raising salaries in those fields.

25. See *Academe* 81,5(1995):5. Also see Gary Rhoades, "Retrenchment Clauses in Faculty Union Contracts: Faculty Rights and Administrative Discretion," *The Journal of Higher Education* 64,3(1993):312–47: and Committee A, "Academic Freedom and Tenure: City University of New York: Mass Dismissals Under Financial Exigency," *AAUP Bulletin* 63(1977):60–81.

26. See Sheila Slaughter and Edward T. Silva, "From Serving Students to Serving the Economy: Changing Expectations of Faculty Role Performance," *Higher Education* 14(1985):41–56, on restructuring in New York. Also see Slaughter, *The Higher Learning and High Technology*; Gary Rhoades and Sheila Slaughter, "The Public Interest and Professional Labor: Research Universities," in *Culture and Ideology in Higher Education: Advancing a Critical Agenda*, ed. William G. Tierney (New York: Praeger, 1991b); Sheila Slaughter and Gary Rhoades, "Changes in Intellectual Property Statutes and Policies at a Public University: Revising the Terms of Professional Labor," *Higher Education* 26(1993):287–312.

27. See Daniel S. Hamermesh, "Salaries: Disciplinary Differences and Rank Injustices," *Academe* 74,3(1988):20–24.

28. It is an open question whether different increases for promotion to different ranks serves to increase, maintain, or reduce the differential among ranks. It depends on the size of the differences and the salaries of the faculty in question.

29. One contract enables managers to pay new faculty less than the minimum, in a clear example of a so-called two-tier contract, in which new faculty are hired onto a salary schedule that is lower than the schedule for continuing faculty. The Nebraska State College contract establishes a "new hire rank base" of minimums for each faculty rank. The bases for new hires are lower at every rank than are the bases established for current faculty. Moreover, the negotiated increase in those "rank bases" for the following year is 1 percent less than the increase in the rank bases of current faculty.

30. See Maitland, Hendrickson, and Rhoades, "Bargaining: Restructuring and Labor."

31. At that time, of course, conditions in higher education were very different than they are today: institutions were expanding in terms of both student numbers and faculty lines. The professional labor market arguably made the need for market provisions in recruitment as important as they are today: schools faced the challenge of being able to recruit enough faculty generally, as well as in particular fields.

32. In addition, an entire section is devoted to "Salary Compression/Inversion," and the "Other Salary Increases" subsection mentions increases due to "market inequities" as well as to "additional salary compression/inversion increases." I code such references as equity adjustments and address them in the equity section of this chapter.

33. In the absence of such provisions, individual faculty still may file lawsuits based on federal law and/or state law. However, I am interested in the efforts of union to build and underscore protections into the collective bargaining agreements that afford faculty greater leverage in such matters.

34. The Florida case is a particularly dramatic one, reported at the 1995 NEA Higher Education meetings by union representatives who had designed a system to redress the adverse effects of the market.

35. Many contracts have more than one category of provision: of the eighty-four contracts with provisions either for merit, market, or equity, eighteen have provisions in two areas and twelve have provisions in all three areas. There are thirteen contracts with both equity and market provisions, twenty-four with both equity and merit provisions.

36. See A. M. Konrad and Jeffrey Pfeffer, "Do You Get What You Deserve?: Factors Affecting the Relationship between Productivity and Pay," *Administrative Science Quarterly* 35,2(1990):258–85; and Jeffrey Pfeffer and Alison Davis-Blake, "The Effect of Proportion of Women on Salaries: The

Case of College Administrators," *Administrative Science Quarterly* 32(1987):1–24.

37. See Bellas, "Comparable Worth in Academia." Also see Bellas' 1993 article, "Faculty Salaries: Still a Cost of Being Female?" *Social Science Quarterly* 74(1993):62–75. Also see Pamela S. Tolbert, "Organizations and Inequality: Sources of Earnings Differences between Male and Female Faculty," *Sociology of Education* 59(1986):227–35.

38. See W. Lee Hansen and Thomas F. Guidugli, "Comparing Salary and Employment Gains for Higher Education Administrators and Faculty Members," *The Journal of Higher Education* 61,2(1990):142–59. Despite a rebound in the 1980s from the 1970s, average faculty salaries in constant dollars were 2 percent lower in 1993 than in 1973. See John Lee, "Faculty Salaries, 1993–94," *The NEA 1995 Almanac of Higher Education* (Washington, D.C.: National Education Association, 1995). Over twenty years faculty salary increases have not even equaled cost of living raises in real terms. For a different interpretation, see Daniel S. Hamermesh, "Not So Bad: The Annual Report on the Economic Status of the Profession, 1995–96," *Academe* 82,2(1996):14–22. He argues for an adjustment to the inflated consumer price index in converting nominal to real salary changes. However, he makes this argument on the basis of an unpublished paper and an interim report on the CPI.

39. For example, salaries in law and engineering are at the top of the salary hierarchy. Yet academic law professors are notorious for not wanting—or being able—to leave academe for private practice. Faculty in engineering have often left private practice, and many are unenthusiastic about returning to the private sector. Moreover, engineering is marked by extreme shifts in market demand and employment that do not seem to depress faculty salaries in engineering. So a relationship may be established between salaries in academe and salaries in related fields in the private sector, but the mechanisms by which external professional markets shape academics' salaries have yet to be adequately specified. (My thanks to Ron Oaxaca for helping me think through this point.)

40. See Konrad and Pfeffer, "Do You Get What You Deserve?"

41. See D. R. Morgan and R. C. Kearney, "Collective Bargaining and Faculty Compensation"; Robert Birnbaum, "Unionization and Faculty Compensation"; W. W. Brown and C. C. Stone, "Academic Unions in Higher Education"; J. L. Marshall, "The Effects of Collective Bargaining on Faculty Salaries in Higher Education"; Tei-Wei Hu and Larry L. Leslie, "The Effects of Collective Bargaining on College Faculty Salaries and Compensation";

Larry L. Leslie and Tei-Weh Hu, "The Financial Implications of Collective Bargaining," and Barbara Guthrie-Morse, Larry L. Leslie, and Teh-Wei Hu, "Assessing the Impact of Faculty Unions." Notably, findings about the generally positive effects of unionization on faculty salaries have been obtained *not* by faculty members in unionized institutions, but by faculty in nonunionized institutions, who were not supportive of unions. Also see J. Ashraf, "Recent Trends in the Union Wage Premium," *Journal of Labor Research* 11,4(1990):435–51; and H. G. Lewis, "Union/Non-Union Wage Gaps in the Public Sector," *Journal of Labor Economics* 8,1(1990):260–328.

42. See Bowen and Schuster, *American Professors*; Burton R. Clark, *Academic Life: Small Worlds, Different Worlds* (Princeton: Carnegie Foundation for the Advancement of Teaching, 1987); and Everett C. Ladd and S. M. Lipset, *The Divided Academy: Professors and Politics* (New York: McGraw-Hill, 1975).

43. See Sheila Slaughter and Gary Rhoades, "The Emergence of a Competitiveness Research and Development Policy Coalition and the Commercialization of Academic Science and Technology," *Science, Technology, and Human Values* 21,3(1996):303–39; Gumport, "The Contested Terrain of Academic Program Reduction"; and Brint, *In an Age of Experts.*

44. See Daniel S. Hamermesh, "Plus Ca Change: The Annual Report on the Economic Status of the Profession, 1993–94," *Academe* 80,2(1994):5–14.

45. Moreover, if the invisible hand of the academic market was operating freely, one would expect shifts in the relative salaries of assistant, associate, and full professors. Instead, there is stability in the internal stratification of academic salary by rank. From 1972/73 to 1993/94 assistant and associate professor salaries increased only very slightly as a proportion of full professor salaries. See Hamermesh, "Plus Ca Change."

46. See Robert K. Merton, "The Matthew Effect in Science," in *The Sociology of Science* (Chicago: University of Chicago Press, 1973).

47. See Bellas, "Comparable Worth in Academia"; Mariam K. Chamberlain, ed., *Women in Academe: Progress and Prospects* (New York: Russell Sage Foundation, 1988); Daniel S. Hamermesh, "Treading Water: The Annual Report on the Economic Status of the Profession," *Academe* 79,2(1993):8–14; John B. Lee, "Faculty Salaries, 1993–94," T*he NEA 1995 Almanac of Higher Education* (Washington, D.C.: National Education Association, 1995); Alison J. Wellington, "Accounting for the Male/Female

Wage Gap among Whites: 1976 and 1985," *American Sociological Review* 59,6(1994):839–48.

48. See Lee, "Faculty Salaries, 1993–94."

49. That gap decreased by $2,005. See June O'Neill and Solomon Polachek, "Why the Gender Gap in Wages Narrowed in the 1980s," *Journal of Labor Economics* 11(1993):205–28; and Wellington, "Accounting for the Male/Female Wage Gap among Whites."

50. It can be argued that such patterns are not the conscious design of academic executives, but are a function of "the market." However, even if academic managers do not decide the level of salaries outside academe, which in turn can exercise influence on academic salaries, these managers do decide whether to increase or reduce recruitment and faculty lines in various academic departments. Over the past decade (and in the mid-1970s), presidents and provosts have articulated the need to make "tough choices" about academic programs, to pick and choose which programs to downsize and/or eliminate, and which ones to create/expand. The consequence is the same dispersion organizationally of academic units' economic conditions that we see nationally in academic fields' average faculty salaries.

51. There are some interesting similarities and differences in the rankings of fields in the two sectors. Among the top ten fields in average salary there are only two fields in each sector that are not in the top ten of the other (educational administration and physical sciences in nonunionized, and agribusiness and educational counseling in unionized institutions). Among the bottom ten fields, there are three fields in each sector that are not in the bottom ten of the other (English, foreign language, and library science in nonunionized, and physical therapy, special education, and teacher education in unionized). In ranking the forty-nine fields in each sector from 1–49, there are differences of ranking that are twenty points or greater in four cases, and ten points or greater in eleven cases—so there are considerable differences in the rankings within the two extremes of top and bottom ten fields. In looking at those fields that differ markedly in ranking, a very interesting pattern emerges. The fields that rank ten points or higher in unionized institutions are agribusiness, English, foreign languages, library science, mathematics, public health, and social sciences. The fields that rank ten points or higher in nonunionized colleges and universities are architecture, education, engineering related techs, and speech. In other words, salaries in many traditional liberal arts fields tend to rank much higher in unionized institutions, whereas the salaries that rank much higher in nonunionized institutions are in professional fields.

52. See Teresa L. Smith, "The Impact of University-Faculty Unionization on the Male-Female Wage Differential," *Journal of Collective Negotiations in the Public Sector* 21,2(1992):101–10. Also see D. R. Balkin, "Union Influences on Pay Policy: A Survey," *Journal of Labor Research* 10,3(1989):299–310, on the reduced gender gap in unionized settings generally. Also see Jeffrey Pfeffer and J. Ross, "Unionization and Female Wage and Status Attainment," *Industrial Relations* 20,2(1981):179–85, on unionized women workers.

53. That would be consistent with a recent finding regarding women's salaries in Sweden. See Alice H. Cook, *The Most Difficult Revolution: Women and Trade Unions* (Ithaca: ILR Press, 1992). The key to reducing the gender gap may be less to institute gender-based adjustments than to reduce overall salary dispersion.

54. See Hansen and Guidugli, "Comparing Salary and Employment Gains for Higher Education Administrators and Faculty Members."

55. See David C. Montgomery and Gwendolyn Lewis, "Administrative Staff: Salaries and Issues," *The NEA 1995 Almanac of Higher Education* (Washington, D.C.: National Education Association, 1995).

56. See Gary Rhoades, "Managerial Professionals," paper presented at meetings of the Association for the Study of Higher Education, Memphis, October 1996.

57. See Montgomery and Lewis, "Administrative Staff: Salaries and Issues."

Chapter 3. Retrenchment and Reorganization:
Managing Academic Work(ers) for Productivity

1. For an example of two public research universities, see Patricia Gumport, "The Contested Terrain of Academic Program Reduction," *The Journal of Higher Education* 64,3(1993):283–311. Also see reports on academic freedom in *Academe* for retrenchment cases in various types of institutions.

2. See Gary Rhoades, "Retrenchment Clauses in Faculty Union Contracts: Faculty Rights and Administrative Discretion," *The Journal of Higher Education* 64,3(1993):312–47.

3. This number is based on a draft version of NCES, *Fall Staff in Postsecondary Institutions* (Washington, D.C.: National Center for Education

Statistics, 1993), tables B7a–c, compiled by Ernst Benjamin. NCES, *Digest of Education Statistics, 1995* (Washington D.C.: National Center for Education Statistics, 1995), indicates that 64 percent of faculty are tenured, but that appears to be a percentage only of tenure track faculty.

4. See Sheila Slaughter, "The 'Danger Zone': Academic Freedom and Civil Liberties," *The Annals of the American Academy of Political and Social Science* 448(1980):46–61.

5. See Matthew W. Finkin, *The Case for Tenure* (Ithaca: Cornell University Press, 1996). Also see Sheila Slaughter, "Political Action, Faculty Autonomy, and Retrenchment: A Decade in Academic Freedom, 1970–1980," in *Higher Education in American Society*, ed. Philip G. Altbach and Robert O. Berdahl (Buffalo, New York: Prometheus Books, 1981).

6. See Sheila Slaughter, "Retrenchment in the 1980s: The Politics of Prestige and Gender," *The Journal of Higher Education* 64,3(1993):250–82. In earlier years, *Academe* was the *AAUP Bulletin*.

7. See Michael Olivas, *The Law and Higher Education: Cases and Materials on Colleges in Court* (Durham, North Carolina: Carolina Academic Press, 1989), and Kenneth P. Mortimer, "Chambers Data for 1983–84," *Chronicle of Higher Education* 27,26 (October 1983):13.

8. See Slaughter, "Retrenchment in the 1980s."

9. See Sheila Slaughter, "Political Action, Faculty Autonomy, and Retrenchment.

10. See AAUP, *1976 Recommended Institutional Regulations on Academic Freedom and Tenure* (Washington, D.C.: American Association of University Professors, 1976), and AAUP, *1940 Statement of Principles on Academic Freedom and Tenure* (Washington, D.C.: American Association of University Professors, 1940).

11. See Olivas, *The Law and Higher Education.*

12. See ibid.

13. See two articles by Todd W. Furniss, "Prescriptions for Institutions in the Eighties: Beyond Institutional Survival," *Review of Higher Education* 3(1980):5–8, and "The 1976 AAUP Retrenchment Policy," *Educational Record* 57(1977):133–39. Also see William M. Fulkerson, *Planning for Financial Exigency in State Colleges and Universities* (Washington, D.C.: American Association of State Colleges and Universities, 1973).

14. See S. A. Veazie, "University Collective Bargaining: The Experience of the Montana System," *Journal of College and University Law* 9(1982-83):51–67, p. 59.

15. See Walter Metzger, "Tenure," invited address presented at the National Education Association Higher Education Conference, Tampa, March 1995.

16. See Elaine El-Khawas, *Campus Trends* (Washington, D.C.: American Council on Education, 1994). In 28 percent of the institutions, from one to three graduate programs had been cut; in 15 percent of the institutions, more than four such programs had been cut. In 67 percent of the institutions, from one to three undergraduate programs had been cut; in 25 percent of the institutions, more than four such programs had been cut.

17. See Gumport, "The Contested Terrain of Academic Program Reduction." Also see C. Berger, "The Erosion of Professional Schools: The Right Blend in a Time of Decline," *Journal of Educational Thought* 19(1985):24-28; Kim S. Cameron, "Strategic Responses to Conditions of Decline: Higher Education and the Private Sector," *The Journal of Higher Education* 54,4(1983):359–80; Cynthia Hardy, "The Rational Approach to Budget Cuts: One University's Experience," *Higher Education* 17(1988):151–73; Wolf Hydebrand, "Sociology at Washington University," *The American Sociologist* 20(1989):330–35; C. L. Manns and James G. March, "Financial Adversity, Internal Competition, and Curriculum Change in the University," *Administrative Science Quarterly* 23(1978):541–52; James R. Mingle and Associates, *Challenges of Retrenchment: Strategies for Consolidating Programs, Cutting Costs, and Reallocating Resources* (San Francisco: Jossey-Bass, 1981); Kenneth P. Mortimer and Michael L. Tierney, *The Three "R's" of the Eighties: Reduction, Reallocation, and Retrenchment*, AAHE-ERIC Higher Education Report No.4 (Washington, D.C.: American Association for Higher Education); Sheila Slaughter and Edward T. Silva, "Towards a Political Economy of Retrenchment: The American Public Research Universities," *Review of Higher Education* 8(1985):295–318; Raymond F. Zammuto, "Managing Decline in American Higher Education," in *Higher Education: Handbook of Theory and Research, vol.2*, ed John C. Smart (New York: Agathon Press, 1986).

18. See especially Slaughter, "Retrenchment in the 1980s," and Gumport, "The Contested Terrain of Academic Program Reduction," on the pattern of cuts. Slaughter, in particular, concentrates on the role not just of corporate markets, but also of gender.

19. See William F. Massy and Robert Zemsky, "Faculty Discretionary Time: Departments and the 'Academic Ratchet,'" *The Journal of Higher Education* 65,1(1994):1–22.

20. See William F. Massy and Andrea Wilger, "Productivity in Postsecondary Education: A New Approach," *Educational Evaluation and Policy Analysis* 14(1992):361–76. One of the major shortcomings of this analysis is that it speaks generally of research versus teaching, failing to disaggregate the analysis. Yet that disaggregation is critical to understanding the internal reallocation taking place within institutions. It is not simply that teaching is traded off for research. Rather, it is that in some fields graduate programs and research are downsized relative to undergraduate education, whereas in other fields graduate education and research are expanded relative to undergraduate education.

21. See Patricia J. Gumport and Brian Pusser, "A Case of Bureaucratic Accretion: Context and Consequences," *The Journal of Higher Education* 66,5(1995):493–520; and Larry L. Leslie and Gary Rhoades, "Rising Administrative Costs: Seeking Explanations," *The Journal of Higher Education* 66,2(1995):187–212.

22. See Gary Rhoades, "Rethinking Restructuring," *Journal for Higher Education Management* 10,2(1995):17–30.

23. Martha Ellis, William Drake, Pat LaPoint, and Kimberly Russell, "Retrenchment Policies in Public Two-Year Community Colleges in the State of Texas," *Community College Journal of Research and Practice* 19(1995):537–48.

24. See D. J. Julius and M. K. Chandler, "Academic Bargaining Agents in Higher Education: Do Their Achievements Differ?" *Journal of Collective Negotiations in the Public Sector* 18(1989):9–58, G. W. Williams and P. A. Zirkel, "Academic Penetration in Collective Bargaining Contracts in Higher Education," *Research in Higher Education* 28(1988):76–95. Also see G. G. Lozier, "Negotiating Retrenchment Provisions," in *Handbook of Faculty Bargaining*, ed. G. W. Angell and E. P. Kelley, Jr. (San Francisco: Jossey-Bass, 1977) for an analysis of retrenchment clauses in their own terms.

25. See Rhoades, "Retrenchment Clauses in Faculty Union Contracts."

26. Comparisons with the 1993 findings are problematic because the AAUP was very much overrepresented in the sample of contracts from the 1980s. By contrast, the HECAS sample is heavily weighted toward the NEA. It is striking, then, that the findings are nevertheless comparable.

27. See Rhoades, "Retrenchment Clauses in Faculty Union Contracts"; Sheila Slaughter, "Retrenchment in the 1980s: The Politics of Gender," *The Journal of Higher Education* 54,3(1993):250–83; and Barbara A. Lee, *Collective Bargaining in Four-Year Colleges*, AAHE-ERIC Higher Education Research Report No.5 (Washington, D.C.: American Association for Higher Education, 1978).

28. This pattern points to the significance of state law, which is sometimes invoked in the retrenchment clauses of contracts. The contracts of these nine Washington institutions, two- and four-year institutions alike, invokes Washington statutes.

29. Although most provisions do not speak to issues of retrenchment, it is useful to briefly review matters covered in twenty-four provisions that refer to reorganization. Some speak to issues of bargaining unit jurisdiction. For example, the contracts of the Universitys of Nebraska at Kearney and at Omaha call for management to notify the union in case of any reorganization. This is a matter of ensuring that the new departments are included in the bargaining unit. "Northern Michigan University shall notify the Presidents of the AAUP and the NMUFA of creation of new academic departments in the reorganization of faculty into new academic departments in writing. The notice will also indicate the University's determination as to which bargaining agent shall represent the faculty assigned in each department" (Northern Michigan University, Memorandum of Understanding). Several contracts deal with the rights of faculty in reorganized units. For example, the contract of the California State University System indicates that reorganization will not affect staff seniority. The Illinois Board of Governors contract has an entire section about the notification and rights of faculty in reorganized units. Affected faculty's rights are also dealt with in the contracts of Central Michigan University, the Florida State University System, Mt. Hood Community College, and Youngstown State University. Macomb Community College's contract restricts board actions in reorganization. "The Board shall make no changes in hours, wages, or working conditions of teachers incorporated in this agreement or institute any reorganization affecting such hours, wages, and working conditions except after good faith negotiation and agreement between the Board and MCCFO." (Article 1). The union position is that faculty are not to be speeded up by reorganization activities. Given the extent of reorganization activity in higher education, the limited measure of provisions, procedures, or constraints on managerial discretion is very significant. For better or worse, reorganization is no longer, if it ever was, primarily an academic matter. It is instead largely a managerial domain driven by considerations of market responsiveness and centrality, not of academic quality. A few contracts (such as those of

the Montgomery County Community College and the Moraine Valley Community College) provide for the involvement of faculty and/or the union in decision making surrounding reorganization. However, the initiative and the ultimate decision lie with management.

30. I do not, as I did in my 1993 analysis, focus on the length of different sections of the retrenchment clauses. Such analysis is somewhat unwieldy with 178 retrenchment articles. Moreover, as one union official noted, length of clauses is not always positively related to constraint on managerial discretion. The greatest restriction on managerial flexibility is a one line, "thou shalt not" sentence. Further, although my previous analysis did point to the focus of the provisions on matters that come after the decision to retrench, it offered more of an indirect indicator of faculty involvement in decision making. Here I focus directly on the extent and nature of faculty involvement in each of the areas of decision making.

31. See Burton R. Clark, *The Distinctive College: Antioch, Reed, and Swarthmore* (Chicago: Aldine Publishing Company, 1970).

32. See Gumport, "The Contested Terrain of Academic Program Reduction."

33. NCES data on full- and part-time male/female and tenured male/female.

34. That gendered pattern is enhanced by the fact that retrenchment is more likely in fields in which there are relatively larger numbers of women faculty and students. See Slaughter 1993.

35. See Rhoades, "Retrenchment Clauses in Faculty Union Contracts," 340.

36. See ibid.

37. Conversation with Ernst Benjamin, of the AAUP.

Chapter 4. Reorganizing the Faculty Work Force for Flexibility: Part-Time Professional Labor

Much of the material in this chapter has been published in Gary Rhoades, "Reorganizing the Faculty Work force for Flexibility: Part-Time Professional Labor," *The Journal of Higher Education* 67,6(1996):624–59. However, I have revised the article in various ways, rewriting several passages and supplementing the original analysis with additional data.

1. Among the classic studies on the rise of professions generally are Burton Bledstein, *The Culture of Professionalism: The Middle Class and the Development of Higher Education in America* (New York: Norton, 1976); and Robert H. Wiebe, *The Search for Order, 1877–1920* (New York: Hill and Wang, 1967). For different interpretations of the rise of academe, see Walter Metzger, "The Academic Profession in the United States," in *The Academic Profession: National, Disciplinary, and Institutional Settings*, ed. Burton R. Clark (Los Angeles: University of California Press, 1987); and E. T. Silva and Sheila Slaughter, *Serving Power: The Making of a Social Science Expert, 1865–1921* (Westport, Connecticut: Greenwood Press, 1984).

2. See chapter 3. Also see the American Association of University Professors, "Report: On the Status of Non-Tenure Track Faculty," *Academe* 78,2(1992):39–48; David Montgomery and Gwendolyn Lewis, "Administrative Staff: Salaries and Issues," *The NEA 1995 Almanac of Higher Education* (Washington, D.C.: National Education Association, 1995); and National Center for Education Statistics, *Digest of Education Statistics* (Washington, D.C.: U.S. Government Printing Office, 1994a). Numbers of part-time faculty are based on a conversation with Ernst Benjamin, of the AAUP, and NEA *Higher Education Research Center's Update*, volume 3, number 1, entitled "Part-Time Employment in Academe."

3. Christopher Jencks and David Riesman, *The Academic Revolution* (New York: Doubleday, 1968).

4. See Ernest L. Boyer, *Scholarship Reconsidered: Priorities of the Professoriate* (Princeton, New Jersey: Carnegie Foundation for the Advancement of Teaching, 1990) on different conceptions of scholarship. Also see James Fairweather, *Faculty Work and Public Trust: Restoring the Value of Teaching and Public Service in American Academic Life* (Boston: Allyn and Bacon, 1994) on research versus teaching and the public interest. Of course, there are a host of popular critiques of the academy, particularly of left-wing academics. Also see William F. Massy and Robert and Zemsky on the "academic ratchet"—"Faculty Discretionary Time: Departments and the 'Academic Ratchet,'" *The Journal of Higher Education* 65,1(1994):1–22. Finally, see Jencks and Riesman, *Academic Revolution*, who in tracing the rise of the national academic profession identify some problems that require reform, presaging much of the current critique of faculty.

5. See Judith M. Gappa and David W. Leslie, *The Invisible Faculty: Improving the Status of Part-Timers in Higher Education* (San Francisco: Jossey-Bass, 1993), and Howard P. Tuckman, "Who is Part-Time in

Academe?" *AAUP Bulletin* 64(1978):305–15, for leading examples of this work.

6. See Gappa and Leslie, *The Invisible Faculty.* Also see David W. Leslie, Samuel E. Kellams, and G. M. Gunne, *Part-Time Faculty in American Higher Education* (New York: Praeger, 1982).

7. . See Judith M. Gappa, *Part-Time Faculty: Higher Education at a Crossroads.* ASHE-ERIC Higher Education Research Report No. 3 (Washington, D.C.: Association for the Study of Higher Education, 1984); and Kenneth P. Mortimer, M. Bagshaw, and Anthony T. Masland, *Flexibility in Academic Staffing: Effective Policies and Practices*, ASHE-ERIC Higher Education Report No. 1 (Washington, D.C.: Association for the Study of Higher Education, 1985).

8. For this argument see George E. Biles and Howard P. Tuckman, *Part-Time Faculty Personnel Management Policies* (New York, London: American Council on Education/Macmillan, Collier Macmillan, 1986). Also see Gappa and Leslie, *The Invisible Faculty*; and David W. Leslie and Jane Ikenberry, "Collective Bargaining and Part-Time Faculty: Contract Content," *CUPA Journal* 30,3(1979): 18–26.

9. Gappa and Leslie, *The Invisible Faculty*, 229–30.

10. For a previous example of this approach, see Gary Rhoades and Sheila Slaughter, "Professors, Administrators, and Patents: The Negotiation of Technology Transfer," *Sociology of Education* 64(1991):65–77.

11. The most recent example of such a stratification approach is Steven Brint, *In an Age of Experts: The Changing Role of Professionals in Politics and Public Life* (Princeton: Princeton University Press, 1994).

12. The classic statement of this perspective is Magali Sarfatti Larson, *The Rise of Professionalism: A Sociological Analysis* (Berkeley: University of California Press, 1977). More recent examples of sociological studies articulating and modifying this perspective are Andrew Abbott, *The System of Professions: An Essay on the Division of Expert Labor* (Chicago: University of Chicago Press, 1988); and Anne Witz, *Professions and Patriarchy* (London and New York: Routledge, 1992).

13. On temporary workers see Robert E. Parker, *Flesh Peddlers and Warm Bodies: The Temporary Help Industry and Its Workers* (New Brunswick, New Jersey: Rutgers University Press, 1994), and Bennett Harrison and Barry Bluestone, *The Great U-Turn: Corporate Restructuring and the Polarizing of America* (New York: Basic Books, 1988). On the "end of

work," see and Jeremy Rifkin, *The End of Work: The Decline of the Global Labor Force and the Dawn of the Post-Market Era* (New York: G. P. Putnam's Sons, 1995).

14. See NCES, *Digest of Education Statistics*. For a more recent analysis based on 1993 faculty survey data (National Survey of Postsecondary Faculty), see the *NEA Higher Education Research Center Update*.

15. See NCES, *Faculty and Instructional Staff: Who Are They and What Do They Do?* Survey Report of 1993 National Study of Postsecondary Faculty (Washington, D.C.: U.S. Department of Education, Office of Educational Research and Improvement, 1994b).

16. Conversation with Ernst Benjamin, of the AAUP. Also see David C. Montgomery and Gwendolyn L. Lewis, "Administrative Staff: Salaries and Issues," *The NEA 1994 Almanac of Higher Education* (Washington, D.C.: National Education Association, 1994). Also see the *NEA Higher Education Research Center Update*.

17. See Perry Robinson, *Part-Time Faculty Issues* (Washington, D.C.: American Federation of Teachers, 1994).

18. See ibid.

19. Sheila Slaughter, "Retrenchment in the 1980s: The Politics of Gender," *Journal of Higher Education* 64,3(1993):250–82, 260.

20. ibid., 266.

21. Committee A, "Report: Academic Freedom and Tenure, University of Bridgeport," *Academe* 79,6(1993):37–45. The ultimate outcome was that the two senior faculty members in psychology returned to work. At the time, Bridgeport was in the midst of a labor dispute. The administration had proposed major changes in the 1987–1990 collective bargaining agreement to enable it to "deal effectively with the financial crisis" the university was allegedly experiencing. In addition to asking faculty to agree to a 30 percent reduction in overall compensation (in return for a promise not to lay off any faculty), the administration sought changes in notice provisions (to give thirty days' notice with no additional severance pay) and to eliminate grievance and arbitration on governance and personnel matters. The union countered, offering to continue the nonsalary provisions of the previous contract and to submit salary to binding arbitration. The administration rejected that offer, and the faculty went on strike. The university then notified the faculty that it would begin to hire "permanent replacements."

22. See Academe, "In Brief," *Academe* 77,2(1991):7.

23. See Committee A, "Report: Academic Freedom and Tenure, Alaska Pacific University," *Academe* 81,3(1995):32–39.

24. See Committee A, "Report: Academic Freedom and Tenure, St. Bonaventure University," *Academe* 81,4(1995):65–73.

25. See Committee A, "Report: Academic Freedom and Tenure, Essex Community College," *Academe* 81,3(1995):40–50.

26. See Committee G, "Report: On the Status of Non-Tenure Track Faculty," *Academe* 78,6(1992):39–48.

27. See ibid., 39.

28. Robinson, *Part-Time Faculty Issues*.

29. ibid., 48.

30. *NEA, Resolutions, Legislative Program, and New Business 1994-95* (Washington, D.C.: National Education Association, 1994), 80, Resolution F.41. Also see NEA, *NEA and Higher Education: Policies and Programs* (Washington, D.C.: National Education Association, 1994).

31. See Gappa and Leslie, *The Invisible Faculty*, for this argument.

32. As I am interested in full-time faculty's control over the use of part-timers, I do not focus on those HECAS contracts that cover only part-time faculty.

33. Leslie and Ikenberry, "Collective Bargaining and Part-Time Faculty," found that the NEA represents about 53 percent of all units that include part-time faculty (compared to about 41 percent of units overall). By contrast, the AAUP and AFT, which represented about 12 and 31 percent, respectively, of all units, accounted for 11 and 28 percent of units including part-timers.

34. In each of the coding categories described below, the unit of analysis is a phrase or substantive mention rather than a straight count of every time the term *part-time* appeared. For example, if *part-time* appears several times in a sentence/paragraph dealing with only one substantive dimension of appointment, it is coded as one reference.

35. See, Gary Rhoades, "Retrenchment Clauses in Faculty Union Contracts: Faculty Rights and Administrative Discretion," *Journal of Higher Education* 64, 3(1993):312–47.

36. That result holds if two-year and technical colleges are collapsed into one category ($x2=1.9$, not significant). No technical college contracts have

clauses. An analysis of incidence by institutional type that separates two-year and technical colleges yields a dependent association ($x2=4.8$, significant at the .05 level), reflecting the absence of appointment/release provisions in technical college contracts.

37. My thanks to Ernst Benjamin, of the AAUP, for this and many, many other insights.

38. In about 15 percent of the contracts the retrenchment clause might cover some or all part-time faculty indirectly or residually. For example, layoff order might give preference to permanent contract faculty over fixed-term, nonrenewable contract faculty. However, fixed-term faculty are not necessarily part-time. Moreover, many such references are vague—for example, they refer to the priority of tenured faculty over nontenured and other. The national unions increasingly are devoting attention not just to part-time faculty, but to what are being identified as "contingent" faculty, a category that includes part-time faculty, but that also includes other nontenure-track categories of faculty that are not part-time. However, in coding, I decided that it was significant whether part-timers were identified explicitly in matters such as order of lay-off.

39. See Rhoades, "Retrenchment Clauses in Faculty Union Contracts."

40. Eight contracts explicate legitimate uses. For example, "temporary faculty may be employed each year in all ranks. These temporary appointments may be caused by such conditions as . . . the absence of faculty, sickness, study or sabbatical leave, or emergency personal situations. The period of service for such an appointee shall not exceed one year in length. . . . Part-time appointments by the College shall not be used to circumvent the intent of this Agreement by eliminating the hiring of full-time personnel. When a department has in two consecutive years the full-time equivalent of one and one-half positions, exclusive of replacements created by leaves or emergencies, the Board shall make every effort to fund an additional full-time position for that department." (Rhode Island College, Section 7.12)

41. In 1979, Leslie and Ikenberry, "Collective Bargaining and Part-Time Faculty," found that 38 percent of the fifty contracts they studied had clauses limiting the hiring of part-timers, a considerably higher incidence than I found. The divergent findings might partly be a result of the fact that Leslie and Ikenberry included clauses that do not constitute collective work-force provisions as I have defined them. For example, they included provisions that restrict part-time faculty members to no more than 60 percent of a full-time load; I code that simply as a provision that defines what constitutes a part-time faculty member. The divergent findings might also be due to differences in the

samples. In particular, contracts covering only full-time faculty are only 36 percent of my sample, as opposed to about 60 percent of Leslie and Ikenberry's sample. However, although one might expect that such contracts would be more likely to have collective work-force limitations on the numbers and proportions of part-time faculty than would contracts that cover at least some part-time faculty, chi-square analysis suggests this is not necessarily the case.

42. My thanks to Ernst Benjamin for making this point.

43. If the cells of two-year and technical colleges are collapsed together, there is a dependent association between the incidence of ratio provisions and institutional type ($x2=4.25$, significant at .05 level). However, the association is not dependent either for order ($x2=.82$) or for replacement ($x2=1.9$) provisions.

44. See NCES, *Faculty in Higher Education Institutions* (National Center for Education Statistics, Washington, D.C.: U.S. Government Printing Office, 1988). The literature suggests that the limited representation of part-time faculty is largely a result of the reluctance of full-time faculty to include them in bargaining units. Yet institutions have also resisted including part-timers in bargaining units. Inclusion is also a function of state statute (which varies by state) and of the National Labor Relations Board (NLRB) rulings (which vary over time) on the eligibility of part-time faculty. See Gappa, *Part-Time Faculty*, and Leslie, Kellams, and Gunne, *Part-Time Faculty in American Higher Education*. Gradations of professional status, then, are partly matters of legal judgment.

45. Of course, what this cross-sectional analysis of contracts does not reveal is the general decline over time in colleges and universities' provisions of fringe benefits, for full- as well as part-time faculty. Hutchinson Community College's contract offers a variation of such benefits deductions, in the form of a two tier contract. New part-timers will not get a right/perquisite enjoyed by current part-time faculty.

46. See Leslie and Ikenberry, "Collective Bargaining and Part-Time Faculty."

47. Conducting a chi-square analysis including all 183 contracts in my sample, the statistical association is not significant ($x2=3.84$). Given that few full-time only contracts have such provisions, however, it might be useful to eliminate them from the analysis. For the 118 contracts that cover full and part-time faculty, there is a dependent relationship between leave provisions and institutional type ($x2=6.08$, significant at the .05 level).

48. Of course, in community colleges, in some states and fields, part-time faculty who have been employed by the institution for some time have an inside track on hiring for full-time positions—not formally, but informally.

49. See Patricia Gumport, "The Contested Terrain of Academic Program Reduction," *Journal of Higher Education* 64,3(1993):283–311; Gary Rhoades, "Rethinking Restructuring," *Journal for Higher Education Management* 10,2(1995b):17–31; and Sheila Slaughter, "Retrenchment in the 1980s."

50. See Gappa, *Part-Time Faculty*; and Leslie, Kellams, and Gunne, *Part-Time Faculty in American Higher Education.*

51. See NCES, *Faculty and Instructional Staff*; and *Faculty in Higher Education Institutions.*

52. See NCES, *Faculty and Instructional Staff.*

53. See Gary Rhoades, "Rising Administrative Costs in Instructional Units." Thought and Action 11, 1 (1995): 7–24.

Chapter 5. The Production Politics of Teaching and Technology: Deskilling, Enskilling, and Managerial Extension

1. See Barry Bluestone and Bennett Harrison, *The Deindustrialization of America: Plant Closings, Community Abandonment, and the Dismantling of Basic Industry* (New York: Basic Books, 1982), and Harry Katz, *Shifting Gears: Changing Labor Relations in the U.S. Auto Industry* (Cambridge: MIT Press, 1985).

2. See Steven P. Vallas, *Power in the Workplace: The Politics of Production at AT&T* (Albany: State University of New York Press, 1993); and Rosemary Crompton and Gareth Steadman Jones, *White Collar Proletarians: Deskilling and Gender in Clerical Work* (Philadelphia: Temple University Press, 1984).

3. My thanks to the anonymous reviewers on an earlier draft of this chapter that was submitted to the *Administrative Science Quarterly.*

4. For example, see the program of the 1996 annual meetings of the American Association of Higher Education.

5. See Sandra S. Ruppert, *The Politics of Remedy: State Legislative Views on Higher Education* (Washington, D.C.: NEA, 1996). Indeed, 95 per-

cent of education committee chairs believe that legislative action to this effect is likely in the next three to five years.

6. On the "rapture of technology," see Stephen C. Ehrmann, "Asking the Right Questions: What Does Research Tell Us about Technology and Higher Learning?" *Change* 27,2(1995):20–27. On "potential and performance," see Steven W. Gilbert and Kenneth C. Green, *Information Technology: A Road to the Future?* (Washington, D.C.: National Education Association, 1995). On related matters see Stephen C. Ehrmann, "Making Sense of Technology: A Dean's Progress," *Change* 26,23(1994):35–38; Steven W. Gilbert and Kenneth C. Green, "Great Expectations: Content, Communications, Productivity, and the Role of Information Technology in Higher Education," *Change* 27,2(1995):8–18; and Kenneth C. Green, "Paying the Digital Paper," *Change* 27,2(1995):53–54.

7. NEA, *Resolutions, Legislative Program, and New Business, 1994–95* (Washington, D.C.: National Education Association, 1994), pp.41–42.

8. AFT, *How Unions Can Harness the Technology Revolution on Campus* (Washington, D.C.: AFT, 1996), 2

9. AFT, *How Unions Can Harness the Technology Revolution*, 9.

10. See *Higher Education Leader* 4,1(March 1996). It is worth noting that one year earlier (stemming from an American Association of Higher Education roundtable organized to address technology issues) a review committee on strategic planning for technology published an article in *Change* magazine (27,2(1995); 49). The article was entitled, "Report from a Committee of Hope" (by Bob Aiken), but it indicated that "although administrative and research computing have benefitted from university-wide planning, there has been no planning for the use of technology to improve teaching and learning. Thus, despite the dollars spent, faculty have experienced Temple's policy as what Steve Gilbert has characterized as 'lurch, crisis, lurch, crisis.' The result is a system that is out of whack."

11. On manufacturing, see Peter Blau et al, "Technology and Organization in Manufacturing," *Administrative Science Quarterly* 21(1976):20–40. On retail firms, see John P. Walsh, "Technological Change and the Division of Labor: The Case of Retail Meatcutters," *Work and Occupations* 16(1989):165–83. On accounting and financial services, see Tom Jewett and Rob Kling. "The Work Group Manager's Role in Developing Computing Infrastructure," in Proceedings of the ACM Conference on Office Information Systems, Boston, Massachusetts, 1990. On social services in governmental agencies, see Rob Kling, "Computerization and Social Transformations,"

Science, Technology, and Human Values 16,3(1991):342–67. On hospitals, see Stephen Barley, "Technology as an Occasion for Structuring: Evidence of Observations of CT Scanners and the Social Order of Radiology Departments," *Administrative Science Quarterly* 31(1986):78–108.

12. See Stephen Barley, "Technology as an Occasion for Structuring."

13. See Marlene E. Burkhardt and Daniel J. Brass, "Changing Patterns or Patterns of Change: The Effects of a Change in Technology on Social Network Structure and Power" *Administrative Science Quarterly* 35(1990):104–27. Also see William Form et al. "The Impact of Technology on Work Organization and Work Outcomes," in *Industries, Firms, and Jobs: Sociological and Economic Approaches*, ed. George Farkas and Paula England (New York: Plenum, 1988) 303–28; Arndt Sorge and Wolfgang Streeck, "Industrial Relations and Technical Change: The Case for an Extended Perspective," in *New Technology and Industrial Relations*, ed. Richard Hyman and Wolfgang Streeck (Oxford: Basil Blackwell, 1988) 19–47; and Kenneth I. Spenner, "Deciphering Prometheus: Temporal Changes in the Skill Level of Work," *American Sociological Review* 48(1983):824–37.

14. The classic statement of this position is Harry Braverman, *Labor and Monopoly Capital: The Degradation of Work in the Twentieth Century* (New York: Monthly Review, 1974). Also see Rosemary Crompton and Gareth Steadman Jones, *White Collar Proletarians*; David Noble, *Forces of Production: A Social History of Industrial Automation* (New York: Knopf, 1984); Harley Shaiken, *Work Transformed: Automation and Labor in the Computer Age* (New York: Holt, Rinehart, and Winston, 1984); and Michael Wallace and Arne L. Kalleberg, "Industrial Transformation and the Decline of Craft: The Decomposition of Skill in the Printing Industry, 1931–1978," *American Sociological Review* 47(1982):307–24.

15. An important variation of the neo-Marxian approach to technology and social relations is hegemony theory, grounded in Gramscian conceptions of ideological control. According to this perspective, the subordination of labor stems from processes and structures that legitimate management's authority and engender workers' acceptance of prevailing social relations of work. See Michael Burawoy, *Manufacturing Consent: Changes in the Labor Process under Monopoly Capitalism* (Chicago: University of Chicago Press, 1979); Daniel Cornfield, *Workers, Managers, and Technological Change: Emerging Patterns of Labor Relations* (New York: Plenum Cornfield, 1987); Richard C. Edwards, *Contested Terrain: The Transformation of the Workplace in the Twentieth Century* (New York: Basic Books, 1979); and Claus Offe, *Industry and Inequality: The Achievement Principle in Work and*

Social Status (New York: St. Martin's Press, 1976). In the case of technology, such hegemony involves workers buying into management's promotion of technology's value and benefits.

16. See two articles by Paul Adler, "Marx, Machines, and Skill," *Technology and Culture* 31,4(1990):780–812; and "Automation and Skill: Three Generations of Research on the N.C. Case," *Politics and Society* 17,3(1989):377–402. Also see Larry Hirschhorn, *Beyond Mechanization* (Cambridge, Mass: MIT Press, 1984); Paul Strassman, *Information Payoff: The Transformation of Work in the Electronic Age* (New York: Basic Books, 1985); and Shoshana Zuboff, *In the Age of the Smart Machine: The Future of Work and Power* (New York: Basic Books, 1988).

17. See Maryellen R. Kelley, "New Process Technology, Job Design, and Work Organization: A Contingency Model," *American Sociological Review* 55(1990):191–208.

18. Barley, "Technology as an Occasion for Structuring," 78. Also see Burkhardt and Brass, "Changing Patterns or Patterns of Change."

19. Of course, technology may not be an initiating factor at all, the effects of which are contingent on some intervening variable(s). Instead, other factors, such as cost pressures, may lead to the adoption of technology, which in turn has some independent effect. My thanks to a reader of an early version of this chapter for making this point.

20. See Sorge and Streeck, "Industrial Relations and Technical Change." Also see Arndt Sorge, *Microelectronics and Manpower in Manufacturing* (Aldershot: Gower, 1983); Spenner, "Deciphering Prometheus"; and M. Warner, "Microelectronics, Technical Change, and Industrialized Economies," *Industrial Relations Journal* 16(1985):9–11.

21. See Form et al., "The Impact of Technology"; and Kelley, "New Process Technology, Job Design, and Work Organization."

22. On "structuration" see Anthony Giddens' books, *Central Problems in Social Theory* (Berkeley: University of California Press, 1979), and *New Rules of Sociological Method* (London: Hutchinson, 1976). Also see Patricia Riley, "A Structurationist Account of Political Cultures," *Administrative Science Quarterly* 28(1983):414–37. On occasions for restructuring, see Barley, "Technology as an Occasion for Structuring"; and Kling, "Computerization and Social Transformations."

23. See Kelley, "New Process Technology, Job Design, and Work Organization;" Robert Price, "Information, Consultation, and the Control of

New Technology," in *New Technology and Industrial Relations*; and J. S. Solomon, "Union Responses to Technological Change: Protecting the Past as Leading to the Future," *Labor Studies Journal* 12 (1987): 51–64.

24. See Kelley, "New Process Technology, Job Design, and Work Organization."

25. See Vallas, *Power in the Workplace*; and Kling, "Computerization and Social Transformations."

26. See Harland Prechel, "Transformations in Hierarchy and Control of the Labor Process in the Post-Fordist Era: The Case of the U.S. Steel Industry," in *The Labor Process and Control of Labor: The Changing Nature of Work Relations in the Late Twentieth Century*, ed. Berch Berberoglu (Westport, Connecticut: Praeger, 1993) 44–58; Helen Rainbird, "New Technology, Training, and Union Strategies," in *New Technology and Industrial Relations*, ed. Richard Hyman and Wolfgang Streeck (Oxford, Basil Blackwell, 1988) 174–88.

27. For example, see Barbara Garson, *The Electronic Sweatshop: How Computers Are Transforming the Office of the Future into the Factory of the Past* (New York: Simon and Schuster, 1988); and Navid Mohseni, "The Labor Process and the Control of Labor in the U.S. Computer Industry," in *The Labor Process and Control of Labor: The Changing Nature of Work Relations in the Late Twentieth Century*, ed. Berch Berberoglu (Westport, Connecticut: Praeger, 1993) 59–78.

28. For an exception, see Gary Rhoades and Sheila Slaughter, "Professors, Administrators, and Patents: The Negotiation of Technology Transfer," *Sociology of Education* 64,2(1991):65–77. For an analysis of the informally negotiated relations between professionals and semiprofessionals, see Barley, "Technology as an Occasion for Structuring."

29. See W. Baumol and S. A. B. Blackman, "Electronics, the Cost Disease, and the Operation of Libraries," *Journal of the American Society for Information Sciences* 34(1983):181–91.

30. See Martin Finkelstein, *The American Academic Profession* (Columbus: Ohio State University Press, 1984). In fact, teaching is the preferred activity of most faculty in all sectors except research universities. Even there, over one-third of faculty's interests lie primarily in teaching. See Martin Finkelstein, "College Faculty as Teachers," in *The NEA 1995 Almanac of Higher Education* (Washington, D.C.: National Education Association, 1995).

31. It is interesting that recent research on unions would lead to the same proposition. Many scholars have noted unions' accommodationist strategy in regard to technology: unions have largely accepted management's right to determine work methods (for example, choice of production technology), trading control over work design and process for wages and benefits (see Steven Vallas, *Power in the Workplace*). Such research has concentrated on blue-collar and clerical workers, not unionized professionals, who might be less disposed to concede the design and control of the work process to managers. Of course, unions may want input into decisions about technology but simply be unsuccessful in negotiating such provisions. Unfortunately, I lack systematic data on strategies of local union negotiators.

32. See Kenneth P. Mortimer and T. R. McConnell, *Sharing Authority Effectively* (San Francisco: Jossey-Bass, 1978). I would point out that particularly in the current climate of restructuring the two decision-making domains are not separate: most decisions about curriculum are also financial decisions, and many if not most financial decisions have curricular/academic dimensions or implications to them. I would also point out that "shared governance" is more an ideology and goal than an empirical reality.

33. See Burton R. Clark, *Academic Life: Small Worlds, Different Worlds* (Princeton: Carnegie Foundation for the Advancement of Teaching, 1987).

34. See Christine Maitland, Rachel Hendrickson, and Gary Rhoades, "Bargaining: Restructuring and Labor," in *The NEA 1995 Almanac of Higher Education* (Washington, D.C.: National Education Association, 1995).

35. Search terms such as *technol** and *tele** identified all words, such as *technology, telecourses, television,* and *telecommunications,* starting with those letters. I have also read through all the contracts for referent terms that would target relevant provisions. I am interested only in curriculum that is delivered *primarily* through the use of new teaching technology. For example, courses that include lab time or that have computer-based components are not of interest to me in this analysis.

36. The 1996 agreement, alluded to previously, goes even further, stating that the college must "arrange and pay for" the costs of special training.

37. That runs counter to some research on private-sector unions and training programs. Some research has suggested a negative relationship between unionization and extent of job training, although other work has pointed to unions' neutral or positive effects in establishing job-training programs. See David Knoke and Yoshito Ishio, "Occupational Training, Unions, and Internal Labor Markets," *American Behavioral Scientist* 37(1994):992–1016; and

David Knoke and Arne L. Kalleberg, "Job Training in U.S. Organizations," *American Sociological Review* 59(1994):537–47.

38. See John Yrchik, "Bargaining Distance Education Issues in Higher Education," paper presented at annual National Education Association Higher Education meetings, Orlando, March 1995.

39. The 1996 agreement restricts class size to maximum class limits for regular classes.

40. See NEA, *Resolutions*, B-56, 41.

41. My search on text- and other books found only three cases of contractual provisions prohibiting or limiting faculty's ability to profit from required curricular materials. However, sixteen other contracts had other limitations on faculty's choice of textbook—either department head or dean approval or phrasing such as "in accordance with college policies and guidelines."

42. As detailed as the provision is, and as protective as it is of faculty rights in instructional technology, the decisions of the Office of Telecourse Programs review committee (two faculty appointed by the chapter and two appointed by the university) "shall be final and cannot be grieved" (Article 30.2.5.5).

43. There is one example of a contract that accords faculty lesser property claims to some such materials than to other forms of intellectual property: "Twenty-five percent of all net proceeds from the sale or licensing of college supported written materials will go to the college and 75 percent will be retained by the originating bargaining unit member. Seventy-five percent of all net proceeds resulting from the sale or licensing of college supported recorded materials and inventions will go to the college and 25 percent will be retained by the originating bargaining unit member." (Johnson County Community College, Article 7.5.A).

44. See Vallas, *Power in the Workplace*.

45. See John Levin, "Professionalizing the Management of Community College Curriculum: Educational Technology and Distance Education," in Gary Rhoades ed. *Managerial Professionals in Higher Education: Restratifying and Reorganizing the Non-Faculty Professional Workforce*, unpublished manuscript, to be submitted for review, fall 1997.

46. In many blue-collar union contracts, for example, unions negotiate provisions for workers whose positions are downgraded to retire early or to have wage cuts phased in over time. See Greg Bamber, "Technological Change and Unions," in *New Technology and Industrial Relations*, ed.

Richard Hyman and Wolfgang Streeck (Oxford, Basil Blackwell, 1988) 204–19.

Chapter 6. Managerial Domain and Academic Employees: Outside Employment, Intellectual Property, and Faculty's Own Time

1. See William H. Whyte, Jr., *The Organization Man* (New York: Simon and Schuster, 1956).

2. See W. Lee Hansen and Thomas F. Guidugli, "Comparing Salary and Employment Gains for Higher Education Administrators and Faculty Members," *The Journal of Higher Education* 61,2(1990):142–59; and David C. Montgomery and Gwendolyn L. Lewis, "Administrative Staff: Salaries and Issues," *The NEA 1994 Almanac of Higher Education* (Washington, D.C.: National Education Association, 1994).

3. In self-report surveys, faculty claim to work about fifty-three hours a week—the exact number varies by institutional sector. See Henry L. Allen, "Faculty Workload and Productivity in the 1990s: Preliminary Findings," *The NEA 1996 Almanac of Higher Education* (Washington, D.C.: National Education Association, 1996). But faculty control when and where most of those hours are worked.

4. See Carol M. Boyer and Darrell R. Lewis, *And on the Seventh Day: Faculty Consulting and Supplemental Income*, ASHE-ERIC Higher Education Report No.3, (Washington, D.C.: Association for the Study of Higher Education, 1985).

5. For perhaps the most well known of the popular critiques, see C. J. Sykes, *Profscam: Professors and the Demise of Higher Education* (Washington, D.C.: Regnery Gateway, 1988). For the most well known of the scholarly critiques, see William F. Massy and Robert Zemsky, "Faculty Discretionary Time: Departments and the 'Academic Ratchet,'" *The Journal of Higher Education* 65,1(1994): 1–23.

6. See Gary Rhoades and Sheila Slaughter, "Professors, Administrators, and Patents: The Negotiation of Technology Transfer," *Sociology of Education* 64,2(1991a):65–77, and "The Public Interest and Professional Labor: Research Universities," in *Culture and Ideology in Higher Education: Advancing a Critical Agenda*, ed. William G. Tierney (New York: Praeger, 1991b); Sheila Slaughter, *The Higher Learning and High Technology: Dynamics of Policy Formation* (Albany: State University of New York Press,

1990); and Sheila Slaughter and Gary Rhoades, "Renorming the Social Relations of Academic Science," *Educational Policy* 4,4(1990): 341–61.

7. See James Fairweather, *Entrepreneurship and the University: The Future of Industry-University Liaisons*, ASHE-ERIC Higher Education Report (Washington, D.C.: Association for the Study of Higher Education, 1988). Also see Sheila Slaughter and Gary Rhoades, "Changes in Intellectual Property Statutes and Policies at a Public University: Revising the Terms of Professional Labor," *Higher Education* 26(1993):287–312; Michael Olivas, "The Political Economy of Immigration, Intellectual Property, and Racial Harassment: Case Studies of the Implementation of Legal Changes on Campus," *The Journal of Higher Education* 63(1992):570–98; and Patricia Chew, "Faculty Generated Inventions: Who Owns the Golden Egg?" *Wisconsin Law Review* (1992):259–314.

8. See Gary Rhoades and Sheila Slaughter, "Professors, Administrators, and Patents," and "The Public Interest and Professional Labor"; and Slaughter and Rhoades, "Renorming the Social Relations of Academic Science."

9. See Boyer and Lewis, *And on the Seventh Day*.

10. There is one other contract with provision for committee involvement in decision making. Western Michigan University's contract refers to a review committee of the Office of Telecourse Programs that addresses issues surrounding the revision and use of materials—for example, if an instructor requests that the materials be revised.

11. For property provisions in general, $x2=.22$. For what property is mentioned, whether patents, copyrights, or tapes, again there is no relationship between incidence and unit membership ($x2=.17$, .01, and .05 respectively). For who owns, $x2=.55$. For faculty autonomy in conditions of ownership, $x2=.43$. For process provisions, $x2=.24$. And for profit provisions that accord monies to faculty, $x2=.63$.

12. See Kristine E. Dillon and Karen L. Bane, "Consulting and Conflict of Interest: A Compendium of the Policies of Almost One Hundred Major Colleges and Universities," *Educational Record* 61,2(1980):52–72; and Gerald V. Teague, "Faculty Consulting: Do Universities Have Control?" *Research in Higher Education* 17,2(1982):179–86.

13. Calculated from the appendix in Roger Geiger and Irwin Feller, "The Dispersion of Academic Research in the 1980s," *The Journal of Higher Education* 66,3(1995):336–60.

14. Christopher Jencks and David Riesman, *The Academic Revolution* (Chicago: University of Chicago Press, 1969); Steven Brint, *In an Age of Experts: The Changing Role of Professionals in Politics and Public Life* (Princeton: Princeton University Press, 1994); and Sheila Slaughter and Larry L. Leslie, *Academic Capitalism: Politics, Policies, and the Entrepreneurial University* (Baltimore, Maryland: Johns Hopkins University Press, 1997).

15. See J. P. Heinz and Edwin O. Laumman, *Chicago Lawyers: The Social Structure of the Bar* (New York and Chicago: Russell Sage Foundation and American Bar Foundation, 1982).

16. See Steven Brint. Also see Slaughter and Rhoades, "Renorming the Social Relations of Academic Science," and "Changing the Intellectual Property Statutes and Policies at a Public University."

17. Christine Maitland, Rachel Hendrickson, and Gary Rhoades, "Bargaining: Restructuring and Labor," *The NEA 1995 Almanac of Higher Education* (Washington D.C.: National Education Association, 1995).

Chapter 7. Unionized Faculty: Managing the Restructuring of Professionals and Production Work in Colleges and Universities

1. See Sheila Slaughter and Gary Rhoades, "The Emergence of a Competitiveness Research and Development Policy Coalition and the Commercialization of Academic Science and Technology," *Science, Technology, and Human Values* 21,3(1996):303–39.

2. Christine Maitland, Rachel Hendrickson, and Gary Rhoades, "Bargaining: Restructuring and Labor," *The NEA 1995 Almanac of Higher Education* (Washington, D.C.: National Education Association, 1995).

3. On the regulation of work load and presence on campus, see ibid. On contact hours in the classroom, and time on campus, see Henry L. Allen, "Faculty Workload and Productivity in the 1990s: Preliminary Findings," *The NEA 1996 Almanac of Higher Education* (Washington, D.C.: National Education Association, 1996), and Martin J. Finkelstein, "College Faculty as Teachers," *The NEA 1995 Almanac of Higher Education* (Washington, D.C.: National Education Association, 1995). In 1988, for all two-year institutions, the average hours per week spent in classroom teaching were 15.2; for four-year institutions, 8.5 (in comprehensive universities and liberal arts colleges, 10.6).

4. See Andrew Abbott, *The System of Professions: An Essay on the Division of Expert Labor* (Chicago: University of Chicago Press, 1988);

Steven Brint, *In an Age of Experts: The Changing Role of Professionals in Politics and Public Life* (Princeton: Princeton University Press, 1994); Harold Perkin, *The Rise of Professional Society: England Since 1880* (London and New York: Routledge, 1989); and Anne Witz, *Professions and Patriarchy* (London and New York: Routledge, 1992).

    5. See Jack Schuster et al., (Phoenix: American Council of Education, Oryx Press, 1994), 17.

    6. See Christopher Jencks and David Riesman, *The Academic Revolution* (New York: Doubleday, 1968); Burton R. Clark, *Academic Life: Small Worlds, Different Worlds* (Princeton: Carnegie Foundation for the Advancement of Teaching, 1987); Howard R. Bowen and Jack H. Schuster, *American Professors: A National Resource Imperiled* (New York: Oxford University Press, 1986); Sheila Slaughter and Larry L. Leslie, *Academic Capitalism: Politics, Policies, and the Entrepreneurial University* (Baltimore, Maryland: Johns Hopkins University Press, 1997).

    7. See Jencks and Riesman, *The Academic Revolution.*

    8. See Slaughter and Leslie, *Academic Capitalism.*

    9. See Bowen and Schuster, *American Professors.*

    10. See Allan M. Cartter, *PhD's and the Academic Labor Market* (New York: McGraw-Hill, 1976); and Richard B. Freeman, *The Market for College Trained Manpower: A Study in the Economics of Career Choice* (Cambridge: Harvard University Press, 1971).

    11. See Clark, *Academic Life: Small Worlds, Different Worlds. Also see his The Higher Education System: Academic Organization in Cross-National Perspective* (Los Angeles: University of California Press, 1983).

    12. See Burton R. Clark, *Places of Inquiry: Research and Advanced Education in Modern Universities* (Los Angeles: University of California Press, 1995).

    13. See Paul Johnston, *Success While Others Fail: Social Movement Unionism and the Public Workplace* (Cornell: ILR Press, 1994).

    14. See Gary Rhoades, ed., *Managerial Professionals in Higher Education: Restratifying and Reorganizing the Non-Faculty Professional Workforce* (unpublished manuscript, to be submitted for review, fall 1997). Also see Gary Rhoades, "Managerial Professionals: The Rise and Restratification of Professionals in Higher Education," paper presented at the

Association for the Study of Higher Education meetings, Memphis, November 1996.

15. Wallace Clement and John Myles, *Relations of Ruling: Class and Gender in Postindustrial Societies* (Montreal and Kingston: McGill-Queen's University Press, 1994).

16. See Jencks and Riesman, *The Academic Revolution.* Also see Kenneth P. Mortimer and Michael L. Tierney, *The Three 'R's' of the Eighties: Reduction, Reallocation, and Retrenchment* (Washington, D.C.: American Association for Higher Education, 1979); George Keller, *Academic Strategy: The Management Revolution in American Higher Education* (Baltimore: Johns Hopkins University Press, 1983); and Slaughter and Leslie, *Academic Capitalism.*

Bibliography

AAUP. 1992. "Report: On the Status of Non-Tenure-Track Faculty." *Academe* 78,6:39–48.

———. 1976. *1976 Recommended Institutional Regulations on Academic Freedom and Tenure.* Washington, D.C.: American Association of University Professors.

———. 1946. *1940 Statement of Principles on Academic Freedom and Tenure.* Washington, D.C.: American Association of University Professors.

Abbott, Andrew. 1988. *The System of Professions: An Essay on the Division of Expert Labor.* Chicago: University of Chicago Press.

Academe. 1991. "In Brief." *Academe* 77,2:7.

Adler, Paul. 1990. "Marx, Machines, and Skill." *Technology and Culture* 31,4: 780–812.

———. 1989. "Automation and Skill: Three Generations of Research on the N.C. Case." Politics and Society 17,3: 377–402.

AFT. 1996. *How Unions Can Harness the Technology Revolution on Campus.* Washington, D.C.: American Federation of Teachers.

Aiken, Bob. 1995. "Report from a Committee of Hope." *Change* 27,2:49.

Allen, Henry L. 1996. "Faculty Workload and Productivity in the 1990s: Preliminary Findings." *The NEA 1996 Almanac of Higher Education.* Washington, D.C.: National Education Association.

Annunziato, Frank. 1995. *Directory of Faculty Contracts and Bargaining Agents In Institutions of Higher Education, v.21,* January. The National Center for the Study of Collective Bargaining in Higher Education and the Professions, School of Public Affairs, Baruch College, City University of New York.

Ashraf, J. 1990. "Recent Trends in the Union Wage Premium." *Journal of Labor Research* 11,4:435–51.

Baldridge, J. Victor, and Frank Kemerer. 1976. "Academic Senates and Faculty Collective Bargaining." *The Journal of Higher Education* 47:391–441.

Balkin, R. 1989. Union Influences on Pay Policy: A Survey." *Journal of Labor Research* 10,3:299–310.

Bamber, Greg. 1988. "Technological Change and Unions." In *New Technology and Industrial Relations.* ed. Richard Hyman and Wolfgang Streeck. Oxford: Basil Blackwell.

Barley, Stephen. 1986. Technology as an Occasion for Structuring: Evidence of Observations of CT Scanners and the Social Order of Radiology Departments." *Administrative Science Quarterly* 31:78–108.

Baumol, W. and S.A.B. Blackman. 1983. "Electronics, the Cost Disease, and the Operation of Libraries." *Journal of the American Society for Information Sciences* 34:181–91.

Bellas, Marcia L. 1994. Comparable Worth in Academia: The Effects on Faculty Salaries of the Sex Composition and Labor Market Conditions of Academic Disciplines." *American Sociological Review* 59,6:807–21.

———. 1993. "Faculty Salaries: Still a Cost of Being Female?" *Social Science Quarterly* 74:62–75.

Berdahl, Robert D. 1971. *Statewide Coordination of Higher Education,* Washington, D.C.: American Council on Education.

Berger, C. 1985. "The Erosion of Professional Schools: The Right Blend in a Time of Decline." *Journal of Educational Thought* 19:24–8.

Biles, G. E., and Howard P. Tuckman. 1986. *Part-Time Faculty Personnel Management Policies.* New York, London: American Council on Education/Macmillan, Collier Macmillan.

Birnbaum, Robert. 1970. "Unionization and Faculty Compensation." *Educational Record* 51:405–9.

Blau, Peter, Cecilia McHugh Falbe, William McKinley, and Phelps K. Tracy 1976. "Technology and Organization in Manufacturing." *Administrative Science Quarterly* 21:20–40.

Bledstein, Burton. 1976. *The Culture of Professionalism: The Middle Class and the Development of Higher Education in America.* New York: Norton.

Bloom, Alan. 1987. *The Closing of the American Mind.* New York: Simon and Schuster.

Bluestone, Barry, and Bennett Harrison. 1982. *The Deindustrializatlon of America: Plant Closings, Community Abandonment, and the Dismantling of Basic Industry.* New York: Basic Books.

Bowen, Howard R., and Jack H. Schuster. 1986. *American Professors: A National Resource Imperiled.* New York: Oxford University Press.

Boyer, Carol M., and Darrell R. Lewis. 1985. *And on the Seventh Day: Faculty Consulting and Supplemental Income.* ASHE-ERIC Higher Education Report No. 3. Washington, D.C.: Association for the Study of Higher Education.

Boyer, Ernest L. 1990. *Scholarship Reconsidered: Priorities of the Professoriate.* Princeton, New Jersey: Carnegie Foundation for the Advancement of Teaching.

Braverman, Harry. 1974. *Labor and Monopoly Capital: The Degradation of Work in the Twentieth Century.* New York: Monthly Review.

Brint, Steven. 1994. *In an Age of Experts: The Changing Role of Professionals in Politics and Public Life.* Princeton: Princeton University Press.

Brown, W. W., and C. C. Stone. 1977. "Academic Unions in Higher Education: Impacts on Faculty Salary, Compensation, and Promotions." *Economic Inquiry* 15:385–96.

Burawoy, Michael. 1979. *Manufacturing Consent: Changes in the Labor Process under Monopoly Capitalism.* Chicago: University of Chicago Press.

Burkhardt, Marlene E., and Daniel J. Brass. 1990. "Changing Patterns or Patterns of Change: The Effects of a Change in Technology on Social Network Structure and Power." *Administrative Science Quarterly* 35:104–27.

Cameron, Kim S. 1983. "Strategic Responses to Conditions of Decline: Higher Education and the Private Sector." *The Journal of Higher Education* 54,4:359–80.

Caplow, Theodore, and Reece McGee. 1958. *The Academic Marketplace.* New York: Basic Books.

Carr-Saunders, M., and P. A. Wilson. 1933. *The Professions.* London: Oxford University Press.

Cartter, Allan M. 1976. *PhD's and the Academic Labor Market.* New York: McGraw-Hill.

Chamberlain, Mariam K., ed. 1988. *Women in Academe: Progress and Prospects.* New York: Russell Sage Foundation.

Chew, Patricia. 1992. "Faculty Generated Inventions: Who Owns the Golden Egg?" *Wisconsin Law Review* 1992:259–314.

Clark, Burton R. 1995. *Places of Inquiry: Research and Advanced Education in Modern Universities.* Los Angeles: University of California Press.

———. 1987. *Academic Life: Small Worlds, Different Worlds.* Princeton: Carnegie Foundation for the Advancement of Teaching.

———. 1983. *The Higher Education System: Academic Organization in Cross-National Persective.* Los Angeles: University of California Press.

Clement, Wallace, and John Myles 1994. *Relations of Ruling: Class and Gender in Postindustrial Societies.* Montreal and Kingston: McGill-Queen's University Press

Cobble, Dorothy Sue, ed. 1993. *Women and Unions: Forging a Partnership.* Ithaca: ILR Press.

Cohen, Arthur M., and Florence B. Brawer. 1982. *The American Community College.* San Francisco: Jossey-Bass.

Committee A. 1995a. "Report: Academic Freedom and Tenure, St. Bonaventure University." *Academe* 81 4:65–73.

———. 1995b. "Report: Academic Freedom and Tenure, Alaska Pacific University." *Academe* 81,3:32–9.

———. 1995c. "Report: Academic Freedom and Tenure, Essex Community College." *Academe* 81,3:40–50.

———. 1993. "Report: Academic Freedom and Tenure, University of Bridgeport" 79,6.

———. 1977. "Academic Freedom and Tenure: City University of New York: Mass Dismissals under Financial Exigency." *AAUP Bulletin* 63:60–81.

Committee G. 1992. "Report: On the Status of Non-Tenure Track Faculty." *Academe* 78,6:39–48.

Cornfield, Daniel. 1987. *Workers, Managers, and Technological Change: Emerging Patterns of Labor Relations.* New York: Plenum.

Crompton, Rosemary, and Gareth Steadman Jones. 1984. *White Collar Proletarians: Deskilling and Gender in Clerical Work.* Philadelphia: Temple University Press.

Dillon, Kristine E., and Karen L. Bane. 1980. "Consulting and Conflict of Interest: A Compendium of the Policies of Almost One Hundred Major Colleges and Universities." *Educational Record* 61,2:52–72.

Douglas, J. M., and N. B. Goldsmith, "Analytical Survey of Contractual Salary and Compensation Methodology in Higher Education Collective Bargaining," in Monograph No.4, National Center for the Study of Collective Bargaining in Higher Education and the Professions, Baruch College-City University of New York, 1981.

d'Souza, Dinesh. 1991. *Illiberal Education: The Politics of Race and Sex on Campus* New York: Free Press.

Dubofsky, Melvyn. 1994. *The State and Labor in Modern America.* Chapel Hill: University of North Carolina Press.

Durkheim, Emile. 1957. *Professional Ethics and Civic Morals.* London: Routledge and Kegan Paul.

Edwards, Richard C. 1979. *Contested Terrain: The Transformation of the Workplace in the Twentieth Century.* New York: Basic Books.

Ehrenreich, Barbara, and John Ehrenreich. 1979. "The Professional-Managerial Class." In *Between Labor and Capital*, ed. Pat Walker. Boston: South End Press.

Ehrmann, Stephen C. 1995. "Asking the Right Questions: What Does Research Tell us about Technology and Higher Learning?" *Change* 27,2:20–27.

———. 1994. Making Sense of Technology: A Dean's Progress." *Change* 26,23:35–38.

Ellis, Martha, William Drake, Pat LaPoint, and Kimberly Russell. 1995. "Retrenchment Policies in Public Two-Year Community Colleges in the State of Texas." *Community College Journal of Research and Practice* 19:537–48.

England, Paula. 1992. *Comparable Worth: Theories and Evidence*. New York: Aldine de Gruyter.

Environmental Systems Research. 1996. "The Politics of Remedy: State Legislatures and Higher Education." Washington, D.C.: National Education Association.

Erikson, Jane. 1997. "Doctor Sues HMO for Sending Clients to Low-Cost Docs." *Arizona Daily Star*, March 15, 1997, Section B, pp. 1–2.

Etzkowitz, Henry. 1989. "Entrepreneurial Science in the Academy: A Case of the Transformation of Norms." *Social Problems* 36:14–19.

Fairweather, James. 1994. *Faculty Work and Public Trust: Restoring the Value of Teaching and Public Service in American Academic Life.* Boston: Allyn and Bacon.

————. 1988. *Entrepreneurship and the University: The Future of Industry-University Liaisons.* ASHE-ERIC Higher Education Report. Washington, D.C.: Association for the Study of Higher Education.

Finkelstein, Martin. 1995. "College Faculty as Teachers." *The NEA 1995 Almanac of Higher Education.* Washington, D.C.: National Education Association

————. 1984. *The American Academic Profession.* Columbus: Ohio State University Press.

Finkin, Matthew. 1996. *The Case for Tenure.* Ithaca: Cornell University Press.

Finnegan, Dorothy E. 1993. "Segmentation in the Academic Labor Market: Hiring Cohorts in Comprehensive Universities." *The Journal of Higher Education* 64,6:621–56.

Form, William, Robert L. Kaufman, Toby L. Parcel, and Michael Wallace. 1988. The Impact of Technology on Work Organization and Work Outcomes." In *Industries, Firms, and Jobs: Sociological and Economic Approaches*, ed. George Farkas and Paula England. New York: Plenum.

Freeman, Richard B. 1993. "What Does the Future Hold for U.S. Unionism?" *The Challenge of Restructuring: North American Labor Movements Respond*, ed. Jane Jenson and Rianne Mahon. Philadelphia: Temple University Press.

————. 1971. *The Market for College Trained Manpower: A Study in the Economics of Career Choice.* Cambridge: Harvard University Press.

Freeman, Richard B., and James C. Medoff. 1984. *What Do Unions Do?* New York: Basic Books.

Furniss, Todd W. 1980. Prescriptions for Institutions in the Eighties: Beyond Institutional Survival." *Review of Higher Education* 3:5–8.

———. 1977. "The 1976 AAUP Retrenchment Policy." *Educational Record* 57:133–39.

Gappa, J. M. 1984. *Part-Time Faculty: Higher Education at a Crossroads.* ASHE-ERIC Higher Education Research Report No. 3. Washington, D.C.: Association for the Study of Higher Education.

Gappa, J. M., and D. W. Leslie. 1993. *The Invisible Faculty: Improving the Status of Part-Timers in Higher Education.* San Francisco: Jossey-Bass.

Garson, Barbara. 1988. *The Electronic Sweatshop: How Computers are Transforming the Office of the Future into the Factory of the Past.* New York: Simon and Schuster.

Geiger, Roger, and Irwin Feller. 1995. "The Dispersion of Academic Research in the 1980s." *The Journal of Higher Education* 66,3:336–60.

Gibbons, Michael, Camille Limoges, Helga Nowotny, Simon Schwartzman, Peter Scott, and Martin Trow. 1994. *The New Production of Knowledge: The Dynamics of Science and Research in Contemporary Societies.* London: Sage.

Giddens, Anthony. 1979. *Central Problems in Social Theory.* Berkeley: University of California Press.

———. 1976. *New Rules of Sociological Method.* London: Hutchinson.

Gilbert, Steven W., and Kenneth C. Green. 1995a. *Information Technology: A Road to the Future?* Washington, D.C.: National Education Association.

———. 1995b. "Great Expectations: Content, Communications, Productivity, and the Role of Information Technology in Higher Education." *Change* 27,2:8–18.

Goode, William J. 1957. "Community within a Community: The Professions." *American Sociological Review* 22:194–200.

Gouldner, Alvin. 1957. "Locals and Cosmopolitans." *Administrative Science Quarterly* 1,2:444–80.

Green, Kenneth C. 1995. "Paying the Digital Piper." *Change* 27,2:53–54.

Gumport, P. 1993. "The Contested Terrain of Academic Program Reduction." *Journal of Higher Education* 64,3:283–311.

Gumport, Patricia J., and Brian Pusser. 1995. "A Case of Bureaucratic Accretion: Context and Consequences." *The Journal of Higher Education* 66,5:493–520.

Hamermesh, Daniel S. 1996. "Not So Bad: The Annual Report on the Economic Status of the Profession, 1995–96." *Academe* 82,2:14–22.

———. 1994. "Plus Ca Change: The Annual Report on the Economic Status of the Profession, 1993–94." *Academe* 80,2:5–14.

———. 1993. "Treading Water: The Annual Report on the Economic Status of the Profession." *Academe* 79,2:8–14.

———. 1988. "Salaries: Disciplinary Differences and Rank Injustices," *Academe* 74,3:20–24.

Hansen, W. Lee. 1988. "Merit Pay in Higher Education." In *Academic Labor Markets and Careers* ed. David W. Breneman and Ted I. K. Youn. New York: The Falmer Press.

Hansen, W. Lee, and Thomas F. Guidugli. 1990. "Comparing Salary and Employment Gains for Higher Education Administrators and Faculty Members." *The Journal of Higher Education* 61,2:142–59.

Hardy, Cynthia. 1988. "The Rational Approach to Budget Cuts: One University's Experience." *Higher Education* 17:151–73.

Hardy, Thomas. 1961 edition. *Jude the Obscure*. New York: Signet.

Harrison, Bennett, and Barry Bluestone. 1988. *The Great U-Turn: Corporate Restructuring and the Polarizing of America*. New York: Basic Books.

Heinz, J. P., and E. O. Laumann. 1982. *Chicago Lawyers: The Social Structure of the Bar*. New York and Chicago: Russell Sage Foundation and American Bar Foundation.

Higher Education Leader. 1996. *Higher Education Leader* iv,l.

Hirschhorn, Larry. 1984. *Beyond Mechanization*. Cambridge, Mass: MIT Press.

Hoffman, L. M. 1989. *The Politics of Knowledge: Activist Movements in Medicine and Planning*. Albany: State University of New York Press.

Hu, Tei-Wei, and Larry L. Leslie. 1982. "The Effects of Collective Bargaining on College Faculty Salaries and Compensation." *Applied Economics* 14:269–77.

Hughes, Everett C. 1958. *Men and Their Work.* Glencoe, Illinois: The Free Press.

Hydebrand, Wolf. 1989. "Sociology at Washington University." *Sociologist* 20:330–5.

Jencks, Christopher, and David Riesman. 1968. *The Academic Revolution.* New York: Doubleday.

Jensen, Jane, and Rianne Mahon, eds. 1993. *The Challenge of Restructuring: North American Labor Movements Respond.* Philadelphia: Temple University Press.

Jewett, Tom, and Rob Kling. 1990. "The Work Group Manager's Role in Developing Computing Infrastructure." In Proceedings of the ACM Conference on Office Information Systems. Boston, Massachusetts.

Johnston, Paul. 1994. *Success While Others Fail: Social Movement Unionism and the Public Workplace.* Cornell: ILR Press.

Julius, D. J., and M. K. Chandler. 1989. "Academic Bargaining Agents in Higher Education: Do Their Achievements Differ?" *Journal of Collective Negotiations in the Public Sector* 18:9–58.

Katz, Harry 1985. *Shifting Gears: Changing Labor Relations in the U. S. Auto Industry.* Cambridge: MIT Press.

Keller, George. 1983. *Academic Strategy: The Management Revolution in American Higher Education.* Baltimore: Johns Hopkins University Press.

Kelley, Maryellen R. 1990. "New Process Technology, Job Design, and Work Organization: A Contingency Model." *American Sociological Review* 55:191–208.

Kelly, Gail P., and Sheila Slaughter, eds. 1991. *Women's Higher Education in Comparative Perspective.* Dordrecht: Kluwer Academic Publishers.

Kemerer, Frank, and J. Victor Baldridge. 1975a. "Senates and Unions: Unexpected Peaceful Coexistence." *The Journal of Higher Education* 52:256–64.

———. 1975b. *Unions on Campus* San Francisco: Jossey-Bass.

Kimball, R. 1990. *Tenured Radicals: How Politics has Corrupted our Higher Education.* New York: Harper and Row.

Kling, Rob. 1991. "Computerization and Social Transformations." *Science, Technology, and Human Values* 16,3:342–67.

———. 1978. "Automated Welfare Client Tracking and Services Integration The Case of Riverville." *Communications of the ACM* 21:484–93.

Knoke, David, and Yoshito Ishio. 1994. "Occupational Training, Unions, and Internal Labor Markets." *American Behavioral Scientist* 37:992–1016.

Knoke, David, and Arne L. Kalleberg. 1994. "Job Training in U.S. Organizations." *American Sociological Review* 59:537–47.

Kuhn, T. 1962. *The Structure of Scientific Revolutions.* Chicago: University of Chicago Press.

Ladd, Everett C., and S. M. Lipset. 1975. *The Divided Academy: Professors and Politics.* New York: McGraw-Hill.

Larson, Magali Sarfatti. 1977. *The Rise of Professionalism: A Sociological Analysis.* Berkeley: University of California Press.

Lee, Barbara A. 1982. "Contractually Protected Governance Systems at Unionized Colleges." *Review of Higher Education* 5:69–85.

———. 1979. "Governance at Unionized Four-Year Colleges: Effect on Decision Making Structures." *The Journal of Higher Education* 50:565–84.

———. 1978. *Collective Bargaining in Four-Year Colleges.* AAHE-ERIC Higher Education Research Report No.5. Washington, D.C.: American Association for Higher Education.

Lee, John B. 1996. "Faculty Salaries, 1994–95." *The NEA 1996 Almanac of Higher Education.* Washington, D.C.: National Education Association.

———. 1995. "Faculty Salaries, 1993–94." *The NEA 1995 Almanac of Higher Education.* Washington, D.C.: National Education Association.

Leslie, David W. 1975. *Conflict and Collective Bargaining.* AAHE-ERIC Higher Education Research Report No.9. Washington, D.C.: American Association for Higher Education.

Leslie, David W., and D. J. Ikenberry. 1979. "Collective Bargaining and Part-Time Faculty: Contract Content." *CUPA Journal* 30,3:18–26.

Leslie, David W., Samuel E. Kellams, and G. M. Gunne. 1982. *Part-Time Faculty in American Higher Education*. New York: Praeger.

Leslie, Larry L., and Tei-Weh Hu. 1977. 'The Financial Implications of Collective Bargaining." *Journal of Educational Finance* 3-32–53.

Leslie, Larry, and Gary Rhoades. 1995. "Rising Administrative Costs: Seeking Explanations." *The Journal of Higher Education* 66,2:187–212.

Levin, John. "Professionalizing the Management of Community College Curriculum: Educational Technology and Distance Education," In *Managerial Professionals in Higher Education: Restratifying and Reorganizing the Non-Faculty Professional Workforce*, ed. Gary Rhoades. Unpublished manuscript, to be submitted for review, fall 1997.

Lewis, H. G. 1990. "Union/Non-Union Wage Gaps in the Public Sector." *Journal of Labor Economics* 8,1:260–328.

Lewis, Lionel. 1988. *Cold War on Campus: A Study of the Politics of Organizational Control*. New Brunswick, New Jersey: Transaction Books.

————. 1975. *Scaling the Ivory Tower: Merit and Its Limits in Academic Careers*. Baltimore: Johns Hopkins University Press.

London, Howard B. 1978. *The Culture of a Community College*. New York: Praeger Publishers.

Lozier, G. G. 1977. "Negotiating Retrenchment Provisions." In *Handbook of Faculty Bargaining*, ed. G. W. Angell and E .P. Kelley, Jr. San Francisco: Jossey-Bass.

Maitland, Christine, Rachel Hendrickson, and Gary Rhoades. 1995. "Bargaining: Restructuring and Labor." In *The NEA 1995 Almanac of Higher Education* Washington, D.C.: National Education Association.

Manns, C. L., and James G. March. 1978. "Financial Adversity, Internal Competition, and Curriculum Change in the University." *Administrative Science Quarterly* 23:541–52.

Marshall, J. L. 1979. "The Effects of Collective Bargaining on Faculty Salaries in Higher Education." *The Journal of Higher Education* 50,3:310–22.

Massy, William F., and Andrea Wilger. 1992. "Productivity in Postsecondary Education: A New Approach." *Educational Evaluation and Policy Analysis* 14:361–76.

Massy, William F., and Robert Zemsky. 1994. "Faculty Discretionary Time: Departments and the 'Academic Ratchet.'" *The Journal of Higher Education* 65,1:1–22.

Metzger, Walter. 1995. "Tenure." Invited address presented at National Education Association Higher Education Conference, Tampa, March.

———. 1987a. "The Academic Profession in the United States." In *The Academic Profession: National. Disciplinary. and Institutional Settings*, ed. Burton R. Clark. Los Angeles: University of California Press.

———. 1987b. "A Spectre Haunts the Professions." *Educational Researcher* 16,6:10–19.

Meyer, John W., and Brian Rowan. 1978. "The Structure of Educational Organizations." In *Environments and Organizations*, ed. Marshall Meyer and Associates. San Francisco: Jossey-Bass.

Meyer, John W., and W. Richard Scott. 1983. *Organizational Environments: Ritual and Rationality*. Beverly Hills: Sage Publications.

Michels, Robert, ed. 1978. *Political Parties*. Gloucester, Massachusetts: P. Smith.

Mingle, James R., and Associates. 1981. *Challenges of Retrenchment: Strategies for Consolidating Programs, Cutting Costs, and Reallocating Resources*. San Francisco: Jossey-Bass.

Mohseni, Navid. 1993. "The Labor Process and the Control of Labor in the U.S. Computer Industry." In *The Labor Process and Control of Labor: The Changing Nature of Work Relations in the Late Twentieth Century*, ed. Berch Berberoglu. Westport, Connecticut: Praeger.

Montgomery, David C., and Gwendolyn L. Lewis. 1995. "Administrative Staff: Salaries and Issues." In *The NEA 1995 Almanac of Higher Education*. Washington, D.C.: National Education Association.

———. 1994. "Administrative Staff: Salaries and Issues." In *The NEA 1994 Almanac of Higher Education*. Washington, D.C.: National Education Association.

Morgan, D. R., and R. C. Kearney. 1977. "Collective Bargaining and Faculty Compensation." *Sociology of Education* 50-28–39.

Mortimer, Kenneth P. 1983. Chambers Data for 1983–84." *Chronicle of Higher Education* 27,26 (October):13.

————. 1982. A Decade of Campus Bargaining: An Overview," *Campus Bargaining at the Crossroads*, ed. J. M. Douglas, Proceedings of the Tenth Annual Conference, National Center for the Study of Collective Bargaining in Higher Education and the Professions, Baruch College-City University of New York, April.

Mortimer, Kenneth P., M. Bagshaw, and Anthony T. Masland. 1985. *Flexibility in Academic Staffing: Effective Policies and Practices.* ASHE-ERIC Higher Education Report No.1. Washington, D.C.: Association for the Study of Higher Education.

Mortimer, Kenneth P., and T. R. McConnell. 1978. *Sharing Authority Effectively.* San Francisco: Jossey-Bass.

Mortimer, Kenneth P., and Michael L. Tierney. 1979. *The Three "R's" of the Eighties: Reduction. Reallocation, and Retrenchment.* AAHE-ERIC Higher Education Report No. 4. Washington, D.C.: American Association for Higher Education.

Murphy, Marjorie. 1990. *Blackboard Unions: The AFT and the NEA. 1900-1980.* Ithaca: Cornell University Press.

NCES. 1995. *Digest of Education Statistics, 1995.* Washington D.C.: National Center for Education Statistics.

————. 1994a. *Digest of Education Statistics.* Washington, D.C.: U.S. Government Printing Office.

————. 1994b. *Faculty and Instructional Staff: Who Are They and What Do They Do?* Survey Report of 1993 National Study of Postsecondary Faculty, Washington, D.C.: U.S. Department of Education, Office of Educational Research and Improvement.

————. 1988. *Faculty in Higher Education Institutions.* Washington, D.C.: U.S. Government Printing Office.

NEA. 1997. *NEA Higher Education Research Center Update: Part-Time Employment in Academe*, 3,1.

————. 1994a. *Resolutions. Legislative Program, and New Business 1994–95.* Washington, D.C.: National Education Association.

————. 1994b. NEA and Higher Education, Policies and Programs. Washington, D C.: National Education Association.

Neave, Guy, and Gary Rhoades. 1987. "The Academic Estate in Western Europe." In *The Academic Profession: National. Disciplinary, and*

Institutional Settings, ed. Burton R. Clark. Los Angeles: University of California Press.

Noble, David. 1984. *Forces of Production: A Social History of Industrial Automation.* New York: Knopf.

Offe, Claus. 1976. *Industry and Inequality: The Achievement Principle in Work and Social Status.* New York: St. Martin's Press.

Olivas, Michael. 1992. "The Political Economy of Immigration, Intellectual Property, and Racial Harassment: Case Studies of the Implementation of Legal Changes on Campus." *The Journal of Higher Education* 63:570–98.

———. 1989. *The Law and Higher Education: Cases and Materials on Colleges in Court.* Durham, North Carolina: Carolina Academic Press.

Parker, Robert E. 1994. *Flesh Peddlers and Warm Bodies: The Temporary Help Industry and its Workers.* New Brunswick, New Jersey: Rutgers University Press.

Parsons, Talcott. 1958. "The Professions and Social Structure." In *Essays in Sociological Theory*, ed. Talcott Parsons. New York: Free Press.

Perkin, Harold. 1989. *The Rise of Professional Society: England Since 1880.* London and New York: Routledge.

Pfeffer, Jeffrey, and J. Ross, "Unionization and Female Wage and Status Attainment." *Industrial Relations* 20,2:179–85.

Prechel, Harland. 1993. Transformations in Hierarchy and Control of the Labor Process in the Post-Fordist Era: The Case of the U.S. Steel Industry." In *The Labor Process and Control of Labor: The Changing Nature of Work Relations in the Late Twentieth Century*, ed. Berch Berberoglu. Westport, Connecticut: Praeger.

Price, Robert. 1988. "Information, Consultation, and the Control of New Technology." In *New Technology and Industrial Relations*, ed. Richard Hyman and Wolfgang Streeck. Oxford: Basil Blackwell.

Rainbird, Helen. 1988. New Technology, Training, and Union Strategies." In *New Technology and Industrial Relations*, ed. Richard Hyman and Wolfgang Streeck. Oxford: Basil Blackwell.

Reskin, B. 1979. "Academic Sponsorship and Scientist Careers." *Sociology of Education* 52:129-46.

Rhoades, Gary. 1996a. "Managerial Professionals: The Rise and Restratification of Professionals in Higher Education." Paper presented at the Association for the Study of Higher Education meetings, Memphis, November 1996.

——. 1996b. "Negotiating the Restructuring of Academic Labor." Paper presented at the American Association for Higher Education meetings, Atlanta, January.

——. 1996c "Reorganizing the Faculty Workforce for Flexibility: Part-Time Professional Labor." *The Journal of Higher Education* 67,6:624–59.

——. 1995a. "Rethinking Restructuring." *Journal for Higher Education Management* 10,2:17–31.

——. 1995b. "Rising, Stratified Administrative Costs: The Place of Student Services." In *New Directions for Student Services. Budgeting as a Tool for Restructuring*, ed. Dudley Woodard. San Francisco: Jossey-Bass.

——. 1995c "Rising Administrative Costs in Instructional Units." *Thought and Action* 11,1:-7-24.

——. 1993 "Retrenchment Clauses in Faculty Union Contracts: Faculty Rights and Administrative Discretion." *The Journal of Higher Education* 64,3:312–47.

——. ed. *Managerial Professionals in Higher Education: Restratifying and Reorganizing the Non-Faculty Professional Workforce* unpublished manuscript, to be submitted for review, fall 1997.

Rhoades, Gary, and Sheila Slaughter. 1991a. "Professors, Administrators, and Patents: The Negotiation of Technology Transfer." *Sociology of Education* 64,2:65–77.

——. 1991b. "The Public Interest and Professional Labor: Research Universities," In *Culture and Ideology in Higher Education: Advancing a Critical Agenda*, ed. William G. Tierney. New York: Praeger.

Riesman David. 1958. *Constraint and Variety in American Education*. Garden City, New York: Doubleday Anchor.

Riesman, David, Joseph Gusfield, and Zelda Gamson. 1970. *Academic Values and Mass Education*. New York: McGraw-Hill.

Rifkin, Jeremy. 1995. *The End of Work: The Decline of the Global Labor Force and the Dawn of the Post-Market Era.* New York: G. P. Putnam's Sons.

Riley, Patricia. 1983. "A Structurationist Account of Political Cultures." *Administrative Science Quarterly* 28:414–37.

Robinson, Perry. 1994. *Part-Time Faculty Issues.* Washington, D.C.: American Federation of Teachers.

Ruppert, Sandra S. 1996. *The Politics of Remedy: State Legislative Views on Higher Education.* Washington, D.C.: National Education Association.

Schrecker, Ellen. 1986. *No Ivory Tower: McCarthyism and the Universities.* New York: Oxford University Press.

Schuster, Jack H., Daryl G. Smith, Kathleen A. Corak, and Myrtle M. Yamada. 1994 *Strategic Governance: How to Make Big Decisions Better.* Phoenix: American Council on Education, Oryx Press.

Selznick, Philip. 1966. *TVA and the Grass Roots: A Study in the Sociology of Formal Organization.* New York: Harper and Row.

Shaiken, Harley. 1984. *Work Transformed: Automation and Labor in the Computer Age.* New York: Holt, Rinehart, and Winston.

Silva, Edward T., and Sheila Slaughter. 1984. *Serving Power: The Making of a Social Science Expert, 1865–1921.* Westport, Connecticut: Greenwood Press.

Slaughter, Sheila. 1993. "Retrenchment in the 1980s: The Politics of Gender." *The Journal of Higher Education* 64,3:250–82.

———. 1990. *The Higher Learning and High Technology: Dynamics of Higher Education Policy Formation.* Albany: State University of New York Press.

———. 1988. "Academic Freedom in the 1980s." *In Higher Education in American Society*, ed. Philip G. Altbach and Robert O. Berdahl. Revised edition. Buffalo, New York: Prometheus.

———. 1981. "Political Action, Faculty Autonomy, and Retrenchment: A Decade in Academic Freedom, 1970–1980." In *Higher Education in American Society*, ed. Philip G. Altbach and Robert O. Berdahl. Buffalo, New York: Prometheus Books.

————. 1980. "The 'Danger Zone': Academic Freedom and Civil Liberties." *The Annals of the American Academy of Political and Social Science* 448:46–61.

Slaughter, Sheila, and Larry L. Leslie. 1997. *Academic Capitalism: Politics. Policies. and the Entrepreneurial University.* Baltimore, Maryland: Johns Hopkins University Press.

Slaughter, Sheila, and Gary Rhoades. 1996. "The Emergence of a Competitiveness Research and Development Policy Coalition and the Commercialization of Academic Science and Technology." *Science, Technology. and Human Values* 21,3:303–39.

————. 1993. "Changes in Intellectual Property Statutes and Policies at a Public University: Revising the Terms of Professional Labor." *Higher Education* 26:287–312.

————. 1990. Renorming the Social Relations of Academic Science." *Educational Policy* 4,4:341–61.

Slaughter, Sheila, and Edward T. Silva. 1985. "Towards a Political Economy of Retrenchment: The American Public Research Universities." *Review of Higher Education* 8:295–318.

Smith, Teresa L. 1992. "The Impact of University Faculty Unionization on the Male-Female Wage Differential." *Journal of Collective Negotiations in the Public Sector* 21,2:101–10.

Solomon, J. S. 1987. "Union Responses to Technological Change: Protecting the Past or Looking to the Future." *Labor Studies Journal* 12:51–64.

Sorge, Arndt, G. Hartmann, M. Warner, and I. Nicholas. 1983. *Microelectronics and Manpower in Manufacturing.* Aldershot: Gower.

Sorge, Arndt, and Wolfgang Streeck. 1988. "Industrial Relations and Technical Change: The Case for an Extended Perspective." In *New Technology and Industrial Relations*, ed. Richard Hyman and Wolfgang Streeck. Oxford: Basil Blackwell.

Spenner, Kenneth I. 1983. "Deciphering Prometheus: Temporal Changes in the Skill Level of Work." *American Sociological Review* 48: 824–37.

Starr, P. 1982. *The Social Transformation of American Medicine.* New York: Basic Books.

Strassman, Paul. 1985. *Information Payoff: The Transformation of Work in the Electronic Age.* New York: Basic Books.

Swenson, Norman. 1996. "The Unions and Change." Paper presented at NEA Higher Education Conference, Phoenix.

Sykes, C. J. 1988. *Profscam: Professors and the Demise of Higher Education.* Washington, D.C.: Regnery Gateway.

Teague, Gerald V. 1982. "Faculty Consulting: Do Universities Have Control?" *Research in Higher Education* 17,2:179–86.

Tokarczyk, Michelle M., and Elizabeth A. Fay. 1993. *Working Class Women in the Academy: Laborers in the Knowledge Factory.* Amherst: University of Massachusetts Press.

Tolbert, Pamela S. 1986. "Organizations and Inequality: Sources of Earnings Differences between Male and Female Faculty." *Sociology of Education* 59:227–35.

Tuckman, Howard P. 1978. "Who Is Part-Time in Academe?" *AAUP Bulletin* 64: 305–15.

Vallas, Steven Peter. 1993. *Power in the Workplace: The Politics of Production at AT&T.* Albany: State University of New York Press.

Veazie. S. A. 1982–83. "University Collective Bargaining: The Experience of the Montana System." *Journal of College and University Law* 9:51–67.

Voss, Kim. 1993. *The Making of American Exceptionalism: The Knights of Labor and Class Formation in the Nineteenth Century.* Ithaca: Cornell University Press.

Wallace, Michael, and Arne L. Kalleberg. 1982. "Industrial Transformation and the Decline of Craft: The Decomposition of Skill in the Printing Industry, 1931–1978." *American Sociological Review* 47:307–24.

Walsh, John P. 1989. Technological Change and the Division of Labor: The Case of Retail Meatcutters." *Work and Occupations* 16:165–83.

Warner, M. 1985. "Microelectronics, Technical Change, and Industrialized Economies." *Industrial Relations Journal* 16:9–11.

Weis, Lois. *Between Two Worlds: Black Students in an Urban Community College.* Boston: Routledge and Kegan Paul.

Wellington, Alison J. 1994. "Accounting for the Male/Female Wage Gap Among Whites: 1976 and 1985." *American Sociological Review* 59,6:839–48.

Whyte, William H., Jr. 1956. *The Organization Man*. New York: Simon and Schuster.

Wiebe, Robert H. 1967. *The Search for Order, 1877-1920*. New York: Hill and Wang.

Williams, G. W., and P. A. Zirkel. 1988. "Academic Penetration in Collective Bargaining Contracts in Higher Education." *Research in Higher Education*, 28:76–95.

Wilson, Logan. 1942. *The Academic Man*. New York: Oxford University Press.

Witz, Anne. 1992. *Professions and Patriarchy*. London and New York: Routledge.

Yrchik, John. 1995. "Bargaining Distance Education Issues in Higher Education." Paper presented at annual National Association of Education Higher Education meetings, Orlando, March.

Zammuto, Raymond F. 1986. "Managing Decline in American Higher Education." In *Higher Education: Handbook of Theory and Research, vol.2*, ed. John C. Smart. New York: Agathon Press.

Zuboff, Shoshana. 1988. *In the Age of the Smart Machine: The Future of Work and Power*. New York: Basic Books.

Zumeta, William, and Janet Looney. 1994. "State Policy and Budget Development." *The NEA 1994 Almanac of Higher Education*. Washington, D.C.: National Education Association.

Index

Abbott, Andrew, 21, 22, 269, 284n, 285n, 317n, 321
American Association of University Professors, 3, 6, 11, 27, 28, 35, 83–86, 91–93, 127, 136–38, 283n, 286n, 289n–91n, 297n, 299n, 301n–5n, 321
American Federation of Teachers, 6, 17, 27, 28, 45, 91, 139, 177, 179, 289n, 290n, 305n, 309n, 321

Bowen, Howard, 274, 286n, 289n, 290n, 294n, 318n, 323
Brint, Steven, 23, 35, 285n, 289n, 294n, 303n, 317n, 318n, 323

Clark, Burton, 273, 274, 281n, 286n, 301n, 302n, 313n, 318n, 324
collective bargaining agreements, 6, 9, 10, 12 . *See also* the relevant substantive focus—e.g., salary structures
conflict of commitment. *See* outside employment, conflict of commitment
conflict of interest. *See* outside employment, conflict of interest

deprofessionalization, 161, 184, 185, 193, 201
deskilling, 8, 174, 179, 180, 182–6, 192, 193, 199, 201, 205–7

enskilling, 8, 174, 179–186, 189, 190, 193, 199, 205, 206, 208

financial exigency:
    and layoff, 7, 84–87, 125, 126
    by institutional type, 91, 92
    bona fide, 92
    contractual clauses, 91, 98, 125, 260
    courts and, 85, 86
    definition of, 86, 87, 91–94, 99
    definition of, by institutional type, 94
    faculty involvement, 7, 94–96
    faculty involvement, by institutional type, 96
    managerial discretion, 7, 85–87, 96, 97
    managerial discretion, by institutional type, 93, 94
    part-time faculty and, 136

Gappa, Judith, 282n, 302n, 303n, 305n, 307n, 308n, 327
grievances and arbitration, 71, 97, 108, 114, 144, 217, 218, 225, 230, 231, 245, 255, 304n, 314n
Gumport, Patricia, 10, 283n, 289n, 294n, 296n, 298n, 299n, 301n, 308n, 328,

Higher Education Contract Analysis System (HECAS), 6, 12, 14, 15, 28, 91, 140, 282n
Hughes, Everett, 25, 286n, 329

instructional technology:
    choice of, 174, 175, 177, 178, 182, 183, 185–190, 205
    contractual clauses, 13, 175, 179, 186, 190, 193–195, 198, 200–202, 205, 208, 264, 313n, 314n
    contractual clauses by institutional type, 187, 190, 194, 195, 205
    costs of, 176, 178, 188–91, 196, 209, 277
    curriculum and curricular control, 174, 178, 183, 185, 193, 195, 197, 200–202, 206–8, 265, 313n
    decision to use (*see* choice of)

341

displacement and retrenchment, 177,
178, 184, 189, 194–96, 200, 202
evaluation, 177, 178, 185, 199, 200,
208, 209, 277
faculty involvement, 22, 174, 177,
178, 182, 183, 185, 187–89, 193,
197, 200, 205, 208
managerial discretion, 22, 174, 175,
182, 183, 185, 187, 190, 193–6, 200,
201, 203, 205, 207, 264, 265
managerial strategy, 175, 176, 207,
209
ownership (*see* intellectual property)
part-time faculty and, 174, 184, 193–5,
201, 203, 206–8, 266
pay, 177–9, 184, 193, 194, 206
privacy (*see* evaluation)
productivity, 176, 182, 185, 208
professional constraints, 195–7, 209
quality, 178, 184, 193, 209, 277
retrenchment and (*see* displacement
and retrenchment)
skills and hiring, 174, 177, 183, 184,
190, 192, 206
stratification and, 174
surveillance (*see* evaluation)
technology policy, 179
training, 177, 178, 184, 186, 190, 191,
206, 313n
unions and, 175, 177, 178, 186
work load and, 177–9, 184–6, 189,
195–9
intellectual property:
conditions of production, 218, 238,
241–3
conflict of interest, 213
contractual clauses, 205, 217, 237–240
contractual clauses by institutional
type, 205, 219, 238–242, 247, 249,
250, 253, 254, 316n
contractual clauses by unit
membership, 250, 252, 316n
faculty as independent professionals,
22, 211, 214, 215, 218, 238, 241,
242, 244, 250, 252–5, 258, 267
faculty involvement, 244–7, 252, 316n

managerial claims, 8, 22, 211, 213–5,
242, 243, 247, 250, 254
managerial discretion, 218, 243, 244,
246, 247, 255
own time (*see* time, faculty's own in
intellectual property)
ownership, 8, 178, 186, 202–5, 214,
218, 238, 240–3, 247, 252
process for determining ownership,
218, 238, 244–6
profits (*see* royalties)
royalties, 202, 203, 214, 218, 238, 247,
248, 252, 314n
type of property, 215, 218, 238–240,
253, 254, 316n
union and nonunion settings, 215, 219,
242, 250–3, 255
use of institutional resources, 203, 204,
218, 242, 244
use and control of the product, 178,
186, 202–4, 218, 219, 238, 249,
314n

Jencks, Christopher, 131, 272, 279, 285n,
302n, 317n–19n, 329
Johnston, Paul, 27, 36, 276, 287n, 290n,
318n, 329

layoff. *See* retrenchment
Leslie, David, 282n, 284n, 299n, 302n,
303n, 305n–7n, 330, 331
Leslie, Larry, 273, 274, 285n, 286n,
288n, 293n, 294n, 317n–19n, 329,
331, 337

managed professionals, 4, 5, 6, 9, 21, 28,
257, 279
managerial discretion. *See* the relevant
substantive focus (e.g., retrenchment,
managerial flexibility), 5, 6, 13–15, 19,
21, 28, 257, 279
managerial extension, 8, 181, 182, 185,
186, 199, 200, 205–7, 275
managerial flexibility. *See* the relevant
substantive focus (e.g., retrenchment,
managerial flexibility), 5, 6, 13, 28,
257, 258, 269, 279

managerial professionals, 277, 296n, 318n, 335

management rights, 18, 107, 141, 187, 190

marginalization of faculty, 8, 33, 80, 201, 203, 205–8, 264–6, 270, 271, 277–9

National Education Association, 3, 11, 17, 27, 28, 91, 92, 139, 140, 176, 177, 197, 199, 283n, 287n–290n, 292n, 294n, 296n, 299n, 302n, 304n, 305n, 309n, 312n–15n, 317n, 333

National Labor Relations Board, 18, 307n

nonfaculty support professionals. *See* professionals, nonfaculty support

outside employment:
  conflict of commitment, 216, 221–4, 227, 233, 236, 251
  conflict of interest, 216, 217, 232–4, 237
  contractual clauses, 216, 220, 223, 236, 251
  contractual clauses by institutional type, 235–7, 251, 252, 266
  contractual clauses by unit membership, 236, 237
  institutional claim, 8, 22, 211, 212, 221–3, 226, 227, 229
  managerial discretion, 216, 217, 223, 224, 228–231, 234, 235, 236, 251, 255
  notice, 217, 227–9, 236, 237, 251
  one day a week rule, 212, 217, 234, 235, 251
  own time (*see* time, faculty's own in outside employment)
  prior approval, 217, 226, 227, 229, 231, 232, 237, 251
  professional right, as a, 22, 211, 212, 216, 222, 225, 227, 230, 254, 255, 258
  sabbatical /leave, 216, 225, 226, 236
  time limitations, 217, 234, 235, 237, 267

union and nonunion settings, 217, 219, 250, 251, 254, 255, 266, 267
use of facilities, 217, 229, 231, 232, 237, 251

part-time faculty:
  appointment/release of, 140, 142–4, 262
  appointment/release by institutional type, 142, 143, 166, 306n
  appointment/release by unit membership, 143, 166
  collective workforce (*see* workforce ratio)
  contractual clauses, 142, 156, 164, 305n
  curricular control and, 120, 149, 153, 163, 165, 170, 171
  displacement, 145
  duties, 141, 159, 167, 263
  duties, by institutional type, 159
  duties by unit membership, 161, 167
  evaluation of, 141
  experience, 141, 161, 167, 263, 264
  faculty involvement, 7, 22, 132, 141, 144, 145, 164–6, 168, 263
  gender and, 264
  individual workforce (*see* retrenchment)
  managerial discretion, 7, 22, 132, 141, 143–151, 155, 164–168, 170, 260, 263
  managerial strategy, 132, 136–8, 155, 168, 169, 269, 279
  numbers and percentages of, 131, 134–6, 169
  numbers/percentages of by field, 169, 170
  numbers/percentages of by gender, 170
  numbers/percentages of by institutional type, 136, 169
  order of layoff, 109, 110, 122, 137, 143, 145, 150, 307n
  priority, 141, 162, 163, 167

professional constraint, 7, 141, 147, 151, 152
professional strategy, 168, 263, 264
quality, 143–5, 161, 165, 166, 168, 263, 278
reassignment, 145
recall, 146
retrenchment, 136–8, 140, 145, 148, 150, 304n, 306n
retrenchment by institutional type, 146, 147, 166
retrenchment by unit membership, 146, 147, 166
rights and perquisites, 141, 157, 164, 167, 168, 263, 278
rights and perquisites by institutional type, 157–9, 307n
rights and perquisites by unit membership, 157, 158
rights of, 145, 146, 153, 154, 158, 165, 166, 263, 278
salaries, 168, 169, 287n
stratification and, 109, 110, 122, 133, 134, 141, 156, 157, 164, 169, 170, 264
tenure and, 133, 136–8
unions and, 22, 138–40, 156, 307n
unit membership and, 142, 156, 166
workforce ratio, 7, 119, 120, 140, 147–153, 263, 278, 306n, 307n
workforce ratio by institutional type, 154, 155, 166, 307n
workforce ratio by unit membership, 154
past practices: clauses in contracts, 14, 15, 190
professional autonomy. See the relevant substantive focus (e.g., retrenchment, faculty involvement), 5–8, 13, 14, 19, 20, 28, 257, 273, 275, 279
professional constraint. See the relevant substantive focus (e.g., retrenchment, faculty involvement), 6, 13, 19, 28, 257, 275
professional involvement. See the

relevant substantive focus (e.g., retrenchment, faculty involvement), 5, 6, 20, 28, 257, 275
professional stratification (see the relevant substantive focus—e.g., salaries, stratification in), 3, 6, 7, 9, 19, 20, 23–5, 28, 121, 257, 258, 266, 272–5, 279, 287n
professionals:
    higher education studies of, 9–11, 24, 35, 131, 132, 270–4, 285n, 302n
    managed professionals (see managed professionals)
    managerial professionals (see managerial professionals)
    nonfaculty, support, 8, 33, 80, 88, 96, 97, 119, 120, 171, 174, 207, 265–266, 270, 274, 277, 278
    sociology of, 9, 20–6, 35, 36, 182, 254, 255, 268–270, 272, 284n, 285n, 302n, 303n, 312n
    unions and, 3, 10, 24, 26–8, 33, 36, 40, 45, 71, 72, 79, 271, 286n
program discontinuation. See retrenchment: rationales, academic
program elimination. See retrenchment: rationales, academic
public interest, 23, 27, 168, 276, 277, 278, 302n

reorganization:
    and part-time faculty, 7, 131, 133, 134, 164, 171, 278, 279
    and retrenchment, 3, 4, 7, 85, 90, 94, 100, 116, 117, 126, 131, 300n, 301n
    and technology, 182, 183, 196
restructuring:
    academe, 1, 2, 4, 9, 11, 12, 19, 25, 33, 35, 36, 75, 76, 80, 84, 85, 100, 101, 124, 126–29, 131, 164, 170, 171, 173, 182, 183, 205–8, 258, 259, 260, 266, 268–75, 278, 279, 295n, 313n
    medicine and physicians, 2
    professions, 1, 21–23, 35, 36, 131, 278, 279

retrenchment:
  conditions, 4, 84, 98, 103, 125, 126, 260
  contractual clauses, 18, 98
  courts and, 83, 85, 86
  faculty involvement, 7, 22, 88, 90, 103, 104, 114–16, 126, 261, 301n
  faculty involvement, by institutional type, 104, 105, 126, 262
  faculty involvement, committees, 95, 96, 103, 105, 106, 114
  faculty involvement, consultation, 94, 103, 105, 106
  faculty involvement, meet and discuss, 103, 105, 106
  gender and, 122, 123, 128, 262, 298n, 301n
  instructional technology and, 173, 176–78, 194–97
  managerial flexibility, 7, 22, 84–90, 103, 104, 106–8, 111, 112, 114, 115, 125, 126, 128, 260, 261, 301n
  managerial flexibility, by institutional type, 104, 258, 262
  managerial flexibility, exceptions to rules, 107, 108, 111, 126, 261
  notice, 111, 112, 122, 123, 127
  notice, by institutional type, 111, 112, 122
  numbers of faculty, 85, 87, 88, 298n
  order of layoff, 107, 109, 110, 121, 122, 127
  order of layoff, by institutional type, 109
  order of layoff, part-time faculty (*see* part-time faculty, order of layoff)
  part-time faculty (*see* part-time faculty, retrenchment)
  professional strategies, 84, 86, 95, 96, 108, 109, 111, 114, 116–118, 120, 121, 127, 129, 261
  professional strategies, displacement, 112, 118, 124
  professional strategies, displacement of part-time faculty (*see* part-time faculty, displacement)
  professional strategies, workforce ratios, 119, 120, 128
  professional strategies, workforce ratios of full and part-time faculty (*see* part-time faculty, workforce ratios)
  rationales, 98, 103, 126
  rationales, by institutional type, 98, 99, 262
  rationales, academic, 4, 88, 98, 100, 126
  rationales, academic, by institutional type, 98, 100, 260
  rationales, economic, 88, 98, 99, 126, 260
  rationales, economic, by institutional type, 98, 99
  rationales, market, 23, 98, 101, 102
  rationales, market, by institutional type, 101
  reassignment, 112–14, 124
  reassignment, by institutional type, 113
  reassignment, part-time faculty (*see* part-time faculty, reassignment)
  recall, 116, 117, 124, 125
  recall, by institutional type, 116, 117, 125
  recall, part-time faculty (*see* part-time faculty, recall)
  retraining, 115, 116, 124
  stratification of rights, 90, 109, 110, 121–25, 128, 262
  stratification of rights, by institutional type, 118, 122, 125
  unions and, 10, 11, 83–87, 127
  union and nonunion, 261, 273
Rhoades, Gary, 281n–85n, 288n, 291n, 292n, 294n, 296n, 299n–301n, 303n, 305n, 306n, 308n, 312n–18n, 331, 333, 335, 337
Riesman, David, 24, 131, 272, 279, 285n, 286n, 302n, 317n, 318n, 319n, 329, 335

salaries:
  administrators, 5, 30, 80, 131, 212
  centrality of faculty salaries, 7, 33, 80,
    89, 131, 171
  compression, 32, 66, 70, 179, 292n
  differentiation, 46, 55–57, 61
  dispersion, 7, 55–58, 61, 62, 74–79,
    260, 273, 275
  faculty, by field, 31–3, 72, 74–79, 275,
    288n, 293n, 295n
  faculty, by gender, 31, 32, 72, 76, 79,
    260, 275, 287n, 288n, 295n, 296n
  instructional technology and, 177, 184,
    193, 194
  merit pay, 34, 35, 45, 259, 290n, 291n
  part-time faculty, 142, 161, 169, 287n
  seniority, 33, 42, 71, 72
  stratification in academe, 30–4, 55–57,
    61, 74, 77–79, 260, 275, 287n, 291n
  unionization and, 10, 25, 26, 29, 34,
    35, 71, 72–74, 77–79, 81, 179, 275,
    288n, 289n, 293n, 293n–296n
salary structures and adjustments:
  across the board, 37, 55, 57, 61, 71,
    259
  contractual clauses, 287n, 292n
  equity, by institutional type, 62, 63, 68,
    70, 71, 73, 259
  equity, contractual clauses, 7, 36, 62,
    68, 70, 73, 290n, 292n
  equity, gender based, 27, 32, 63,
    68–70, 79, 259
  equity, general, 64–66, 70, 259
  equity, market based, 32, 66, 69, 71,
    79, 259, 292n
  equity, over time, 70
  faculty involvement in, 22, 29, 30, 32,
    38, 42, 44–46, 51, 52, 60, 62, 63–5,
    67, 70, 71
  managerial discretion in, 22, 29, 30,
    32, 33, 36, 39, 40, 43, 45–49, 51, 52,
    57–62, 71, 75, 76, 81, 258, 259,
    291n, 292n
  market based, by institutional type, 46,
    47, 50, 61, 73, 259, 262

  market based, collective adjustments,
    48, 52–54
  market based, contractual clauses, 7,
    23, 46, 50, 61, 73, 291n, 294n
  market based, increased emphasis, 54,
    55, 58–60, 62
  market based, initial salaries, 48, 57,
    58
  market based, recruitment and
    retention, 50, 288n, 291n, 292n
  merit based, by institutional type, 37,
    40–45, 73, 259, 262
  merit based, contractual clauses, 7, 37,
    40, 73, 290n
  non-discrimination clauses, 67, 68
  professional strategies, 35–7, 42–6, 49,
    51, 53–5, 61, 64–6
  promotion, 37, 43, 44, 57, 61, 291n
  proxy measures of merit, 37, 42, 43,
    45, 290n
  salary schedules, 42–44, 50, 51, 58, 59,
    61, 71, 259, 262
  step or ladder increases, 38
  unions and, 71, 73, 81, 259
Schuster, Jack, 26, 274, 286n, 289n,
  290n, 294n, 318n, 323, 336
Slaughter, Sheila, 11, 136, 273, 274,
  281n, 283n–86n, 289n, 291n, 294n,
  297n, 298n, 300n–304n, 312n,
  315n–19n, 329, 335–37
state legislature: and collective bargaining, 17, 18
strikes:
  and technology, 195
  in academe, 15, 18, 27, 304n
  no-strike clauses, 15–17
  no-strike clauses by institutional type,
    16, 17
  no-strike, no lockout, 16
  sympathy strikes, 16
tenure:
  challenges to, 3, 4, 84–86, 138
  part-time faculty use, 132–34, 136–9,
    155, 304n

retrenching tenured faculty, 3, 83–86,
  89, 125–9, 136–39, 261, 304n
time:
  academic employment, 8, 22, 23, 211,
    212, 254, 255, 267, 268, 317n
  faculty's own in intellectual property,
    8, 22, 23, 214, 215, 218, 238, 242,
    252
  faculty's own in outside employment,
    8, 22, 23, 212, 217, 220, 223, 227,
    251
  gender and, 256

unionized faculty:
  challenges confronting, 3, 7–9, 17–19,
    21, 27
  compared to non-unionized (*see also*
    the relevant substantive focus—e.g.,
    salaries and/or salary structures,
    unionization and), 11, 12, 25, 26,
    258, 266, 273
  numbers of, 9, 10, 12

official positions of national unions
  (*see* the relevant substantive
  focus—e.g., instructional technology, unions and)
unions:
  higher education literature and, 10, 11,
    25, 26, 35
  sociology of, 26, 27, 35, 287n
  strategies of (*see also* the relevant sub-
    stantive focus—e.g., retrenchment,
    professional strategies), 9, 11,
    13–17, 19, 20, 36, 84, 86, 108, 109,
    117, 120, 121, 127, 128, 138–40,
    153, 165, 166, 168, 175, 177, 178,
    181, 186, 202, 207, 257, 259, 261–6,
    268, 271, 275–9, 313n, 314n

Vallas, Steven, 206, 207, 308n, 312n,
  313n, 314n, 338

Witz, Anne, 36, 284n, 290n, 303n, 318n,
  339

SUNY Series: Frontiers in Education

Philip G. Altbach, editor

List of Titles

Class, Race, and Gender in American Education—Lois Weis (ed.)

Excellence and Equality: A Qualitatively Different Perspective on Gifted and Talented Education—David M. Fetterman

Change and Effectiveness in Schools: A Cultural Perspective—Gretchen B. Rossman, H. Dickson Corbett, and William A. Firestone

The Curriculum: Problems, Politics, and Possibilities—Landon E. Beyer and Michael W. Apple (eds.)

The Character of American Higher Education and Intercollegiate Sport—Donald Chu

Crisis in Teaching: Perspectives on Current Reforms—Lois Weis, Philip G. Altbach, Gail P. Kelly, Hugh G. Petrie, and Sheila Slaughter (eds.)

The High Status Track: Studies of Elite Schools and Stratification—Paul William Kingston and Lionel S. Lewis (eds.)

The Economics of American Universities: Management, Operations, and Fiscal Environment—Stephen A. Hoenack and Eileen L. Collins (eds.)

The Higher Learning and High Technology: Dynamics of Higher Education and Policy Formation—Sheila Slaughter

Dropouts from Schools: Issues, Dilemmas and Solutions—Lois Weis, Eleanor Farrar, and Hugh G. Petrie (eds.)

Religious Fundamentalism and American Education: The Battle for the Public Schools—Eugene F. Provenzo, Jr.

Going to School: The African-American Experience—Kofi Lomotey (ed.)

Curriculum Differentiation: Interpretive Studies in U.S. Secondary Schools— Reba Page and Linda Valli (eds.)

The Racial Crisis in American Higher Education—Philip G. Altbach and Kofi Lomotey (eds.)

The Great Transformation in Higher Education, 1960–1980—Clark Kerr

College in Black and White: African-American Students in Predominantly White and in Historically Black Public Universities—Walter R. Allen, Edgar G. Epps, and Nesha Z. Haniff (eds.)

Textbooks in American Society: Politics, Policy, and Pedagogy—Philip G. Altbach, Gail P. Kelly, Hugh G. Petrie, and Lois Weis (eds.)

Critical Perspectives on Early Childhood Education—Lois Weis, Philip G. Altbach, Gail P. Kelly, and Hugh G. Petrie (eds.)

Black Resistance in High School: Forging a Separatist Culture—R. Patrick Solomon

Emergent Issues in Education: Comparative Perspectives—Robert F. Arnove, Philip G. Altbach, and Gail P. Kelly (eds.)

Creating Community on College Campuses—Irving J. Spitzberg and Virginia V. Thorndike

Teacher Education Policy: Narratives, Stories, and Cases—Hendrick D. Gideonse (ed.)

Beyond Silenced Voices: Class, Race, and Gender in United States Schools— Lois Weis and Michelle Fine (eds.)

Troubled Times for American Higher Education: The 1990s and Beyond— Clark Kerr (ed.)

Higher Education Cannot Escape History: Issues for the Twenty-first Century—Clark Kerr (ed.)

The Cold War and Academic Governance: The Lattimore Case at Johns Hopkins— Lionel S. Lewis (ed.)

Multiculturalism and Education: Diversity and Its Impact on Schools and Society— Thomas J. LaBelle and Christopher R. Ward (eds.)

The Contradictory College: The Conflicting Origins, Impacts, and Futures of the Community College—Kevin J. Dougherty (ed.)

Race and Educational Reform in the American Metropolis: A Study of School Decentralization—Dan A. Lewis (ed.)

Professionalization, Partnership, and Power: Building Professional Development Schools—Hugh Petrie (ed.)

Ethnic Studies and Multiculturalism—Thomas J. LaBelle and Christopher R. Ward

Promotion and Tenure: Community and Socialization in Academe—William G. Tierney and Estela Mara Bensimon (eds.)

Sailing against the Wind: African Americans and Women in U.S. Education—Kofi Lomotey (ed.)

The Challenge of Eastern Asian Education: Implications for America—William K. Cummings and Philip G. Altbach (eds.)

Conversations with Educational Leaders: Contemporary Viewpoints on Education in America—Anne Tumbaug Lockwood